Destination Marketing

1-6
7-9

Destination Marketing

An Integrated Marketing Communication Approach

Steven Pike

AMSTERDAM • BOSTON • HEIDELBERG • LONDON • NEW YORK • OXFORD
PARIS • SAN DIEGO • SAN FRANCISCO • SINGAPORE • SYDNEY • TOKYO
Butterworth-Heinemann is an imprint of Elsevier

Butterworth-Heinemann is an imprint of Elsevier
Linacre House, Jordan Hill, Oxford OX2 8DP, UK
30 Corporate Drive, Suite 400, Burlington, MA 01803, USA

First edition 2008

Library of Congress Cataloging-in-Publication Data
A catalogue record for this book is available from the Library of Congress

British Library Cataloguing-in-Publication Data
A catalogue record for this book is available from the British Library

ISBN: 978-0-7506-8649-5

For information on all Butterworth–Heinemann publications visit our website at books.elsevier.com

Printed in the United States of America

10 11 12   10 9 8 7 6 5 4 3

To Louise, Jesse and Alexandra
– Arohanui

With thanks to Don and Pearl

Contents

Prologue – It's a bloody shocking ad!

In early 2006, Tourism Australia launched a new destination brand positioning campaign. Even though the brand was designed for use in overseas markets, controversy surrounding the new positioning slogan ensured that the topic of destination marketing would be a key topic of conversation around the nation for weeks. Never before had a tourism campaign stirred so much debate in Australia.

The Australian campaign sets the context for this text in so many ways. The branding initiative, and ensuing publicity, encapsulates many key aspects of the issues related to the theory and practice of destination marketing. For example, much of the public (and I daresay private) discussion about the appropriateness of the new slogan seemed to be based on personal opinions, rather than an objective assessment of what makes for a successful destination brand. Other themes inherent in the campaign process that are addressed in the text include:

- the importance of differentiation in the marketplace
- the politics of destination marketing decision-making
- the high profile nature of destination marketing in the community
- the value of publicity in creating awareness of destination marketing activity

- the difficulty in developing a succinct destination slogan that encapsulates a sense of place in a few words
- the difficulty in developing a one brand positioning theme for use in different markets
- public criticism of destination marketing efforts
- the challenge of measuring brand campaign performance.

It is not being unkind to suggest that neighbouring country New Zealand stole a march on Australia in destination branding at the beginning of the new millennium. Indeed it has been suggested by others that Australia failed to capitalise on the global attention of the 2000 Sydney Olympic Games. Critics have lamented the lack of a destination brand that captures the spirit of the Aussie culture. The last campaign to do so was during the 1980s when the star of the hit movie *Crocodile Dundee*, Paul Hogan, urged American and British TV audiences to 'throw another shrimp on the barbie'. The campaign succeeded in getting Australia noticed in crowded international travel markets. Arguably, as important as the success in attracting international visitors, the campaign also struck a cord at home...most Australians were proud of the way the ads portrayed their part of the world.

Since 2000, the *100% pure New Zealand* brand campaign has been widely regarded as one of the most successful destination marketing initiatives. However, not many realise the strong connection between the New Zealand brand and the new Australian campaign. Not so long ago the marketing director responsible for Tourism New Zealand's *100% pure New Zealand* campaign moved to Australia to become CEO of Gold Coast Tourism, the regional tourism organisation responsible for promoting Australia's best known resort destination. Building on the experience of the *100% pure New Zealand* campaign, the new CEO initiated a re-branding for the Gold Coast. Re-branding is nothing new for the Gold Coast. After all, the place we now call Surfers Paradise was originally known as Elston.

The Gold Coast's new brand positioning launched in 2005 was *Very GC*, which attracted a lot of attention locally for a number of reasons, including the use of cartoon imagery (http://www.verygc.com/gold_coast_tourism_press_releases/very_gold_coast_very_innovative.html):

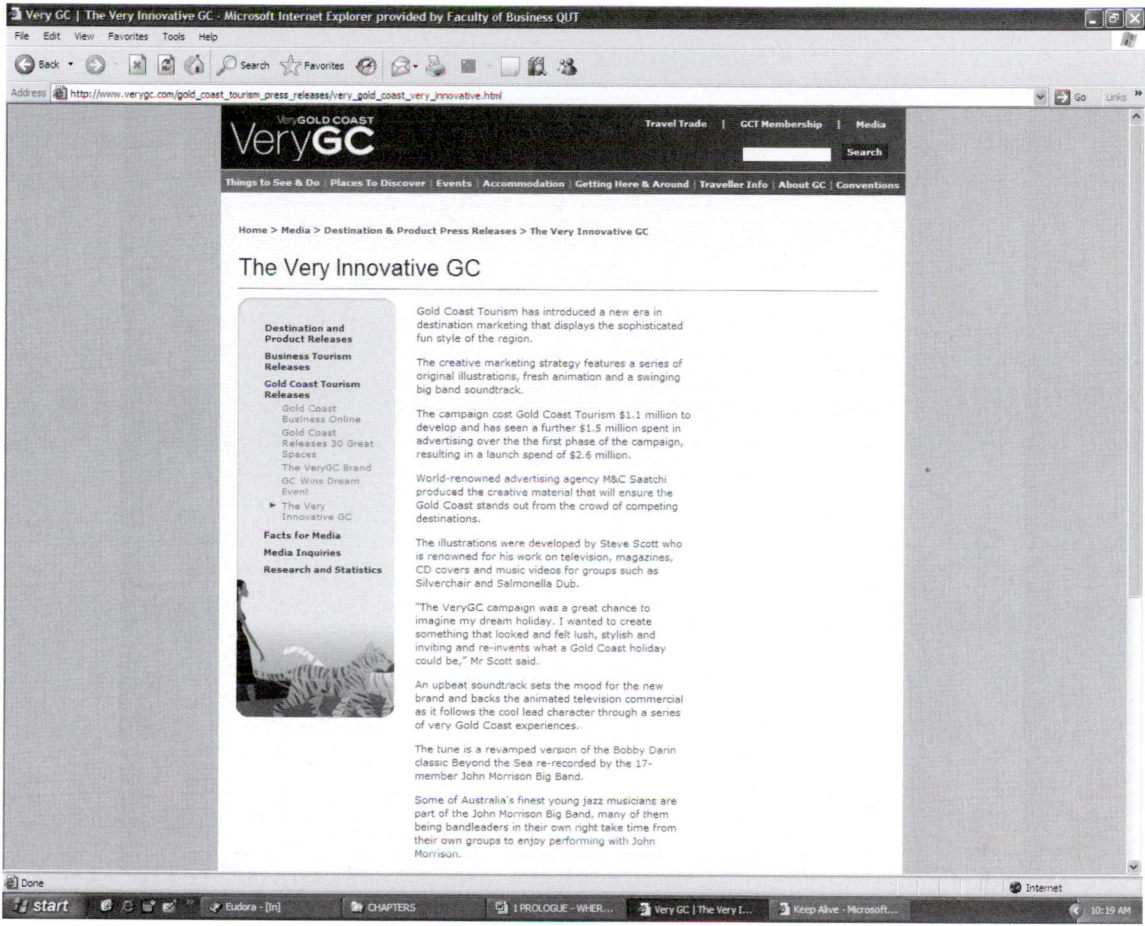

Not long after the launch, the CEO departed Gold Coast Tourism to take up the position of Marketing Director for Tourism Australia, the national tourism office. Now building on the experience of the *100% pure New Zealand* and *Very GC* initiatives, the Marketing Director coordinated the development of a new destination brand for Australia. Tourism Australia's rationale for the new brand was (http://www.tourism.australia.com/Marketing.asp?lang=EN&sub=0413):

> *The new destination campaign has been developed in recognition of the fact that it is no longer enough for our customers to have a positive awareness of Australia as a great place for a holiday. Whilst Australia is highly desired by tourists worldwide, we need to convert this positive yet passive predisposition towards Australia into an actual intention to travel to the country.*
>
> *To do this Australia needs to cut through the clutter of sameness in tourism destination marketing, by presenting a compelling single brand proposition about Australia to consumers in all markets.*

The launch of the *So where the bloody hell are you* campaign (see www.wherethebloodyhellareyou.com) attracted a flury of media publicity in Australia and overseas, with opinions very much divided. Elements of the campaign also received mixed reviews from the advertising industry. For example, the decision by the advertising agency to use a 'foreigner' to shoot the new campaign was labelled 'appalling' and 'idiotic' (see Nguyen, 2006). Australian Commercial and Media Photographers national president described the decision as a 'slap in the face' for local creatives.

Some of the many negative media headlines included:

- 'Better bloody work – why does the tourism industry need taxpayer help?' – *The Australian* (Editorial) 24/2/06, p. 17.
- 'Just too bloody stupid' – *The Courier-Mail*, 27/2/06, p. 11.
- 'Ad campaign suffering from vernacular disease' – *The Courier-Mail*, 25–26/2/06, p. 5.
- 'Tourism Australia chief defends advert' – *The Australian Financial Review*, 10/4/06, p. 16.

And some of the positive media headlines included:

- 'Bloody crass, but a bloody good viral campaign' – *B&T*, 3/3/06, p. 1.
- 'Tourism's $180m bloody well spent' – *The Australian Financial Review*, 27/2/06, p. 46.
- 'True blue language sells Australia to the world' – *The Courier-Mail*, 24/2/06, p. 5.

A number of overseas governments, such as Canada and Britain, objected to the campaign. Some of the headlines about overseas reactions included:

- 'Ads use swearing to attract tourists down under' – *China Daily*, 24/2/06, p. 6.
- 'Bloody Brits censure ads' – *The Australian Financial Review*, 10/3/06, p. 15.
- 'No bloody swearing, we're British' – *The Courier-Mail*, 10/3/06, p. 3.
- 'Bloody difficult job for Minister' – *The Sunday Mail*, 12/3/06, p. 34.

One of the problems inherent in the debate about the new brand was that so much of it appeared to be based on personal views, and not on an objective assessment of what these types of campaigns try to achieve. At one point, Tourism Australia's Managing Director (formerly Director of the New Zealand Office of Tourism and Sport) was forced to point out: '... its just a bloody ad, not a cultural essay'.

The tourism market is fiercely competitive. No other marketplace has as many brands competing for attention and yet only a handful of countries account for 75% of the world's visitor arrivals. The other 200 or so are left to fight for a share of the remaining 25% of traffic. Destination marketers at city, state, and national levels have a far more challenging role than other services or consumer goods marketers. This is no place for the fainthearted, and launching a new destination brand slogan is usually a courageous move, for a number of reasons (see Pike, 2005):

- Destinations are multi-dimensional. That is, the destination product is an amalgam of a diverse and often eclectic range of attractions, activities, people, scenery, accommodation, amenities, and climate. And yet to get noticed in the market, that diversity has to be synthesised into a statement of around seven words that capture the spirit of the place, with some focused imagery that will fit on to a billboard or magazine page. This is an almost impossible task for a city like Los Angeles or Manchester, so imagine the challenge facing marketers of a land mass the size of Australia. That's why we see so many broad-scoped brand slogans such as *Take time to discover Bundaberg, Coral Coast and Country*, and *Ohio – so much to discover*. It is not often we see a focused destination slogan such as *Snowy Mountains – Australia's high country*.
- Local tourism businesses don't all share the same market interests. For example, some target American backpackers, while others might be more interested in Japanese honeymooners or German campervanners. Is one slogan, such as *Idaho – great potatoes, tasty destinations*, likely to be meaningful in every market?
- Related to the previous points is the issue of tourism industry politics. Naturally, all tourism businesses would like to see advertising that features their type of product, so the issue of who decides the brand slogan and how they are held accountable is important. Often a neutral stance is adopted, such as *Greece – beyond words*. I have personally been involved in a destination brand campaign that was scrapped after a six-year investment, purely on the whim of one influential stakeholder.
- There must be a balance between brand theory and community consensus about what is an acceptable campaign, because a top-down approach won't work. Destination marketers lack any direct control over the actual delivery of the brand promise. Instead they need buy-in from local tourism businesses so that all are 'flying in formation'. Many Australians interact with tourists at some point, so it helps if members of the host community feel part of a potentially stereotypical brand promise such as *So where the bloody hell are you?* Apparently, focus group testing in Australia found only one person who objected to the use of the word bloody. An NTO spokesperson advised in true Aussie fashion that this participant was firmly told by the others to 'pull your head in mate'.

With these points in mind, what makes for an objective assessment of a destination brand slogan? From an analysis of over 200 destination slogans from around world the following considerations are offered, in no particular order of importance (see Pike, 2004):

1. Does the slogan have a clear proposition? That is, is it quickly evident what value is being suggested to travellers? In the majority of cases, such as *Brisbane – its happening*, there is a clear proposition. In other cases, such as *Utah!*, there isn't.
2. Who will find the proposition meaningful? Will it be obvious to all our target markets, because what we should be trying to do is make the consumer's decision-making easier by tapping benefits they seek, such as *Be inspired by Wales*. If we have to sit down and explain the meaning, such as in *Slovenia – the grown place of Europe*, or *Blackall – there's more than stuff all!*, we will have lost their attention.
3. Does the slogan differentiate us from the thousands of other destinations offering similar beaches, theme parks, museums, clubs etc.?
4. Is the message likely to be memorable? Staying in the hearts and minds of consumers is an expensive and long-term venture. Once the initial publicity has waned, will the theme last for a decade or so, such as in *I ♡NY*? Simplicity, such as *Nicaragua – a water paradise,* and courage under fire are paramount.
5. Finally, can the host community deliver the brand promise? Creativity must be tempered with reality because we travellers aren't stupid. Do we really believe the claims of *Barbados – just beyond your imagination,* or *England's North Country – the perfect package,* or *Greenland – out of this world*?

The quickest route to becoming memorable in the consumer's mind is to reinforce positively held perceptions, and not to try and change people's minds. The uniqueness of the Australian people is a big part of the travel experience here, and Tourism Australia's aim to inject that spirit into the campaign to differentiate it could be a sound choice. At the end of the day what will matter is not the publicity gained from the shock value. The decision-makers at Tourism Australia know that the true success of this campaign is not going to be judged by the amount of publicity gained or the number of advertising creativity awards. The government, taxpayers, and tourism businesses will be looking for evidence that the campaign generates more visitors who stay longer and spend more. In this regard, expectations are huge. But how do you measure the number visitors to Australia who are here as a direct result of the campaign, as opposed to those who are here as a result of word-of-mouth referrals from friends, a movie, a cheap airfare deal, a sporting event etc.? Read on.

Postscript

It has been said that imitation is the sincerest form of flattery. In light of the publicity surrounding Tourism Australia's campaign, the Irish Tourism Board ran advertisements in Australia with the headline "Get your ass over here"!

Further reading

Pike, S. (2004). Destination brand positioning slogans – Towards the development of a set of accountability criteria. *Acta Turistica, 16*(2), 120–124.

Pike, S. (2005). Tourism destination branding complexity. *Journal of Product & Brand Management, 14*(4), 258–259.

Tourism Australia. (2006). A uniquely Australian invitation – Strategy & execution. http://www.tourism.australia.com/content/ Destination %20Campaign/Strategy%20and%20Execution.pdf

Discussion questions

- Why do you think Tourism Australia selected such a potentially controversial positioning theme?
- Why do you think Tourism Australia conducted focus groups of Australian residents, when the campaign was designed for use in overseas markets?

Accompanying Resources

To support **Destination Marketing** we have provided you with the downloadable PowerPoint slides and Word documents to accompany this book. These contain solutions for all discussion questions, review questions and case studies found in this book and will provide you with a useful teaching aid when using the book in your classes.

CHAPTER 1

The study of destination marketing

Effective tourism managers who are able and willing to apply appropriate management techniques are increasingly needed. They should possess an understanding of the specialised management functions such as financial management, human resource management, as well as an appreciation of the structure, economics, and historical development of the tourism industry.

Witt & Moutinho (1994)

Aims

The aims of this chapter are to enhance understanding of:

- the rationale for the study of destination marketing
- a range of gaps in the destination marketing literature
- the need to bridge the divide between tourism practitioners and academics.

Perspective

The study of destination marketing is essential for anyone who is currently working in, or contemplating, a managerial or entrepreneurial career in tourism, travel or hospitality. The success of individual businesses is often as reliant on the competitiveness of the destination in which they are located, just as the success of any destination is reliant on the competitiveness of individual businesses. Opportunities to develop mutually beneficial relationships between destination marketers and tourism businesses are plentiful, but often untapped by both parties. The politics, challenges and constraints facing destination marketers are quite different to those faced by individual businesses. An understanding of such issues enables stakeholders to take advantage of opportunities in promotion, distribution, and new product development, thereby enhancing their own success as well as contributing to the effectiveness of their destination marketing organisation (DMO). The chapter sets the context for the study of destination marketing. I conclude the chapter with a brief discussion on the perspective from which I have approached the text. From careers as both a destination marketer and tourism academic I lament the divide between tourism practitioners and academics, acknowledge the wealth of academic theory of practical value to marketers, but provide a warning that due to the complexity of destination marketing much of this theory can be *easier said than done.*

Introduction

Most tourism activities take place at destinations. Not surprisingly then, destinations have emerged as 'the fundamental unit of analysis in tourism' (WTO, 2002), and form a pillar in any modelling of the tourism system, as shown, for example, in Leiper's (1979) outline of the geographic elements of tourism in Figure 1.1. Travellers are now spoilt for choice of destinations, which must compete for attention in markets cluttered with the messages of substitute products as well as rival places.

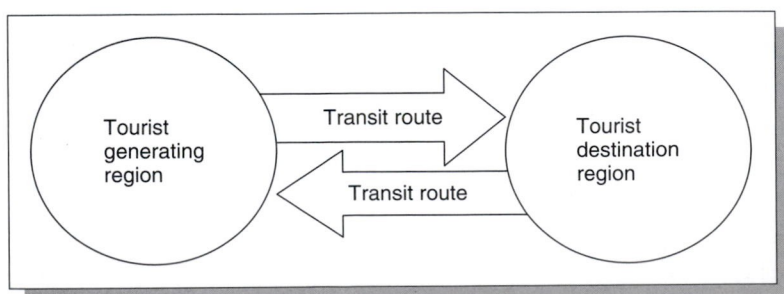

Figure 1.1
Geographical elements
of tourism

Destination marketing texts

Destination marketers are concerned with the selling of places, a field of study that has only recently attracted significant research attention. Given the prominent place of destinations in the tourism system it is surprising there have been relatively few texts to date that have focused on the operations of destination marketing organisations (DMO). While tourism has been around, in an organised form at least, since the late 19th century, texts concerned with destination planning, marketing and management have only emerged in earnest since the 1990s. Notable contributions are highlighted in Table 1.1. My previous text, *Destination Marketing Organisations*, was published in 2004 (see Pike, 2004b).

Table 1.1 Texts related to destination marketing

Topic	Author(s)
Destination planning and management	Lickorish (1992), WTO (1994), Laws (1995), Godfrey & Clarke (2000), Howie (2003)
Urban destinations	Page (1995)
Case studies of tourist organizations	Pearce (1992)
CVB functions	Harrill (2005)
Destination marketing	Wahab et al. (1976), Ashworth & Goodall (1990a), Goodall & Ashworth (1990), Heath & Wall (1992), Nykiel & Jascolt (1998), Kolb (2006)
Place promotion	Ashworth & Voogd (1990), Gold & Ward (1994)
Destination branding	Morgan et al. (2002, 2004)
Conference marketing	Davidson & Rogers (2006)
Destination crisis marketing	Beirman (2003a)

Destination marketing conference themes

A growing number of academic conferences featuring the destination marketing theme have also emerged since the 1990s:

- In 1990 the topic of the third international tourism workshop organised by the Geographical Institutes of the University of Groningen and the University of Reading was selling tourism destinations (see Ashworth & Goodall, 1990).

- The 1993 Association Internationale d'Experts Scientific du Tourisme (AIEST) conference addressed the issue of the competitiveness of long-haul destinations (see Ritchie & Crouch, 2000a).
- In 1996 the Fundacion Cavanilles for Advanced Studies in Tourism organised the Second International Forum on Tourism, themed the future of traditional tourist destinations (see Buhalis & Cooper, 1998).
- In 1998 the 48th Congress of the International Association of Scientific Experts in Tourism (AIEST) focused on 'Destination marketing – scopes and limitations' (see Keller, 1998).
- The 1999 TTRA Europe conference was themed 'Tourism destination marketing – gaining the competitive edge' (see Ruddy & Flanagan, 1999).
- Also in 1999, the Centro Internazionale di Studi Économia Turitica (CISET) conference on destination marketing and management was held in Venice.

Since 2000, the number of conferences featuring destination marketing in the core themes has increased remarkably, as has the number of marketing conferences featuring a destination marketing track. In 2005, the first conference focusing on destination branding was hosted by the Macau Institute for Tourism Studies in conjunction with Perdue University. At the time of writing the organisors were planning to stage the conference biennially (see www.ift.edu.mo/conference/index.html).

Destination marketing journal publications

There has been a wealth of material related to destination marketing published in academic journals. For example, I reviewed 142 papers published in the literature between 1973 and 2000 that were concerned with just one aspect of destination marketing – that of destination image analysis (see Pike, 2002a). While there is not yet a dedicated destination-marketing journal, the journal *Place Branding and Public Diplomacy* was launched in 2004.

Research gaps

This text synthesises the current extent of academic knowledge in the field. For teaching purposes the discussion is linked to real world industry examples and case studies. However, as we progress through the chapters, many research gaps relating to destination marketing issues will be highlighted. The following are some examples of areas in which DMOs face practical opportunities, challenges and constraints, and would benefit from more published research:

Governance and the politics of decision-making

Who decides on the priority of target market selection and the destination's positioning theme? Is this the domain of impartial DMO staff or the role of a committee or board that may or may not be representative of the local tourism industry? Will those businesses whose market interests or products do not feature in destination promotions accept the decisions for the holistic good of the destination? For example, the launch of the *Where else but Queensland* campaign in Australia attracted criticism from the Queensland Textile, Clothing and Footwear Union over the destination's use of branded thongs (jandals) that leave the imprint 'Queensland' in the sand, because they were made in China (Barrett, 2006). Who decides the governance structure and membership of the board of directors? Should directors be democratically elected or hand picked on the basis of expertise? What is the optimum number of directors for an effective board?

Effective organisation structure

How should a DMO be structured? Fast moving and entrepreneurial, or consultative and conservative? Public or private sector? A public–private partnership? Is there still a place for small community-based DMOs, or does competition dictate greater efficiencies and effectiveness through macro-region entities? Should structure be designed to enable a competitive strategy, or does structure dictate strategy?

Destination management

To what extent are DMOs representative of destination *marketing* organisations or destination *management* organisations?

Alternative funding sources

If the government withdraws funding, as in the recent cases of Colorado and California in the USA and Waikato in New Zealand, what alternative funding sources are available? What are the expectations of the funders, and will they be independent of strategic and operational decisions?

Strategic planning and implementation

To what extent are DMOs able to engage in long-term strategic planning versus the priority of short-term tactical initiatives?

Brand positioning

Will one brand positioning slogan suit the needs of all markets? Or does market heterogeneity demand consideration of the design of different themes? Should the brand theme represent the interests of all local tourism businesses and intermediaries? How well does the brand encapsulate the host community's sense of place? How well will the theme(s) be delivered by stakeholders and intermediaries? How is it possible to represent a multi-attributed destination with a promotional message that is succinct enough to fit on a billboard or postcard? To what extent is the brand identity congruent with the actual brand image? What is the life expectancy of an effective destination brand?

Human resources

To what extent is there a career path for aspiring destination marketers? Should staff representing the DMO in overseas markets be a local or be from the destination? In 2005 ANTOR estimated half of the overseas tourist offices based in Britain were operated by representation companies (www.travelmole.com, 8/6/05). Will all staff adopt a holistic and independent approach towards promotion of the destination, or are informal alliances formed with more active, aggressive or better-funded stakeholders? Why have relatively few women made it into the ranks of DMO senior management?

Communication with stakeholders

How should a DMO best engage in effective two-way participative communication with stakeholders, in a manner that does not grind down to a bureaucratic nightmare? What balance should there be between the amount of scarce time spent with stakeholders, and communicating with the market.

Relationships between national, state and regional DMOs

To what extent are national, state and regional DMOs able to work together in a way that enhances brand equity at each level?

Marketing research

If a market orientation is now essential for all organisations, how feasible is it to expect a DMO to engage in data collection and analysis in all of the markets and travel segments of interest to their local tourism businesses? To what extent do stakeholders appreciate the need for market research as a priority, relative to promotional activities?

Integrated marketing communication (IMC) implementation

Is IMC possible for a destination, given the range and diversity of stakeholders and intermediaries?

Visitor relationship management (VRM)

Is communicating with previous visitors a more efficient use of resources than traditional above-the-line advertising? How is it possible for DMOs, who have no direct contact with visitors, to engage in meaningful dialogue to stimulate repeat visitation and destination loyalty?

Performance measures and accountability

How is it actually possible to quantify the success of DMO promotional activities over the long term? With the increasing investment in destination branding initiatives, how should brand equity measured? Should performance metrics include factors such as yield and environment impacts?

Bridging theory and practise

Information that has a limited audience is bound by formal considerations. Scientific information appears in scholarly monographs; political information in speeches, pamphlets, editorials and wall posters; commercial information in advertisements and catalogues; news in reports. Each special informational format presupposes a set of methods and has its own version of reliability, validity and completeness. Becoming a scientist or a politician means, in part, learning and adhering to, even 'believing in', the standards and techniques of one's profession (MacCannell, 1976, p. 135).

This statement, from MacCannell's seminal work, *The Tourist*, suggested that the process of becoming a tourist is akin to the learning process involved in becoming a member of a profession. The proposition also serves to introduce the second key theme underpinning the text, which is the divide between tourism academics and practitioners (ironically the term practitioner is not one used by members of the tourism industry to describe themselves). Admittedly, this mention of a divide is a generalisation and is likely to be a contentious point, since some tourism academics do engage in research with tourism organisations.

In an ideal world the academic literature would inform industry while DMO best practise would inform the literature, in a mutually beneficial cycle. However, a significant divide prevents this. Academics have written about the problem (see, for example, Jafari, 1984; Taylor et al., 1994; Baker et al., 1994; Selby & Morgan, 1996; Jenkins, 1999), and practitioners have spoken about it. For example, in a plenary session at the 2004 Council for Australian University Tourism and Hospitality Education (CAUTHE) conference, Managing Director of Brisbane's *The Day Tour Company* Wayne Clift lamented:

In the aftermath of September 11 and the Ansett collapse, we nearly drowned in a sea of research data and information churned out by every well-intentioned organisation known to man . . . As an industry we certainly said enough is enough, we can't handle it – we don't have time to read all this stuff! And therein lies the problem. We don't see the benefits – therefore we don't make the time.

As observed by MacCannell, different professions have different requirements in terms of the ways in which information is written, controlled and disseminated. Therefore it could be expected that, if tourism is now a profession, and it was as recent as 1976 when MacCannell (p. 176) referred to the new term 'tourist industry' being used at the time, then it would be fair to assume that all those associated with this profession would confer using a common dialogue. The reality is that the information needs of tourism academics and practitioners are usually different, and are provided for in different types of forums and publications. It is suggested, therefore, that MacCannell's statement also applies to the difference in discourse between tourism academics and practitioners. While the work of many academics and practitioners could be subsumed under the terms tourism, travel, leisure and hospitality, the assumption should not be made that academics and practitioners work together in some sort of organised and symbiotic fashion. There is no common tourism discourse. Calls have been made for more engagement between tourism academics and practitioners, particularly at a destination level:

> *. . . our understanding of place promotion is, like the activity itself, partial and fragmentary . . . yet if place promotion is to become an established and useful practice, it requires some real intellectual engagement between critic and practitioner* (Ward & Gold, 1994, p. 15).

In this regard, the World Tourism Organisation (WTO, 2002a) noted that their 2002 think tank on destination competitiveness was the first time that a group of practitioners and knowledge experts had met in a WTO forum on destination management. For the most part, separate conferences are held for the two groups, often unfortunately with only small overlaps in attendance by the other.

Publish or perish

Academics must publish to gain recognition from peers, in an environment of *publish or perish*. Some are rewarded for the level of output rather than the level of contribution to either theory or practice. Even though numerous studies in the tourism literature have practical implications, the vast majority of practitioners will never actually read the academic papers relevant to their business operations. Academics gain credibility by being published in peer reviewed academic journals, textbooks and academic conference proceedings. Increasingly, due to government funding policies and the proliferation of publishing opportunities, papers must be seen to be in the right journals. Many parts of the world are adopting a tiered system of journal rankings and academic rewards. At one prominent Australian university, for example, academics are rewarded with a $12,000 research grant for an article published in a Tier 1 journal such as *Annals of Tourism Research*.

At last count there were at least 40 academic journals related to tourism. Fortunately, for practitioners used to the confidentiality of privately commissioned research reports, these journals are in the public domain, available by subscription, and through university electronic databases. Also, the peer double-blind refereed rigour of the academic literature is one of the very reasons for its value. Top journals boast a rejection rate of over 80%. However, the review process results in lengthy delays between manuscript submission and journal publication, and it is not unusual for data reported to be three or four or more years old by the time it is published.

Theory

The practical downside of the academic literature is that journal articles usually involve lengthy theoretical and methodological discussions, with complicated formulae and terminology that will be unfamiliar to those without research training, such as epistemology, periodicity, multivariate analysis, and principal components analysis with orthogonal rotation. It's enough to scare some academics, let alone a busy tourism manager, but a journal article must make a contribution to knowledge, preferably theoretical. The reality is that practitioners, particularly those in small businesses that make up the majority of the tourism industry, have a busy operational focus. Tomorrow's cash flow concentrates the mind in the fiercely competitive market place. Realistically, how many practitioners are aware of, let alone have time to keep up to date with, the extant literature?

For busy practitioners, the expanse and variety of the tourism literature can be overwhelming. If they are aware in the first place, the difficulty lies in the complex, multidisciplinary and fragmented nature of the tourism system as well as the sometimes turgid nature of academic writing, relative to other information sources. Clift summarised the industry's view of research in general as: 'We don't believe it, we don't know where to look, and we're not sure how to use it'. In New Zealand, Coventry (1998) cited an RTO spokesperson from the country's leading resort destination who was particularly critical of an academic destination image report by Kearsley et al. (1998):

> Why don't academics produce meaningful research which adds value to debate . . . they just produce this academic, trite stuff which simply occupies shelves and gives academics something to do.

This type of comment is surprising given the richness of academic tourism marketing information, including the aforementioned report. For example, Ritchie (1996, pp. 51–52) argued that tourism research 'from its very beginning, has been driven by individuals having a strong market orientation'. Nevertheless, in a case of *perception is reality*, the example above demonstrates a real world belief held by a destination marketer.

The issue has also been raised in other parts of the world. Three decades ago in the UK, Riley and Palmer (1975) lamented that their study recommendations had not been adopted by destination marketers. They suggested that the benefits of marketing research must therefore be better promoted to industry. Others have suggested that more research needs to provide practical recommendations for tourism practitioners (Baker et al., 1994; Selby & Morgan, 1996; Taylor et al., 1994). In discussing the gap between researchers and practitioners, Taylor et al. suggested that the key to research not ending up collecting dust on a shelf, as was much of what was produced by Canada's tourism researchers, lay in improving interpretation and presentation. Similarly, Hall (1998) claimed Australia was yet to develop close ties between the tourism industry and academia. In the USA, Plog (2000) lamented the lack of consulting opportunities for tourism academics, observing that it was amazing the number of tourism operators who continue to make decisions 'by the seat of their pants', instead of based on research.

However, it should be anticipated that the value of the literature will be more widely accepted by the next generation of tourism managers, as a higher percentage will have had exposure to tourism marketing theory through participation in the tourism and hospitality degree courses that have emerged only since the 1990s.

In practise

From a large focus group meeting with managers of destination marketing organisations (DMO) in the USA, Gretzel et al. (2006) summarised the following challenges faced:

- Adapting to technological change.
- Managing expectations of stakeholders.
- The shift from destination marketing to destination management.
- Confronting new levels of competition.
- Recognising creative partnering as the new way of life.
- Finding new measures of success.

In terms of the reverse situation of reporting DMO best practice in the literature, there are also constraints. For example, why should DMOs share confidential insights based on their own significant investment of resources? What incentives exist for busy practitioners to prepare detailed case studies? Even if there were more case collaboration by academics and practitioners, one journal editor privately regretted to me the decreasing space available for case studies. This is a shame in that if ever there was a potential mechanism to encourage practitioners to read academic research, it is a case study that addresses a real world problem.

One notable recent initiative in the attempt to bridge the academic/ practitioner divide is the online publication *e-Review of Tourism Research (eRTR)*, launched in April 2003. A cooperative venture between Texas A & M University, the Travel & Tourism Research Association (TTRA), and the Canadian Tourism Commission, the publishers promote *eRTR* as creating a platform for the dissemination of ideas and research in a "user friendly manner". During 2006 the average number of visits per issue was 10,000. These visitors were from 81 countries. The journal focuses on presenting short pieces, of less than 1000 words, which have an applied focus. Contributions in the following areas have been particularly encouraged (see http://ertr.tamu.edu):

- non-technical summaries of current research
- applied tourism research notes

- practitioner perspectives on tourism research
- best practices
- case studies
- conference reports.

Recognising the practical value of so much of the academic literature, the second theme of this text therefore is an attempt to present a synthesis of the literature relating to DMOs, in a manner that will be of value to, and decipherable by, students and practitioners of tourism alike. Case Study 1.1 highlights a problem at a resort destination in Turkey, which demands academic and industry collaboration.

Case study 1.1   From heaven to hell: Alanya, Turkey

It is customary at tourism conferences for local officials to welcome delegates to their destination, and to extol the local tourism strengths. Therefore it was a surprise at the opening session of the International Tourism Conference held in Alanya, Turkey, during November 2006, to hear the rector of the host university share his views on the local tourism industry's problems. Clearly passionate about Alanya, he nevertheless lamented that his destination had gone 'from heaven to hell'.

Alanya is a tourism resort area situated in the Antalya region on the Mediterranean coast of Turkey. The destination is nestled between coastline and mountains, and enjoys an almost sub-tropical climate suited to an all-year destination.

Following the rector's speech I became more observant of the local tourism scene, which was all but closed for the winter... hotels were shut, the streets, tourist bazaar and sea promenade appeared almost deserted for most of the day. This was a destination with a lot to offer off-season visitors, but was clearly at the mercy of travel intermediaries selling all-inclusive summer sun and sand packages:

> In terms of economy, productivity is decreasing not increasing. The competition of the foreign tour monopolists is kept on by decreasing the price and marketing all-inclusive packets, which causes the best hotels to be marketed at very low prices. Only about 25% of this income stays in Alanya and 75% of it goes out of the city.

The social and economic impacts were everywhere... the often desperate pleas of shopkeepers in the bazaar for cash flow, the many people out of work, lines of empty taxis, and the ubiquitous coloured wristbands that identified the all-inclusive tourist. As I waited with a German tourist for one more paying passenger to join a one-hour boat tour, the captain confided to the two of us: 'Alanya is now shit tourism.' He despised the lower class of visitor that was now attracted to the all-inclusive packages at that time of year. A similar unsolicited comment from a café owner later in the day left me wondering for how long the naturally friendly and hospitable nature of these warm hosts would last.

Alanya is a naturally beautiful destination, with much to offer visitors from around the world. However, a number of important strategic decisions need to be made, including how to reposition away from an all-inclusive summer sun and sea commodity resort at the mercy of overseas intermediaries.

> **Discussion questions**
>
> - What are the disadvantages of all-inclusive packages for destinations?
> - Discuss the potential for your destination to reach the situation faced by Alanya.
> - Can you find evidence of case studies in the academic literature of (1) this situation occurring at other destinations, and (2) any destinations that have been successfully repositioned?

Purpose of the text

The purpose of this text is to expand my previous text *Destination Marketing Organisations*, which was published in 2004 as part of Elsevier Science's 'Advances in Tourism Research' series. The aim of *Destination Marketing Organisations* was to provide a synthesis of the key literature related to destination marketing. As such, this was a research text rather than a teaching text, and primarily aimed at providing a resource for advanced undergraduate and postgraduate tourism students involved in destination research. Nevertheless, I was advised that many aspects of the book were being used for teaching in various parts of the world. As a marketer I am naturally interested in feedback from customers, and in this regard I received numerous comments about the need for a destination marketing teaching textbook. So, following suggestions from colleagues in the USA, UK and Australasia, this new text represents an expanded and updated transformation of *Destination Marketing Organisations*. Key content and resources deemed useful to research students has been retained. This has been supplemented by a wealth of new material, formatted as a teaching text. The result is a strategic overview of the study of destination marketing, which, while global in outlook, uses theory and cases to highlight just how uniform the challenges, constraints and opportunities facing DMO management are, whether in Branson Missouri, Southampton England, or Macau China.

One of the consequences of publishing any type of book is that published writing is open to public criticism. I have attempted to respond to constructive criticism, which is one of the strengths of the academic community, where colleagues have pointed out limitations and provided suggestions. For example, in his review of *Destination Marketing Organisations*, Professor Nigel Morgan (see Morgan, 2006) suggested that "like so many tourism academics" I had omitted to acknowledge the extensive work produced by Walton (1983, 2000) regarding the history of tourism. This proved a very useful resource, which I have duly incorporated in Chapter 3. To improve future editions I welcome your suggestions and comments.

Key learning outcomes

This text is primarily designed for use by undergraduate students of tourism, travel and hospitality. The rationale is that an understanding of the nature of DMO operations and challenges should not only be a prerequisite for those seeking a career in destination marketing, but should also be regarded as essential for those who will become active stakeholders of such organisations. It is strongly argued that such an understanding is required by managers of tourism, travel and hospitality businesses such as hotels, attractions, adventure operators and airlines, as well as local government politicians and policy-makers.

As future tourism industry managers, students will almost certainly interact with DMOs at national, state and/or local levels during their career. Opportunities exist for even the smallest of tourism operators to participate in, benefit from, and contribute to DMO planning and operations in some way. All DMOs share a common range of political and resource-based challenges not faced by private sector tourism businesses. Understanding these constraints and challenges will be of benefit to those who will be dealing with DMOs. Without this knowledge, initial encounters with DMO staff can be frustrating, which can then inhibit a long-term relationship with the organisation marketing their region. Private sector tourism managers must understand that the principles guiding public sector managers, such as in DMOs, are often quite different to their own, and that by considering these they will be able to work more effectively with them for mutual benefit.

The aim should be to develop relationships that both create opportunities to further their own business interests more effectively, and contribute positively to the competitiveness of the destination. After all, the success of these individual tourism businesses will ultimately be reliant to a large extent on the attractiveness of the destination, and the success of the destination will be reliant on the competitiveness of individual tourism businesses. At one extreme the very viability of tourism enterprises at destinations in crisis, such as Fiji, Beirut, the former Yugoslavia, Bali, and New Orleans, have been wiped out by exogenous events, such as war, terrorism and acts of God, which have rendered the destination uncompetitive overnight. Clearly, hotel managers cannot stop a hurricane or military coup. What they can do however is work with the DMO to prepare an emergency contingency plan.

The key learning outcomes of the text are to enhance understanding of the fundamental issues relating to the:

- multidimensional nature of destination competitiveness
- rationale for the establishment of DMOs
- structure, roles, goals and functions of DMOs
- the shift in thinking towards destination management
- key opportunities, challenges and constraints facing DMOs
- complexities of marketing multi-attributed destinations as tourism brands
- philosophy of integrated marketing communications
- design, implementation and monitoring of effective destination marketing communication strategies
- the potential for visitor relationship management
- necessity of disaster response planning
- destination marketing performance metrics

Two clear themes underpin the discussion throughout the text. The first, involving both the demand-side and supply-side perspectives of marketing, is concerned with the challenges involved in promoting multi-attributed destinations in dynamic and heterogeneous markets. The second theme concerns the need to provide more effective bridges linking academic theory and research outputs with real world DMO practice.

My position as author

This text has been motivated by my first-hand experience of the political and marketing challenges involved in marketing destinations at both the national tourism office (NTO) and regional tourism organisation (RTO) levels. In January of 1989 I was allocated a desk and a phone in a quiet second floor corner of the Rotorua District Council's (RDC) Civic Centre, a local authority responsible for the public administration of one of New Zealand's leading tourism resort areas. A few months earlier, the board members of the district's poorly funded local tourism association, the Rotorua Promotions Society, had resigned en masse, effectively terminating a contract with the RDC to act as the DMO. RDC recognised that the tourism community in Rotorua, for so long the flagship of New Zealand's tourism industry, was in crisis, and had committed to taking a more direct and proactive role in destination promotion. I had been employed, at age 28, to establish a new RTO, which became known as Tourism Rotorua (see www.rotoruanz.com). Previously I had spent nine years with the New Zealand Tourism Department, in New Zealand and Australia.

Rugged individuals

My experience as the Tourism Rotorua CEO was never dull, due to local tourism industry politics and the challenges of marketing a multidimensional destination to a dynamic and heterogeneous world. While the marketing challenges were exciting, the politics were frankly frustrating and boring. However, the two issues of marketing and politics are inextricably linked at the destination level. I recall the then Rotorua mayor, John Keaney, counselling me that tourism operators were like farmers, of which he was one, because they were 'rugged individuals' with plenty of strong opinions. From experience I learnt that tourism operators are happy to be led during a crisis, but demand increasing involvement when progress is being made and the budget is increasing. The more operators are involved in destination marketing planning, the more they must be empowered in RTO decision-making. However, the more they are empowered, the more bureaucratic the process becomes, and the slower the decision-making. A fast-moving entrepreneurial approach during a crisis (see Ateljevic & Doorne, 2000) can evolve into a politically correct bureaucracy. This can in turn be a source of frustration for entrepreneurial RTO staff and the rugged individuals alike.

The challenge

It would be an understatement to suggest that the task of establishing the Rotorua RTO was recognised as representing a significant challenge. One senior airline official commented at the time: 'If you can turn Rotorua around you will be able to write your own ticket!' With the benefit of hindsight, Wahab et al.'s (1976, p. 92) reflections on negative images were certainly appropriate in Rotorua's case:

> *It is easy to downgrade a product or allow it to deteriorate; but it is the devil's own work to upgrade a low-image product.*

Once-proud Rotorua was suffering serious image problems, not only in the market place but within the host community. Aspects of the history leading to this crisis point has been reported previously (see, for example, Ateljevic, 1998; Ateljevic & Doorne, 2000; Horn et al., 2000), and is presented as a case study in Chapter 6 of this volume. One of the problems noted during my initial meetings with local industry groups was the disparate nature of the tourism community. In particular there was a strong feeling that Rotorua Promotion Society promotions had only focused on the larger tourism businesses, which were referred to as 'the fat cats'. The larger operators explained to me that since they contributed the majority of funding, it was only fair to expect more promotional exposure. It was also implied that any future destination promotions should continue to feature their product. Ironically, one of these businesses was from outside the district boundary, and therefore not a contributor to the local authority rates (tax), which funded the new RTO. Another offered to provide a fund of $1000 every month to our office to ensure their product featured in all destination advertising. I learnt from countless discussions with counterparts in New Zealand and overseas that this was certainly not a situation unique to Rotorua.

By the time I handed over the reins of Tourism Rotorua in 1996, the organisation had won two national tourism awards for 'Best RTO'. The office also won again in 1997 and became the first RTO to win a distinction, which is granted to those organisations that have won an award category three times. Through a team effort between our staff and local tourism operators, Tourism Rotorua had progressed from being the lowest funded RTO in New Zealand in 1989 to the best resourced in 1996.

Rotorua attracts approximately 1.3 million visitors each year, and tourism is the leading employer. This has always been a tourist town, and most locals have an opinion on how tourism works, what the opportunities are, and how they should be delivered to the community. The range of RTO stakeholders is not therefore limited to those directly involved in the tourism industry. Everyone in Rotorua knows someone in the tourism industry. In my case my mother Pearl worked at Rainbow Springs wildlife sanctuary for 30 years and my late father-in-law, Ben Hona, was the Kaumatua (elder) at the New Zealand Maori Arts & Crafts Institute for over a decade. I therefore felt it important to include this section to acknowledge the perspective from which I approached this text. I enjoyed 17 years experience as a tourism practitioner, in Australia and New Zealand, and participated in destination promotions in North America, Australasia, the Pacific, Asia and Europe. I have attempted to provide an objective analysis, but acknowledge that I have brought to the research my own experiences and potential biases.

I became an academic almost by accident. While completing an MBA as the Tourism Rotorua CEO I became impressed with the rich resource of information for destination marketers that existed in the literature, and I wondered why this was not being disseminated by academia to industry directly. I changed careers, became an academic, began consulting to RTOs, and completed a PhD in destination marketing. The text has therefore been written by someone who does not claim to be an expert in the topic, but rather one who understands and appreciates, from experience, both sides of the divide – the perspectives of destination marketing practitioners and tourism academics.

Easier said than done

While academic theory offers a wealth of opportunities for tourism practitioners, my own experience suggests that implementation for DMOs responsible for coordinating a diverse range of stakeholders in multiple markets is problematic. My interest in theory is motivated by the desire to identify practical solutions for DMOs. However, my recommendations to industry and students have always been made with the explicit acknowledgement that this is often *easier said than done*.

Personal lessons

My own personal lessons about DMO leadership can be simply summarised as follows:

- Develop a long-term view, show commitment, and champion a vision.
- Be your own person. Seek counsel of course, but don't sit in the pocket of any stakeholders.
- Understand your organisation's reason for being. Be prepared to make trade-offs to maintain that core focus.
- Appoint staff who have a passion for the mission, and get out of their way. Run cover for them when needed.
- Foster open and two-way communication with stakeholders. Always.
- Acknowledge mistakes and learn from the experience.
- Develop clear performance measures. Be accountable.
- Enjoy yourself – tourism is meant to be fun.

Key points

1. The rationale for the study of destination marketing

Understanding the complexity of challenges, opportunities, and constraints facing DMOs is as important to the management of individual tourism businesses as it is to those seeking a career in destination marketing. An understanding of such issues enables stakeholders to take advantage of opportunities in promotion, distribution, and new product development, thereby enhancing their own prospects of success as well as contributing to the effectiveness of their destination marketing organisation (DMO).

2. A range of gaps in the destination marketing literature

For teaching purposes the text attempts to link discussion related to theory with real world industry examples and case studies. In doing so, many research gaps relating to destination marketing issues will be highlighted. These relate to areas in which DMOs face practical opportunities, challenges, and constraints, and would benefit from more published research.

3. The need to bridge the divide between tourism practitioners and academics

Ideally, best practice should inform theory, and theory should inform practice in a symbiotic cycle. However, practitioners and academics alike acknowledge the general divide between theory and practice. More collaboration and information dissemination forums are required for mutual benefit.

Review questions

- Explain why it is important for the general manager of a major hotel to have an understanding of the opportunities, challenges and constraints facing DMOs.
- What initiatives do you think could be developed to stimulate more engagement between academics and practitioners?

CHAPTER 2

Definitions

All tourism involves travel, yet not all travel is tourism. All vacation travel involves recreation, yet not all tourism is recreation. All tourism occurs during leisure time, but not all leisure time is spent on tourism activities.

Mill & Morrison (2002, p. 1)

Aims

The aims of this chapter are to enhance understanding of:

- the challenge of defining tourism
- different types of destinations
- the importance of a marketing orientation.

> **Perspective**
>
> While tourism has been around for centuries, it is only recently that this field of study has been taken seriously. Not surprisingly, perhaps, there is still a lack of agreement about some of the common terms in use today. Nevertheless, to set the context for the text, it is important to clarify the meanings ascribed to key terms. The chapter begins therefore with an attempt to define the terms tourism, destination, and marketing. Of particular practical importance, for any study in the field of marketing, is an understanding of the role and importance of what constitutes a marketing orientation.

Defining tourism

Is there really such a thing as the tourism industry? The term comprises hospitality (broken down further into accommodation, wining/dining, gaming), travel, tour operations, entertainment, and leisure, where members of each participate in their own industry. An industry is generally viewed as groups of firms engaged in the same kind of productive activities. However, there has been a lack of agreement about what constitutes a tourism business. For example, many businesses in other services sectors, such as entertainment (e.g. movie theatre) and transport (e.g. taxi), would not generally be classified as a tourism firm. And yet at many destinations these businesses will service visitors as well as locals. For more discussion on the complexities of this, see Vanhove (2005) and Ermen and Gnoth (2006).

An Internet exploration of the word 'tourism', using a search engine such as www.google.com, will generate over one million references. The word is so often used in everyday language that few adults in the developed world would have difficulty articulating some interpretation of its meaning. All of us have been somewhere on holiday, know someone working in hospitality, travel or tourism, and have seen coach loads of visitors from other places. So it is a surprise for many students to learn that there is no universally accepted definition of tourism.

Instead, there have been almost as many different definitions as there are researchers (Smith, 2001). It has even been suggested that defining tourism is almost conceptually impossible (Smith, 1988; Holloway, 1994). Complications arise from the multidisciplinary nature of tourism research, the ambiguity of what constitutes a tourist and tourism business, and overlaps with the concepts of travel, hospitality and leisure. Tourism is a relatively new academic discipline, and as such Leiper (1979, p. 392) found that few academics had devoted effort towards defining what it is:

> *The study of tourism as a focal subject has sometimes been treated with derision in academic circles, perhaps because of its novelty, perhaps because of its superficial fragmentation, perhaps because it cuts across established disciplines.*

Tourism research has drawn extensively from theories in other disciplines such as geography, economics, sociology, psychology, business and anthropology. Thus, as has been pointed out by Hall (1998) and Leiper (1995), most tourism texts offer a different definition. Table 2.1 presents a selection of tourism definitions from the academic literature.

Table 2.1 Definitions of tourism

Author	Definition
Hunziker (1951, in Collier 1997, p. 2)	". . . the sum of the phenomena and relationships arising from the travel and stay of non-residents, in so far as they do not lead to permanent residence and are not connected with any earning activity".
Leiper, (1979, p. 403–404)	"It is the system involving the discretionary travel and temporary stay of persons away from their usual place of residence for one or more nights, excepting tours made for the primary purpose of earning remuneration from points en route."
Mill & Morrison (1992, p. 9)	"Tourism is the term given to the activity that occurs when people travel. This encompasses everything from the planning of the trip, the travel to the destination area, the stay itself, the return and the reminiscences about it afterwards. It includes the activities the traveller undertakes as part of the trip, the purchases made, and the interactions that occur between host and guest in the destination area. In sum it is all of the activities and impacts that occur when a visitor travels."
Heath & Wall (1992, p. 4)	"The study of tourism is the study of people away from their usual habitat, of the establishments that respond to the requirements of travellers, and of the impacts they have on the economic, physical, and social well-being of their hosts. It involves the motivations and experiences of the tourists, the expectations of and adjustments made by residents of reception areas, and the roles played by the numerous agencies and institutions that intercede between them."
Holloway (1994, p. 3)	". . . someone who travels to see something different, and then complains when he finds things are not the same!"
Gunn (1994, p. 4)	". . . tourism is defined as encompassing all travel with the exception of commuting".
WTO (1995, p. 12)	". . . the activities of persons travelling to and staying in places outside their usual environment for not more than one consecutive year for leisure, business and other purposes".
Hall (1998, p. 6)	"Tourism is a commercial phenomenon of industrial society which involves a person, either individually or in a group, travelling from place to place (the physical component of tourism), and/or journeying from one psychological state to another (the re-creating component of tourism)."
Sharpley (2002, p. 22)	"It is, in short, a social phenomenon which involves the movement of people to various destinations and their (temporary) stay there."

The definition used will also depend on the purposes for which it is to be applied, which most commonly are to define markets and analyse visitor impacts and statistics. For DMOs, these include, for example, reports that seek to:

- promote the economic and social benefits of tourism to a community in a bid to enlist government funds for destination promotion
- promote the scale and growth of tourism in a business investment prospectus
- highlight potentially negative environmental impacts at a proposed development site
- report negative sociocultural impacts at a destination.

Following Buck's (1978) assertion that tourism scholarship was organised across two distinctive streams, economic development and tourism impacts, Leiper (1979) sought to develop a general framework for tourism that would bridge the two. In reviewing previous attempts at defining tourism, Leiper identified three approaches. The first was economic, where definitions only recognised business and economic aspects, such as:

> Tourism is an identifiable nationally important industry. The industry involves a wide cross-section of component activities including the provision of transportation, accommodation, recreation, food, and related services. (Australia Department of Tourism and Recreation, 1975, in Leiper, 1979, p. 392.)

Leiper criticised this approach for the lack of a number of elements, the most important being the human dimension. The second approach was technical, where the interest was in monitoring the characteristics of tourism markets, such as describing tourists, travel purpose, distance travelled and length of time away. For example, the first of these was that adopted by the League of Nations Statistical Committee in 1937, which defined an international tourist as someone who 'visits a country other than that in which he habitually lives for a period of at least twenty-four hours' (OECD, 1974, in Leiper, 1979, p. 393). Most definitions have used this approach, usually as a basis for collection of comparable statistics. The third approach was holistic, where the attempt was made to capture the whole essence of tourism, such as:

> Tourism is the study of man away from his usual habitat, of the industry which responds to his needs, and of the impacts that both he and the industry have on the host's sociocultural, economic and physical environments (Jafari, 1977, in Leiper, 1979, p. 394).

Many historians (see, for example, Shaffer, 2001, p. 11) cite the Oxford Dictionary explanation of the origin of the word 'tour' as originating from the Latin *tornus*, which came from the Greek word for a 'tool describing a circle'. This is representative of a circular journey away from home, from site to site, and then returning home. Shaffer suggested that the verb *tour* first emerged in the English language during the 17th century. According to Sigaux's (1966, p. 6) overview of the history of tourism, the word first appeared in the 19th century. Sigaux cited the Dictionnaire Universal du XIX Siecle of 1876, which defined tourists as 'people who travel for the pleasure of travelling, out of curiosity and because they have nothing better to do'. Sigaux (p. 92) also limited the scope of tourism to preclude domestic travel: 'One can almost say that national tourism, at home in one's own country, hardly counts as tourism.'

Such perspectives clearly don't encompass all categories of temporary visitors to a destination, who would otherwise still contribute to the coffers of businesses whose managers consider they are in the tourism industry. Other than travel for general pleasure, many other types of tourism which may or may not fit the category of a holiday have been documented. These include:

- business travel, including attendance at conferences or exhibitions or trade fairs
- attendance or participation at sporting events, the arts and entertainment
- visiting friends or relatives
- sex and romance
- gambling
- educational field trips
- adventure sports
- hunting and fishing
- spiritual events and pilgrimages
- day excursions.

Although some of the above could be subsumed under the heading of pleasure travel, it is doubtful whether all participants would regard themselves as *tourists*. Consider the case of travel for health or recuperation, such as spa visits. For example, a report in the *News Mail* (22/1/04, pp. 18–19), entitled 'Nip and Tuck Holiday', discussed the potential of the Queensland coastal resort Noosa to become Australia's cosmetic surgery capital. Leading Melbourne cosmetic surgeon Professor Gerard Sormann spends 12 days a month at his practice in Noosa to cope with demand from visitors from around Australia and overseas:

> *I should be nominated for a Noosa tourism award. Why wouldn't people who want cosmetic surgery come here, it's a fantastic destination and only makes sense to combine the two – surgery and holiday.*

Tourism then is concerned with the activities and interactions of people as they visit different places. Importantly, people not only include travellers, but also the travel trade at the origin and the host destinations and residents of the host communities. Visiting involves travel by various modes while transiting and temporarily residing. Places include destinations at various levels from continents to visitor attractions. That there is no commonly accepted definition is neither problematic nor unique to tourism

(Leiper, 1995). For the purpose of this text, no new definition is offered, other than to state an interest in:

> *The activities and interactions of people, other than regular commuters, and the resultant impacts on both the demand and supply sides, while visiting places away from home.*

Types of destinations

A destination is a geographical space in which a cluster of tourism resources exist, rather than a political boundary. A cluster is:

> *...an accumulation of tourist resources and attractions, infrastructures, equipments, service providers, other support sectors and administrative organisms whose integrated and coordinated activities provide customers with the experiences they expected from the destination they chose to visit* (Rubies, 2001, p. 39).

Some clusters exist within a section of a political boundary, others are a political boundary, while others cross political boundaries. Examples of these are shown in Table 2.2.

Other terms for clusters identified in a literature review by McDonnell and Darcy (1998) include: precinct, recreational business district, peripheral tourism area, tourism destination zone, enclave, integrated beach-resort development, tourism shopping village, and tourist district. Their analysis of the competition between Bali and Fiji in the Australian short-haul market, suggested that one of the key reasons for the latter losing 50% of its market share between 1982 and 1995 was the lack of tourism clusters. This was in part due to a non-interventionist approach to tourism development by the Fijian government. Without a proactive development policy private-sector driven all-inclusive resorts are scattered over a wide area, with no distinct tourism precincts offering a cluster of other attractions and services.

From the demand perspective, destinations are places that attract visitors for a temporary stay, and range from continents to countries, to states and

Table 2.2 Destination cluster types

Section of a political boundary	A political boundary	Across political boundaries
• The French Quarter, New Orleans, USA • Darling Harbour, Sydney, Australia • Fisherman's Wharf, San Francisco, USA	• The Gold Coast, Australia • Rotorua, New Zealand • Las Vegas, USA	• The Algarve, Portugal • Outback Queensland, Australia • European Alps

Figure 2.1
The author's son at
Peel Island

provinces, to cities to villages, to purpose-built resort areas, to uninhabited islands. Regarding the latter, consider the case of Peel Island shown in Figure 2.1. Accessible only by private boat, this subtropical island off the coast of Brisbane in Queensland's Moreton Bay is a year-round retreat featuring a beautiful beach, bush walks, snorkelling, fishing, and wildlife such as eagles, dolphins and dugong (sea cow). Once housing a leper colony, the island is now uninhabited and is protected from commercial development. The only facility on the island is an eco-toilet. So, even though there is no opportunity to spend money on the island, this is seen as a competing destination by nearby places, since on any given weekend you will find a small fleet of pleasure craft moored or beached at the island, and maybe a few tents pitched on the beach.

At the foundation level, destinations are essentially communities based on local government boundaries. With regard to the multidimensional nature of destinations, it has been suggested that the smaller the destination region, the greater the likelihood of internal homogeneity (Kelly & Nankervis, 2001). Intuitively this appears logical since a town or city would likely be more compact and less geographically diverse than an entire country. However, a diversity of natural features and tourism facilities also represents both a strength and a challenge for many smaller regions. In fact, the operating environment is a microcosm of that faced by NTOs. The WTO (2002a) think tank offered the following working definition of a local tourism destination:

> *A local tourism destination is a physical space in which a visitor spends at least one overnight. It includes tourism products such as support services and attractions and tourism resources within one*

> *day's return travel time. It has physical and administrative boundaries defining its management, and images and perceptions defining its market competitiveness. Local destinations incorporate various stakeholders, often including a host community, and can nest and network to form larger destinations.*

Since the majority of tourism activity takes place at destinations, they can be described as:

> *. . . a place at which visitors temporarily base themselves to participate in tourism related interactions and activities.*

Marketing orientation

Tourism features a negotiation between two forces: a supply-side and a demand-side. The supply-side is the travel and tourism industry, which seeks to stimulate demand for products and services. The demand-side represents consumer-travellers, who seek travel products and services to satisfy certain needs. Marketing is an exchange process between the two forces:

> *Marketing is a social and managerial process by which individuals and groups obtain what they need through creating and exchanging products and value with others* (Kotler et al., 1999, p. 12).

What is not explicit in many definitions of marketing is whether it is a strategy, a series of processes, or a philosophy. Ideally, marketing should be viewed as an organisational philosophy, not the sole responsibility of the marketing department. After all if a firm fails to sell its wares, there won't be any need for accountants or human resource managers, except to close the business. On this basis it could be argued that marketing is the most important function of an organisation. A *marketing orientation* should therefore pervade the entire organisation. The focus in this approach is based on the principle of making decisions with the customer's needs in mind:

> *A marketing orientation is a philosophy that recognises the achievement of organisational goals requires an understanding of the needs and wants of the target market, and then delivering satisfaction more effectively than rivals* (Kotler et al., 2003).

This represents the third stage in the evolution of marketing. Medlik and Middleton (1973) proposed that tourism was following the traditional three-stage process towards a marketing orientation, which had been experienced by other industries. The three stages were identified as:

1. **Production orientation** This stage is characterised by a shortage of available goods and services, and is therefore a seller's market. The main problem is to increase output. Until the 1950s tourism was, in general, at this stage.

2. **Selling orientation** This occurs when technological progress enables mass production, leading to increased competition, lower prices and a supply in excess of demand. This is therefore a buyer's market with a sales orientation from the producer to sell the increased output. The development of wide-bodied jets and large hotels in the 1960s and 1970s are examples of the second phase in tourism.

3. **Marketing orientation** Increased competition and sophistication of buyers in an affluent society leads to the recognition of the necessity to identify consumer needs. Selling will not be sufficient since consumer needs become the starting point for what is produced. 'Modern marketing is designed to achieve optimal satisfaction of the consumer and to do so at an appropriate return to the producer' (p. 34). Tourism has been slow to achieve the full potential of moving from the selling orientation to a marketing orientation.

A fourth level that has since been introduced to the hierarchy is the *societal marketing orientation*, which dictates a market orientation, but operationalised in a way that also considers the well-being of society and the environment. DMOs, as representatives of a host community and natural environment as well as commercial tourism services, have such a wider societal obligation. For DMOs, marketing may be considered as representing:

> . . . *the process of matching destination resources with environment opportunities, with the wider interests of society in mind.*

Case Study 2.1 summarises a government-funded initiative in one rural area of South Africa to enhance tourism as a means for community development. Heath (2003, p. 20) is a proponent for tourism as a means of reducing poverty in South Africa, and to 'improve the quality of life of millions' through the capacity to create new jobs in small-scale developments. A key inhibitor to harnessing the potential of tourism in South Africa has been the lack of coordinated efforts in policy, planning, development and marketing between stakeholders holding generally myopic attitudes about their own personal interests.

Case study 2.1 Mbombela Local Municipality, South Africa

Dr Mathilda van Niekerk, Tshwane University of Technology, South Africa

South Africa, situated on the southern tip of the continent and known as the rainbow country, is synonymous with Nelson Mandela, the Big Five, the Bafana–Bafana soccer team, the Protea cricket team and the Springbok rugby team. *The South African Yearbook* boasts that the country's unique combination of people, landscape, scenery, history and the different cultures makes this one of the most enchanting countries in the world to visit.

The Mbombela Local Municipality is situated within the Mpumalanga province. Mpumalanga, the place of the rising sun, is one of South Africa's nine provinces. The province is positioned as the newest and fastest-growing province for tourism in South Africa. Tourist attractions in the province are numerous and vary from game viewing, such as the 'Big Five' and world-famous Kruger National Park, to spectacular natural wonders created by the escarpment of the Drakensberg Mountains. The province also offers hunting safaris, farm holidays, lodges, caves, cultural heritage and traditional African trials, arts and handicrafts (see http://www.mii.co.za).

It is not possible for all provinces in South Africa to cater for all tourists, and so it is important to help provinces segment markets so that they can develop, manage, plan and market tourist attractions more effectively. Existing and potential tourism market segments were identified through government-funded research in order to determine the appropriate tourism strategies. The tables below indicate the broad markets to be considered, based on market trends and the visitor demand for the Mbombela area. They include the distinguishing characteristics of the market, and an indication of the growth potential for each segment.

Foreign target market segments for Mbombela

Target market	Geography	Length of stay	Growth potential
Holidaymakers	Primarily UK, Mozambique & Swaziland	Medium	Medium
VFRs	Primarily UK, Mozambique & Swaziland	Short	Medium
Shoppers	Primarily Mozambique & Swaziland	Short	High
Business tourists	Primarily Mozambique & Swaziland	Short	High

Domestic target market segments for Mbombela

Target market	Geography	Length of stay	Growth potential
Holidaymakers	Primarily Mpumalanga, Gauteng, KZN, Limpopo, Western Cape	Long	High
VFRs	Primarily Mpumalanga, Gauteng, KZN, Limpopo, Western Cape	Long	Low
Shoppers	Primarily Mpumalanga	Short	High
Business tourists	Primarily Gauteng	Short	High
Transit tourists	Primarily Gauteng, Limpopo, KZN	Short	Medium

Potential products

The Product/Market matrix shown below provides an overview of the existing products which meet a market need as identified in the target market segments above. The matrix indicates the strongest market segments for Mbombela are holiday and VFR for both the domestic and foreign markets. The strongest products on offer are entertainment and recreation, shopping and arts & crafts. This matrix is unweighted and merely provides an overview for discussion purposes.

Products	DOMESTIC					FOREIGN				TOTAL
	Holiday	VFRs	Shoppers	Business	Transit	Holiday	VFRs	Shoppers	Business	
Entertainment and recreation (19%)	√	√	√	√	√	√	√	√	√	9
Scenic drives and nature (17%)	√	√			√	√	√			4
Shopping (12%)	√	√	√	√		√		√	√	7
Adventure (9%)	√	√				√	√			4
Conservation & wilderness (7%)	√	√				√	√			4
Industrial tourism (7%)				√					√	2
Agricultural tourism (6%)				√		√	√		√	4
Fishing and hunting (5%)	√	√				√				3
Arts and crafts (4%)	√	√	√			√	√	√	√	7
Sport (4%)	√	√								2
Historical interest (4%)	√	√								2
Cultural interest (4%)	√	√				√	√	√		5
TOTAL:	10	10	3	4	2	7	7	4	4	

Product-market readiness

In terms of product development and improvement it was necessary to evaluate and determine the readiness of the product for the markets as identified above. Most products are reasonably ready for the market while in some areas improvements are required. Attention is required to the grading of products as only 40% of products in the study area as indicated by owners are graded. This will become increasingly important for the 2010 Football World Cup, and as the South African Tourism Grading Council grading system becomes more widely accepted.

The next stage of the project is to develop a marketing plan for the Mbombela Local Municipality. The destination's marketing resources are limited, and remain reliant on government support.

Discussion question

How does the planning approach used in the case relate to the proposed definition of a marketing orientation?

Further reading

http://www.mii.co.za (Mpumalanga Investment Initiative)
van Niekerk, M., & Geldenhuys, S. (2005). Developing a tourism sector plan for the Mbombela Local Municipality. In *International Conference on Destination Branding and Marketing for Regional Tourism Development*. Macau: Institute for Tourism Studies.

Note: The research was carried out by the Tshwane University of Technology, Tourism Department, Nelspruit Delivery Site for the Mbombela Local Municipality in South Africa.

Destination marketing organisations

Organisations have been defined as 'formal entities in which a complex interaction of people, materials, and money is used for the creation and distribution of goods and services' (Inkson & Kolb, 1998, p. 6). All organisations, whether in business, the public sector, or not-for-profit sector, share a common set of characteristics. Each usually has a range of objectives, a chairperson and governing board, a chief executive officer, and staff. The study of organisational behaviour emerged during the 1940s, and was primarily undertaken by psychologists interested in job satisfaction (Lawrence, 1987, in Kolb et al., 1995). Since then the field has expanded to cover a broad range of macro- and micro-issues relating to the external and internal environments in which organisations operate, such as: productivity, ethics, open systems, strategic management, innovation, leadership, governance, organisational culture, change management, human resource management, outsourcing, communication, networks, and organisational learning.

At a country level there are often three quite distinctive types of tourism organisations with interests in destination tourism development. These are a destination marketing organisation (DMO) responsible for promotion, a government ministry providing policy advice to government, and a private sector umbrella industry association that champions the causes of member organisations. The focus of the text is on the activities of organisations responsible for marketing the destination. A destination marketing organisation is:

> *The organisation responsible for the marketing of an identifiable destination. This therefore excludes separate government departments that are responsible for planning and policy, and private sector umbrella organisations.*

National tourism office (NTO)

The WTO (1979, p. ii) introduced the term national tourism administration (NTA) as: 'the authorities in the central state administration, or other official organisation, in charge of tourism development at the national level'. The term 'NTA' was used to distinguish it from national tourist organisation and national tourist office. For consistency in the text, the term national tourism office (NTO) is used to represent:

> *The entity with overall responsibility for marketing a country as a tourism destination, whether purely a DMO or an NTA.*

State tourism office (STO)

A state tourism office is:

> *The organisation with overall responsibility for marketing a state (e.g. USA), province (e.g. Canada) or territory (e.g. Australia) as a tourism destination, in a country that has a federal political system.*

Regional tourism organisation (RTO)

The term region has a number of different meanings, ranging in geographic scope from a transnational area such as South East Asia to a local area. For the text the term is used to represent 'concentrated tourism areas' (Prosser et al., 2000, p. 4), such as cities, towns, villages, coastal resort areas, islands and rural areas. This level of DMO is also known by other titles in different parts of the world, such as convention and visitor bureau (CVB), RTP in Wales, regional tourism boards (RTB) in the UK and area tourism boards (ATB) in Scotland. A regional tourism organisation is defined as:

> *The organisation responsible for marketing a concentrated tourism area as a tourism destination.*

Local tourism administration/Local tourism association (LTA)

Not all local tourism areas, as defined by a local authority boundary, have a standalone RTO. Instead they may have an LTA, which is a term used to represent both a local tourism administration and a local tourism association. The former may be the local government authority, while the latter is a form of cooperative association of tourism businesses.

Glossary

ATB	Area tourist board
BHAG	Big hairy audacious goal
CAM	Commercial accommodation monitor
CBBE	Consumer-based brand equity
CVB	Convention and visitors bureau
DMO	Destination marketing organisation
EAV	Equivalent advertising value
IMC	Integrated marketing communication
LTA	Local tourism administration/Local tourism association
Marcom	Marketing communication
MDP	Management decision problem
M.I.C.E	Meetings, incentives, conventions, exhibitions
MRP	Marketing research problem
NTA	National tourism administration
NTO	National tourism office
PPP	Public-private partnership
PR	Public relations
ROI	Return on investment
RTB	Regional tourist board
RTO	Regional tourism organisation
STO	State tourism office
ToMA	Top of mind awareness
TTRA	Travel and Tourism Research Association
USP	Unique selling point
VIC	Visitor information centre
VFR	Visiting friends and/or relatives
VMP	Visiting media programme
VRM	Visitor relationship management

Key points

1. The challenge of defining tourism

Although tourism has been around for centuries, it is only recently that the field of study has been taken seriously. Due to the complexity of tourism, and the intertwining of concepts such as tourism, travel, leisure, recreation, and hospitality, the definition used will differ according to the writer's purpose. Commonly, definitions have been based on technical, economic or holistic terms.

2. Different types of destinations

A DMO is often established or funded by the government of a political boundary. However, travellers do not necessarily view a destination as being based on such a political space. Therefore, a destination may be a section of a political boundary, an entire political boundary, or across political boundaries.

3. The importance of a marketing orientation

It has been suggested that the tourism industry has been slow to evolve towards a marketing orientation. A marketing orientation is a philosophy which should pervade the entire organisation that is based on making all decisions with the consumer in mind. Marketing is seen as an exchange process between the demand side and supply side, in a way that matches organisation resources with environment opportunities.

Review questions

- What is a market orientation? To what extent does your DMO demonstrate a marketing orientation?
- For your favourite destination, what type of cluster does it represent?
- When you are on holiday, do you regard yourself as a tourist? Does the term sound derogatory?

Destination marketing organisations

The primary reason cities created destination marketing organizations hasn't changed in more than 100 years: "Bring in the business".

John A. Marks, President and CEO, San Fransisco Convention & Visitors Bureau (in Marks, 2004).

Aims

The aims of this chapter are to enhance understanding of:

- the proliferation of DMOs
- the rationale for the establishment of DMOs
- the challenge of marketing multi-attributed destinations in dynamic and heterogenous markets.

> **Perspective**
>
> DMOs are the result of a tourism community becoming organised. The first were established over a century ago, although a large number only emerged in the 1970s and 1980s. The early DMOs were predominantly promotion oriented, focusing on booster policies. Increasingly, communities are recognising that a foundation of their destination's competitiveness is the establishment of a partnership approach between stakeholders with a vested interest in the impacts of visitors; and that the partnership recognises the importance of the local environment, an effective market position, the visitor experience, the profitability of tourism businesses, and local residents' views. In today's market place it is doubtful that destination competitiveness could be attained, let alone sustained, without an organisation committed to such a holistic and long-term perspective. This chapter provides an introduction to the politics, opportunities, challenges, and constraints faced by DMOs. In the history of DMO development, the rationale has been the quest for destination competitiveness.

A brief history of DMO development

Recognition by tourism communities of the need to become organised, to foster a *cooperate to compete* approach to achieve destination competitiveness has led to a proliferation of DMOs, particularly since the 1980s.

Table 3.1 Historical analyses of tourism

Author	Topic	Country
Sigaux (1966)	History of tourism	France
Walton (1983)	Seaside resorts in the 18th and 19th centuries	UK
Stafford (1986, 1988)	Development of a resort area in the 19th and 20th centuries	New Zealand
Sears (1989)	Tourist attractions in the 19th century	USA
Black (1992)	The Grand Tour of the 18th century	UK
Aron (1999)	History of vacations	USA
Richardson (1999)	A history of Australian travel and tourism	Australia
Walton (2000)	Seaside holidays in the 20th century	UK
Davidson & Spearritt (2000)	Tourism in Australia since 1870	Australia
Shaffer (2001)	Tourism and national identity, 1880–1940	USA
Cross & Walton (2006)	Pleasure places in the 20th century	UK, USA
Berger (2006)	Development of Mexico's tourism industry	Mexico

Although no one knows exactly how many DMOs exist on the planet, after seeking input from academics on the global TRInet listserv in 2003, Professor Bob McKercher's estimate was over 10,000.

The history of DMOs is relatively short, with the first emerging in the late 19th century. While there is a growing body of literature interpreting the development of modern tourism in general, a selection of which is shown in Table 3.1, disappointingly the published literature on the evolution of DMOs around the world is sparse.

National tourism offices

The establishment of the New Zealand Department of Tourist and Health Resorts in February 1901 represented the world's first NTO (NZTPD, 1976). This was a remarkably forward-thinking initiative for a small, fledgling and far-flung South Pacific colony, at a time when only four New Zealand towns had electricity. At the same time, New Zealand was the first country to introduce government tourist bureaux (Coventry, 2001), which were a vertical integration of overseas sales and promotion office, tour wholesaler, travel agent, and visitor information centre. The first regional Government Tourist Bureau was built in Rotorua, on the southern end of the city's current visitor information centre, and was funded and operated by the NZTPD for almost 90 years. The first overseas sales mission was a visit to the 1904 St Louis Exposition in the USA. In 1906 the department opened a bureau in Australia (NZTPD, 1976), and by 1910 honorary agents had been appointed in England, USA, Canada, and South Africa (TNZ, 2001). Interestingly, it would be another fifty years before a national umbrella association of private-sector tourism interests was formed in New Zealand (Staniford & Cheyne, 1994).

Many nations did not establish an NTO until decades after New Zealand. For example, of the key neighbouring competitors to New Zealand in European markets, Australia's federal government did not become involved in tourism marketing until 1929 when a grant was provided to the newly-formed Australian National Tourist Authority (Carroll, 1991). The nearby Samoa Visitors Bureau was not established in 1986 (Pearce, 1999).

In Europe, the French NTO was established in 1910 (Sigaux, 1966). By 1919, when the Italian NTO was established (Osti & Pechlaner, 2001), the Alliance Internationale du Tourisme had been formed in Brussels, bringing together 30 European NTOs. In Britain, the government provided financial support for the 1929 establishment of the Travel Association of Great Britain and Ireland (Elliott, 1997). However, the organisation was no more than embryonic until after World War II, when the publicly supported British Tourism and Holiday Board was formed in 1947 (Jeffries, 1989). Predating this was the English Channel island state of Jersey, where a tourism committee was empowered to promote the destination in 1937 (Cooper, 1997). In a case of unfortunate timing, both the Irish Tourism Board and the Belgium General Commission for Tourism were established in 1939 (WTO, 1979). The Northern Ireland Tourist Board was established through the Development of Tourism Act of 1948 (Davidson & Maitland, 1997). The first statutory legislation in Britain did not occur until the Development of

Tourism Act of 1969 (English, 2000), which paved the way for the national tourist boards of Scotland, Wales, and England, as well as the British Tourist Authority (BTA). It has been suggested that in Scotland tourism had not been seriously addressed until this time (Kerr & Wood, 2000).

Following World War II the International Union of Official Tourism Organisations, the predecessor of the World Tourism Organisation, had around 100 member NTOs in 1946 (Vellas & Bécherel, 1995). In Asia the Hong Kong Tourism Association was established in 1957 (Gartrell, 1994), Japan and Thailand established NTOs in 1959, and Singapore in 1964 (Choy, 1993). The Barbados Tourism Board was formed in 1958. In Africa the Ghana Tourist Board and Ivory Coast Ministry of Tourism were established in 1960, and the Nigerian Tourist Association was formed in 1962 (WTO, 1979). The first official NTO in Sweden was not established until 1976 (Pearce, 1996).

The Mexican federal government created the Mixed Pro-Tourism Commission in 1928, which brought together representatives from government ministries and the private sector, to develop a tourism industry (Berger, 2006). The Cuban National Tourism Commission was also formed in the 1920s (Berger, 2006), while the Canadian Bureau of Tourism was established in 1934 (Go, 1987; Jenkins, 1995). The government of the USA did not become seriously involved in international tourism promotion until 1961, when the International Travel Act was passed by congress (Mill & Morrison, 1986). This enabled the establishment of the United States Travel Service as a division of the Department of Commerce, which would later be changed to the US Travel and Tourism Administration (USTTA). The USTTA folded in 1996 due to a lack of funding (Brewton & Withiam, 1998). Morrison et. al. (1998) observed that CVBs such as Las Vegas had larger budgets than the fledgling NTO. Congress then established the National Tourism Organisation, a smaller NTO, to encourage public/private sector cooperation, which was in turn scrapped (Blalock, 2000). The USA became actively involved at a national level again in 2003 with the formation of the new Tourism and Travel Promotion Advisory Board (Hoover, 2003).

By 2006, WTO membership included 150 countries, seven territories and 350 affiliate organisations (www.world-tourism.org/):

> With its headquarters in Madrid, Spain, the UNWTO plays a central and decisive role in promoting the development of responsible, sustainable and universally accessible tourism, with the aim of contributing to economic development, international understanding, peace, prosperity and universal respect for, and observance of, human rights and fundamental freedoms. In pursuing this aim, the Organization pays particular attention to the interests of developing countries in the field of tourism.

State tourism organisations

The Hawaii Visitors Bureau was established in 1903, following tourism promotional visits to the US mainland in 1901 and 1902 by the Honolulu Chamber of Commerce and Merchants Association (Choy, 1993). Most other American state tourism marketing did not occur until much later. Doering (1979) suggested that some state tourism marketing offices were being established during the 1940s in anticipation of a post-war surge in domestic tourism. Of the then 48 states, 26 had become involved in tourism promotion by 1946. It would not be until the 1970s that all states had STOs.

The state government of Tasmania in Australia initiated the Tasmanian Tourist Association in 1893 (Davidson & Spearritt, 2000), although little has been reported about its activities. Spurred on by the success of the Tasmanian group in creating a tourism profile, the Governor of the state of New South Wales convened a conference of government officials in 1905 to initiate the establishment of a tourism division that was curiously called the Intelligence Department. The states of South Australia and Victoria followed in 1908. However, the first STOs to be formed as separate government agencies, rather than as part of other departments, did not occur in Australia until 1919 (New South Wales), 1921 (Western Australia), and 1934 (Tasmania).

Regional tourism organisations

The reported history of regional tourism promotion significantly predates that for NTOs and STOs. For example, the first travel guidebook for Cambridge in England was published in 1758 (Davidson & Maitland, 1997), while visitor guidebooks for English seaside resorts were also in use around this time (Walton, 1983). In Switzerland, the first RTO was established at St Moritz in 1864 (Lässer, 2000). In 1879 the Blackpool Municipal Corporation obtained British government authority to levy a local property tax for advertising the destination's attractions (Walton, 1991, in Cross & Walton, 2005). This was a unique privilege as competing British resort areas only obtained lesser powers four decades later when the Local Authorities (Publicity) Act (1931) legislated to give local government the opportunity to engage in destination promotion (Lavery, 1990). Following the establishment of the English Tourist Board (ETB) in 1969, 12 English RTBs were created, jointly funded by the ETB, local government, and the private sector (Davidson & Maitland, 1997). Old industrial cities such as Bradford, Sheffield, Birmingham, and Manchester did not establish DMOs until the 1980s (Bramwell & Rawding, 1994).

The establishment of RTOs in Spain occurred only slowly from the 1980s (Pearce, 1996b). Similarly, in New Zealand most RTOs were established in the 1980s when local government became more proactive in economic development; although there had been various other forms of destination promotion since the 1880s. In Australia, Dredge (2001) suggested that the New South Wales local government were given legislative power to develop leisure and recreation facilities as early as 1858, at a time when demand was increasing for such facilities by excursionists and holiday-makers, and by 1908 were given powers to stimulate tourism through advertising. However, for a number of reasons, including a legacy of paternalistic and centralised state government, there had been, in general, a "timid approach" towards direct involvement in tourism development initiatives.

Convention and visitor bureaus (CVB)

While Sheehan and Ritchie's (1997) survey of 134 North American CVBs identified 15 that had been in existence for over 50 years, the average was only 23 years. Tourism Vancouver, however, is over 100 years old (Vallee, 2005). Even though infrastructure developments enabled regional tourism in north-eastern USA during the late 1700s and early 1800s (see Shaffer, 2001), the development of place promotion organisations did not occur for another century. Interestingly, at Coney Island, which had attracted visitors since the early 1800s, there was no attempt to collectively advertise the destination until 1902 when a Board of Trade was formed (Cross & Walton, 2005). In the interim, travel advertising in many parts of the USA was organised by boosters and the railways. The CVB format emanated in the USA, where the first was set up in Detroit in 1896 (Gartrell, 1992). The next CVBs to be established were in Atlantic City in 1908, Denver in 1909, and Atlanta in 1913 (wee.iacvb.org). Well-known cities to set up CVBs much later include New York in 1934, Chicago in 1943, Las Vegas in 1955, Anaheim in 1961, Orlando and Orange County in 1984.

Destination competitiveness

The rationale for the development of DMOs, at all levels, has been as a means for enhancing destination competitiveness. While destination competitiveness has been described as "tourism's holy grail" (Ritchie & Crouch, 2000a), this field of research only emerged during the 1990s. An issue on tourism and travel competitiveness in *Tourism* (see Volume 47, Issue 4, 1999) featured three papers at the destination level: price competitiveness (Dwyer et al., 1999), the role of Spanish public administrations (Bueno, 1999), and the competitiveness of alpine destinations (Pechlaner, 1999). *Tourism Management* then devoted a special issue to 'The Competitive Destination' (see Volume 21, Issue 1, 2000). The range of topics covered in this issue highlights the multidimensional nature of destination competitiveness:

- sustainable competitiveness (Ritchie & Crouch, 2000b)
- price competitiveness (Dwyer et al., 2000)
- managed destinations (d'Hauteserre, 2000)
- responding to competition (Kim et al., 2000)
- the destination product and its impact on traveller perceptions (Murphy et al., 2000)
- the role of public transport in destination development (Prideaux, 2000)
- environmental management (Mihali, 2000)
- integrated quality management (Go & Govers, 2000)
- regional positioning (Uysal et al., 2000)
- marketing the competitive destination of the future (Buhalis, 2000).

From these works, along with a review of other papers on the topic (see Australian Department of Industry, Tourism and Resources, 2001; Ahmed & Krohn, 1990; Crouch & Ritchie, 1999; Dwyer, Livaic & Mellor,

2003; Enright & Newton, 2005, 2006; Faulkner, Oppermann & Fredline, 1999; Fayos-Sola. 2002; Heath, 2003; Kozac, 2002; March, 2003; Melian-Gonzalez & Garcia-Falcon, 2003; Poon, 1993; Ritchie & Crouch, 2000a, 2003; Ritchie, Crouch & Hudson, 2000; Rubies, 2001; Smeral, 1996, 2004; Smeral & Witt, 2002; Vanhove, 2006), it is clear that while there is not yet a widely accepted causal model of destination competitiveness, there is agreement that the construct comprises economic, social, cultural, and environmental dimensions. A competitive destination is one that features profitable tourism businesses, an effective market position, an attractive environment, satisfactory visitor experiences, and supportive local residents.

In practice

During 2004 the WTTC developed a destination competitiveness index, in conjunction with the Christel de Haan Tourism and Travel Research Institute at the University of Nottingham. The index tracked the extent to which each of over 200 countries provided a competitive environment for travel and tourism development. The data is summarised through a traffic-light colour-coded system for each country across eight indices. These provide a measure out of 100 that is relative to the other countries rather than one that is absolute. Green, amber, and red lights indicate above average, average, and below average performance. For example, the assessments for Australia and China across the eight measures are compared in Table 3.2. Australia was judged a world leader in terms of infrastructure, technology, human resources and social, but lagged in a number of areas such as price competitiveness and openness. China, on the other hand, was regarded as a leader in price competitiveness but fell short in areas such as environment, openness and human tourism.

Table 3.2 WTTC competitive indices for Australia and China

Index	Australia index value	China index value	Australia rank	China rank
Price competitiveness	35 (red)	89 (green)	95	3
Human tourism	32 (red)	9 (red)	68	107
Infrastructure	100 (green)	34 (red)	1	93
Environment	60 (orange)	38 (orange)	42	133
Technology	100 (green)	51 (orange)	24	93
Human resources	100 (green)	50 (orange)	1	82
Openness	56 (orange)	35 (red)	89	127
Social	96 (green)	53 (green)	6	93

Given the multidimensional nature of destination competitiveness, it is doubtful in today's competitive travel marketplace that a destination could sustain, even attain, competitiveness without effective organisation. Regardless of whether the first DMOs held a holistic perspective regarding the environment, visitors, businesses, and residents, which I referred to as a societal-marketing orientation in Chapter 1, or were essentially boosters limited to a promotion orientation such as in Spain during the 1960s and 1970s (see Bueno, 1999) and Mexico today (see Cerda, 2005), the purpose has been to enhance market competitiveness of a destination in a manner that could not be achieved by individual stakeholders working in isolation.

Booster is a term used to describe '. . . a simplistic attitude that tourism development is inherently good and of automatic benefit to the hosts' (Hall, 1998, p. 248). Getz (1987, in Hall, 1998) argued that boosterism is practised by two groups: politicians seeking economic development and those benefiting financially from tourism. In boosterism little planning consideration is given to the wider issues of potential negative economic, social, and environment impacts. The first major booster campaign in the USA was probably the 1906 *See America First* concept, which originated in Salt Lake City (see Shaffer, 2001). The campaign endeavoured to convince Americans to see 'The West' of the USA instead of travelling to Europe, which was in vogue at the time. The idea was for the formation of an alliance of railways, governments, and businesses to advertise the West's tourist attractions, as well as develop infrastructure. While a lack of funding quickly derailed the original plans, the *See America First* theme continued to be used for many years by various Western booster groups:

> . . . *See America First expressed the desires of western boosters interested in promoting scenery for the sake of increasing investment and settlement in the West.*

For many destinations, maintaining competitiveness is now a major challenge (WTTC, 2001, in Australian Department of Industry, Tourism and Resources, 2001). Competition is intensifying due to maturing tourism growth rates, increasing numbers of DMOs, and increasing budgets of NTOs (Ritchie & Crouch, 2000). A number of destinations in decline or stagnation have been reported, including Hamm (Buckley & Witt, 1985), Majorca (Morgan, 1991), Canada (Go, 1987), Bermuda (Conlin, 1995), Amsterdam (Dahles, 1998), Spain during the 1970s (Bueno, 1999), USA during the 1980s (Ahmed & Krohn, 1990), Rotorua, New Zealand (Pike, 2007), Australia's Gold Coast (Faulkner, 2002), and Fiji during the 1980s and 1990s (McDonnell & Darcy, 1998). As observed by Rubie (2001, p. 38):

> *There are many tourist destinations that produce little richness, low prosperity, and high social and environmental costs. Some were prosperous in the past and today hardly survive and face very strong social or economic problems. Others see their future with pessimism. And all wonder the keys to sustainability .*

What have you got that I can't get anywhere else?

At the 2005 Tourism & Travel Research Association conference in New Orleans (just prior to Hurricane Katrina), keynote speaker Peter Greenberg, well known to Americans as 'the travel detective' on one of the national television networks, challenged the audience with the same question he poses to destination promoters who lobby him to film a segment at their place: 'Tell me what experience you offer me that I can't find anywhere else'. This gets to the heart of the challenge of destination marketing, which is differentiating amidst an almost endless list of competitors. Greenberg argued that most destinations struggle to do this. One of the greatest obstacles to achieving destination competitiveness is the challenge of marketing multi-attributed destinations in dynamic and heterogeneous markets.

Marketing multi-attributed destinations in dynamic and heterogeneous markets

The tourism industry (in New Zealand) is so fragmented, diverse, unfocused, self-seeking, and disorganised that PhD theses have been written on its structural complexities. It's got more separate working parts than a 747's Rolls Royce engine and only some of them are vaguely headed in the same direction (Chamberlain, 1992).

While Chamberlain's (1992) observations were made in the context of the New Zealand tourism industry, there will be few if any countries where a multiplicity of divergent tourism interests, and therefore potential for fragmentation to occur, does not exist. Consider also the small scale of the New Zealand tourism industry, with an estimated 13,500 to 18,000 small businesses (OTSP, 2001), compared to Europe with an estimated 1.5 million tourism businesses, of which 95% employ less than 10 people (Wason, 1998), and the issue is magnified. A key theme readers will find recurring throughout the text is the DMO challenge of promoting a multi-attributed destination in dynamic and heterogeneous and global marketplace. From the supply-side marketing perspective, a DMO represents a large, diverse and even eclectic range of destination attributes, including natural features, commercial, and not-for-profit facilities and amenities. Consider the following for example:

- commercial visitor attractions such as theme parks and wildlife sanctuaries
- water-based activities such as day cruises, whitewater rafting, and boat hire
- accommodation suppliers such as hotels, exclusive lodges, backpacker hostels, and bed and breakfast guest houses
- outdoor adventure activities such as parachuting, bungy jumping, and bridge climbs
- dining and nightlife, such as restaurants, cafes, pubs, and clubs
- shopping precincts, malls, and craft markets
- archaeological and historic sites

- castles and palaces
- battlefields and scenes of disaster
- cathedrals, churches, temples, and mosques
- beaches, harbours, lakes, rivers, and waterfalls
- museums and art galleries
- picnic and barbecue amenities
- children's playgrounds
- forests, parklands, flora, and fauna
- sporting facilities such as football stadiums and golf courses
- festivals and special events
- mountains and landscape vistas
- ski fields
- theatres and cinemas
- host population characteristics such as language, customs, and indigenous culture
- climate.

The key tenet of this theme is that a DMO usually has no direct control over the products they represent, nor the packaged offerings of intermediaries such as airlines, tour wholesalers, and travel agencies. From the supply perspective, the often eclectic collection of destination features must somehow be presented to the market in a way that not only cuts through the clutter of crowded markets to offer benefits desired by travellers, but also satisfies the interests of the host community, local businesses, and travel intermediaries. DMO and stakeholder opinions on how this can be achieved are rarely congruent. It is not being cynical to suggest the natural self-interest of many businesses will instinctively be to expect their market of interest to be the target of promotions, which in turn feature their product. The politics of DMO decision-making can, and does, inhibit implementation of marketing theory. In this respect, destination marketing requires a certain amount of courage!

On the demand-side of destination marketing, the global market of consumer-travellers is not homogenous in terms of needs (Wahab et al., 1976). Travellers from different geographic areas, socio-demographic groups, and lifestyle clusters will respond to different offers at different times, for a complex array of reasons, including the purpose of travel, individual motivation(s), time available, the time of year, and availability of other discretionary spending opportunities. Consumers will engage in different types of travel at different times of the year and their lifetime. Thousands of DMOs now compete for the attention of busy consumers through communication channels cluttered with noise from rival and substitute offerings. The greatest challenge facing DMOs is to effectively differentiate their offering at decision time.

Travel might be considered a psychological necessity for some individuals. However, for others travel and tourism involves discretionary spending, where a new car, stereo or wedding will compete for scarce funds. Not even the largest NTOs have the resources to match the promotional spend of corporate heavyweights from other product categories, such as Coke, Sony, and BMW. Increasingly, marketers must communicate meaningful but focused messages at the right time and place to gain 'cut through' to the right people. How can a DMO produce succinct messages that (1) encapsulate the essence of place, (2) differentiate the destination from the myriad of competitors offering the same features, (3) at the time households are making holiday decisions, and (4) be meaningful to heterogeneous and dynamic markets? Destination marketing is not for the faint-hearted, and this core challenge, faced by every destination globally, has implications for every aspect of DMO operations, including: funding, strategy, organisation, politics, finance and budgeting, human resources, crisis management, branding, communication, market research, promotions and performance measures.

Career opportunities

In the post-industrial era, the success of a corporation lies more in its intellectual and systems capabilities than in its physical assets (Quinn et al., 1996, p. 71). As with any organisation, staff are an important asset for any DMO. This is important at all levels, from the frontline staff at visitor information centres to the CEO. DMOs usually enjoy a high profile within the destination community, and this carries political implications for customer services skills. DMOs are now recognised as providing serious career opportunities. For example, a survey of IACVB members (IACVB, 2001, in Fenich, 2005) found that the average staff size of CVBs was 14 full-time employees. However there is a dearth of literature relating to human resource management in DMOs.

In Australia, McKercher and Ritchie's (1997) study of local government tourism officers raised questions about levels of professionalism in the field. They found, for example, a lack of formal tourism qualifications, little prior tourism industry experience, and turnover of up to 50% of staff each year. Given the nature of the challenges discussed and the high turnover, McKercher and Ritchie questioned whether local government tourism management is seen as a valid career in its own right or merely a stepping stone to other opportunities. Some of the difficulties faced by local government tourism officials included:

- working in small organisations with no internal promotion opportunities
- isolation from counterparts
- under-staffing
- under-funding
- unrealistic expectations from elected council representatives.

Ultimately the impact of a high turnover is disruption to what are predominantly small teams. McKercher and Ritchie (1997) identified three primary reasons for the high turnover of staff. First, many local authority tourism staff aspire to higher positions within the tourism industry and use the LTA as a stepping stone to other organisations such as STOs. Such moves offer higher salaries as well as greater status within the tourism hierarchy. Second, LTA roles are generally very high profile within the community, and managers are likely to become public property. As a result the role is forced to become involved in a broader range of activities than tourism promotion, which can be seen as being invasive. Third, LTA roles require constant innovation as well as ongoing lobbying of local politicians. Therefore it can be easier to move and transfer existing ideas to a new community.

Research snapshot 3.1 Management characteristics

Morrison et al.'s (1998) 1992/93 survey of 254 member CVBs of the IACVB found executives of the highest funded organisations were more likely to be males over 55 years with a university degree and an average of 16 years experience:

- **Gender** The executives of 59% of CVBs were male and 41% were female. Female executives tended to work with smaller budgets than male executives.
- **Education** Two-thirds of executives had university degrees, with three holding doctorates. 80% of male executives had degrees but only 49% of females.
- **College major** Less than 2% indicated a tourism major. Of the 66 majors listed the most common were business administration (18%), marketing (10%), and education (8%).
- **Tourism work experience** Two-thirds of executives indicated prior tourism industry experience, while 45% had previously worked in a CVB.
- **Income** Two-thirds of executives had salaries of US$50,000 or more. Incomes tended to rise in relation to age and education. Males averaged US$70,000–$74,999, while females averaged US$45,000–$49,999. 14% of males earned over US$110,000 compared to 1% of females.
- **Job titles** A total of 19 different titles were reported, with the most common being Executive Director (50%) and President (15%). 41% of males were listed as President/CEO, in comparison to only 12% of females.
- **Period of tenure** The average period of tenure for the current executives was 5.6 years, from a range of 1 to 25 years.

Source: Morrison, A., Bruen, S. M. & Anderson, D.J. (1998). Convention and visitor bureaus in the USA: A profile of bureaus, bureau executives, and budgets. *Journal of Travel & Tourism Marketing*, 7(1), 1–19.

Given the noticeable gender differences identified in Research Snapshot 3.1, Morrison et al. (1998) proposed a worthwhile project of identifying the characteristics of successful female executives. Likewise, McKercher and Ritchie (1997) found a gender imbalance among LTAs in the Australian states of Victoria and New South Wales. Women tended to be relegated to lower status positions of managing VIC units, while the management of larger local authority tourism departments were more likely to be male. There was also a significant gender salary gap, even though males were generally no better qualified than women.

Skills and qualifications

Sims' (1990) survey of 79 CVBs identified a mean of seven professional staff, of which five were male and two female. The paper listed respondents' views on desirable attributes for service level, sales, and administration positions. Frequently mentioned personal qualities were: creativity, flexibility, friendliness, honesty, motivation, outgoing personality, and honesty. The majority of respondents felt a university degree was a prerequisite for employment. In a survey of STO and CVB management, O'Halloran (1992) found 76% and 80% respectively held university degrees. Both groups considered people as the most important DMO resource. The most important DMO management skills were leadership and employee relations, followed by marketing and other technical skills. O'Halloran summarised the following essential characteristics of a successful DMO manager:

- At least six years experience with a DMO, with additional prior business experience.
- A minimum of a bachelor's degree, preferably in tourism or business.
- Excellent communication skills.
- The ability to work well with people at all levels.
- Knowledge of the tourism system and its potential impacts on the community.
- Leadership and strategic planning.
- Political savvy, in terms of the political system and the relationship between the public and private sectors.

It is one of the great business myths that visionary organisations are great places to work (Collins & Poras, 1997). Rather, they are great places to work for those who fit the culture of the organisation. Prospective DMO staff should do their homework to find out everything they can about the culture of the organisation. In return candidates should expect a rigorous screening process. In many communities the DMO is a high-profile organisation, and so there is usually strong competition for advertised positions. Students seeking a career in destination marketing might be interested to note O'Halloran's (1992, p. 90) curriculum recommendations for DMO management training:

> Subject areas for study should be communication (persuasion and negotiation, advertising, business writing, oral communication, and inter-personal communication), business (tourism systems, management skills, policy, services management, economics, planning and development, marketing, finance and accounting), social sciences (geography, anthropology, psychology, sociology, and political science). Other critical skills include research methods and management, information systems, transportation and international studies.

In terms of professional development training for DMO staff, the IACVB offers a Certified Destination Management Executive Program (CDME):

> Recognized by the CVB industry as its highest educational achievement, CDME is an advanced educational program for veteran and

career-minded CVB executives looking for senior-level professional development courses. The focus of the program is on vision, leadership, productivity and the implementation of business strategies (www.iacvb.org/iacvb/view_page.asp?mkey=&mid=100, 23/4/04).

Key points

1. Proliferation of DMOs

DMOs have been in existence for over a century. The first RTO and STO were established in the 19th century and the first NTO at the beginning of the 20th century. Many, however, have only been established relatively recently as communities have recognised the need for a coordinated approach to place promotion. Recognition of the positive impacts of tourism, and the need for a coordinated destination promotion effort, has led to a proliferation of DMOs worldwide.

2. The rationale for the establishment of DMOs

The rationale for the development of DMOs, at all levels, has been as a means for enhancing destination competitiveness. Given the multidimensional nature of destination competitiveness, it is doubtful in today's competitive travel marketplace that a destination could sustain, even attain, competitiveness without effective organisation.

3. The challenge of marketing multi-attributed destinations in dynamic and heterogeneous markets

One of the consistent themes in the text is the challenge of marketing multi-attributed destinations in dynamic and heterogenous markets. From the supply-side marketing perspective, a DMO represents a large, diverse, and even eclectic range of destination attributes. On the demand-side of destination marketing, the global market of consumer-travellers is not homogenous in terms of needs. Travellers from different geographic areas, socio-demographic groups, and lifestyle clusters will respond to different offers at different times, for a complex array of reasons. Cutting through the competitive noise with a meaningful proposition at consumer decision time is arguably the DMO's greatest challenge.

Review questions

- Summarise the key dimensions of destination competitiveness.
- If there wasn't a DMO at your destination, what would the likely impacts on the local tourism industry be?

Organisation structure

The continual stream of great products and services from highly visionary companies stems from them being outstanding organizations, not the other way around.

Collins and Poras (1997, p. 31)

Aims

The aims of this chapter are to enhance understanding of:

- the variety in DMO legal entity
- public–private partnerships
- governance challenges.

> **Perspective**
>
> In terms of being organised for the quest of destination competitiveness, it is worthwhile considering whether good strategy emerges from an effective organisational structure, or whether the organisation should be structured to implement an innovative strategy. After all, it has been suggested that being organised will increasingly be the basis for gaining competitive advantage in the future. The management literature is divided on the issue on the relationship between structure and strategy. On one hand there is the view that strategy is paramount, and therefore structure, processes, and culture should be designed to enable it. On the other hand is the view that a value-oriented organisation is first required to underpin the development of an effective strategy. What is evident from an analysis of DMO evolution is a general shift in structure that has taken place, with DMOs generally moving from bureaucratic government departments to more entrepreneurial and accountable private-public partnerships (PPPs). Such PPPs represent a maturing in attitudes of both the public and private sectors.

DMO legal entity

Is structure the quintessential management tool? Alternatively, should structure be designed to enable a competitive strategy? Galbraith and Lawler (1993), for example, argued that organisational structure will be the basis for gaining competitive advantage in the future. This view suggests that as sustainable competitive advantage becomes increasingly difficult to achieve through unique strategies, it will be the well-structured organisations that will be the most effective in implementing new strategy. Treacy and Wiersema (1995) on the other hand argued that strategy is paramount, and should be based on excelling in one of three value propositions: (1) best total cost, (2) best product, or (3) best total solution. Structure, processes, and culture should be designed to enable continually improving superior value of the strategy. Porter (1996) also promoted the view that operational effectiveness is necessary but not sufficient, and argued that a serious problem is the failure to distinguish operational effectiveness from strategy. Tourism businesses need to cultivate organisational learning and in doing so align processes with customer expectations through effective feedback systems. Organisational creativity therefore represents an important resource-based advantage due to the difficulty in replicating. The challenge is clear:

> *The challenge for managers in the future will be to balance the need for efficiency and consistency with the need for constant innovation. Organisations will need to 'learn how to learn' (Gilbert, 1995, p. 350).*

If constant innovation is necessary, organisations may need to create flexible structures. Market niches are becoming smaller, thus favouring flexible specialised companies:

> *Competitive advantage has, in recent years, tended to shift away from firms with large size and long experience toward firms with unique knowledge and swift response capabilities (Oviatt, 1995).*

However, there has been little research into the relationships between organisation, strategy, and effectiveness of DMOs to guide destination marketers on effective organisation. Indeed there has been little published at all about the structure of NTOs (Choy, 1993; Morrison et al., 1995). What is apparent is that no universally accepted model for DMO structure currently exists. This is evidenced by the great variety in existence (Morrison et al., 1995, p. 606):

> *This variety is reflected in different organisational names (e.g. authorities, commissions, boards, tourist organisations, bureaux, tourist offices, corporations, departments, councils, ministries, etc.), relationships to national governments, budget levels, tourism policies, goals, objectives, responsibilities, and foreign office locations. It is clear that no typical 'model' for an NTO can be suggested because of the great diversity that there is in existing organisational types.*

At the RTO level, different models exist in different countries. In some cases a system is imposed from the national or state level, such as in England and in Queensland, Australia. The incentive for regions to participate is usually access to government funding. In other cases, such as in Sweden (see Pearce, 1996a) and in New Zealand, regions are free to establish, or not establish, any RTO structure desired. Little or no direct financial support is available from central government, and RTOs will be at the mercy of their local government for funding. A hybrid of these approaches is also evident. For example, in Scotland the Area Tourist Boards are statutory bodies, coming under the control of the Scottish Tourism Board (Kerr & Wood, 2000). However, they do not receive statutory funding, relying instead on grants from the NTO and local government. Some RTOs have been based on a single country, such as in Sweden, while others have been based on macro-regions, such as in Wales.

In terms of geographic scale, the largest DMOs are those that have been established to market the tourism interests of a group of countries. In this regard there have been calls for increased cooperation between countries in many parts of the world, including for example: Scandinavia (Flagestad & Hope, 2001), central and eastern Europe (Davidson & Maitland, 1997; Hall,

1998), East Africa (Beirman, 2003b), and Australasia (Tourelle, 2003). In other areas, such collaboration has been formalized. Examples include:

- The Caribbean Tourism Organisation (CTO, see www.onecaribbean.org) is a cooperative approach to marketing the region's small island nations. Formed over 50 years ago, the CTO comprises 32 member governments.
- The European Travel Commission (ETC, see www.etc-europe-travel.org) is the Brussels-based headquarters for Europe's 37 NTOs. The roles of the ETC are to market Europe as a tourism destination, and to provide advice to member NTOs. A key aspect of the organisation's structure has been the formation of 'Operations Groups' of member NTOs in North America, Japan, and Latin America.
- The South Pacific Tourism Organisation (SPTO, see www.tcsp.com) was formed in the 1980s to promote tourism to the region. SPTO represents 12 Pacific island NTOs, and, interestingly, China.
- The Asia Pacific Tourism Organisation (see www.apto.org) was formed in 2004, and currently has 43 member countries.
- During 2003 the Irish government established a new national tourism development authority, Fáilte Ireland (see www.failteireland.ie), to replace Bord Fáilte and CERT. Previously the countries of Ireland and Northern Ireland operated separate NTOs.
- Visit Britain was also established in 2003, to replace the British Tourist Authority (BTA) and English Tourism Commission (ETC). Visit Britain represents England, Scotland, and Wales.
- The Confederación de Organizaciones Turísticas de la America Latina (see www.cotal.org.ar).
- The ASEAN tourism association (see www.aseanta.org).
- The Indian Ocean Tourism Organization (see www.cowan.edu.au).

Public–private partnerships

At an NTO level, DMOs have historically been government departments. By the 1970s however it was evident a shift was emerging away from direct government involvement in DMO operations. From a survey of 95 NTOs in 1975, the WTO (1975) found only 6 that were non-governmental. The WTO (1979) also found that of 100 recognised NTAs, 68 were part of the country's government administration, which the WTO suggested provided the advantage of being able to directly influence government tourism policy in addition to undertaking promotional work. The remaining 32 NTAs were operating outside the central administration. Although still linked to, and funded by, central government, these organisations had a separate legal identity. A benefit of this structure was greater financial and administrative independence:

> *The proper solution for each country can only be found within the framework of the national situation, but the main point is that the NTA should be able to work closely with, and obtain the active support and cooperation of, all government authorities whose responsibilities affect*

various aspects of tourism, as well as the private sector, if it is to help develop balanced travel plant and an effective tourism development programme (WTO, 1979, p. 3).

This is representative of a public–private partnership (PPP), which is becoming the most common form of DMO at NTO, STO, and RTO levels. For example, most provincial and territorial DMOs in Canada are now industry led and publicly funded (National Tourism Strategy, 2003, in Vallee, 2005). Smith (2003) described the evolution of Canada's NTO to a new public–private partnership, the Canadian Tourism Commission (CTC), in 1995. A major impetus for change was complaints by industry that the previous administration was under-funded and not market driven. In Australia, STOs have commonly been formed as statutory authorities, which are established by an Act of Parliament.

In the UK, private-public partnerships (PPPs) became a means towards generating larger budgets for local destination marketing during the 1980s and 1990s when tight spending restrictions on local governments were applied by central government (Bramwell & Rawding, 1994). For example, in 1993 Leicester Promotions Ltd was established as a non-profit RTO with a £1.1 million grant from the local council (Miller, 2003). A decade later and partnerships with the private sector have led to the council funding representing less than 50% of the annual budget.

The WTO adopted the theme of 'Public–private sector partnership: the key to tourism development and promotion' for world tourism day in 1998. Some DMOs were quick to embrace the concept, such as Visit Florida, which celebrated 10 years of PPP status in 2006. The STO was established in 1996 when the Department of Commerce was disbanded to make way for a PPP to promote tourism to Florida (www.travelindustryreview.com, 1/3/06). Others have yet to pursue this approach. For example, during 2006 there were strong calls by the government opposition in Bermuda to replace the Ministry of Tourism with a PPP that would be 'more in tune . . . forward thinking and fiscally prudent . . . we don't want politicians running tourism' (www.travelindustryreview.com, 9/3/06).

In practice

Jeb Bush, the Governor of the state of Florida bemoaned the state's pre-1996 tourism promotion efforts as operating 'under cumbersome, bureaucratic rules and policies that hindered its effectiveness' (Bush, 2004, p. 123). Florida's tourism industry welcomes over 70 million visitors each year, employs 860,000 people, and generates over $3 billion in annual sales tax revenue. Bush strongly argued that the industry deserved a more effective structure. Before 1996, the state's tourism marketing was run as a government office, which was a division of the Florida Department of Commerce. The office had no initiatives to encourage private sector financial involvement, which in turn limited marketing strategies.

> By the late 1980s, increasing competition led to the recognition of the need for more resources. In 1991, the state moved to transition the responsibility for tourism marketing from the government to the private sector. The first step was a dedicated government funding source, initially as a rental car levy, which would 'free the new organisation from the annual scramble for general revenue dollars that had plagued its predecessor' (p. 123). The new structure however was still operating under a government model, which prohibited any fast-moving entrepreneurial marketing activity.
>
> In response to an industry-led lobby for change, the Florida government formed a new PPO in 1996. The new STO, which would become known as Visit Florida, was able to adopt a business model and operate with less vulnerability to government pressures. The head of the STO is still accountable to the Governor for management of the government's financial contribution. However, the PPO structure enabled new revenue streams to be generated through partnerships with industry, resulting in more effective marketing.

Poetschke (1995, pp. 57–58) proposed the following benefits of a cooperative public–private sector cooperative tourist authority:

- reduced antagonism through representation of all stakeholders
- avoidance of duplication through enhanced communication channels between represented sectors
- combined areas of expertise, such as private sector efficiency and public sector holistic benefit-seeking
- increased funding potential through the reduction in duplicated efforts as well as industry-based taxes
- the creation of a win/win situation through an increase in industry profitability and ensuing increase in government tax revenue.

Poetschke (1995) also suggested a typology of public–private partnership models, depending of the level of industry involvement, ranging from lobby group, to advisory group, to general commission, to tourist authority. Lobby groups provide input to the government, which is responsible for designing and implementing tourism policies. Such lobbying efforts are often antagonistic. An advisory group provides input through a formal council. However, government remains in full control of setting and implementing policy. In a general commission, the tourism industry plays a formal role in policy decision-making at a strategic level. A tourist authority is commonly a separate entity controlled by a board of directors comprising members from industry and government. The board of an authority is involved in more detailed planning than a commission. Advantages for the private sector include larger budgets and increased access to government policymakers.

In North America, CVBs are usually one of four types (Morrison et al., 1998, p. 3): independent, non-profit associations/business leagues; chambers of commerce as non-profit associations or non-independent subsidiaries; local government agency, department or public authority; or a special legal entity/authority. Sheehan and Ritchie's (1997) survey of 134 North American CVBs found that 75% of the sample were independent organisations, with the remainder being part of a chamber of commerce, economic development agency, or city department.

In other parts of the world RTOs have commonly been formed as statutory bodies, trusts, local authority departments, and, more recently, as private companies. For example, the latter applies to England's 12 RTBs (Greenwood, 1993) and to Wales where the original RTBs were rationalised into three private companies (Davidson & Maitland, 1997). There have been moves in recent years towards such rationalisation, in order to improve the efficiency of resources. In Scotland the 32 area tourist boards (ATB) established during the 1980s were amalgamated into 14 in 1996, following a 1993 government review of tourism (Davidson & Maitland, 1997; Kerr & Wood, 2000). A similar restructuring strategy was announced in Western Australia during 2004 (www.tourism.wa.gov.au/media/discussion_03.asp, 22/2/04). As part of the 'New Concept for State Tourism Strategy', the number of official RTOs in the state would be reduced from ten to five. A commitment of A$3.25 million annual funding for the five RTOs was announced by the Western Australian state government to 'increase economies of scale, and empower the regions'.

Implementation of such rationalisation can be problematic. For example, a reduced number of RTOs was called for in the New Zealand Tourism Strategy released in 2001 (see Tourism Strategy Group, 2001). One of the strategy goals was for a smaller number of new RTOs to be established from the existing 25 RTOs. Through sharing common back-office functions, it was suggested that the reduced number of RTOs would make significant savings in overhead costs, which could then be more effectively used in promotion. However, the strategy did not discuss how the proposal would be implemented, and in particular how the political implications would be addressed. Three years later the issue remained problematic despite the efforts of a Regional Tourism Organisations New Zealand (RTONZ) taskforce, as explained to me by the then RTONZ chair Paul Yeo: 'Obviously it's a delicate one with lots of political overtones, but it has to be addressed.' Interestingly, by 2007 the number of RTOs had actually increased, to 29 (see http://www.tianz.org.nz/Industry-Facts/NZ-Tourism-Partners.asp#RTO).

DMO governance

In the actual practice of management there is always a danger of politicians, public and private organisations, and managers becoming self-serving and failing in their official responsibilities. Public organisations and resources can be used for private purposes. There can

*be financial corruption but more insidious is organisational corrup-
tion, where public objectives and principles are displaced by private
objectives (Elliott, 1997, p. 7).*

Politics in decision-making is a significant aspect of DMO governance,
and may even be unavoidable. From one perspective, politics may be
viewed as the art of getting things done. From another perspective, politics
has been described as 'the striving for power, and power is about who
gets what, when and how in the political and administrative system and
in the tourism sector' (Elliott, 1997, p. 10). The political environment in
tourism at national and local levels includes governments and ministers,
bureaucratic cultures, competing entrepreneurs, the media, other industry
sectors, the host community, and special interest groups. The industry is
made up of a diverse range of organisations and individuals involved
in a complex array of relationships, and it is the challenge of the manager to understand this and work within the system to achieve objectives
(Elliott, 1997).

Working through the minefield of tourism politics is a challenging reality. The best-laid plans of well-meaning destination marketers can come
unstuck due to the differences in opinions of influential stakeholders.
While this occurs at national, state, and regional levels, the political coal-
face can be most challenging at a local community level, where there
is little escape from daily interactions with stakeholders. The discussion
of tourism politics in the academic literature has been rare (Hall, 1994),
and there have been calls for increased coverage of the study of the politics in tertiary tourism education (see Hollingshead, 2001; Dredge, 2001).
There has been little research attention towards the influence exerted by
special-interest groups on DMO governance. Greenwood (1993) suggested
that interest groups are usually more successful the less they use public channels of communication. Media is only used as a last resort. In
tourism, groups with an active interest in DMO governance at all levels include sector associations and local/national tourism umbrella associations. In some cases there are organised lobby groups such as the
Tour Operators Study Group in the UK. An interest group has been
defined as:

*Domain-based in economic fields of operation, operating with a degree
of permanence, where membership is restricted to organisations such
as firms and pressure is exerted through developing permanent relations with government, often in 'behind closed doors' environments
(Greenwood, 1993, p. 336).*

The Case Study 4.1 provides an insight into the politics of decision-making
in Barbados.

Case study 4.1 Barbados Tourism Authority: The challenge of inclusion

Michael Scantlebury, PhD, Rosen College of Hospitality Management, University of Central Florida

The 1950s was a special period in the history of tourism in Barbados. There was the passage of the Hotel Aids Act (1956), designed to stimulate the development of the hospitality sector, and the formation of the Barbados Hotel Association in 1952, a private-sector agency representing its hotel members' interests. In 1958 the Barbados Tourist Board Act was passed. This created a statutory corporation to promote Barbados tourism. In 1997 the Barbados Tourism Authority (BTA) Act was passed, giving the NTO a mandate to:

1. promote, assist and facilitate the efficient tourism development
2. design and implement suitable marketing strategies for effective promotion
3. make provision for adequate and suitable air and sea passenger transport services
4. encourage the establishment of amenities and facilities
5. carry out market intelligence
6. register, license and classify tourist accommodation according to the standard of amenities provided
7. register and classify restaurants catering primarily to tourists, according to the standard of cuisine and amenities provided
8. register and regulate such forms of service for tourists as the Minister determines
9. do such other things that in the opinion of the Authority would facilitate the proper discharge of its functions or would be incidental or conducive thereto.

The Act established a board of directors responsible for the execution of the policy and the general administration of the BTA. To execute such policy the Board developed a system of five committees: (1) Marketing, (2) Public relations, (3) Establishments, (4) Hotel registration and classification, and (5) Budget and finance. These committees review and approve proposals submitted by the executive, and then submit the proposals to the Board. Board meetings ratify committee decisions and only then can the executive officially implement Board decisions. Directors are appointed by, and sit at the discretion of, the Minister.

In a 1990s initiative to have directors that represented all sector interests, the Minister appointed a 19-member board. As a result, proposals coming forward were discussed at committee level and subsequently the Board and each representative's opinion had to be documented. This resulted in long Board and committee meetings, some taking two days to complete! While the representational initiative may have been commendable, it was not highly effective in expediting decision-making.

Discussion question

Is there anything that the Chairman of the Board might have done to expedite decision-making? How could the committee decision-making approach have been more effectively engineered?

Further information

Laws of Barbados (1997) Barbados Tourism Authority Act, CAP 342, Government Printery, Bay Street Bridgetown, Barbados, http://www.barbadosbusiness.gov.bb/miib/Legislation/documents/barbados_tourism_authority_act_cap342.pdf

As seen in Case Study 4.1, some boards can be quite large and cumbersome. Bramwell and Rawding (1994) reported that in the UK, Birmingham's RTB board comprised 25 directors, with seven representatives from the local authority and 18 from industry. The first CTC board in Canada contained 26 members, of which 16 were from the private sector and the remainder from the public sector (Smith, 2003). The large size of the board reflected the effort to ensure all regions of Canada were represented. A survey of IACVB members (IACVB, 2001, in Fenich, 2005) found the average size of CVB boards was 16 voting directors. Lathrop (2005, pp. 198–199) reported the case of Townsville in the USA, where the CVB had a board of directors with 60 members. Lathrop's case study of how one group of dissatisfied stakeholders who were excluded from decision-making, concluded with the following governance lessons:

- Bylaws must clearly define the role, responsibility, and code of conduct for the board and staff. The importance of effective bylaws cannot be overstated.
- Do not exclude key community constituents simply because they might not agree, or because it is easier not to deal with them. The old adage 'keep your friends close and your enemies closer' holds true in the case of board composition.
- Limit the size of the board. Because of the sheer size of the board in this case study, it was virtually impossible for the chair or executive to manage it effectively.
- Board turnover is a good thing and should be a key aspect of the bylaws. As long as there is a nucleus of experienced board members and an effective orientation process, the regular introduction of new members should not be a problem.
- Embrace board governance as an effective management and leadership tool.

In the USA (see Lathrop, 2005) and Canada (see Vallee, 2005), most CVBs are required by federal and state regulations to have an elected non-compensated board and a set of bylaws dictating governance and fiduciary responsibilities. Typically a CVB board is responsible for the following (Lathrop, 2005, p. 191):

- defining the purpose of the bureau and establishing its governing principles
- providing advice and consent with respect to overall policy
- approving the annual operating budget and monitoring the bureau's finances
- approving the membership structure and fees
- providing direction and oversight for the bureau's operations
- monitoring the performance of the CEO
- representing the bureau's interests among external audiences and serving as an advocate for tourism and destination management issues.

Table 4.1 Key responsibilities of CVB directors and senior management

Duty of care
Requires exercising ordinary and reasonable care when making decisions, with all decisions made in the best interests of the organisation. There is also an obligation to protect confidentiality.

Duty of loyalty
Requires undivided allegiance to the organisation, and in doing so avoid real, perceived, or potential conflicts of interest.

Duty of obedience
Requires following federal and state laws and corporate governing documents such as articles of incorporation and bylaws.

McMillan (2005, p. 186) recommended that CVB board members and senior management have three key responsibilities: duty of care, duty of loyalty, and duty of obedience. These are outlined in Table 4.1

It has been suggested that governance of globally competitive destinations features five critical success factors (Poetschke, 1995, pp. 62–63):

- a significant level of private sector control over authority spending
- understanding of the need to incorporate public sector objectives to achieve a balance between marketing and new product development
- a dedicated revenue stream that is not subject to annual government control
- a broad, integrated mandate encompassing all functions critical to developing a strong tourism industry, such as marketing, education, research, and infrastructure development.

Selection of directors

The two main options for selecting directors are by appointment or by election. A danger in any board election system is the appointment of those who are popular, or even articulate, incompetents, rather than those best qualified. An articulate incompetent is someone who is great at expressing issues and explaining solutions, but fails to act on them (Wintermans, 1994). Bramwell and Rawding (1994, p. 431) suggested that when appointments are made to public-funded RTOs by selection, the organisation is 'less democratic and less accountable to the local electorate'. However, local government representatives on the board can serve this purpose. If government representatives are not included on the board, the issue of accountability needs to be carefully addressed in the funding contract and government reporting process. For example, Tourism New Zealand has a board of 9 directors appointed by the government's Minister of Tourism for a term of three years. Directors receive an annual fee of NZ$15,000.

Table 4.2 Government expectations of Tourism New Zealand directors and operations

Expectations of Tourism New Zealand operations	Skills and experience of directors
• integrity • frugality and due care in the use of taxpayer money • advancing activities beneficial to the tourism sector and wider community rather than to any individual business • focusing on medium- to long-term strategies rather than short-term gains • showing openness and having good communication with the Minister, the Ministry of Tourism, and other government agencies • partnering with the private sector to add value rather than displace or duplicate private businesses	• a wide perspective on issues • good oral and written communication • understanding of public sector governance and accountability • previous experience as a company director • ability to work in a team and work collaboratively • strategic skills • experience in developing and maintaining partnerships with other organisations and companies • experience with financial statements • understanding of and/or experience in the tourism sector at a senior level • understanding the importance of value creation, innovation and international best practice comparisons • experience of marketing issues

The qualities sought in directors and expectations of Tourism New Zealand by the government are highlighted in Table 4.2.

In 2003, the USA Commerce Department secretary appointed 15 travel and tourism executives to the new Travel and Tourism Promotion Advisory Board (Hoover, 2003). When the British Travel Association was replaced by the BTA, a key difference was in the selection of the governance structure (Jeffries, 1989). The former had a large board of predominantly tourism industry representatives elected from member organisations with a government appointed chair, whereas the new organisation comprised a small group appointed by the government.

Gee and Makens (1985) provided a candid explanation of the opportunities, challenges, and conflicts that face members of tourism boards:

> *Tourism boards can be an effective force for a community's hospitality industry, and the hotel manager is a crucial part of such a board. But to do its job, the board may have to resist the influences of politics, unrealistic community 'cheerleading', and intra-industry competition (Gee & Makens, 1985, p. 25).*

While Gee and Makens were writing specifically for hotel managers, their paper is a worthwhile read for any prospective DMO board member, as is the paper summarised in Research Snapshot 4.1. Another account of DMO governance issues likely to be faced was provided in Kelly and Nankervis'

(2001) observations of the challenges in Australia faced by one of the state of Victoria's RTOs, the Yarra Valley, Dandenong and the Ranges Tourism Board:

- the diversity of features
- board representatives not focused on the 'big picture'
- operator's suspicions of others' sectoral interests
- cumbersome organisational name to reflect all areas covered
- a regional community not fully informed on the advantages of tourism
- lack of reliable visitor statistics.

Research snapshot 4.1   Governance styles

Palmer's (1998) review of the governance literature identified a loose-tight or informal-formal continuum of managing organisational relationships. Loose styles are likely to be more suited to creative tasks, and important considerations are trust and levels of access to resources. Informal relationship controls are self-control, based on financial or psychological incentives, and sociocultural control, based on group norms. Tight styles are governed by more formal legal controls. The former might signal unclear objectives and strategy, but be more flexible, creative, and fast moving. The tight style, on the other hand, is more likely to generate clear and formal goals, contractual rights and obligations, but also be more bureaucratic, particularly in terms of decision-making. This approach can be frustrating to entrepreneurial tourism operators.

Palmer (1998) hypothesised that while a loose style might suit a local tourism association because of the dynamic nature of tourism markets, a tight governance style would be more effective in terms of maintaining a strategic focus. In a survey of 172 members of 13 English LTAs, there was evidence to suggest a strong link between a tight governance style and organisation effectiveness. The most effective local tourism associations were ones with formal rules governing relationships between members, an efficient and effective secretariat, and a lack of opportunities for discussing the management of the association.

Source: Palmer, A. (1978). Understanding the governance style of marketing groups. *Annals of Tourism Research*, *25*(1), 185–201.

DMO names

When Visit Britain (see www.visitbritain.com) was chosen as the name for the UK's new DMO, it had to be purchased from a company that had owned it for 25 years (TravelMole.com, 16/4/03). The chairman of Visit Britain discussed some of the difficulties associated with selecting an appropriate name (TravelMole.com, 26/3/03):

> *You have no idea how much trouble goes into creating a new name. It has to be legal, we have to make sure it means the same thing in different languages, and that it sounds good over the phone, and works in different media.*

As with so many aspects related to DMOs there is no consistency in names used. There currently exists a myriad of types of DMO names:

- agency (Latvian Tourism Development Agency)
- authority (The Gambia Tourism Authority)
- board (British Virgin Islands Tourist Board)
- bureau (Hawaii Visitors Bureau)
- centre (Le Centre Gabonais de Promotion Touristique)
- coalition (North Carolina Travel & Tourism Coalition)
- commission (Nevada Commission on Tourism)
- company (New York City and Company)
- corporation (Virginia Tourism Corporation)
- council (Swedish Travel & Tourism Council)
- department (Dubai Department of Tourism and Commerce Marketing)
- destination (Destination Northland)
- development (Northern Tasmania Development)
- directorate (Crete Tourism Directorate)
- institute (Nicaraguan Institute of Tourism)
- ministry (Israel Ministry of Tourism)
- office (China National Tourism Office)
- organization (Cypress Tourism Organization).
- region (Bundaberg Region Limited)

Since the early 1990s, new types of names have emerged, such as those incorporating 'travel' (Travel Alberta), 'tourism' (Falkland Islands Tourism), 'destination' (Destination Lake Taupo), and 'visit' (Visit Heart of England) to denote organisation focus, and then others that are difficult to categorise such as Maison de la France, Fáilte Ireland, Latitude Nelson, and Positively Wellington Tourism. While there is no one naming theme common to DMOs, there has been a shift in recent years away from the more bureaucratic sounding names that are representative of government divisions. A selection of examples is provided in Table 4.3, which compares the current name to one used in the past.

Table 4.3 DMO name changes

Current name	A previous name
Tourism Australia	Australian Tourist Commission
Tourism New Zealand	New Zealand Tourist and Publicity Department
Tourism Queensland	Queensland Tourist and Travel Corporation
Visit Britain	British Tourist Authority

Key points

1. The variety in legal entity

There is a plethora of DMO structures, with no widely accepted model. Historically, DMOs emerged either as government departments or as industry association collectives.

2. Public–private partnerships

More recently there has been a shift towards the establishment of public–private partnerships (PPPs), as a way of ensuring destination marketing programmes are industry driven but also accountable to public funders. PPPs, at both a national and local level, are generally governed by a private sector board that is appointed by, and reports to, a government representative.

3. Governance challenges

The politics of decision-making is a critical element of DMO effectiveness. Of concern to government funders is the need for industry expertise and accountability from the board of directors. However, stakeholders also demand fair representation in decision-making, which can lead to large and cumbersome boards and slower decision-making. A critical question is whether directors should be appointed on the basis of expertise, or be democratically elected.

Review questions

- Design an effective board structure for your local DMO. How many directors are appropriate? Who would be most effective, and should directors be appointed on merit or democratically elected? Who should make the appointment decisions? What length of term should directors serve?
- The chapter discussed the failure in New Zealand's tourism strategy to reduce the number of RTOs. Summarise the potential advantages for doing so, and discuss the potential disadvantages that have stalled the initiative.
- What are the key advantages of a PPP?

DMO funding

Going forward, the lazy or unimaginative will continue to wait for members' dues checks to arrive, and pray that their municipality continues to fund them at the same, or (with a little luck) at an even higher level through the room tax or city's general fund. Their days are numbered.

Marks (2004, p. 141)

Aims

The aims of this chapter are to enhance understanding of:

- the importance of securing long-term funding
- the reliance on public-sector funding
- other funding sources

> **Perspective**
>
> Fundraising has been a perennial challenge for many DMOs. The majority of DMOs, at all levels, and regardless of how they are structured, rely to a large extent on government support. Government funding is commonly provided through annual grants or through some form of levy on visitors or businesses. The over-reliance on government funding has been a concern to many DMOs, given the often long-term uncertainty of political commitment towards tourism. The withdrawal of state government funding in Colorado serves as a warning to all DMOs. More research into alternative forms of funding is required. John Marks, CEO of the San Francisco CVB, suggests that the key to future funding lies in developing a more entrepreneurial spirit among staff. Marks (2004) sees the entrepreneurial spirit as being critical to developing alliances with non-traditional partners as well as tourism businesses. The San Francisco CVB, for example, has partnered with a diverse range of companies, such as Visa, See's Candies, Colavita Olive Oil, Buick, and the San Francisco Giants. Similarly, New York City and Company has partnered with American Express, Coca-Cola, and the National Football League to leverage budgets (Nicholas, 2004).

Long-term funding security

In Colorado, a state government referendum in 1993 resulted in the abolishment of the tax that funded the Colorado Tourism Board (CTB). Without such government funding the CTB was closed (Bonham & Mak, 1996). The state became the only one that did not have an STO. At the time tourism was the state's second largest industry, worth an estimated $6.4 billion annually (La Page et al., 1995). The effects in the marketplace were significant, with estimates that Colorado slipped from 3rd to 17th in terms of traveller recognition of state destinations, and that pleasure travellers decreased by up to 10% (Donnelly & Vaske, 1997). McGehee et al. (2006) cited a report indicating that Colorado's share of domestic pleasure travel declined by 30% between 1993 and 1997.

In 2004, the Illinois governor's office proposed a 54% cut in tourism funding to help offset the state deficit (Bolson, 2005). This was successfully opposed in an aggressive campaign by the tourism industry, led by the state's CVB association. Such a withdrawal of government funding can lead to a tourism crisis. For example, in 2006 Tourism Waikato, one of New Zealand's regional tourism organisations (RTO), had its budget unexpectedly cut in half by the local government (see Coventry, 2006, p. 1). Tourism Waikato's Chief Executive Officer lamented: 'It's a very gut wrenching situation. Marketing of the whole of Waikato will be suspended until funding regenerates.'

The world average for NTA budgets was estimated at US$19 million in 1997, which pales into insignificance in the global marketplace in comparison to leading consumer goods brands such as Sony and Philips. DMOs compete with such brands for a share of voice in discretionary spending categories. Morgan and Pritchard (2001) compared Sony's annual advertising budget of US$300m with a WTO estimate of the total tourism advertising spend of all governments in the world to be US$350 million.

Marketing destinations in a dynamic environment requires significant financial and management resources. However, destination marketing is undertaken by organisations that often have no direct financial interest in the visitor industry, and therefore have no income of their own. A key exception is in places where a bed tax regime operates, such as North America, where increased accommodation revenue can lead to an increased budget for CVBs. Of course the reverse also applies, as in the 9/11 aftermath when accommodation revenue decreased in many places. For example, in Las Vegas, a 10% decrease in visitors following 9/11 resulted in a similar decrease in the CVB's $250 million annual budget.

While Vallee (2005) reported Canada's largest CVBs, such as Montreal, Toronto, and Vancouver, have budgets ranging from $10 million to $25 million, many DMOs have limited budgets. For example, Rogers (2005) found only one in five British CVBs had a budget greater than £100,000. Relative to RTOs in other major cities, the London Tourist Board (LTB) is poorly funded by government (Hopper, 2002). At the time the LTB received £1.85 million from central government and £241,000 from local authorities annually. The remainder of the £6 million annual budget was contributed by the private sector through subscriptions, partnership marketing, and sponsorship.

Funding is a critical issue for DMOs. In fact for any marketing organisation without products or services of its own to gain sales revenue it is arguably the most important consideration. Non-business organisations usually cannot cover costs through sales, and often devote ongoing efforts to generate new tax revenues, sponsorships, and/or contributions from members. The high reliance on government funding leaves many DMOs at the mercy of political masters. A survey of USA CVBs identified the main impediment to financial management was future funding security (Sheehan & Ritchie, 1997).

Security of long-term government funding is not only a challenge faced by STOs and RTOs. WTO (1999a) estimated that collective worldwide NTA budgets declined during the 1993–1997 period, from US$2,224 million to US$1,791 million. The problem is global. RTO budgets in Australia have generally been modest, and in New South Wales many have struggled to survive (Jenkins, 2000). Carson et al. (2003) found local authority budget contributions to tourism in the state of Victoria, Australia, ranged from A$2,000 to A$6.5 million, with a median of $232,000. They found 40% of councils surveyed indicated a tourism budget of less than A$150,000. In Scotland, Kerr and Wood (2000) reported on the financial difficulty, including near bankruptcy, for some ATBs due to reduced levels of local government funding. They cited the example of the Dumfries and Galloway Tourist Board, which was £1.2 million in debt in 1998. One of the problems was that the ATB areas did not match local government boundaries, and so ATBs were forced to lobby several councils for funding support.

Multiple accountability

The challenge of spending scarce resources lobbying several local authorities in an RTO's 'regional' catchment area is common. Consider, for example, Outback Queensland (www.outbackqld.com.au) in Australia. The RTO's catchment area represents 50% of the state's land area and includes 21 local government authorities. The structure of local government can make a regional approach to regional problems extremely difficult. Clearly, managing relationships with multiple-funding agencies is time-consuming. Tourism Auckland CEO Graeme Osborne strongly lamented to me the impact of the resultant multiple accountability and multiple governance, where the RTO reports to the committees of each council as well as to the tourism industry.

> It prevents truly visionary leadership being exercised at a regional level, which of course is the correct approach for destination marketing. The fundamental flaw then is the structure and (ridiculously excessive) scale of local government, the ensuing lack of regional vision, the 'sovereignty driven', duplicative, parochial leadership offered by generally low-average-quality local government politicians.

Tourism Auckland received NZ$2.1 million in local authority funding for the 2003/2004 financial year. As can be seen in Table 5.1 most of this was from one local authority. However, it has been estimated that while the Auckland City Council contributes 79% of the RTO's funding, the city area receives only 55% of the economic contribution of tourism to the Auckland region (Tourism Auckland, 2002).

Auckland is New Zealand's largest population centre, and its most visited destination. Auckland International Airport facilitates 71% of all visitor arrivals to New Zealand. Given the prominent status of the region,

Table 5.1 Local authority funding for Tourism Auckland

Local authority	Population base	2003/04 contribution	Per capita
Auckland City Council	377,382	$1,645,000	$4.36
Manukau City Council	281,604	$300,000	$1.07
Waitakere City Council	167,172	$0	$0.00
North Shore City Council	184,287	$90,000	$0.49
Rodney District Council	77,001	$10,000	$0.13
Papakura District Council	40,035	$5,000	$0.12
Franklin District Council	51,450	$20,000	$0.39

Table 5.2 Comparison of local authority contributions to major New Zealand RTOs

RTO	Population base	Local authority contribution	Per capita
Auckland	1,178,931	$2,000,000	$1.70
Christchurch	316,224	$2,600,000	$8.22
Wellington	163,827	$4,600,000	$28.08
Rotorua	64,473	$1,212,000	$18.08
Queenstown	17,040	$1,600,000	$93.90
Mean	581,895		$18.24

Tourism Auckland's budget might be considered low relative to other New Zealand RTOs, as shown in Table 5.2.

Manchester's CVB, in the UK, reports to 10 local authorities (Bramwell & Rawding, 1994), Bundaberg Region Ltd, an RTO in Australia, reports to 10 local authorities (www.bundabergregion.info), the former West Country Tourist Board in the UK was responsible to six and a half counties (Meethan, 2002). At the state level, Pennsylvania has more RTOs than any other in the USA, with 59 agencies in 67 counties (Goeldner et al., 2000).

There is no common model for determining the appropriate level of funding for a DMO. In an examination of government policy of European Community member countries, Akehurst et al. (1993) found little correlation between central government tourism expenditure and international receipts on a per capita basis. For example, Greece, which had the highest government spend per capita, was at the lower end of international tourism receipts per capita. Comparisons can be made between DMO budgets from different regions using many different measures, including:

- host population
- visitor numbers
- as a ratio of visitor spend
- number of commercial accommodation beds/rooms
- number of taxpayers/ratepayers.

Ultimately the funding decision process will depend on the local situation, with influences including:

- local politics
- community acceptance of tourism
- destination life-cycle stage and industry maturity
- economic importance of tourism relative to other industries
- DMO history and current structure.

A key management challenge for DMOs is finding the optimal balance between fixed costs and promotional spend (WTO, 1999a). The WTO found that the average marketing allocation was 74% for those NTOs with budgets over US$50 million and for those with budgets between US$10 and $20 million. For NTOs with budgets between US$20 and US$50 million, the average was 64%. In the USA, IACVB (1993, in Morrison et al., 1998) estimated that of all room taxes collected, approximately 27% is used for the convention centre construction, debt servicing and operations, 25% for CVB marketing, and 48% for 'non-visitor uses'. McKercher and Ritchie's (1997) study of local government tourism units in New South Wales and Victoria, which identified a median operating budget of A$215,000, found over half of average budgets were allocated to staffing, with the median marketing allocation only A$70,000.

Sources of revenue

The most common sources of revenue for DMOs are: accommodation tax, tax on business, member subscriptions, commercial activities, cooperative campaigns, and government grants.

Accommodation bed/room taxes

Key advantages of accommodation taxes are that they directly target the visitor industry, and can generate large amounts of revenue for a relatively low cost. Room taxes, which are additional to any other local, state, or national general sales taxes, have existed in the USA since at least the 1940s (Migdal, 1991 in Morrison et al., 1998). A survey of IACVB members (IACVB, 2001, in Fenich, 2005) found that the average city hotel tax was 11.6%. An average of 56% of the tax collected is dedicated to funding the CVB. Visitor taxes are a way for governments to shift the financial burden of funding DMOs and infrastructure from local taxpayers. While many countries, such as the UK, Australia, and New Zealand do not have a bed tax system, Sheehan and Ritchie's (1997) survey of USA CVBs found that the largest source of revenue was hotel room taxes, generating a mean 72% of revenue. The next level of funding sources were modest by comparison: membership fees (7% – the highest was 58%), government grants (6% – highest 90%), local authority taxes (2.6% – highest 100%), cooperative programmes (2% – highest 41%), restaurant taxes (2% – highest 60%). Other sources, representing an average of 8%, included: convention centre grants, merchandise, advertising sales, county tax, events, admissions, in-kind services, and a provincial or state tax. In Mexico, federal government legislation in 1996 enabled the states to levy up to a 5% hotel room tax (Cerda, 2005). Just over half of Mexico's CVBs are now funded by room taxes. In Europe, Vienna introduced a bed tax of 2.8% in 1987.

However, the hotel room tax is far from universally lauded. The repeal of the 5% bed tax in the state of New York was hailed by some in the tourism industry as the removal of an inhibitor to destination marketing (Cahn, 1994). The tax, which was introduced in 1990, was the subject of strong criticism from industry, with one executive likening it to 'economic suicide' for the meetings sector. In a survey of delegates attending the 1999 Scottish

Hospitality Industry Congress, Kerr and Wood (2000) found a resounding 93% of respondents against the concept of a bed tax, although 35% did indicate possible support if all the revenues were devoted to the tourism industry. A variation of this, reported by the *The News Mail* (31/503, p. 3), was used in Queensland's Wide Bay region. Around A$80,000 was collected from a visitor levy during the 2002 whale-watch season, which was being used on an advertising campaign to promote the 2003 season.

In light of the criticism by some in industry that visitor taxes damage destination competitiveness through forced price increases, a number of studies have investigated the impact such levies have on traveller demand (see Aguilo et al., 2005; Bonham & Gangnes, 1996; Bonham et al., 1991; Hiemstra & Ismael, 1992, 1993; Mak, 1988; Mak & Nishimura, 1979).

Tax on business

An alternative tax, which may become more common in the future, is one that is levied on local business' turnover or capital value. This can be used as an effective means of raising revenue for RTOs, and an alternative to funding through the general household tax or rates base, or through member subscriptions. The efficacy of this approach has been demonstrated in smaller resort areas where tourism has a high profile. Examples include the New Zealand resort destinations of Lake Taupo and Queenstown. These local governments charge a levy to all local businesses, thereby avoiding the challenge of defining tourism businesses at a percentage rate of the business' capital value. The mechanism provides the main source of funds for the RTOs in both areas. Another example is Monaco, which with no income taxes relies to a large extent on levies on casinos (Bull, 1995).

Bonham and Mak (1996) reported that the Oklahoma Tourism Promotion Act (1991) levied a tourism promotion tax of 0.1% of gross turnover of accommodation, rental car, restaurant and bar operations. The intent was for the state government to collect the tax from the tourism industry to be used solely by the industry, for which the state would charge a 3% collection fee. Prior to its demise in 1993 the Colorado STO had a similar tax of 0.2% (Bonham & Mak, 1996). A downside of this approach is a reduction in funding during periods of crisis when visitation levels have fallen, even though such periods demand more marketing funds. For example, in Canada, the *Calgary Herald* (13/1/03, p. B4) reported that a fall in the Banff/Lake Louise Tourism Bureau's 2003 revenue was likely to result in a reduction in marketing spend of C$168,000, which would directly impair the organisation's ability to promote Banff in their traditional secondary markets such as New Zealand and Australia.

Member subscriptions

In the UK, 58% of CVBs receive funding from membership fees (Rogers, 2005). The IACVB (1993, in Morrison et al., 1998) found that while half of their member CVBs received membership subscription fees, for those responding to a survey, the level of subscriptions was only 5% of their collective budgets. Bonham and Mak (1996) found that only Alaska, Hawaii, and Washington DC received significant private-sector contributions such as through membership subscriptions. Their analysis of private versus public funding of the Hawaii Visitors Bureau is summarised in Research Snapshot 5.1. This is a common problem for RTOs, many of which have abandoned attempts to generate subscriptions due to low returns relative to costs incurred in the process.

Research snapshot 5.1   Public versus private-sector funding

The Hawaii Visitors Bureau (HVB), which has one of the longest histories of private membership, has offered a range of incentives to financial members, including: monthly newsletters, HVB posters and brochures, reduced fees for HVB meetings, participation in trade promotion and cooperative advertising, listings in information guides, and a copy of the annual report. In its early years the organisation received more in private-sector contributions than from government. However, by 1988 only an estimated 7% of all businesses were financial members of the HVB, and by 1994 private-sector contributions represented less than 10% of the annual budget. One of the reasons offered by Bonham and Mak (1996) was extensive 'free riding' by tourism operators. They cited Mok's (1986) PhD thesis, which estimated HVB memberships representing 78% of airlines, 66% of hotels, 32% of banks, 24% of restaurants, and only 4% of retail outlets. Since membership is voluntary the organisation was forced to spend up to $500,000 to generate $2 million in membership dues (Rees, 1995, in Bonham & Mak, 1996).

Source: Bonham, C. & Mak, J. (1996) Private versus public finance of state destination promotion. *Journal of Travel Research*, Fall, 3–10.

A survey of IACVB members (IACVB, 2001, in Fenich, 2005) found that half of the CVBs were a membership organisation, with an average of 663 members. Membership fees may be based on tiered sponsor categories, a standard arbitrary amount, tiered based on organisation turnover level or number of employees or per room for accommodation establishments. Donnelly and Vaske (1997) investigated the factors influencing membership of the voluntary organisation, the Colorado Travel and Tourism Authority (CTTA), established to replace the previously state-funded DMO. The CTTA targeted businesses that directly benefited from tourism, such as hotels, restaurants, and attractions. Their review of the literature relating to voluntary organisations identified two participative incentive themes: instrumental and expressive. Instrumental incentives are those public goods, such as promotion of the destination, that are obtained by both members and non-members. Expressive incentives are resultant benefits that will only be obtained by membership, such as access to a database of consumers who have requested tourism information from the DMO. Donnelly and Vaske (p. 51) suggested that the value placed on expressive incentives to join a DMO will depend on an individual's:

- financial ability to pay membership dues
- beliefs about tourism and destination marketing
- level of perceived importance about the costs and benefits of membership.

> ## In practice
>
> The following story was relayed to me a number of years ago by a member of an RTO subscriptions committee who was frustrated by the lack of support from businesses in a tourism resort area. Two LTA directors were attempting to enlist the modest financial support of one of the region's busiest gas stations. They were told, very bluntly, by the business owner that he was not in the tourism business and therefore refused to subscribe to the LTA. Standing directly behind the gas station owner were two 40-seat sightseeing coaches, filling up with diesel fuel.

Commercial activities

Some DMOs have developed an income stream from their own activities to fund destination marketing. In the UK, 63% of CVBs receive some funding from commercial activities (Rogers, 2005). Pritchard (1982) reported an innovative approach used by Alaska to stimulate industry contributions to the STO budget. For every dollar contributed by an individual business, the STO would provide one name and address from the consumer database for direct marketing. The database was tailored to provide contacts from segments of interest to the contributing tourism business. *Marketing News* (29/9/97) reported that the new logo developed by Florida's STO in 1997 would be used to generate royalties of 6% of the wholesale price of items featuring the logo. The report claimed that universities such as Florida State and Notre Dame earned millions of dollars annually from such royalties. In some cases, however, legal issues can prevent some types of DMOs from maximising their earning potential. In the USA, most CVBs have been structured as non-profit associations, qualifying for tax-exempt status. These organisations promote the business interests of their members but are not permitted to engage in regular profit-making business activities.

It is also not uncommon for RTOs to earn commission from their member hotels for conference bookings. However, this approach can lead to the DMO focusing on conference promotion, business travel, and short-break hotel packages to the exclusion of other destination products (Bramwell & Rawding, 1994).

Other RTOs earn commissions through subsidiary visitor information centre (VIC) sales. Net returns are often modest, even with a substantial turnover, if there is an absence of big-ticket items. In New Zealand, local government regulations prohibited many local authority-owned VICs to trade commercially, other than sales of sightseeing tickets and postcards. However, the greater empowering provisions of the Local Government Act (2002) have enabled enhanced trading opportunities. VICs are labour intensive, and, as their title suggests, a large component of visitors are there seeking 'information'. Travellers seek advice, collect brochures, make a decision, and then book direct with the tourism provider, from the comfort of their accommodation.

Even with a multi-million dollar turnover, it is difficult for VICs to generate a profit when relying on sightseeing sales paying on average 10% commission. However, many of these VICs could be profitable if they adopted private-sector practices used by travel agencies, such as preferred suppler agreements. This might involve, for example, one operator per service category receiving preferential treatment and in return providing commissions up to 25–30%. A tiered system of commissions might be used to rank providers in terms of preference levels and prominence of brochures on display. For example, in Canada travel agents represent on average only four tour wholesalers (Statistics Canada, 1999, in Hashimoto & Telfer, 2001). However, it would be hypocritical for an RTO that receives government funding for the purpose of developing tourism in the region to then preclude the majority of suppliers from receiving VIC bookings in a preferential system. In some parts of the world this type of activity would leave the DMO open to litigation from disadvantaged businesses. Many local authorities understand the need for a trade-off and provide an operating grant for the VIC on the basis that the contribution is for the public good.

In Australia, Tourism Queensland recently licensed the STO's wholesale travel division, Sunlover Holidays, to a private sector firm, earning what the outgoing CEO Ian Mitchell described in 2007 as 'millions of dollars of new income through licensing fees for the purposes of international marketing'.

Cooperative campaigns

Tourism Consultant Ken Male lamented the problem that the British Treasury measures the success of NTO activity by the level of private-sector participation (www.travelmole.com, 30/9/03). Indeed, cooperative campaigns managed by the DMO can be an effective vehicle for demonstrating to government the level of industry contributions. In this regard, the government grant is seen as seeding funding to attract private-sector contributions. Cooperative campaigns include a diverse range of initiatives such as sales missions, travel exhibitions participation, media advertising features, and visiting media programmes.

Government grants

Due to the significant resources often required to attract and retain membership funding, it can be more cost-effective to lobby for government funds. For example, two decades ago, as a direct result of the STO lobbying state political candidates in the 1978 Pennsylvania election, the elected governor tripled the destination marketing budget between 1979 and 1982 (Pritchard, 1982). Bonham and Mak reported that the HVB employed three political lobbyists. In the UK, 90% of CVBs receive funding from local government, with 25% also receiving funding from the European Union (Rogers, 2005).

Key points

1. The importance of securing long-term funding

Marketing destinations in a dynamic environment requires significant financial and management resources. However, destination marketing is undertaken by organisations that often have no direct financial interest in the visitor industry, and therefore have no income of their own. It is critical to secure a long-term funding agreement, since the more that resources are spent on fundraising activities the less resources are available for marketing.

2. The reliance on public-sector funding

The majority of DMOs, at all levels, and regardless of how they are structured, rely to a large extent on government support. Government funding is commonly provided through annual grants or through some form of levy on visitors or businesses. The over-reliance on government funding has been a concern to many DMOs, given the long-term uncertainty of political commitment towards tourism. The withdrawal of state government funding in Colorado serves as a warning to all DMOs. Commonly, public-sector funding is sourced through grants, accommodation taxes, or levies on businesses.

3. Other funding sources

It has been suggested that DMOs need to be more creative in sourcing funding, to overcome the over-reliance on the public sector. However, this has proved problematic at many destinations and more research into alternative forms of funding is required. Other options available to DMOs include: member subscriptions, commercial activities, and cooperative campaigns.

Review questions

- Why should the DMO not receive all the revenue from an accommodation tax, since it was generated by visitors at tourism businesses?
- What are the key benefits for a business becoming a member of a DMO?

CHAPTER 6

The role of government

Governments are a fact in tourism and in the modern world. The industry could not survive without them.

Elliott (1997, p. 2)

Aims

The aims of this chapter are to enhance understanding of:

- government intervention in tourism
- the key arguments for government funding of destination marketing
- the key reasons why governments might not support tourism development.

Perspective

In the history of DMO development it is clear that the majority, including those cooperatives established by the private sector, would not have succeeded without the support of government. However, the issue of whether governments should or should not use public funds to support the tourism industry remains contentious. Why should taxpayers subsidise tourism businesses? An important issue in the development and survival of DMOs has been the role played by governments at national, state, and local levels. While entrepreneurs in many areas have been catalysts for stimulating cooperative destination promotions, rarely have they become effective in the long term without government intervention. Increasingly, DMOs are taking the form of public-private partnerships, utilising public funds and private sector expertise. It behoves anyone with an interest in tourism management to be able to articulate the rationale for the existence of DMOs and the key arguments for and against government intervention.

The case for government intervention in tourism

Case Study 6.1 summarises how the fortunes of one resort destination has risen and fallen and risen in line with government intervention. The case, which I present in more detail in the *Journal of Marketing for Travel & Tourism* (see Pike, 2007), can be used to highlight, on one hand, the difficulty in stimulating an effective cooperative approach to place promotion without government support, and, on the other hand, the damage that can take place when stakeholders become complacent through an over-reliance on a paternalistic government. Rotorua is one of New Zealand's two most popular resort areas, attracting 1.2 million visitors each year. Tourism is a key element of the local economy, employing one in every five workers.

Case study 6.1 A destination's rise and fall and rise in line with government support

Rotorua was New Zealand's first tourism destination, rising to prominence a hundred years ago on the back of the government of the country's vision for a South Pacific spa to rival those of Europe. In 1902 the government was convinced to invest all available resources in the development of one spa, at Rotorua, rather than spread resources around the nation. To support the spa development, government resources were used to develop and support Rotorua's infrastructure and tourism industry, like no other in the British Commonwealth, for the best part of the 20th century. This included: airports, drainage, water supply, roads, parks and gardens, railways, hotel development, spa facilities, electricity, visitor information, swimming pools, lake launches, deer and possum release, administration of Maori villages, licensing of tourist guides, development of the New Zealand Maori Arts & Crafts Institute, and geothermal tourist attractions. For many decades, Rotorua was New Zealand's premier tourism destination.

Although a town board was formed in 1880, Rotorua was to be managed by the New Zealand Department of Tourist & Health Resorts, the world's first NTO established in 1901. The reliance on government resources was such that Rotorua did not have an independent council, devoid of government representatives, until 1950. The town's visitor information centre was managed by the NTO for 90 years. Rotorua's rise as a tourism destination occurred on the back of New Zealand government intervention during the first half of the 20th century.

Rotorua's decline took place gradually over the next 30 years. The attempt to make it the great spa of the southern hemisphere floundered during the depression years and World War Two, and by the 1950s the government had dispensed with the concept. Rotorua's increasingly forced independence from central government from the 1950s onwards coincided with a steady decline in destination image, due to a lack of infrastructure maintenance and the lack of a DMO. Examples of negative publicity included:

- In 1965 the president of the Travel Agents Association of New Zealand described Rotorua as 'the most squalid place in the country'.
- The local council had developed the town's rubbish tip on the Lake Rotorua foreshore, adjacent to the central business district, and released sewerage into the lake after only partial treatment. An overseas scientist gained national media coverage when he labelled the lake an 'unflushed toilet' in the 1970s.
- In 1978, 200 people attending a tourism conference reached consensus that Rotorua was 'losing its oomph' against other destinations.
- In 1986, a major newspaper and national television network described the situation as 'the death of a tourist town'.

Attempts to develop a private sector destination promotion organisation ultimately failed due to infighting and a lack of funding. A crisis point was reached during the 1980s when entrepreneurs and the local council recognised that the destination was losing ground to unheralded competition. Rotorua had been firmly established on the blue ribbon route of coach tour itineraries, and thus assured of a steady flow of group tourists. However, a 1980s shift away from coach touring towards self-drive holidays opened up more destinations to travellers, and shifted distribution control away from a small group of inbound tour operators, on which Rotorua relied so heavily. There was also a sense of NTO abandonment of Rotorua in overseas promotions, in favour of the South Island's snowy mountain scenes and the emergence of Queenstown as a leading resort destination.

Ultimately, the 1988 crisis would lead to Rotorua's rise again as a destination. Finally acknowledging a tourism crisis, the local council agreed to take responsibility for destination marketing. The council's financial commitment to establishing an RTO, an economic development unit, and a much needed $30 million infrastructure redevelopment saw Rotorua rekindle the interest of entrepreneurs, hotel developers and intermediaries. Tourism Rotorua, the RTO, undertook local pride campaigns, extensive television advertising in the domestic market, organised coordinated marketing opportunities for local tourism businesses, and established stronger links with the NTO, other RTOs, and key wholesalers in international markets.

By 1996, Tourism Rotorua comprised a marketing office with six staff and an annual budget of $1 million, a visitor centre with 11 staff and turnover in excess of $3 million, and the redeveloped Rotorua Convention Centre. That year, Tourism Rotorua released the district's first strategic plan for tourism. In 1997 Tourism Rotorua became the first RTO to achieve a distinction at the New Zealand Tourism Awards for winning the 'Best RTO' award on three occasions. The district has also been a recipient of New Zealand's 'most beautiful city' award in 1999, 2000, and 2002. The local council's philosophical and financial commitment led to a new spirit of cooperation among the private sector, and between industry and local government. The turnaround in destination image has been such that few visitors to Rotorua today would be aware of the negative publicity of the 1960s, 1970s, and 1980s.

Discussion questions

1. What key lesson(s) do you draw from this case which could serve as a message to your local DMO?
2. Why might the local government not have taken a proactive approach earlier?
3. What theory or conceptual framework could be applied to this case?

Further reading

Ateljevic, I. & Doorne, S. (2000). Local government and tourism development: issues and constraints of public sector entrepreneurship. *New Zealand Geographer. 56*(2), 25–31.
Pike, S. (2007). A cautionary tale of a resort destination's self-inflicted crisis. *Journal of Travel & Tourism Marketing. 23*(3/4).
Stafford, D. (1986). *The Founding Years in Rotorua: A History of Events to 1900.* Auckland: Ray Richards.
Stafford, D. (1988). *The New Century in Rotorua.* Auckland: Ray Richards.

While it has been entrepreneurs such as Thomas Cook who have been responsible for the rapid growth of mass tourism, this would not have been possible without government support in the form of security, stimulation of increased affluence and leisure time, and infrastructure development (Elliott, 1997). Government intervention has been necessary to guide the actions of both the private sector and the public sector. In Canada, over 20 government agencies have an active interest in tourism (Vallee, 2005). Mill and Morrison (1986) noted in the USA during the 1980s that there were over 150 government programmes across 50 departments that directly affected tourism. Similarly, in the UK a 1982 report identified over 70 pieces of legislation that affected tourism (Jeffries, 2002). Such fragmentation clearly requires coordination, which can only occur with government support.

Why should taxpayers subsidise tourism businesses?

It is not uncommon for those outside the tourism industry to question why taxpayers should subsidise the tourism industry. A diverse range of groups can pose this challenge, from retiree associations that have no vested interest in business to representatives of other industries such as horticultural/agricultural producer boards. This issue has been a major hurdle for tourism interests in the USA, where a lack of Congress support for an NTO had been attributed to strong political views that this would represent corporate welfare (Gatty & Blalock, 1997).

Globalisation of competition has impacted on the ability of democratic governments to provide traditional services, due to a resistance by residents to accept high tax levels (Wanhill, 2000). There have been increasing calls for the public sector to focus on the core tasks required to operate in a market economy. These include the provision of essential services, assurance of macro-environment stability and protection of the environment. Implications of this include a smaller state enterprise sector, the privatisation of infrastructure, and a user-pays approach to the operation of museums and parks. Tourism would rarely be regarded as an essential government service such as health, education, and security.

The case for government intervention in tourism may be made through the following:

- economic development
- market failure
- provision of infrastructure
- fiscal revenue
- border controls
- spatial redistribution
- protection of resources
- regulatory safeguards
- exogenous events
- social benefits.

Tourism as an enabler of economic development

In the Bahamas, 70% of foreign exchange earnings are generated by tourism (Edgell, 1999). Attracting visitors has long been recognised as a means of stimulating economic growth. For example, the emergence of a bathing season for visitors to Margate during the 1730s is credited with rescuing the English port town from ruin, following tough economic times (Walton, 1983). Opportunities exist for the smallest communities to benefit from tourism as a vehicle for economical development. Ioannides (2003) offered the examples of Pigeon Forge in Tennessee, Branson in Missouri, and Jackson in Wyoming, as places with populations of less than 5,000 that attract over five million tourists each year. Such opportunities have long been the prime motivation for government intervention in tourism. In Australia, the enthusiastic endorsement of tourism in government policy documents has traditionally espoused the benefits of encouraging tourism solely on the grounds of economic benefits (Craik, 1991).

Tourism has generally proved a stable investment vehicle, with overall global growth averaging 6% annually during the 1960s–1990s (Bull, 1995). International tourism receipts grew faster than world trade during the 1980s, and by the 1990s constituted a higher proportion of the value of world exports than all sectors other than petroleum products and motor vehicles (WTO, 1995). Also, for developing nations, tourism is usually free of the artificial constraints of other export industries where import quotas and tariffs can limit trade (Jenkins, 1991).

One of the essential services provided by governments is the stimulation of opportunities for the unemployed, and tourism as a service industry is labour intensive. Long's (1994) survey of over 100 British local authorities, which had an appointed tourist officer, identified increased employment opportunities as the most important benefit of tourism. In the USA, tourism is the first, second or third largest employer in 32 states (Goeldner et al., 2000). Globally, tourism employment has been estimated at one in every 12 jobs, representing around 8% of all jobs (WTTC, 2005). The WTTC estimated that the tourism industry was responsible for 215 million jobs and 10% of global GDP. Table 6.1 highlights the ratio of full-time equivalent jobs for a selection of macro-regions, countries, and communities. In general terms, it is useful to consider tourism as contributing *1 in 10*. For example, approximately 10% of world GDP and approximately 10% of world jobs are generated by tourism.

Table 6.1 Full-time equivalent tourism jobs

Destination	Ratio of full-time equivalent tourism jobs in the economy	Source
The world	8%	WTTC (2003)
European Union	6%	Akehurst, Bland & Nevin (1993), Jeffries (2001)
Central and Eastern Europe	12%	WTTC/WEFA (1997, in Hall, 2002)
England	7%	Elliott (1997)
Australia	6%	Jenkins (1995)
USA	6%	Goeldner, Ritchie & McIntosh (2000)
Fiji	10%	http://www.tcsp.com/invest/table_A2.shtml, viewed 25/3/04
Cyprus	10%	Ionnides & Apostolopoulos (1999)
Mexico	10%	WTTC (2004, in Berger, 2006)
New Zealand	9%	Tourism Auckland (2002)
Wales	9%	Shipton (1997, in Pritchard & Morgan, 1998)
Scotland	8%	Kerr & Wood (2000)
New Orleans, USA	16%	Dimanche & Lepetic (1999)

Table 6.1   (Continued)

Destination	Ratio of full-time equivalent tourism jobs in the economy	Source
Isle of Thanet, England	15%	Bishop Associates (1987, in Voase, 2002)
Valencia region, Spain	10%	Bueno (1999)
Cambridge, England	6%	Cambridge City Council (1995, in Davidson & Maitland, 1997)
Amsterdam, The Netherlands	6%	Dahles (1998)
Auckland, New Zealand	5%	Tourism Auckland (2002)

Case Study 6.2 examines how investors are returning to the Blackstone Valley, America's industrial birthplace, on the back of government intervention. Beginning in 1790 with cotton manufacturing, the Valley became the place to achieve the American Dream. However, by the 1940s industry was leaving. The Valley went into an economic free-fall, people moved on, and mill villages decayed. In 1986, the National Park Service, with special legislation, began to tell the story about this special landscape. Resultant initiatives have resulted in the Blackstone River becoming cleaner, historic properties being thoughtfully restored, and visitation growing.

Case study 6.2   Federal investments attracting private-sector investments in historic industrial areas

Dr Robert Billington, President, Blackstone Valley Tourism Council Inc, Pawtucket, Rhode Island, USA

The Blackstone River Valley played a 'seminal role in transforming America, from a colonial landscape of farmlands and forests to one of riverside mills and urban factories' (National Tourism Association, 2003). The region is regarded as the 'birthplace of America's industrial revolution' (SMHS, 2002). Situated in New England, 200 miles north of New York City, the Valley rose to prominence in 1790, when English immigrant Samuel Slater built the first successful water-powered cotton-spinning mill in America (Slater Mill Historic Site, 2002).

Slater went on to become known as the father of American manufacturers, establishing several manufactories throughout Southern New England (Rivard, 1974). Hundreds of mills were built throughout the Blackstone Valley after Slater's success, underpinning the United States' progression to world economic leader. Immigrants flocked to the Blackstone's textile industry from all over the world.

After 150 years of growth and prosperity, the textile industry in the Blackstone Valley was hit by hard times. Manufacturers moved south and the mills grew silent. Outdated technology, labour troubles, and the climate were blamed. The region was then plagued with decaying mills, contaminated landscapes, a toxic river, and plunging community morale. This was a place for the economically deprived to live, and a place of disinvestment.

The textile industry that built America eventually killed the Blackstone River, and devastated its environment. With its textile industry decimated, the people of the Valley were faced with increasing high unemployment. The Valley was in an economic free-fall. The social turmoil and restlessness in the United States in the 1960s led to positive action along the Blackstone River. In 1972 change began to emerge. The people of the Valley had enough of their polluted river, and wanted to do something to bring it back to a better day when it ran clear. With leadership from volunteers, Rhode Islanders organised a *ZAP the Blackstone* campaign, and initiated a 10,000-person cleanup project in September of that year.

By 1985, an effort to develop a programme to attract visitors to the Blackstone Valley was launched. Although tourism development was laughable to many in Rhode Island because of the past 200 years of environmental degradation in the Valley, after five years the programmes of the Blackstone Valley Tourism Council began to work, and people started believing in this new industry. The former textile mills were seen as important places of heritage, and key to the future of the Blackstone Valley.

Officials in the State of Rhode Island and the Commonwealth of Massachusetts knew that if the health of the river were to be improved it would have to be accomplished in a different way; it would have to be done across state jurisdictions. In the early 1980s the two states petitioned the National Park Service to review the Blackstone River Valley and all of its historic and cultural resources, to determine any level of national significance. It took several years of work and support by the Rhode Island and Massachusetts US Congressional delegation, and extensive state, local, and organisational support, before President Ronald Reagan signed the Blackstone Valley National Heritage Corridor Act into law in November of 1986. Congress designated the Blackstone Valley a National Heritage Corridor for the purposes of (Public Law 99–647, November 10, 1986):

> ... preserving, and interpreting for the educational, and inspirational benefit of present, and future generations the unique and significant contributions to our national heritage of certain historic and cultural lands.

The Blackstone Valley Tourism Council, in 1989, began to lease small riverboats and eventually raised enough funds to build their own 49-passenger riverboat for the Blackstone River. Their educational staff developed curricula for environmental and historical tours for kindergarten to graduate level education.

Education at all levels of the community has brought about change, both attitudinally and financially. Since the creation of the Blackstone River Valley National Heritage Corridor, approximately $21 million in federal funds has been invested in the Valley. These funds have assisted 24 communities and hundreds of projects in both states. The National Park Service funding has been key in creating a high-profile context for private investors. This federal investment is beginning to shrink as a percentage of what private investors are investing in the historic resources of the Valley. Over $73.5 million in private funds have been attracted to the Rhode Island riverfront portions of the National Heritage Corridor; most of these funds have been invested in the last five years.

Blackstone River Valley National Heritage Corridor, National Park Service Investments Compared to Private Sector, River-related Heritage Project Investments in Rhode Island

Fiscal year	NPS annual	Private sector
1987	50,000	1,200,000
1988	350,000	
1989	325,000	2,000,000
1990	320,600	
1991	696,000	
1992	2,518,000	
1993	1,537,000	
1994	1,047,000	
1995	1,325,000	
1996	860,000	
1997	1,020,000	
1998	1,069,000	
1999	1,330,000	10,000,000
2000	1,727,000	1,300,000
2001	3,391,000	500,000
2002	2,106,000	1,000,000
2003	2,107,000	57,500,000
TOTALS	$21,778,600	$73,500,000

Source: Blackstone River Valley National Heritage Corridor Commission, City of Pawtucket, City of Central Falls, City of Woonsocket. (March 2003).

The Blackstone Valley has risen to the standard where its plans for preservation are deemed worthy of private investment. Several more buildings, in historic districts, are being sought by preservation-minded private investors. This could mean sustainability of the historic fabric of the region, which is vital to residents, their cultural history, and the visitor industry. The work completed in the Blackstone Valley over the last two decades has created a generation with a new awareness of their natural, cultural, and historical resources. Community revitalisation, based on education, historic preservation, landscape improvements, private and public investments, are causing this new-found awareness to ensure the Blackstone Valley is not just a place to make a living, but a place worth living.

Discussion question

How can public place-making investments in infrastructure, culture, the environment, and history, help a visitor destination draw private investments?

Further reading

Boucher, S. M. (1986). *The History of Pawtucket 1635–1986*. West Hanover, MA: The Pawtucket Public Library & The Pawtucket Centennial Committee.

Copping, S. E. (2003). *Report, Leveraging and Resources Information, National Heritage Areas Program.* Washington, DC: National Park Service.
Blackstone River Valley National Heritage Corridor Commission (1999). The next ten years, an amendment to the cultural heritage and land management plan. Woonsocket, RI: JHC Blackstone River Valley National Heritage Corridor Commission.

Recognition that visitor increases lead to new job creation has seen tourism move from the shadows of fiscal policy to a place in centre stage (Hall, 1998). However, some in industry, such as the director of the British Travel Trade Fair, argue the benefits of tourism are not fully recognised by governments (Barnett, 2006, p.1):

> *In marketing terms, tourism's return on investment is exceptional, reaping nearly £50 in income for every £1 spent. It's another example of why MPs of all parties need to wake up to the fact tourism needs to be moved right up the government agenda.*

Kubiak (2002), a senior policy advisor to the Southern Governors' Association in the USA, suggested that the potential of tourism as an economic enabler had been underestimated by state governments, and questioned why more had not been done to promote the benefits offered by tourism. Kubiak (p. 19) referred to tourism as the 'red-headed step-child' of state government policymakers.

Market failure

In New Zealand, Edlin (1999) cited a National Bank report that presented a succinct argument for the government's financial support of the NTO. National Bank economists argued that offshore marketing was required to attract higher-spending tourists, and suggested that an extra $10 million in offshore marketing spend could generate an extra 31,000 annual visitors spending $385 million a year. It was argued that without an NTO, market failure would result. In other words, if left to the private sector, the priority for individual businesses would to do what is best for their own operation rather than the destination.

Competition within a destination is positive when it leads to innovation, quality, and efficiency (Porter, 1991). The one-industry concept recognises that while businesses pursue individual goals, the success of the tourism industry relies on effective interrelationships between stakeholders to produce traveller satisfaction (Collier, 1997). The assumption is that the traveller's perspective of a holiday, while made up of a composite of service encounters, is judged as a total experience (Medlik & Middleton, 1973). At a destination level the implication is that poor service provision by one or more sections of the community, which may or may not be directly involved in the tourism industry, may ultimately impact on the success of other suppliers.

Clearly, developing a cooperative approach towards quality assurance, as well as stimulating a cooperating to compete marketing philosophy/approach requires a champion with a holistic perspective. This is a challenge, since while there may be good vertical integration in tourism, there has been a general lack of horizontal coordination (Lickorish, 1991). Individual businesses tend to first consider the costs, rather than the benefits of collaboration.

Would small tourism businesses survive against unfair competition from larger and better-resourced operators without government intervention? What constitutes membership of the tourism industry? It is extremely difficult for tourism to adopt a cooperative producer board approach, such as is found in the horticulture and agriculture industries, due to the difficulty in delineating those businesses that benefit from tourism spending. Generally, it is for this reason that destination marketers need government support more than other industries. Also, a vast pooling of resources would be required to achieve a reasonable destination marketing budget since the vast majority of tourism businesses are family-owned businesses:

- Around 98% of the one million plus USA travel businesses are classified as small businesses (Edgell, 1999; Jeffries, 2001).
- In the UK, over 75% of tourism businesses are small and medium-sized enterprises (SMEs) with a turnover of less that £250,000 (Frisby, 2002).
- In Europe, about 95% of tourism businesses employ less that 10 staff (Middleton, 1998), and 96% of the 1.3 million hotels and restaurants have less than 9 employees (WTO, 1997, in Jeffries, 2001).
- The mean number of staff in Sweden's 20,000 tourism businesses has been estimated at 10 (Swedish Tourist Board 1990, in Pearce, 1996a).
- An estimated 70% of accommodation houses in England have only 10 or fewer guest rooms (McIntyre 1995, in Davidson & Maitland, 1997).

Torbay, an English seaside destination, is a useful example of the importance of government intervention in tourism. English's (2000) case study presented a snap shot of many of the issues discussed in this chapter. Torbay has been promoted as the English Riviera in reference to its picturesque bay and resort towns. The area suffered a decline in popularity from the 1970s due to the increased affordability and availability of European holiday packages. Tourism has a significant economic impact on the area with an estimated 16,000 people employed in the local tourism industry. English cited a leading local official to highlight the need for government intervention: 'We all know the story of Torbay's decline but its trying to persuade government that we suffer measurable deprivation that's the big challenge' (p. 91). There was a lack of direct involvement by central government, and poor communication between the regional tourism board and local operators. English's synopsis (p. 96) provides sobering reading for one of Britain's leading resort areas, where tourism is the core industry, where standards are declining, and where strong government leadership is lacking:

> Many tourism providers are trying to be all things to all people, and the result is often a lower standard of experience for the tourist. In Torbay the major problem is a lack of professionalism and the belief that they do not need help. Many come to the industry with no prior background or training and very little knowledge . . . Many providers only think short term, few have business plans or tourism development strategies, and these are major failings that result in a lack of professionalism. Businesses also feel they are only in competition locally . . . and thus do not work together. On the whole, few seem to be investing for long-term benefits and standards vary considerably. This research has shown that many supporting the industry would like to see more government involvement and feel that government has an important leadership and coordination role to play.

Provision of infrastructure

Traditionally, governments have been responsible for the development of infrastructure to enable tourism, such as utilities, sewerage, cleaning, health, and fixed communication and transport facilities (Bull, 1995). In recent years India has been investing heavily in infrastructure projects, such as over 18,000 kilometres of highways (D'Sliva & Bharadwaj, 2004). In 2003 the first annual Africa tourism investment summit was announced by the Ugandan Minister of Tourism (TravelMole.com, 23/7/03). One of the principal aims of the forum was to promote infrastructure development, in a continent that was attracting only 2% of global tourism spending.

Hazbun (2000) reported the difficulty faced by Jordan in attracting visitors prior to the 1990s, due to a lack of infrastructure, access, and attractions. Poor-quality infrastructure has also been one of the major challenges to overcome for destinations in Eastern Europe (Davidson, 1992). During 2003 the Albanian government began an ambitious development tourism redevelopment programme in a bid to appeal to international visitors (www.TravelMole.com, 23/6/03). The government organised the demolition of run-down buildings along the best beaches, which would be replaced with 5-star accommodation developments. Albania's Minister of Tourism suggested that only Kosovans were willing to put up with the poor roads and other inconveniences of travelling within Albania. Apparently, hundreds of illegally erected kiosks, shops, and hotels did not have access to water and sewerage facilities (Brown, 2003). A similar problem exists in Kazachstan today, where significant government investment in infrastructure is required to enable the fledgling tourism industry to develop. Likewise, Papua New Guinea's tourism potential will remain untapped unless there is the political will by government to develop necessary infrastructure (Wright, 2006). Papua New Guinea attracted only 15,000 tourists during 2003.

Fiscal revenue

A government has no money of its own, and so the more it can collect in taxes from tourism businesses the more it can spend on enhancing a social, environmental, and economic climate where entrepreneurs can flourish (Owen, 1992). The tourism industry can therefore be a source of increased tax revenue to help fund government's essential services. Examples include:

- The April 2003 newsletter of the Colorado Tourism Office reported the results of a study that estimated every advertising dollar spent by the STO generated US$12.74 in state taxes.
- In the decade 1996–2005, Las Vegas room taxes (9%) generated approximately $321 million for local schools, $247 million for local transport services, and $477 million for local government.
- In Florida, tourism generated US$51 billion in taxable sales during 2002, with the US$3.1 billion in tax representing 20% of the government's total sales tax take (Word, 2003). By 2004 visitor spending of $57 billion generated $3.4 billion in tax revenues to the state (www.travelindustryreview.com, 1/3/06).
- In 1995, total USA tourism-related taxes at federal, state, and local levels was estimated at US$64 billion (Brewton & Witham, 1998).

Most commonly, taxes in tourism take the form of user-pays charges, as discussed in Chapter 5. In some cases the tax is levied across most goods and services, such as the value added tax (VAT) in the UK and Mexico, and the Goods and Services Tax (GST) in Australia and New Zealand. In other cases there may be a special tax levied by federal, state, or local government on specific services such as accommodation. Often this contribution from tourism goes into the government's consolidated fund rather than dedicated to tourism, much to the ire of the tourism industry. For example, the Hawaii state government introduced a 5% room tax in 1986, with all revenue allocated to the state general fund rather than to the HVB (Bonham & Mak, 1996). In other cases a bed tax is used as a dedicated destination marketing fundraiser. For example, the Tokyo metropolitan government collected a bed tax that provides revenue solely for tourism promotion (*The Daily Yomiuri*, viewed online at www.yomiuri.co.jp, 11/8/03).

Taxes also commonly target international travellers at gateways. These include an airport departure fee, such as in Costa Rica and New Zealand, and an arrival tax, such as in Paraguay and Venezuela. In other cases revenue may be raised through visa application fees. A visa fee levied on entry, as is the case in China for example, might also be considered an arrivals tax. Another tax example is permit fees for admission to national and forest parks and marine reserves. Such tourist taxes to help pay for the use of public amenities (Wanhill, 2000), which would otherwise be funded by local taxpayers.

Some taxes can be divisive. Internet news wire service TravelMole.com (10/6/03) reported news of a controversial eco-tax introduced in May 2003 in Spain's Balearic Islands which was in danger of being scrapped only one year later. The purpose of the tax was to offset environmental damage caused by tourism. At the same time as the levy was imposed however, visitor numbers declined significantly, The report cited the spokespersons from the Federation of Tour Operators and the *Majorca Daily News* who suggested strongly that the tax had made a significant negative impact on the affordability of the islands. So there is a paradox in the balance between government realisation of tourism's economic development potential versus tourism as an easy target for taxes. While tourists are a valuable part of the tax base, they are not voters (Wanhill, 2000).

In India the government recently abolished the Inland Air Travel Tax and Foreign Travel Tax (D'Sylva & Bharadwaj, 2004). State governments there have also reduced tourism taxes. For example, Goa reduced the luxury hotel tax from 15% to 8% during the peak season and 4% during the low season, which ironically resulted in an increase of 23% in tax revenue. McMahon and Sophister (1998, in Davidson & Rogers, 2006) cited two examples of negative impacts of bed taxes. In New York a 1990 5% tax on rooms over $100 per night was repealed in 1994 following three years of lobbying by hotels, based on reports that New York lost $2 in related taxes for every $1 in tax revenue. In Ireland an estimated 10% of hotels closed following the 1980s value added tax (VAT) on hotel rooms increasing to 23%. Lobbying by hotels resulted in a decrease in 1985 to 12.5%. In 2004, Mexico became the second country, following Chile, to reduce the VAT rate to zero for international conventions (Cerda, 2005). The initiative, which was proposed by the tourism industry, covers venue hire, accommodation, transfers, and related services.

Border controls

Since so much travel crosses national borders, governments have been forced to develop policies for entry and exit by residents and visitors. Often the tourism industry lobbies for the easing of visa restrictions to improve access from emerging markets. At the 2003 IACVB convention chairman Rick Antonson lamented that the USA's new visa programme was putting off travel to that country (Travelwire News, 4/8/03).

In some cases coordination between tourism policy and immigration policy has resulted in visa regulations designed to enhance international visitor arrivals. For example, a relaxed visa policy introduced by Oman in 2003 was promoted by officials as a measure to boost tourism to the Gulf nation (Rahman, 2003). The European Union is a tourism example of a free trade agreement, where the entry/exit process has been hugely simplified for citizens, much to the envy of tourism interests in most other parts of the world.

Spatial redistribution

The imbalance of the London-centric nature of British inbound tourism has long been controversial in Britain (Jeffries, 1989). Around two-thirds of all holiday visitors to Britain arrive in London (Bowes, 1990). Using redistribution policies involving a combination of taxation and spending, it is possible for governments to spread economic benefits throughout the economy

(Bull, 1995). For example, the government in Egypt introduced a 10-year tax holiday for developments in remote areas (Wahab, 1995, in Gartner, 1996). Malaysia, Italy, Thailand, and the UK have used regionally-variable taxation and development grants as incentives for development in outlying areas.

Tourism can be an effective way of redistributing wealth from prosperous cities to rural and industrial areas that have a narrow economic base. Through increased diversification into tourism, these regions can counter the risk of decline in traditional industries. The resultant employment opportunities also help to reduce the impact of urban drift among younger members of the population. A proactive approach developed in the USA is Civic Tourism (see www.civictourism.org), which aims 'to provide a forum for communities to decide if and how the individual ingredients of place (cultural, built, and natural) can be integrated to create an appealing, dynamic, and distinctive community identity'. The initiative emerged from those concerned about the urban drift from the old mining towns in the country's south west. Rural America has long been in economic decline, and Edgell (1999) cited a number of reports initiated by Congress that promote tourism as a major opportunity for revival. Edgell asserted that most of rural America, which contains 25% of the USA's population and 90% of the natural resources, is conducive to tourism. Other notable examples of spatial redistribution policies to improve regional economic opportunities by government include the Languedoc Roussillon development in France (see de Haan et al., 1990; Jeffries, 2001), Cancun in Mexico (Jeffries, 2001), and Korea's Cheju Island (Jeffries, 2001).

Protection of resources

A completely free market philosophy might not be congruent with a community's wider interests such as the protection of the environment and public goods (Jeffries, 2001). Would an unfettered tourism industry ensure all members of the host and visiting community retained access to natural features such as beaches and rivers? Would unrestricted access to such assets by private sector developers place an undue strain on public sector infrastructure responsibilities? Could we rely on all entrepreneurs to adopt sustainable resource practices without government intervention? While tourism can be used as an economic incentive for protecting native wildlife from poaching (Ritchie & Crouch, 2003), in general there is increasing conflict between the tourism industry and the conservation movement (Carroll, 1991). This conflict has played a role in stimulating government policies relating to the protection of natural resources for sustainable use. These issues are discussed further in Chapter 7.

Regulatory safeguards

Key motives for government policies relating to regulatory safeguards are concerned with economic controls, consumer protection, and orderly markets (Bull, 1995). Economic controls impact on international travel where a generating country might impose restrictions on the export of the local currency or regulations concerning tax deductibility for business travel. Consumer protection areas include the licensing and bonding of goods and services providers, accommodation classification systems, and the fulfilment of contracts. As temporary residents of a community, travellers also have a right to expect protection from unfair practices and to safe passage. For example, ensuring the safety and security of travellers is a major obstacle to Papua New Guinea's tourism growth. Clearly, regulatory safeguards need to avoid unnecessary bureaucracy. In this regard, Bermuda has been labelled 'red-tape island' by the government opposition due to the problems being encountered by hotel developers there (www.travelindustryreview.com, 9/3/06).

Exogenous events

An emerging area of interest in the tourism literature is the impact of disasters on the tourism industry, both at global and local levels. Quick decisions are required in times of crisis. Such decision-making and resultant responses should also be of a cooperative nature and therefore coordinated. Individual businesses are at the mercy of exogenous events, but few have the resources individually to engage in strategic planning for crises, particularly at a destination level. The government therefore has a vested interest in ensuring adequate leadership. The topic of tourism disaster management is discussed in Chapter 18.

Social benefits

A key factor in the rise of tourism during the 1950s and 1960s was the introduction of the social policy of leave with pay from work (WTO, 1983b, p. 3). Jeffries (2001) referred to research by Cadieu (1999), who recorded French government initiatives in the 1930s to promote social tourism through publicly subsidised holidays for low-income earners as part of a welfare programme. Cooper et al. (1993) reported plans in Wales to develop tourism in ways that would optimise the social and economic benefits. Long's (1994) survey of British local authorities found that, after increased employment opportunities, the social benefits of an increase in the range and quality of facilities, services, and events designed for the visitor industry was the next most-cited benefit of tourism development in their community. Bramwell and Rawding (1994, p. 430) cited the head of the Manchester City Council tourism section:

> Tourism can make the city a better place to live, visit, work and invest in and so the standard of living goes up, and the quality of life improves, and the profile of the city is raised, and (this process) goes round in a circle.

The WTO (1983b) analysed the social effects of domestic tourism, on the basis that 80% of the world's tourism movements were domestic at that time. The study broke new ground in terms of addressing the social costs and benefits of tourism at national and local levels. These are summarised in Table 6.2.

Table 6.2 Social cultural benefits of tourism

National benefits	Local benefits
Contact among people from different regions stimulates socio-cultural integration at a national level	Rural areas develop urban infrastructure facilities, medical care, and education
Socio-cultural integration fosters national identity and pride	Tourism income leads to the development of a middle class
Stimulation of educational diversification, in terms of learning national values	Family relations change as a result of increased employment opportunities and therefore economic independence for the younger generation
Travel stimulates progress and modernity	Local cultural values, customs, arts, and monuments can be revitalised
Increased travel opportunities lead to quality of life enhancement	Increased contact with visitors broadens the mind of locals

The case against government funding of tourism

With so many policy areas impacting on tourism it would seem to be very much in a government's interests to support a coordinating body, such as a DMO. However, just as lobbying for government support is undertaken by the tourism industry leaders, other stakeholders can be just as passionate in arguing that government has no place supporting tourism marketing.

Government recognition of the economic value of tourism to communities, as well as subsequent social benefits, has to a large extent been responsible for the proliferation of DMOs worldwide. The focus of DMO operations has generally been selling a place, with the desired end results being increases in visitor arrivals, length of stay, and spending. However, as will be discussed in Chapter 19, one of the problems with destination marketing is that it has been difficult to actually quantify the contribution of DMO efforts to the overall success of the destination.

The lack of performance metrics rightly leaves the industry open to attack from politicians and other industries seeking justification for public funding of place promotion, high costs of infrastructure (sewerage and water) and superstructure (tax breaks for developers), and the impact of export leakage (foreign owned hotels). For example, in the late 1980s, a British government review of the BTA examined the extent to which the private sector should be responsible for overseas marketing. Jeffries (1989, p. 75) cited the then minister responsible as stating the government's wish was 'to see such activities carried out in the private sector wherever possible'. The British government continues to be accused of apathy towards tourism by major tourism industry players such as the CEO of VisitBritain (www.travelindustryreview.com, 9/3/06) and the director of the British Travel Trade Fair who offered this criticism (Barnett, 2006):

> *VisitBritain does an excellent job in marketing the UK around the world and yet 'tourism' is buried within the Department of Culture, Media and Sport and largely ignored by all but a few parliamentarians.*

The USA federal government has traditionally adopted a non-interventionist approach to tourism destination marketing at a national level. However, it has been suggested that any criticism of the devolvement of NTO activities to the states should first consider the significant federal resources committed to the protection of recreation resources such as the National Park Service, the Fish and Wildlife Service, the Forest Service, and the Bureau of Land Management (Jeffries, 2001). In a few cases, state governments have adopted a similar stance to the federal government, such as in Colorado, California, and Maine. In 1976, California and Maine closed their tourism marketing offices, although California reinstated the office in 1978, albeit with almost the lowest budget in the USA (Doering, 1979, p. 312). California, the world's fifth largest economy and home to such globally recognised tourism icons as Disneyland and Hollywood, is not clear of the problem. In 2003 the then governor of California proposed that the state tourism office be closed as a cost-saving measure. The STO had a $7.5 million budget and at the time California faced a $35 billion shortfall (*Inbound*, 13 January 2003, p. 1).

There are essentially two key arguments against public funding involvement in the support of commercial tourism development (Bull, 1995). Firstly, such investments may distort markets. This may occur when a project would not ordinarily succeed in a free market, and the net welfare benefits such as employment creation are used to support commercial inefficiencies. Also, larger entities may receive a larger share of resources. Stimulated by the decline in oil prices in the 1980s and a peace accord with Israel in the early 1990s, tourism was promoted in Jordan as the panacea to that country's economic woes (Hazbun, 2000). Tourism would be the oil of the Jordanian economy. However, Hazbun warned of the danger of false expectations created by unrealistic or overly optimistic projections by the Jordanian state. Jordan, which relied on Arab aid and remittances from expatriates abroad, announced ambitious plans to encourage private sector tourism developments. The strategy was to stimulate a rush of investment in mega projects, such as 30,000 new hotel beds in the Dead Sea area by 2010, to overcome the 'low equilibrium trap' of low visitors arrivals generating little revenue for future tourism development. One of the results of this was a 68% increase in hotel beds during the period 1993–1996. However, by 1997 hotel occupancy rates had decreased to only 38%. Khouri (1998, in Hazbun, 2000, p. 195) cited a Jordanian economist:

> *Hotels, tourist buses and travel agencies are real and sad examples of how parts of the economy went on an investment binge in 1995, only to come down to earth with a thud a year later and then start to wallow in a depression which continues.*

One of the problems with Jordan's 'big push' in stimulating new tourism developments and infrastructure, was a failure to balance this with adequate initiatives to stimulate increased demand for the new products (Hazbun, 2000). Part of the problem was a lack of public or private promotional organisations, resulting in a lack of information flow and cooperation between individual tourism businesses.

Bull's (1995) second argument against funding tourism is that subsidies may ultimately benefit visitors rather than suppliers through lower tariffs. This might not be an issue for domestic tourism, but in such cases governments may in effect unintentionally subsidise international visitors. Unfortunately it is the term *subsidise* that is often used by some to describe government funding of destination marketing.

Even though few countries are self-sufficient and therefore require foreign exchange earnings to purchase necessary imports, not all have embraced the idea of an international tourism trade. Historically, authoritarian regimes have either banned tourism or tightly controlled it (Gartner, 1996). In this regard, readers are referred to Roper (2001) for a comprehensive discussion on the perceived problems with tourism. Roper summarised these points of view as primarily falling into six categories, which are shown in Table 6.3.

While a full discussion on the negative impacts of tourism is beyond the scope of the text, it is important to acknowledge there are often strong arguments by sections of society against tourism. Some of the claims are fair . . . some are not. Students of destination marketing should be aware of the nature of these points of view in order to develop a balanced perspective.

Table 6.3 Perceived problems with tourism

A dislike of strangers and xenophobia
While such views are probably in the minority, there are many closed societies where outsiders are not welcome. The Hawaiian island of Ni'ihau is an example of a place virtually off limits to tourists. Other examples include towns and rural communities that are the base for religious sects such the Jews of Mea Sharim in Israel and the Amish of Ohio.

Changes to the character of the destination
The character of a destination and its people can be negatively affected by the very people who come to experience it. The number, characteristics, morality and behaviour of visitors can spoil the very nature of what attracted interest in the first place.

Negative social and cultural impacts
New visitors not only bring money into a destination, but they can also bring crime, ideas that create disharmony and envy among the host community. To cater to the entertainment tastes of mass tourists, traditional cultures have been replaced with ersatz rituals.

(Continued)

Table 6.3 (Continued)

Economic damage
Critics of tourism argue that the majority of jobs are low paid and servile in nature, and that most of the profits flow out of the community to outside investors.

Negative environmental impacts
Tourism developments have been the cause of damage to the environment. Also, ironically, increasing numbers of eco-tourists are spoiling the very serenity of the nature they seek to enjoy.

Colonialism or external control
It has been argued that tourism is the new form of colonialism, and is even more powerful than any imperial power.

Key points

1. Government intervention in tourism

Governments generally interact with tourism in the following ways: stimulating economic growth, provision of infrastructure, fiscal revenue, border controls, spatial redistribution, protection of resources, regulatory safeguards, managing of exogenous events, stimulating social benefits, and minimising market failure.

2. The key arguments for government funding of destination marketing

Coordination is required within and between government departments, within industry, and between government and industry. Only governments can provide such coordination through their access to taxation revenue and ability to legislate. Many DMOs, at national, state, and local levels, would simply not be able to function in their current form without the resources of government.

3. The key reasons why governments might not support tourism development

Anyone with an interest in tourism management should be able to debate the argument for and against government support of DMOs. Critics argue that this is a form of subsidy. Some stakeholders from other industries see this as unfair, while others in the community suggest tourism benefits a select few.

Review questions

- Why should a government subsidise the tourism industry?
- Apart from finance, what other forms of government support are provided to the tourism industry at your destination?

DMO roles

Competitiveness without sustainability is illusory.

Ritchie & Crouch (2003, p. 9)

Aims

The aims of this chapter are to enhance understanding of:

- the commonality in DMO roles
- the shift in thinking towards DMOs as destination management organisations.

> **Perspective**
>
> Ultimately, the vision and mission of a DMO must be related to enhancing the long-term competitiveness of the destination. Increasingly, it is recognised that without sustainability, competitiveness is illusory, and as a result we are witnessing greater tension between entrepreneurs and conservationists. A competitive destination is one that features a balance between profitable tourism businesses, an effective market position, an attractive environment, positive visitor experiences, and supportive local residents. This chapter focuses on the roles of DMOs in each of these areas. Recognition of the multidimensional nature of competitiveness has led to a desire to see DMOs evolve from destination *marketing* organisations to destination *management* organisations. The latter is indicative of a societal marketing orientation, and yet the tourism industry has been slow to evolve from a promotion orientation to a marketing orientation. So, while the term destination management organisation is being used more frequently, by academics in particular, this represents a paradigm shift in thinking about the role of DMOs; and that might not yet be reality at the coalface for many destination marketers.

The commonality in DMO roles

The roles of a DMO are dictated by the mission, goals, and objectives which, in general, are similar around the world. This is highlighted in the roles of RTBs in the UK (Pattinson, 1990, p. 210) and the roles of CVBs in North America (Morrison et al., 1998, p. 5), which are summarised in Table 7.1. Key themes include: coordination, strategy, stakeholders, economics, marketing, product development, lobbying, information provision, protection, research, and the host community.

Table 7.1 Roles of RTBs and CVBs

Roles of RTBs in the UK	Roles of CVBs in North America
• To produce a coordinated regional tourism strategy in liaison with local authorities and consistent with the broad aims of the English Tourist Board	• An economic driver of new income, employment, and taxes to create a more diversified local economy
• To offer advice to both commercial tourism businesses and local authorities on tourism planning	• A community marketer, communicating the most appropriate destination image, attractions, and facilities to selected markets
• To encourage the development of tourist amenities and facilities which meet the needs of a changing market	• An industry coordinator, providing a clear focus and encouraging less industry fragmentation so as to share in the benefits

Table 7.1 (Continued)

Roles of RTBs in the UK	Roles of CVBs in North America
• To administer the national financial aid scheme for assisting tourism development • To represent the interests of the region at the national level and the interests of the tourism industry within the region • To market the region by providing reception and information services, producing and supplying suitable literature, and undertaking promotional activities	• A quasi-public representative adding legitimacy for the industry and protection to visitors • A builder of community pride by enhancing quality of life and acting as the flag carrier for locals and visitors

In practice

The responsibilities of Tourism Auckland (Tourism Auckland, 2002) in New Zealand:

Developing marketing plans: developing comprehensive plans and strategies for marketing the Auckland Region as a tourist destination, and developing the means of implementing, monitoring, and reviewing those plans and strategies.

Marketing region: marketing in New Zealand and overseas the advantages of the Auckland Region for visitors and tourists, including promoting and coordinating the development of parks, holiday resorts, scenic reserves, and recreational, business and tourist facilities and activities.

Convention location: establishing, maintaining, and marketing the Auckland Region as a premier convention location.

Visitor information services: operating visitor information and entertainment services to ensure visitors and tourists to the Auckland Region are welcomed and given information and assistance.

Reservation services: providing a reservation service for accommodation, travel, and tour services within the Auckland Region.

Information on resources: researching, publishing, and disseminating information on the resources of the Auckland Region in order to encourage and promote the development, coordination, and marketing of commercial, industrial, communication, transportation, recreational, and education interests, services and facilities conducive to tourism.

Coordinating marketing: coordinating joint-venture marketing campaigns with the private sector and publicly-funded regional tourism organisations in order to raise the profile of the Auckland Region and to contribute to sustained tourism growth in the Auckland Region.

Statistical information: researching and recording statistical information on tourism and monitoring visitor numbers in order to provide forecasts of visitor numbers and visitor research information for the Auckland Region.

Promoting events and conventions: promoting, supporting, and bidding for events and conventions that bring economic benefit to, or increase the profile of, the Auckland Region in a cost-effective manner.

General: all such things as are incidental or conducive to the attainment of the charitable objects and purposes.

No limitation: The objects and purposes of the Trust shall not, except where the context specifically or expressly requires it, be in any way limited or restricted by reference or inference from the terms of any other clause or sub-clause or from the name of the Trust and none of the objects or purposes of the Trust shall be deemed subsidiary or ancillary to any other object or purpose of the Trust.

Objects and purposes independent: The Trustees shall be empowered to carry out any one or more of the objects or purposes of the Trust independently of any other object or purpose of the Trust.

Destination management

Should DMO refer to a destination *marketing* organisation or a destination *management* organisation? A lecturer of a tourism (environmental) planning course might argue for the latter, while I currently adhere to the former, for two reasons. First, critics who have suggested a destination marketing orientation implies a narrow marketing viewpoint should consider the evolution of marketing from a product orientation to selling orientation to marketing orientation to societal marketing orientation. The responsibilities of any destination management organisation fits within the societal marketing orientation, which is far from a narrow perspective.

Every DMO must take a proactive interest in stewardship of the destination's resources, which include social, cultural, and environmental dimensions. In doing so a distinction must be made between resources that are renewable, such as hunting and fishing stocks, and those that are not, such as a famous work of art (Ritchie & Crouch, 2003). Achievement of destination competitiveness requires an orientation that is broader than sales and marketing. What is required is a societal marketing orientation, or a destination management approach. However, the societal marketing orientation, the philosophy of which is to make all decisions with the consumer as well as the wider interests of society at heart, sounds admirable in theory, but is difficult to practise. This relates to my second point, which is to suggest that much of the debate about the appropriate name is academic. That is, arguments have been suggested to me that the WTO prefers the term, and that some legislation has been designed to force DMOs into considering sustainability issues.

In the UK the concept of destination management is very much in its infancy (Rogers, 2005), and in Mexico a major challenge for CVBs is that of moving from a promotion orientation to a marketing orientation (Cerda, 2005), let alone a management orientation. In North America there has long been a gap between marketing of destinations and ensuring sustainability

(Getz, Anderson & Sheehan, 1998), where the CVB focus has been sales and marketing. My own experience in Australia, New Zealand, and the Pacific, plus informal discussions with colleagues around the world, suggests this is common.

For all the rhetoric, the vast majority of destination marketers remain concerned with results relating to visitor numbers, length of stay and spend. More research is required to convince otherwise. My hope is that eventually DMOs will be regarded as destination management organisations because it is warranted . . . until that time it is not an accurate term *per se*. For example, while Canada's national, provincial, and regional DMOs have evolved well past the traditional promotion orientation, the nation's tourism industry lacks destination management (Vallee, 2005, p. 229): 'An integrated approach to destination management involving the country's multiple stakeholders has yet to be developed.' At the time of writing, DMAI, the world's oldest association of CVBs and DMOs, was still using the term destination marketing organizations on it's website.

Nevertheless, the DMO modus operandi paradigm is quietly undergoing a revolution. Thomas Kuhn's original thesis on paradigms was as science operating within a largely unquestioned framework, governed by fundamental theoretical models (Gregory, 1987). When a theory is accepted it becomes a paradigm until it is challenged by way of revolution. This concept applies as much to tourism practices as it does to science. The role and activities of DMOs have evolved slowly over time, and there have been few revolutionary shifts.

Ideally, the primary role of a DMO is to act as the coordinating body for the many public and private sector organisations with an interest in tourism (Heath, 2003). Case Study 7.1 highlights the need for an umbrella organisation with a holistic overview of the potential conflicts that can emerge between tourism interests, conservationists, and developers. In this regard it is useful to consider Harrill's (2005, p. xx) observation of the similarities between ecology and destination management. Harril was following Odum (1953), who examined the entire ecosystem rather than the ecology of different parts of nature. Harrill sees a destination management ecosystem including interrelationships within the complex network of stakeholders: 'Much like a natural ecosystem, a change in one area of destination management often significantly affects other parts of the system.'

Case study 7.1   The Greater Yellowstone National Park

Professor Jerry Johnson, Head of Department of Political Science, Montana State University, Bozeman, USA

The Greater Yellowstone Region is home to the world's first national park (Yellowstone), a complete array of large predator/prey relationships, and a place of unmatched recreation and beauty. The communities of the region are clean, safe, and prosperous. Increasing numbers of people are discovering that the region is a wonderful place to live and work.

More than 23,000 square miles demarcate the Greater Yellowstone Region; it is largely defined as the historical range of the Yellowstone grizzly bear. The area is home to two national parks (Yellowstone and Grand Teton) and seven national forests; 80% of the 18-million-acre (7.2 million hectares) land base is publicly owned and the remainder is private land.

The economy is increasingly dominated by nature tourism and recreation (hiking, hunting and fishing, skiing, protected area tourism) and the construction industry; much of it as second home development in pristine river valleys and high alpine regions. The inherent conflict is obvious – as more homes are built in the rural countryside, the natural beauty of the region is potentially compromised until the open spaces and spectacular views are lost to development.

Historically, the western states of Idaho, Montana, and Wyoming have been less well-off than many other states and, typically, have less diversified economies. Tourism provides many jobs but most are part-time and low wage. Construction on the other hand is year around employment and near the top of the labour pay scale. Property taxes paid by owners of expensive homes is a majority basis of public revenues in rural counties.

Politically, the culture of the region is against comprehensive land use planning. Individual property rights prevail with respect to how land is developed. If a rancher chooses, he can subdivide his prime agricultural land into 20-acre (8 hectares) parcels for recreational ranches and block public access to thousands of acres of public land in the process.

Landowner data from the region shows that almost half the private ranch land is owned by amenity owners – those that purchase a large ranch for recreation rather than cattle or crop production. Many are privacy seeking and not in favour of hunting. Taken together, they control nearly 3 million acres (1.2 million hectares). The same study indicated that as amenity ownership has increased, public access to both public and private land for recreation has decreased.

The intent of this case is to encourage thinking of a local economy or market(s) in terms more comprehensive than employment, earnings, and revenues. Rather, a contemporary market in high-amenity locations like the Yellowstone region is comprised of a qualitative value frequently not considered by economists or market strategists. As public officials seek to position their communities in the highly competitive 'amenity market' they will necessarily need to learn to balance both quantitative (i.e. economic) considerations with the qualitative nature of community and local culture.

Discussion questions

1. Identify three possible groups impacted by the above scenario. Describe the problem or issue from their point of view.
2. Identify the direct/indirect and tangible/intangible costs and benefits to the user groups you identified in question 1.
3. Given that the market for the Yellowstone lifestyle is segmented among seemingly competing groups, design a research question that would allow publicly-elected offi-cials to weigh the opportunity costs of both recreation/tourism and construction/amenity development.

Further reading

Johnson, J. (2006). Tourism development and impacts in the Greater Yellowstone Region, USA. Turk-Kazakh International Tourism Conference, November. Alanya Turkey.

In many communities the conservationists and social scientists are not as powerful a lobby as the government sponsor, entrepreneurs, and intermediaries. This is then a matter of balancing stakeholders' expectations, and of being realistic about the extent of destination management that will be possible for DMOs. Even well-financed STOs and NTOs will grapple with this function, given the scale of their environment. The Las Vegas CVB is faced with balancing phenomenal growth in accommodation construction with increased traffic on 'the strip' and a lack of affordable housing for construction workers and the increased number of hospitality staff. DMOs may have a sustainability related committee, may provide submissions to government agencies, and may develop discussion papers. Unless a crisis demands action, the focus will remain marketing.

Dwyer, Livaic and Mellor (2003) included 20 destination management attributes in their destination competitiveness model. Goeldner, Ritchie & McIntosh (2000) promoted 12 elements. Heath's (2003) destination competitiveness model for South African tourism featured six sustainable development policy conditions. Ritchie and Crouch (2000) included eight elements of destination management in their destination competitiveness model. These attributes, which are listed in Table 7.2, support the idea of destination competitiveness demanding a DMO's roles featuring a balance between profitable tourism businesses, an effective market position, an attractive environment, positive visitor experiences, and supportive local residents. The remainder of the chapter discusses these roles.

Stimulating profitable tourism businesses

Since destinations are multi-attributed, a common challenge faced by DMOs is the number of suppliers who make up the destination product. For example, in England the North West Tourist Board conceded that the product range was too diverse to market effectively as a single entity (Alford, 1998). My own research in New Zealand (Pike, 1998) found seven RTOs that identified over 400 local tourism businesses within their territory, while eight RTOs indicated a range of 200 to 400. Even though this is a significant number for the RTOs concerned, the numbers pale in comparison to Tourism Vancouver's 1000 members (see Vallee, 2005) and the Philadelphia CVB's 1300 member businesses (see Walters, 2005).

Although many DMOs do not have paid members as such, it is still in the interests of the destination to enhance upskilling of local businesses. During Tourism New Zealand's 2006 nationwide seminar series involving 1400 participants in 27 centres, one noticeable benefit was the opportunity for new businesses to network with others in the business, according to the NTO's industry communications manager Tracy Johnston: 'These businesses are so dependent on themselves to earn a living, it is hard for them to put aside vital time for training and getting to know others in the business' (Coventry, 2006). The NTO concluded that few tourism businesses in New Zealand are upskilling in the way they should be. During 2006 and 2007 Tourism Queensland in Australia conducted a series

Table 7.2 Destination management attributes

Dwyer, Livaic & Mellor (2003)	Heath (2003)	Ritchie & Crouch (2000b)	Goeldner, Ritchie & McIntosh (2000)
Training programmes	Conducive tourism policy and legislative framework	Resource stewardship	Cultural heritage management
DMO reputation for attracting visitors	Responsible management of resources	Marketing	Visitor management
Public sector recognition of 'sustainable' tourism	Stimulating a positive investment climate	Finance and venture capital	Community management
'Vision' reflecting shareholder values	Implementing strategies to ensure transformation of the industry	Organisation	Water quality management
Commitment to education and training (Public)	Sustainable environmental principles	Human resource development	Park management
Quality of research input	Effective institutional and funding framework	Information/ research	Air quality management
Packaging of destination experiences		Quality of service	Planning
Responsiveness of firms to visitor needs		Visitor management	Marketing
Commitment to education and training (private)			Human resources management
Training responsive to visitor needs			Information management
Private sector recognition of 'sustainable' tourism			Operations management
Clear policies in social tourism			Organisation management
Development responsive to visitor needs			
Development responsive to community needs			
Cooperation between firms			
Extent of foreign investment			
Resident support for development			
Development integration			
Government leadership and commitment			
'Vision' reflecting resident values			

of wine tourism workshops to help local wineries attract the visitor market. Wine tourism is one of Queensland's fastest growing tourism sectors.

Establishing an effective market position

Establishing and defending an effective market position is one of the major aspects of marketing, since all marketing activity should be focused on strengthening the brand's presence in the minds of target groups. Destination positioning is the focus of Chapter 12.

Maintaining an attractive environment

Tourism depends on the protection of environmental and community resources. Is sustainable tourism an oxymoron? There has been increasing criticism about the negative impacts of tourism on societies and environments (Elliott, 1997). Problems include the pressure of mass tourism on communities, natural and built environments, and infrastructure; lack of control over tourist developments; and lack of control over sex tourism. Government intervention is required to identify solutions that are in the public interest. Examples of government leadership in environmental protection have included:

- the establishment of the world's first national park in the USA in 1872 (Elliott, 1997)
- the 1887 establishment of the Rocky Mountains Park by the Canadian federal government (Go, 1987)
- the establishment of Tongariro National Park in New Zealand in 1903, which was the first in the world to be on land gifted by indigenous people for that purpose
- Hawaii's Land Use Law of 1961 in the face of rapid tourism developments (National Tourism Resources Review Commission, 1973, in Doering, 1979).
- the Bruges government's Reien Project, to better manage the quality of the destination's canals (see Vanhove, 2002)
- New Zealand's Resource Management Act (1991), which provides a legislative framework for land use planning, water and soil management, pollution, waste control, coastal management, and land subdivision.

Clearly, the future of tourism relies on sustainable development, even though the short-term focus of many stakeholders will be the results of marketing activity, not long-term sustainability management. The growing responsibility of citizenship means businesses must demonstrate, and not simply espouse, a commitment to the future. Getz (1994, p. 3) argued that in the tourism industry 'planning must be long-term and visionary in nature, not reduced to the greedy pursuit of short-term economic and political benefits . . . return on investment must be redefined.' Examples of environmental guidelines for tourism include: WTTC Environmental Guidelines, Code of Environmental Principles for Tourism in New Zealand, and the

PATA Code for Environmentally Responsible Tourism. Coventry (1997, p. 1) cited the New Zealand NTO market research manager:

> *German visitors to New Zealand are like environmental evangelists. They feel we need to protect the environment and it is almost as though we have a sacred environment that ought to be cherished. They feel that if we do anything that blights the environment in their eyes we are almost being blasphemous.*

Case Study 7.2 introduces the attempt by a community to develop an environmentally sustainable tourism industry through Green Globe benchmarking. Green Globe is the global environmental certification programme for the tourism industry. Douglas Shire in Australia was selected as a pilot in develop the Green Globe Certification process for communities. By 2007, ten other communities had received Green Globe certification.

Case study 7.2   Green Globe Benchmarked Community

Note: This case is based on a report prepared by Mrs Kimberly Christopher, Green Globe Asia Pacific, from material provided by Ms Kirsty Sherlock, Douglas Shire Council, 2001.

With 78% of its land World Heritage listed, the Douglas Shire in Queensland Australia is an attractive gateway to the Wet Tropics areas of Cape Tribulation and the Daintree Rainforest. The Shire is also the only place in Australia where two World Heritage Areas converge, as the Great Barrier Reef World Heritage Area lies off the coast. Townships include the Port Douglas resort area, the sugar cane town of Mossman, and the Daintree Village.

During 2000, the Douglas Shire Council signed an agreement with the Australian Cooperative Research Centre for Sustainable Tourism (CRC), the Centre for Integrated Environmental Protection, Griffith University, and the Queensland Environmental Protection Agency (EPA), to facilitate an ecologically sustainable environment. In doing so the alliance sought to stimulate environmental best practice among local tourism businesses. The council's commitment to helping the community develop in an environmentally and socially sustainable manner is reflected in the achievements against the Green Globe Benchmarking Indicator for Communities. Green Globe offers communities and businesses opportunities to benchmark their environmental performance, and then to gain certification. Green Globe's standard benchmarking indicators are: (1) Total energy consumption, (2) Total water consumption, (3) Total waste production, (4) Community commitment. Checklists are provided to monitor: (5) Water saving, (6) Waste recycling, (7) Paper products, (8) Pesticide products, (9) Community commitment, (10) Chemical products. Douglas Shire became the first Green Globe Benchmarked Community in the Asia Pacific region. Key initiatives and results for the shire included:

Energy

Consumption of electricity per capita is well below the national average, and exceeds the Green Globe best practice level through a range of initiatives, including: incentives for residents to introduce solar hot-water systems, incentives for energy-efficient buildings, and development of renewable energy, such as a by-product of the cane crushing process.

Water consumption

The Shire is rated above best practice level due to initiatives such as ultra-filtration systems. All new rural residential properties must install 20,000-litre rainwater tanks to ensure self-sufficiency in drinking water.

Waste

Through initiatives such as recycling the council aims to reduce landfill by up to 65%. Additionally, the council recycles effluent from the Port Douglas sewerage plant to irrigate local golf courses.

Air quality and noise control

The council is involved in the Cities for Climate Protection programme, which measures energy consumption and greenhouse gas emissions. The Shire aims to lower greenhouse gas emissions through their sustainable farming practices, including cutting cane green rather than burning off. Also, as a part of the Greenhouse Gas Abatement Project, 3000 hectares of planting within the Shire is required for carbon sequestration.

Social commitment

In acknowledging the economic effects of tourism the council supports local goods and services to ensure that the economic benefits remain within the local region. At the time of accreditation, 12% of local tourism operators had environmental performance accreditation. Generally, 10% participation is regarded as an excellent outcome.

Discussion question

Other than positive environment impacts, what potential advantages will the programme offer the destination from a destination marketing perspective?

Further information

Green Globe http://www.greenglobe.org/page.aspx?page_id=46
Douglas Shire Council http://www.dsc.qld.gov.au/

De-marketing • • •

Although the concept of de-marketing is not a new one, it has not been used effectively as a tourism management tool (Benfield, 2001). Benfield claimed almost nothing had been published about de-marketing in tourism until 1989. Benfield and Beeton (in Beeton, 2001) listed the following 11 strategies being practised:

- increasing prices
- increasing advertising that warns of capacity limitations
- reducing promotion expenditure
- reducing sales reps' selling time
- curtailing advertising spend

- eliminating trade discounts
- reducing the number of distribution outlets
- separate management of large group
- adding to the time and expense of the purchaser
- reducing product quality or content
- provision of a virtual tour.

Beeton (2001) argued that by incorporating de-marking strategies into the marketing mix, greater management efficiency and sustainability can be achieved. The following examples of destination de-marketing were offered by Buhalis (2000, p. 100):

- Cambridge, England, aims to attract only visitors who stay overnight, and therefore discourage day trippers by controlling parking processes.
- Mauritius does not allow charter flights, therefore discouraging low-expenditure tourism.
- Venice introduced premium pricing and negative advertising to reduce mass tourism.

Positive visitor experiences

The rationale for sustainable development planning is that the tourist experience is the central element in the tourism market (Hall, 1998). The experiences of tourists influence future travel, and so it is imperative their needs are considered a focal point of destination management. Key roles in this regard are monitoring service and quality standards, and stimulating new product development.

Service and quality standards • • •

The very nature of tourism as a service industry demands a fixation with quality standards: 'The tourist is buying an illusion. He will be embittered by anything or anybody who shatters it' (Wahab et al., 1976, p. 74). Plog (2000) predicted managed destinations, such as resorts and cruise ships, would become increasingly popular in the future due to their ability to manage capacity and maintain consistency of quality. Likewise, d'Hauteserre's (2000) analysis of Foxwoods Casino Resort suggested that the success factors would be much more problematic for destinations than managed resorts. These included, for example, staff empowerment and the reinvestment of earnings into product development.

In the early 1990s, a consultancy commissioned to investigate the state of Northern Ireland's tourism industry reported a 'considerable disparity' between visitor expectations and the actual experience (O'Neill & McKenna, 1994, p. 33). The Tourism (Northern Ireland) Order 1992 incorporated the recommendations of the review, which included the introduction of an accommodation classification registry, to which providers could only be included upon an inspection assessment. Similarly, in 1999 a report tabled in the British parliament criticised the state of the

Table 7.3 Destination quality management programmes

Country	Programme	URL
Austria	Destination Management Monitor Austria (DMMA)	www.dmma.at
Denmark	Destination 21	www.destination21.dk
New Zealand	Qualmark	www.qualmark.co.nz
Switzerland	Vallais Excellence	www.valais-excellence.ch

Scottish tourism product, including poor quality accommodation, unwelcoming hosts, uncompetitive and unattractive prices, poor standards at visitor attractions, and poor accessibility (Kerr & Wood, 2000, p. 287). In New Zealand, Tan et al.'s (1995) survey of tourism businesses from six sectors found 78% had no formal quality system, with 65% having no intention of introducing one.

Table 7.3 lists a number of destination quality management programmes implemented by destinations around the world. Many such programmes are joint ventures between the DMO and other organisations. In New Zealand, for example, Qualmark, which is the official quality agency for the tourism industry, is a joint venture between the NTO and the Automobile Association (see www.qualmark.co.nz).

New product development ● ● ●

Globalisation is increasing the homogeneity and commodification of tourism products. For example, the internationalisation of theme parks, such as through expansion by Disney, and the outsourcing of international consultants is leading to an homogenous approach towards these developments (Swarbrooke, 2001). Likewise, the westernisation of Asia, the standardised format of international hotel chains, the ubiquitous golden arches, and the sale of similar types of souvenirs has decreased the surprise factor for experienced travellers. This is resulting in increasing difficulty in DMOs' ability to differentiate.

Theme parks understand the need to develop a stream of new and innovative products to increase repeat visitation. Likewise, DMOs recognise the need to be able to refresh product offerings. A product has been defined as 'anything that can be offered to a market for attention, acquisition, use or consumption that might satisfy a want or a need' (Kotler, et al., 2003). A product offering comprises core, actual, and augmented elements. The core product is the bundle of benefits sought by the consumer. In the case of destinations these are the ability to cater to travel motivations such as the need for escape and relaxation or adventure and excitement, among others. The actual product is that supplied for purchase, such as a travel package. In this regard a destination is viewed by the consumer as both a product in itself, since in general consumers talk about purchasing travel to a destination such as Paris or Germany, as well as an amalgam of individual tourism services. The augmented product represents the added-value component. For tourism service providers and intermediaries a satisfaction guarantee to overcome perceived risk is a useful example. Other examples include brag value and iconic photo opportunities.

While some DMOs, particularly at the NTO level, have historically been directly involved in developing and managing tourism products, the majority no longer have any direct responsibility, due in the main to the high labour intensity of the activity and the changes in government philosophy towards direct involvement in private business. Getz, Anderson and Sheehan (1998) found most Canadian CVBs lacked formal goals for product development, with only one-quarter reporting having a policy. They found that significant barriers to direct involvement included a lack of resources and a marketing mandate, and of course concerns from existing members. In some cases the DMO abdicates responsibility to an economic development agency, such as in the case of Rotorua, New Zealand, where the product development has been the domain of the local council's business development unit (see http://rotorua-business.com/index.shtml).

Stimulating new developments

Essentially there are three main product development roles played by DMOs. One opportunity is the proactive stimulation of new products. Independent research undertaken during the development of Australia's new tourism strategy in 2006 estimated that A$86 billion of investment, particularly in accommodation and attractions, would be required in the following 10 years to meet forecast increases in demand.

The DMO must determine the extent to which the range of destination products adequately takes advantage of the destination's source(s) of comparative advantage. In Canada the CTC has worked with industry to develop 34 product-based clubs in an effort to increase both the range and quality of tourism products (Vallee, 2005). In New Zealand for many years it has been argued that of all the attributes that country has to offer visitors there is only one that is truly unique on the world stage, and that is the indigenous Maori people and their culture. Everything else, such as fiords and glaciers, geothermal activity, bungee jumping and the like can be found elsewhere. Given that so many travellers are interested in experiencing aspects of other cultures this has been advantageous for New Zealand. However, until very recently there has been a lack of commercial Maori product for visitors to experience, and a lack of access to 'authentic' Maori life on the Marae (tribal meeting place). In terms of a successful proactive initiative, the economic development unit, mentioned in the previous paragraph, commissioned and funded a $30,000 feasibility study that resulted in a much-needed new hotel development called for by the RTO.

A marketing orientation dictates that products are designed to meet the needs of the target. However, a destination's major tourism products are usually rigid in terms of what they can be used for, and may be difficult to adapt to changing demand. For example, Morgan (1991) reported that the late 1980s price wars by UK tour operators, which led to demand for increased accommodation capacity in Majorca, stimulated the development of 70,000 new hotel beds. A later shift in demand from the dominant UK and German markets for self-catering accommodation then led to a surplus of an estimated 50,000 to 70,000 hotel beds on the island.

Stimulating packages

A second DMO role is stimulating the bundling or packaging of products to meet identified market needs. This type of approach can be undertaken through wholesale and retail package sales. For example, during the 1980s, Bradford, categorised as a difficult tourism area, placed a significant emphasis on promoting a series of special interest short-break packages. These were based on the following themes, which generated an estimated 85,000 bed nights a year (Buckley & Witt, 1985):

- The area's mill shops
- 'In the footsteps of the Brontë sisters'
- Television and film themes
- Industrial heritage
- Camera craft with the National Museum of Photography, Film and Television.

Examples from the USA's mid-west include (Carley, 2005, p. 116):

- Europe without a passport. A regional offering of ethnic attractions
- The adventure that Lewis and Clark missed. A tour of the historical attractions in a section of Dakota not visited by the explorers.
- Seeing stars. Opportunities to view stars at both a local planetarium and a restored movie theatre showing vintage films.

Stimulating events

A third area of product involvement by DMOs is special events, which can generate substantial visitor arrivals. For example, during 2003 the Dublin Chamber of Commerce reported an otherwise flat tourism season was 'kept alive' by a series of major events, including the Special Olympics (www.onbusiness.ie, 11/8/04). In the modern era the first examples were probably the Great Exhibitions of the 19th century that were held in London in 1851, Vienna in 1863, and Paris in 1878 (see Elliott, 1997). Today the highest profile events in the world are sports related, and it has been estimated that sports and related recreation make up at least 25% of tourism activity (Research Unit, 1994, in Pitts & Ayers, 2000). A significant component of sports tourism is special events, such as InterHash. This biennial gathering of Hash House Harriers from around the world has since the early 1990s regularly attracted over 4000 participants. The 8th Masters Swimming World Championships held in Munich in 2000 attracted 7406 competitors.

Despite the high profile of national and international sports events, as many, if not more, people attend events related to culture. Cultural events are not the sole domain of the major cities. For example, in the USA the Age of Rubens exhibition attracted 234,000 visitors to Toledo, mostly from interstate (Holcolmb, 1999). Gartrell (1994) reported that the Street Art Fairs in Ann Arbor, Michigan, attracted over 500,000 attendees.

Another event category could be labelled odd, wacky, or off-beat. For example, in August each year the tomato fight in the Spanish town of Bunol attracts around 30,000 participants (http://edition.cnn.com/2000/FOOD/news/08/24/spain.tomato.war.ap, 29/03/04).

Examples of off beat events in the UK include (Ross, 2003):

- The World Bog Snorkelling Championships at Llanwrtyd
- Shrovetide football, with goalposts 4.8 kilometres apart, at Ashbourne
- Up-Helly-Aa Viking festival, which originated in the 19th century, in Lerwick
- The Shrove Tuesday Pancake race at Olney
- The World Coal Carrying Championships at Onsett
- Cheese rolling races, which date back 400 years, at Brockworth
- The World Toe Wrestling Championships at Wetton
- The World Stinging Nettle Challenge at Marchwood
- Gurning competition (pulling grotesque faces) at the Egremont Crab Fair
- Stonehaven Fire Balling Festival.

Examples in other parts of the world include:

- Groundhog Day on 2nd February in Punxsutawney, Pennsylvania, which attracts over 30,000 visitors to see groundhog 'Punxsutawney Phil' emerge from Hibernation.
- Wild cow milking at the Rerewhakaiitu Rodeo, New Zealand
- 'Battle of the Queens' cow fighting, Valais, Switzerland
- The World Cow Chip Throwing Championship in Beaver, Oklahoma.
- The Whitestone Cheese Rolling competition in Wendon Valley, New Zealand.
- The Wife-Carrying World Championships in Sonkajarvi, Finland.
- The Palio of Siena horseraces around the central square in the medieval town of Siena, Italy.
- The Henley-on-Todd regatta in Alice Springs, Australia, where curious looking boats are raced by foot along the dry riverbed. The regatta is only cancelled when rain creates water in the Todd River!

A further event opportunity is place anniversaries such as Quebec City's 400th anniversary in 2008 and Germany's Dresden, which celebrated its 800th anniversary in 2006 by presenting over 400 special events. Anniversaries of people are also employed, such as in Spain during 2006/07 to mark the 125th anniversary of Picasso's birth.

Supportive local residents

DMOs are recognising that tourism planning should be inclusive for the host community. Wherever possible, efforts should be made to advise the community of important tourism developments, to seek feedback, and to address any problem issues raised. Davidson and Rogers (2006), for example, cited a number of urban regeneration programmes based on the construction of new convention centres, such as in rundown sections of Glasgow and San Diego. Edgell (1999) noted the following creative tourism developments that seek to improve the local environment:

- Baltimore's Inner Harbour Place
- Boston's Faneuil Hall and Market Place
- Charleston and Savannah's historic preservation areas
- Old San Juan.

Key points

1. The commonality in DMO roles

The roles of a DMO are dictated by the mission, goals, and objectives, which in general are similar around the world. Key themes include: coordination, strategy, stakeholders, economics, marketing, product development, lobbying, information provision, protection, research, and the host community.

2. The shift in thinking towards DMOs as destination management organisations

The concept of destination management is akin to the societal marketing orientation. In this regard, achievement of destination competitiveness requires an orientation that is broader than sales and marketing. The increasing difficulty in achieving destination competitiveness necessitates DMOs taking a proactive interest in stewardship of the destination's social, cultural, and environmental resources. This is however difficult in practise, and so the concept is in infancy in most parts of the world. Destination management roles feature a balance between profitable tourism businesses, an effective market position, an attractive environment, positive visitor experiences, and supportive local residents.

Review question

Debate the extent to which your nearest DMO is a destination marketing organisation or a destination management organisation.

CHAPTER 8

Marketing strategy development

A company can outperform rivals only if it can establish a difference that it can preserve.

Porter (1996, p. 62)

Aims

The aims of this chapter are to enhance understanding of:

- the purpose of the DMO vision, mission, goals, and objectives
- a strategy design framework
- sources of comparative and competitive advantage.

> **Perspective**
>
> The increasing competitiveness of tourism markets, cluttered with the offers of substitute products and countless destinations promoting similar benefits, forces DMOs at all levels to develop effective differentiation strategies. Strategic marketing planning is a proactive attempt by the DMO to shape a positive future by establishing a differentiated, meaningful and accurate position in the minds of target consumers. In Chapter 1 it was proposed destination marketing is (1) a forward thinking discipline, which (2) involves matching organisational resources with environment opportunities. These two concepts underpin strategy design. Ultimately, the ability to implement strategy is as critical as the quality of the strategy. One of the main shortcomings in strategy implementation is the failure to translate strategic goals into a practical guide about those factors that are critical to the achievement of the targets. While later sections of the text focus on implementation and performance measurement, this chapter provides a framework for developing effective strategic goals and articulating these to stakeholders. Central to the framework are three tools: the SWOT Matrix, STEEPL analysis, and VRIO Resource Model.

Vision and values

Much of marketing planning is about finding opportunities to meet unmet consumer needs. Marketing is therefore a forward thinking exercise, and it is often useful for DMOs to articulate an envisioned future as a way of rallying and motivating stakeholders. A destination vision has been described as an 'inspirational portrait of an ideal future that the destination hopes to bring about at some defined future' (Goeldner et al., 2000, p. 445). Table 8.1 highlights a number of DMO vision statements which tend to articulate aspects of future destination competitiveness.

Following Collins and Poras (1997, p. 87), it is important to understand that vision statements should essentially be verbalising what the organisation already stands for, rather than an attempt to calculate what would be the most pragmatic or popular. An important element in the vision design is therefore an understanding of the organisation's values, which are a small set of deeply held and enduring beliefs. Collins and Poras found visionary organisations tended to have between three and six simply stated core values, but that there was no single common ideology:

> *Our research indicates that the authenticity of the ideology and the extent to which a company attains consistent alignment with that ideology counts more than the content of the ideology.*

Some firms feature customers at the core, others feature staff, some feature services, some feature risk taking, while others feature innovation. The core values of three tourism service-related firms from an extensive list compiled by Collins and Poras (pp. 68–71) is shown in Table 8.2.

Table 8.1 DMO vision statements

NTO	Vision
Tourism Australia	Tourism Australia is a leverage marketing organisation that has adopted the vision to become and remain the best DMO on the planet (www.tourism.australia.com)
Canadian Tourism Commission	Canada will be the premier four-season destination to connect with nature and to experience diverse cultures and communities (Smith, 2003, p. 131)
Tourism New Zealand	New Zealand is known as the ultimate destination for interactive travellers (TNZ, 2004, p. 5)

Table 8.2 Examples of core values

Firm	Values
Walt Disney	• No cynicism allowed • Fanatical attention to consistency and detail • Continuous progress via creativity, dreams, and imagination • Fanatical control and preservation of Disney's 'Magic' image • 'To bring happiness to millions' and to celebrate, nurture, and promulgate 'wholesome American values'
Marriott	• Friendly service and excellent value (customers are guests); 'make people away from home feel that they're among friends and really wanted' • People are number 1 – treat them well, expect a lot, and the rest will follow • Work hard, yet keep it fun • Continual self-improvement • Overcoming adversity to build character
American Express	• Heroic customer service • Worldwide reliability of services • Encouragement of individual initiative

Mission

While a vision statement serves as a motivational aspiration, a mission is a statement about what is expected to be achieved and measured. Management and directors are held accountable to the mission. Even though mission statements are often criticised as being bland, it is important to

Table 8.3 DMO mission statements

Organisation	Mission statement
Canadian Tourism Commission	Canada's tourism industry will deliver world-class cultural and leisure experiences year-round, while preserving and sharing Canada's clean, safe, and natural environments. The industry will be guided by the values of respect, integrity, and empathy (Smith, 2003, p. 130).
Tourism New Zealand	To motivate interactive travellers to come now, to do more, and to come back (TNZ, 2004, p. 5).

clearly articulate to stakeholders the overall purpose of the organisation (Johnson & Scholes, 2002). Given the political dynamics of tourism destination marketing, and the often divergent interests of stakeholders, a succinct and clear mission is important for DMOs. There should be no confusion as to the DMO's reason for being. The structure of mission statements varies, and might range from a narrow focus to one that includes the vision, values, activities, and target market. Examples of DMO mission statements are listed in Table 8.3.

Goals and objectives

Ultimately, organisations are established to achieve goals. Goals are general statements of intent, related to the mission, and are usually qualitative (Johnson & Scholes, 2002). That is, they provide broad indicators of how the mission will be achieved, but are not necessarily quantifiable. Collins and Poras (1997, p. 94) promoted the concept of a big hairy audacious goal (BHAG) as a way of capturing the attention of stakeholders.

> *A BHAG engages people – it reaches out and grabs them in the gut. It is tangible, energising, highly focused. People 'get it' right away; it takes little or no explanation* (Collins & Poras, 1997, p. 94).

Henry Ford's BHAG was to democratise the automobile. Bill Gates held a similar aim for computers. The BHAG of a famous soft drink brand was once to have their beverage on tap in every home, in the same way as water. While such a BHAG might seem impossible, it can stimulate increased creativity. For example, a state-of-the-art car suspension system was designed in the USA by a team of designers who were challenged to design a vehicle that could operate with square wheels. What is a suitable BHAG for your destination?

In practice

Tourism Australia's 'Game Plan' section of their 2005/2008 Corporate Plan lists the following broad goals, for which quantifiable measurements would be complex (http://www.tourism.australia.com/content/About%20Us/Corp_plan0506_0708.pdf):

- Maximise competitiveness
- Target the ideal visitor
- Affirm brand perception
- Increase brand salience
- Realise segment and market opportunities
- Ensure effectiveness
- Engage stakeholders.

Since the key argument for government funding of destination marketing is the potential economic benefits, it would be expected that DMO goals will be related to achieving this. Investigations during the 1990s certainly support this proposition at NTO (see Akehurst, Bland & Nevin, 1993; Baum, 1994), STO (see Hawes, Taylor & Hampe, 1991) and RTO (see Sheehan & Ritchie, 1997) levels.

Whereas goals are broad statements about how to achieve the mission, objectives are the quantifiable targets of the goals, and should clearly describe specific outcomes. Ideally, objectives should be SMART (Tribe, 1997, p. 32):

- specific
- measurable
- agreed with those who must attain them
- realistic
- time-constrained.

A strategy design framework

A major element in striving for competitive advantage in crowded tourism markets is the development and implementation of tourism strategies, since destinations endowed with natural attractions have been forced into competition with places that have developed attractive built environments. In the pursuit of destination competitiveness it has only been relatively recently that DMOs have begun to develop coordinated tourism strategies. The need for an industry-wide tourism strategy has been called for in most parts of the world in recent years, including, for example: Scandinavia (Flagestad & Hope, 2001), Canada (Go, 1987), New Zealand (NZTP, 1989; OTSP, 2001), USA (Ahmed & Krohn, 1990), Central and Eastern Europe (Hall, 1999) and Australia in the federal government's 2004 $235 million white paper (see http://www.atc.net.au/aboutus.asp?sub=1twp, accessed 24/4/04). (*Note*: The new Australian tourism strategy was launched in

March 2006 – see www.industry.gov.au/tourisminvestment). Leslie (1999, p. 40) was particularly critical of the then Northern Ireland Tourist Board for a lack of long-term strategic planning, which had resulted in the destination losing touch with changing patterns of demand:

> *For those involved, to consider publicly that the troubles have masked attention to significant underlying trends counteracting demand for the province would not only bring into question their personal role and job but also that of the value of the organisation.*

In practice

In considering the strategy development stage, it is worth considering the approach used by Tourism Vancouver, which is characterised by five basic principles (Vallee, 2005, pp. 238–239):

1. **Consultative** From client advisory boards to membership input sessions to stakeholder consultations, the intention is for many people and organisations to contribute to the plan.
2. **Dynamic** The annual business plan is focused and directed, but it is not set in stone. The ever-changing nature of business dictates that the plan must be responsive to new opportunities that arise.
3. **Performance-driven** Monthly tracking of some seventy measures and quarterly reporting to the industry were introduced in 1993, featuring the investment effectiveness index that analyses the accomplishment of goals against investment made.
4. **Long-term** The initiatives laid out in the plan have a minimum three-year horizon. Tourism Vancouver's approach was to ensure continuity to both sellers and buyers in the marketplace.
5. **Team-oriented** Initiative teams develop, deliver, and evaluate their initiatives with support from management and the board of directors. The successful execution of the plan is predicated on the basis of highly-qualified and motivated teams delivering superior service to customers.

Figure 8.1 presents a framework for the challenge of formulating strategy to achieve the goals, remembering that the fundamental purpose of the DMO is to enhance destination competitiveness. The approach is based on the philosophies of (1) a future orientation, and (2) matching organisational resources with environmental opportunities. Organisational resources are those assets within the direct control of the DMO that represent potential strengths and weaknesses. Environment opportunities represent factors in the macro-environment over which the DMO has no control, but which represent potential opportunities and threats. The framework facilitates undertaking an environment analysis to identify sources of strengths,

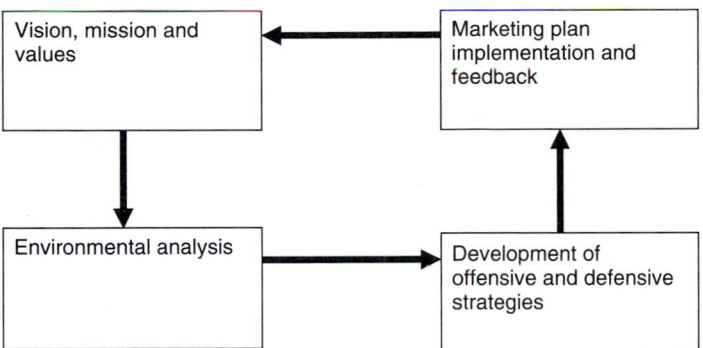

Figure 8.1
Strategy framework

weaknesses, opportunities, and threats, in a manner that leads to the development of offensive and defensive strategies, which will in turn guide the development of the promotional tactics.

Opportunities and threats

A DMO does not operate within a vacuum. The best-laid plans will come unstuck because of events in the environment over which the DMO has little or no control. Determinants of tourism and travel comprise exogenous factors and market forces. Exogenous factors are those that are not directly related to tourism, but have the potential to influence the extent and nature of demand for tourism activity. It is a useful starting point therefore to consider the range of macro-environment influences with the potential to impact on the tourism industry either positively or negatively, and which of these are likely to be most important in the future (Johnson & Scholes, 2002).

As shown in Figure 8.2, it is useful to visualise the environment in the shape of a donut. The outer layer is representative of the macro-environment, the source of opportunities and threats over which the DMO has no control. For example, weather-induced seasonality is a key macro-environment issue affecting Canada's competitiveness (Smith, 2003, p. 125). The macro-environment which surrounds the organisation's internal environment consists of sociocultural, technology, economic, environmental, political, and legal forces. The internal operating environment consists of sources of strengths and weaknesses, over which the organisation has varying degrees of control, such as stakeholders, competitors, and customers. While it can be argued that a DMO does not have control over the actions of customers or competitors, destination marketers do have some control over which segments to target, and in doing so which competitors.

The ideal is to implement strategies, which are not used by existing rivals, that will exploit strengths, neutralise threats, and avoid weaknesses. The desired result is to build a source of sustainable competitive advantage, or a defendable position.

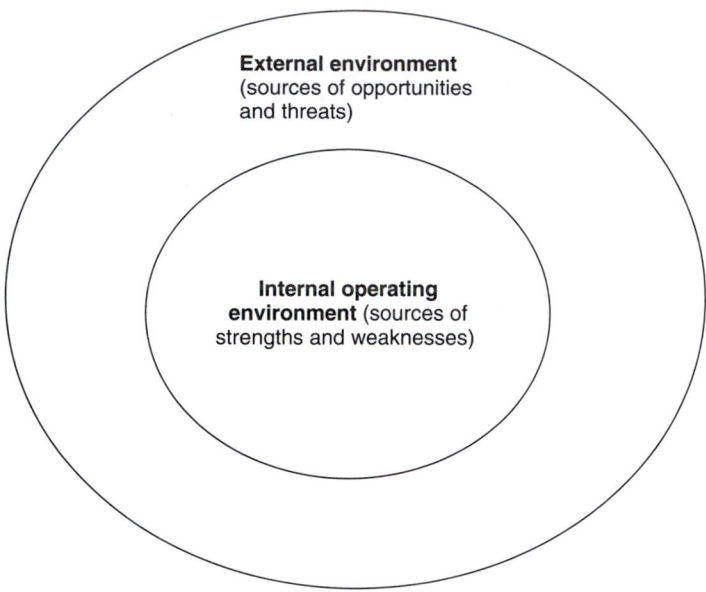

Figure 8.2
Macro-environment and
internal environment

The SWOT matrix

An effective tool for designing and communicating strategic objectives, by matching organisation resources with environment opportunities, is the SWOT matrix as shown in Figure 8.3. The SWOT matrix extends the practical value of the traditional SWOT analysis, which is often not used effectively. Many marketers carefully prepare a bullet point list of strengths, weaknesses, opportunities, and threats, and file it away in the appendices. The SWOT is then usually not explicitly referred to in terms of shaping strategy. The SWOT matrix encourages thinking about offensive strategies that will maximise strengths relative to opportunities, and defensive strategies that will minimise weaknesses in relation to threats.

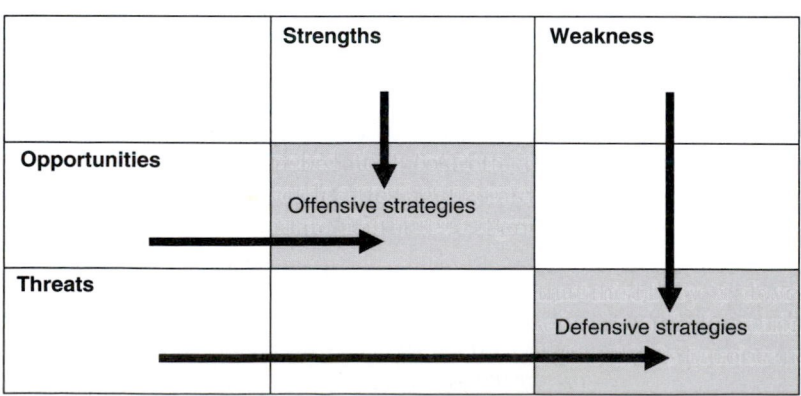

Figure 8.3
SWOT matrix

Forward thinking

Marketing is as much a forward thinking exercise about unmet consumer needs as it is about catering to current needs. Hamel and Prahalad (1994) argued for the importance of devoting time to thinking about the future. They urged organisations to develop a view about the future as an ongoing project sustained by continuous debate, rather than a massive one-time effort. While it would be futile to attempt to predict the future (Drucker, 1995), it is critical that emerging megatrends, which have the potential to shape the future of the tourism industry, either positively or negatively, are identified. In examining the historical time lag from technological invention to market use and acceptance, Drucker suggested that the future is already here, and that we look at the fringes of society to observe future applications that are currently in the design stages. Everything that will be in common use in 30 years time already exists in some form today, perhaps tucked away somewhere in the fringes of society. There exists a rich resource of views offered by futurists. A sample of futurists' thoughts offered over the past 20 years, which may have tourism implications, is provided in Table 8.4.

Table 8.4 Views of the future

Futurist	Trends
World Futurist Society (2007, see www.wfs.org)	• Hydrogen fuel cells will be cost-competitive by 2010 • The era of the Cyborg is at hand • By 2015, New York, Tokyo and Frankfurt may emerge as hubs for high-speed, large-capacity supersonic planes • Schools based on classrooms and a human teacher will dwindle over the next 25 years • Speculation in hydrogen energy stocks could create an investment bubble, as happened with the Internet • Ocean currents may surpass wind as an energy source • A snail may save your life • Weapons of mass destruction will be even easier to obtain over the next 15 years • The convergence of genetic engineering, nanotechnology and robotics will allow humans to change their bodies in profoundly new ways • Robots and smart environments will improve care and independence for the elderly

(Continued)

Table 8.4 (Continued)

Futurist	Trends
Trendwatching.com (2007)	• Status lifestyles • Transparency tyranny • Web N+1 • Trysumers • The global brain
Drucker (1992)	• Decreasing labour requirement • Decreasing raw material cost • Increasing knowledge requirement • Increased consumer spending on leisure, health, education, and retirement savings • Not-for-profit organisations • Decreasing half life of skills • Eroding political power base • Demise of large-scale war • Knowledge as capital • Decreasing management structures • Knowledge society the most competitive ever
Naisbett (1994)	• Booming global economy • Arts renaissance • Free-market socialism • Global lifestyles • Privatised welfare state • Rise of Pacific rim • Rise of women • Age of biology • Religious revival • Triumph of the individual • Global paradox – tribalism • The Asian way • Market-driven economies • Rise of networks • Supercities
Handy (1994)	• Discontinuous change: • Shift from manufacturing to service provision • Knowledge workers versus manual workers • Fewer skilled young • More women in workforce • Longer life span, more aged • Demise of the career path • End of capitalism • Changing structure of organisations • Accounting for intangibles • Uncertainty • Portfolio workers • Need for a new order to replace capitalism

Table 8.4 (Continued)

Futurist	Trends
Popcorn (1996)	• Cocooning • Clanning • Fantasy adventure • Pleasure revenge • Small indulgences • Anchoring • Egonomics • Female think • Mancipation • 99 lives • Cashing out • Being alive • Down-ageing • Vigilante consumer • Icon toppling • Save our society
Kennedy (1993)	• Technology as cure for exploding demography • Shrinking national sovereignty • Increased illegal immigration • Environmental damage • Demise of empires • Rise of women • 18th century as a metaphor for today's challenges • Widening gap between rich and poor countries • Rise of multinationals • Robotics • Knowledge explosion • Integration of science and communication • Transnational alliances
Toffler (1991)	• Static nature of agriculture and manufacturing • Demassification • Knowledge as wealth • Tribalism and conflict • Global market • Electronic cottages • Knowledge gap • Real-time voting • Demise of economies of scale • Acceleration of change
Glenn (1989)	• Humans integrated with technology • Extra-terrestrials • Cyborgs • Communication with plants

(Continued)

Table 8.4   (Continued)

Futurist	Trends
Schwartz (1996)	• Rise of global teenagers • Science and technology shaping the future • Migration waves • Cultural diversity • Ecological issues • Shuffling politics of alliances • Increasing importance of education • Global pragmatism • Global information economy

STEEPL analysis

The STEEPL analysis provides a structure for environment scanning. While a full analysis of key issues, trends, and drivers that confront global tourism is beyond the scope of this chapter, an example of a STEEPL summary is shown in Table 8.5, when 10 key issues are highlighted for each category. The STEEPL provides a systematic approach to the identification of forces that have the potential to impact on tourism in the future, either positively or negatively. These therefore represent environment opportunities and threats for inclusion in the SWOT matrix. (*Note*: An opportunity is not a tactic, as is so often seen in SWOT analysis, but rather a force over which the DMO has no control).

Table 8.5   STEEPL analysis

Sociocultural	• Population growth and aging population • China • Mega-rich • Nostalgia • Busier lives • Increasing growth in travel • Exercise movement • Westernisation of Asia • Changing work and workforce patterns • Consumer sophistication • Virtual shopping and demassification
Technology	• Internet • Rates of obsolescence • Virtual reality • Artificial intelligence

Table 8.5   (Continued)

	• Real-time global media • Robotics • Nanotechnology • Mobile communications • Sub-orbital travel • Medical tourism
Economic	• Business alliances, mergers, and acquisitions • Lessening political control of interest rates and currency exchange rates • Value of information • Virtual networks • Increased competition • Foreign direct investment • Disposable income • Retirement income • Costs and availability of resources • Low cost airlines
Environment	• Climate change • Environmental protection • Recycled water • Renewable energy • Biotechnology • Eco-tourism growth rates • Responsibility of citizenship • Green movement • Recycling • Overcrowding and pollution
Political	• Terrorism • Regional trading blocs • Community-based tourism planning • Government stability • Increasing democracy • Demise of communism • Tribalism • Demise of large-scale war • Decentralisation • Indigenous peoples' land rights
Legal	• Visas and passports • European Union • Illegal migration • Deregulation • Safety standards • Information privacy • Intellectual property • User-pays taxes • Increasing bureaucracy • Insurance liability

Strengths and weaknesses

An important question raised by Ritchie and Crouch (2000a) was whether destination 'stars' are made or born. They offered the example of Russia, well-endowed with natural resources but lacking in deployment, in comparison to destinations such as Singapore, Las Vegas, Branson, and San Antonio, all of which had developed successful tourism strategies with limited endowed resources. Ritchie and Crouch suggested that an understanding of success drivers was of fundamental importance, and categorised these into resources that would represent sources of either comparative or competitive advantage. Endowed resources inherited by a destination, such as climate and scenery, are categorised as sources of *comparative advantage*. However, resources created by the destination, which includes the way in which endowed resources are deployed in the market, represent sources of *competitive* advantage. A practical example of this was provided by Dascalu (1997), who cited comments from a former Romanian Minister of Tourism concerned that his country had enormous tourism resources but that the tourism industry was under-performing. These resources may represent sources of comparative advantage but were not being used to achieve a competitive advantage. Other examples of sources of comparative advantage that perhaps do not yet represent competitive advantage include:

* Ethiopia's Simien Mountains, with spectacular gorges up to 1000 metres deep.
* The world's oldest paintings at Cantabria's Altamaria Caves in northern Spain, which date back 14,000 years.
* Some of the most complete dinosaur remains can be found in the Fossil triangle, which links to outback towns of Winton, Hughenden, and Cloncurry in Queensland, Australia.
* The spectacular terraced Goddess Lake in China's Jiuzhaigou Nature Reserve.

Sustainable competitive advantage

Competitive advantage is expressed in terms of competitors and customers. Porter (1980, 1985) suggested a competitive strategy was one that positioned a business to make the most of strengths that differentiated the organisation from competitors. A firm's success is ultimately achieved through 'attaining a competitive position or a series of competitive positions that lead to superior and sustainable financial performance' (Porter, 1991, p. 96). A sustainable competitive advantage (SCA) is gained when consumers perceive a performance capability gap that endures over time (Coyne, 1986).

Barney (1991, 1996) developed the VRIO model as a tool for determining the competitive status of resources controlled by a firm. The model is based on the assumption that resources are heterogeneous and immobile across firms. Heterogeneity means organisations are not created equal and will vary in terms of the resources they control. Immobility refers to the difficulty of buying resources from the marketplace. To achieve SCA, the VRIO model firstly requires a resource to be valuable (V) to the firm for either increasing revenue or decreasing costs. Secondly, the resource should be rare (R) among competitors. Therefore, resources must be analysed in comparison to the competitive set of destinations. Differentiation alone does not lead to meaningful advantage over others. Exploitation of such organisational strengths must first be converted into (Day & Wensley, 1998): (1) benefits, (2) perceived by a sizeable customer group, (3) which these customers value and are willing to pay for, and (4) cannot readily be obtained elsewhere.

Thirdly, it should be costly for competitors to imitate (I) the resource. Finally, the firm must be organised (O) in such a way that it is able to exploit the resource in the market. An example of the VRIO resource model is provided in Table 8.6. The table shows how answering yes to each denotes that a resource is a source of sustainable competitive advantage. Answering yes to the first two or three qualities indicates a source of temporary competitive advantage. A resource that is valuable, but not meeting the other criteria, represents a source of competitive parity. Finally, a resource that is not valuable represents a source of competitive disadvantage. The VRIO model determines which strengths should be included in the SWOT matrix.

A tourism resource may be viewed as anything that plays a major role in attracting visitors to a destination (Spotts, 1997). Sources of competitive advantage are essentially assets and skills (Aaker, 1991). An asset is a resource that is superior to those possessed by the competition, and a skill is an activity undertaken more effectively than competitors. A resource audit is therefore a key component of marketing planning. However, Ferrario (1979a, 1979b) suggested that the availability of tourism resources was often taken for granted by both practitioners and academics. More recently the process of auditing a destination's resources has received increased attention in the literature (see, for example, Faulkner et al., 1999; Pearce, 1997; Ritchie & Crouch, 2000a; Spotts, 1997). A categorisation of DMO resources representing sources of comparative and competitive advantage is suggested in Table 8.7.

A DMO must then showcase the destination in a way that offers benefits sought by travellers, represents the interests of tourism suppliers, and does not commodify residents' sense of place. Communicating matches

Table 8.6 VRIO resource model

Strength	Valuable?	Rare?	(Un)Imitable?	Organised?	Status
Resource A	yes	yes	yes	yes	SCA
Resource B	yes	yes	yes	no	TCA
Resource C	yes	no			CP
Resource D	no				CD

Notes: CP = competitive parity; TCA = temporary competitive advantage; SCA = sustainable competitive advantage; CD = competitive disadvantage.

Table 8.7 DMO sources of comparative and competitive advantage

Sources of comparative advantage	Sources of competitive advantage
Natural resources Location, landscape features and climate	**Developed resources** Accessibility, infrastructure, and the scale, range, and capacity of man-made attractions and other superstructure
Cultural resources History, language, cuisine, music, arts & crafts, traditions, and customs	**Financial resources** Size and certainty of the DMO budget; private sector marketing resources; influence on government fiscal policy such as taxation, investment incentives and capital expenditure on infrastructure developments; size of the local economy; access to capital for product developments and ability to attract new investment
Human resources Skills and availability of the region's labour force; industrial relations; industry service standards; and attitudes of locals	
Good will resources Travellers' ancestral links to the destination; friends and/or relatives; novelty or fashionability of the destination; ToMA levels; levels of previous visitation and satisfaction; and perceived value	**Legal resources** Brand trademarks, licenses and visa policies
	Organisation resources Governance structure and policies; staffing levels, training, experience, skills and retention; organisational culture; innovation; technology adoption; and flexibility; customer service orientation; fast, flexible and creative response capability
	Information resources Marketing information system, specialised knowledge of segment needs
	Relationship resources Internal/external industry integration and alliances; distribution; stakeholder cooperation; and political influence
	Implementation resources Sustainable tourism development planning; brand development, positioning, and promotion; ease of making reservations; consistency of stakeholders' delivery

	Strength Range and diversity of accommodation	Weakness Small regional airport not serviced by major carriers
Opportunity Increasing level of short breaks by consumers	*Offensive strategy* (matching strength with opportunity) Assist accommodation businesses develop initiatives to keep in touch with previous visitors from the city, to stimulate repeat visitation	
Threat Proliferation of low-cost airlines offering city consumers affordable short-break air packages to new destinations		*Defensive strategy* (matching weakness with threat) Proactively commission feasibility study to identify benefits for low-cost carriers to service the destination

Figure 8.4
SWOT matrix example

between destination resources and travellers' needs is the focus of DMO promotional activities. Figure 8.4 illustrates how the SWOT matrix might be used to develop offensive and defensive strategies for the marketing plan. In this case the examples are drawn from a beach resort area located close to a major city. This matrix provides a simple example of the potential value for guiding stakeholders on the rationale for the DMO's marketing strategies.

Key points

1. Vision, mission, values, and goals

The core purpose of DMOs is enhancing destination competitiveness. Since marketing requires a forward thinking orientation, a vision statement is used to articulate a motivational aspiration. The mission is a summary statement of the purpose of the organisation. The role of goals and objectives is to articulate how the mission will be achieved, and in doing so provide motivational targets, by which the success of the organisation can be monitored.

2. Strategy design framework

The SWOT matrix provides a useful framework for designing strategic goals and articulating these in a practical way to guide stakeholders. The SWOT matrix is based on the philosophy of marketing as matching organisation resources with environment opportunities. A fundamental role in the SWOT matrix development is the macro-environment analysis, which comprises those exogenous forces over which the DMO has no control, but which represents sources of opportunities and threats. The STEEPL analysis provides a structured approach to environment scanning, by systematically identifying those forces that have the potential to impact on tourism, either positively or negatively.

3. Sources of comparative and competitive advantage

A successful strategy achieves a point of difference against competitors on an attribute deemed important by the market. A DMO's resources consist of sources of comparative and competitive advantage. The VRIO resource model helps to identify those resources that represent potential sources of competitive advantage.

Review questions

- What other trends could you add to the STEEPL analysis in Table 8.5?
- Identify what you believe to be the three trends in each STEEPL section that have the potential to impact the most on your destination in the future, either positively or negatively.
- Prepare a SWOT matrix for your destination.
- What is the vision and mission of your DMO? Do the goals adequately address the mission statement?
- Brainstorm possible BHAGs for your DMO.

CHAPTER 9

Marketing research

Where is research going? I think right now it's heading nowhere slowly. Many clients use research as a crutch... research is used for analysis and information... it's not used for insight. It's operating at about 30% of its potency.

Kevin Roberts, CEO Saatchi & Saatchi

Aims

The aim of this chapter is to enhance understanding of:

- the marketing research process
- exploratory, descriptive, and causal research
- limitations of marketing research.

Why conduct marketing research?

Marketing research has been defined as (Malhotra et al., 2006, p. 5):

> *The systematic and objective collection, analysis and dissemination of information for the purpose of assisting management in decision-making related to the identification and solutions (and opportunities) in marketing.*

Clearly, any destination marketer with a market orientation (see Chapter 1) requires a process for staying in tune with consumer-travellers in target markets and gaining insights into the why of buy, to generate information that will aid future decision-making, both for the DMO and for stake-holders. Information reduces uncertainty and so is necessary at each stage of the marketing process from the environmental analysis and planning (see Chapter 8) through to implementation and ultimately performance evaluation (see Chapter 19). Access to the right information enables more effective marketing decision-making.

Times have certainly changed in terms of marketing research adoption by DMOs. Someone involved in the early days of regional destination promotion confided to me during an in-depth interview that many of her resort destination's promotions in the 1960s and 1970s were developed 'over a bottle of gin at two in the morning'. From my own experience in New Zealand I know that most RTOs there only became serious about developing a marketing research programme around the late-1990s. But even then the function was rated secondary to other marketing activities, with one RTO marketing manager admitting to me: 'As you know Steve, research is always the first to get cut in the budget planning.' Around the same time in the USA, Hawes et al. (1991) found that only 10 out of 37 USA STOs commissioned market research on a regular basis. In the UK, Bramwell and Rawding (1996, pp. 213–214) noted the lack of research used by destination marketers there. They cited the following comment by the CEO of a Convention and Visitor Bureau on the development of a city image during the 1990s:

> The image was chosen because it is the facts, it is the reality. We did no market research to create an image . . . We promote the facts, we don't go in for gimmicks.

In examining the priority of research for CVBs in the USA, Masberg (1999) found that the activity was regarded as essential for improving productivity, and yet the bureaus were devoting little time or funding. For example, the person responsible for research was more likely to hold a management position rather than hold the title of research manager, and almost 80% of respondents indicated spending less than 10% of their time on research. Masberg (p. 38) summarised the research findings as 'grim and bleak'. Similarly, in an investigation of the perceived importance of research in Austria by the NTO and RTOs, Dolnicar and Schoesser (2003) found:

- an underestimation of the importance of market research
- minimal research budgets relative to promotional spend
- a lack of formal criteria for evaluating market research needs
- a lack of coordination between research and marketing staff.

Increased competition and greater access to information have contributed to increased marketing research activity by DMOs at all levels. Case Study 9.1 provides an example of a sizable CVB marketing research project, where much was at stake in terms of decision-making based on information generated.

Case study 9.1   Gateway Calgary: Research-driven strategies

Tracey Grindal, Market Research Manager, Tourism Calgary

Gateway Calgary was a research study initiated and project managed by Tourism Calgary on behalf of seven industry partners. The goal of the study was to identify lucrative product-market linkages within the Calgary region's tourism industry from which to develop, package, and promote product clusters. The results are guiding Tourism Calgary's marketing and strategic planning through to 2008. The study began in 2004 and concluded in summer 2005.

Gateway Calgary was a four-phased project. Phase one, information collection, included a thorough scan of Calgary's tourism industry inventory to identify areas of critical mass and gaps in tourism product offerings and an analysis, using demographic as well as psychographic and behavioral tools, of Calgary's current geographic and product-based markets. In phase two, 10 developing and emerging products on which to focus marketing effects in the near and long-term were identified. Phase two identified 10 potential market segments for Calgary and area. Of the 10, three were identified as having immediate potential, which were (1) Western Heritage, (2) Information, and (3) Sport/Major Event Tourism. In phase three, industry was consulted to gather their input, feedback and support of the three segments. Phase four, sustainable implementation, continues to be the most important phase of the project. It involves the focused, strategic marketing of the right products to the right demographics.

To-date, several initiatives relating to the three segments have been completed or are underway. Under Western Heritage, media marketing has been increased on Western heritage and culture. The 'West' messaging and the brand, Experience Calgary Heart of the New West, are used throughout Tourism Calgary's marketing and sales initiatives. Four different Western Heritage experiences – the Old West, the Real West, the Wild West, and the New West – were developed based on the research.

Under Information, Tourism Calgary partnered with the City of Calgary and the Calgary Tower to open a new Visitor Information Centre that services both visitors to Calgary and Calgary residents. Other initiatives include provincial accreditation of visitor information centres and improved visitor-friendly highway signage.

A major component of the Sport and Major Event segment was the development of the Calgary Sport Tourism Authority (CSTA). The CSTA is a volunteer committee of senior level Calgary executives whose purpose is to review and ultimately decide whether to support sport and major event opportunities for Calgary by taking a look at the economic, social, and environmental impacts and merits and its 'fit' with Calgary. In just two short years Tourism Calgary and its partners have made great strides in this area, confirming the 2006 World Figure Skating Championships, 2007 North American OutGames, and the 2008 JUNOS.

Discussion question

How does the Gateway Calgary project relate to the definition of marketing as described in Chapter 1?

Further information

www.tourismcalgary.com

Information clearing house

A key function for DMOs is acting as an information clearing house for local stakeholders, potential investors and developers. The majority of tourism service providers are small family-owned businesses with minimal marketing budgets. DMOs can enhance decision-making of small businesses by providing links to market intelligence and other useful information. Table 9.1 lists the key elements in Ritchie and Crouch's (2003) model of DMO information management.

Table 9.1 Inward and outward flows of DMO information

Inward flow of information	Outward flow of information
• Evolving research methods	• To investors and developers
• Impacts on tourism policy	• To members
• Environment scanning	• To visitors
• Monitoring competitors	• To community stakeholders
• Monitoring performance	
• Monitoring markets	
• Destination image	
• Monitoring sector performance	
• Monitoring visitor impacts	
• Visitor feedback	
• Internal destination information	
• Internal DMO information	

In practice

For an example of a comprehensive research clearing house see Tourism Queensland's corporate site (http://www.tq.com.au/research/index.cfm). The site provides summary fact sheets about key markets and trends, as well as more detailed reports and links to other tourism research providers. Information on the site is freely available. Also in Australia, Tourism Research Australia (www.tra.australia.com) made the move in 2006 to providing fact sheet research summaries, in an effort to appeal to a broader range of stakeholders.

The marketing research process

As future managers, it is important for students of destination marketing to develop a good understanding of the marketing research process, even though many might view the topic as being as scary as management accounting due to an aversion towards anything involving numbers or statistics. My question to any student aspiring to a marketing or management position who tries avoid these topics is this: *When you are responsible for business decision-making, how can you trust what the accountant and marketing researcher are advising you if you don't have an understanding of the basic concepts?* After all, you will be making decisions that involve their input.

What will be particularly valuable is an understanding of the advantages and disadvantages of the various research techniques in relation to the decision problem. Marketing research is increasingly being criticised about its effectiveness, for (1) techniques being selected on the basis of economic efficiency rather that tailored to address a specific problem, and (2) using metrics designed for previous generations that are no longer effective in the Internet age.

In addition to general marketing research texts (see, for example, Aaker et al., 2007; Churchill & Iacobucci, 2005; Malhotra et al., 2006; Zikmund & Babin, 2007) and tourism research texts (see, for example, Jennings, 2001; Veal, 2006), a useful resource is Ritchie, Burns and Palmer (2005), who edited a 17-chapter text on the applicability of various research approaches to tourism. Each chapter has been written by a researcher who has applied the approach in a tourism setting, including for example: Delphi forecasting, depth interviews, mystery shoppers, action ethnography, case studies, focus groups, and content analysis. The text by no means addresses all available research techniques, but it is hoped that the concept will be expanded in the future.

Some types of information required by managers will be informal or indirect in nature, such as the feedback from suppliers dealing directly with visitors and non-visitors. Other aspects will be generated by more formal and direct means, such as intercept surveys of visitor at information centres. There is a place for both types of information in decision-making. Gut feelings or intuition from those on the frontline of tourism services is valuable for some decision-making. For example, the ANZCRO case in Chapter 15 discusses the development of a marketing joint venture based on both research and practitioner experience.

Generally, the more complex the decision the more detailed the information required and this requires a systematic approach. What is important is that the information generated for decision-making purposes has the following qualities (Malhotra et al., 2006): relevance, accuracy, reliability, validity, timeliness, and efficiency.

Marketing research is a six-step process, as highlighted in Figure 9.1. It is important to note that this is not a linear process that stops at step 6. Rather the process is ongoing in a circular manner. In this way, the conclusions in step 6 lead to the identification of new problems and/or opportunities.

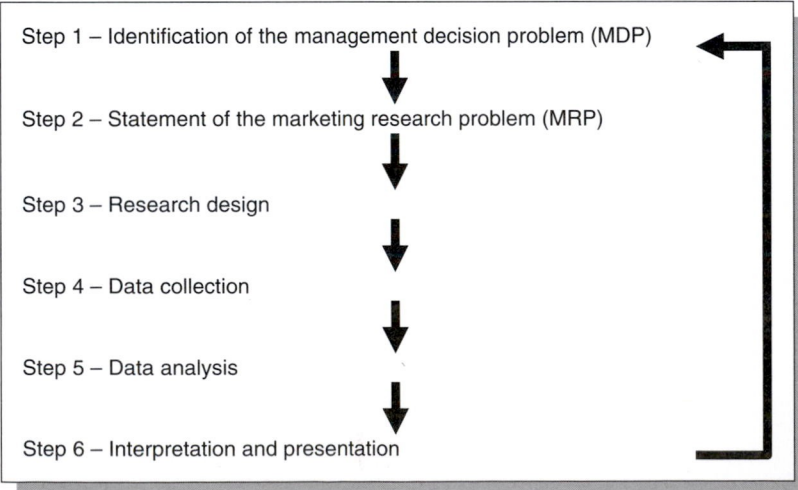

Figure 9.1
Marketing research process

Step 1 – Identification of the management decision problem (MDP)

Step 2 – Statement of the marketing research problem (MRP)

Step 3 – Research design

Step 4 – Data collection

Step 5 – Data analysis

Step 6 – Interpretation and presentation

Management decision problem (MDP) and marketing research problem (MRP)

The first stage in marketing research involves identifying and articulating the management decision problem (MDP). The MDP is a short statement summarising the problem or opportunity facing management. In this section, the terms opportunity and problem are used interchangeably. An example is whether to use the destination's general brand positioning theme when entering a new market such as China. This is a potential marketing opportunity, but represents a decision problem requiring information to design a course of action such as retaining or modifying the theme for the new markets or in markets with English as a second language such as in the case of Tourism Australia's controversial *Where the bloody hell are you* campaign in 2006.

While all steps are important, it is essential that the MDP and MRP are clear, because it is these that lay the foundation for the remaining steps. The MDP is typically expressed as action-oriented, focusing on a practical marketing decision. The type of information required for the decision is then guided by a marketing research problem (MRP) statement. The aim is to focus the researcher's attention on the information required to address the MDP. The MRP usually features a broad statement about the construct of interest, which is then broken down into more manageable research objectives.

The brief

Usually a brief would be provided by management for the marketing researcher, much in the way a client's brief would guide an advertising agency. For example, Appendix 9.1 is a real world 'Request for proposals' (RFP) distributed by Tourism New Zealand in 2005. The RFP invited marketing research firms to submit research design proposals. The MDP and MRP are not necessarily explicit in these documents. In this case, the MDP could read: Is the brand positioning theme still relevant/appropriate in our major markets? Or, does the brand positioning theme need to be changed? This clearly identifies the action/decision faced by management. The MRP to address the MDP could then feature the following broad statement: How is New Zealand positioned as a holiday destination in each major market? The key construct of interest here is market position. This would then be supported by a series of questions to guide the collection of information that would measure this construct, and therefore enable management's decision.

Research design

The research design is sets out the procedures for collecting the required information. Important considerations include (Malhotra et al., 2006, p. 21):

- definition of the target population
- methods of collecting qualitative and quantitative data
- sampling process and sample size

- measurement and scaling procedures
- questionnaire design
- data analysis approach.

The value of mixed methods • • •

Clearly, the level of available resources will dictate the scope and limitations of the research design. Importantly, the focus must remain on designing the collection of information to address the MRP and therefore the MDP. In many cases, the most effective research designs will employ mixed methods, which combine both qualitative and quantitative techniques. Figure 9.2 helps to demonstrate the value of mixed methods. In short, quantitative techniques offer the potential to provide a broad scope of data from a large and representative sample of the population. However, the data is quite shallow given that it is only in the form of numbers. Qualitative techniques on the other hand are not designed to provide a breadth of data, and so the scope is quite narrow with only a small unrepresentative sample of the population. However, qualitative data, in the form of a transcript of the participant's conversation, for example, provides a greater richness and depth of insights.

Qualitative research uses an inductive approach, where the phenomena of interest are observed and then a conclusion or theory is subjectively interpreted. Quantitative research uses a deductive approach, in which hypotheses previously developed from theory are objectively tested through data collection. Qualitative techniques are useful in exploratory research, while quantitative techniques are used in descriptive and causal research designs.

Exploratory research design • • •

Exploratory research is useful when the nature of the problem/opportunity is not fully understood. This is common at the situation analysis stage of marketing planning. Exploratory research approaches might be used

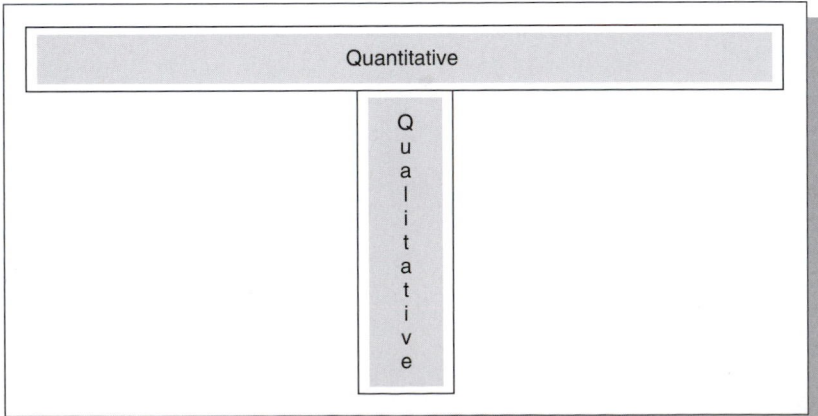

Figure 9.2
The breadth and depth of mixed methods

to diagnose a situation, to screen alternatives, or to discover new opportunities.

Information generated in exploratory research may be in the form of either primary or secondary data. Primary data is originated for the purpose of addressing the MRP. Secondary data on the other hand is that which has been previously collated for purposes other than the current MRP. For example, primary data collected by the DMO and placed on a website for general viewing will become secondary data for those third party organisations accessing it. The first port of call in any research project should be to check secondary data sources in an effort to see if information already exists to address the MRP. The wide range of external secondary data sources of interest to DMOs include:

- government statistics, such as the national/regional census
- tourism industry association reports, such as by the WTTC, WTO, PATA, and IACVB
- specialist industry reports, such as those by Euromonitor
- the academic literature
- the news media
- syndicated marketing research services.

Construct/concept

Effectively defining the construct (also referred to as concept) of interest helps the research team to develop a research design that will effectively measure the construct. Common marketing research constructs of interest to DMOs include brand image, brand awareness, market position, consumer attitudes, and visitor satisfaction. The academic literature review at this stage is particularly useful as it enables the researcher to identify how others have conceptualised (defined) and then operationalised (measured) the construct. In other words, what is the current extent of knowledge? Verbal, graphical, or mathematical models provide a guide to otherwise complex concepts. For example, a common DMO research objective is to identify whether a marketing initiative has resulted in increased awareness of the destination and intent to visit. From a review of the consumer behaviour literature, Fishbein and Ajzen (1975) proposed that any question exploring the relationship between attitude and behaviour must include the following characteristics:

- the behaviour (in this case a holiday)
- the target object at which the behaviour is directed (destinations)
- the situation in which the behaviour is to be performed (type of holiday)
- the time at which the behaviour is to be performed (e.g. in the next 12 months)

These are then incorporated in the following question designed to measure unaided awareness: *Of all the destinations available to you for your next family holiday, which one first comes to mind?* The response to this question can be regarded as qualitative as it will be elicited unaided by the participant.

Although quantitative techniques can be engaged in exploratory research, such as in a pilot study, it is more common for qualitative techniques to be employed. A summary of some qualitative techniques, potential applications, and destination marketing references is provided in Table 9.2.

Qualitative techniques are particularly effective at the questionnaire design stage, in that they aid the researcher in constructing questions and scale items that are relevant to the target group. Following a questionnaire, qualitative techniques can again be useful in helping to clarify any emergent issues and gain in-depth feedback relating to the findings.

Table 9.2 Qualitative approaches

Approach	Applications	Destination marketing references
Focus groups	Stimulating interaction between 8–12 participants at a time in a free-flowing discussion to: • define problems • understand opportunities • screen ideas • brainstorm • interpret prior quantitative results	Mackay & Fesenmaier (1997) Perdue (2000)
Depth interviews	An unstructured or semi-structured conversation with a single participant, to: • elicit expert opinion • discuss sensitive topics • gain a greater depth of insights	Pike (2003) Hudson & Shephard (1998)
Repertory grid analysis	A structured personal interview, commonly using the triad card method, to elicit the dimensions by which the participant differentiates objects such as a competitive set of brands	Pike (2003, 2007) Riley & Palmer (1975) Embacher & Buttle (1989) Young (1995) Walmsley & Jenkins (1993)
Q methodology	A personal interview using a sorting process of a list of statements to gain insights into the participant's meanings and opinions	Fairweather & Swaffield (2001) Stringer (1984)

Descriptive research design • • •

The aim of descriptive research is to describe the characteristics of the phenomena or population of interest. This approach, which takes place after the problem/opportunity has been clearly identified, has been the most popular in the destination marketing literature (see, for example, Research Snapshot 9.1). Descriptive research designs generally employ the use of questionnaires, where numbers are assigned to responses. Observation methods can also be used but are rarely reported in the destination marketing literature. Quantitative techniques are employed to generate findings from a representative sample that can be generalised to the wider population of interest.

Research snapshot 9.1   Destination image by the numbers

The first studies of destination image were reported in the literature in the early 1970s. In the time since, the field has grown into one of the most popular topics for tourism researchers. In a review of 142 destination image papers published in the literature between 1973 and 2000, it was found that the vast majority of papers (114) used quantitative methods to measure the construct. Less than half of the papers reported the use of qualitative methods at any stage in the research. The paper is a useful guide for destination image researchers, as it tables the approaches used in each of the 142 studies.

Source: Pike, S. (2002). Destination image analysis – A review of 142 studies between 1973 and 2000. *Tourism Management. 23*(5): 541–549.

Key attractions of questionnaires to destination researchers include:

- a standardised instrument can be used by multiple interviewers
- ease of administration of large samples
- relatively low cost, particularly using internet-based applications
- large geographic flexibility
- availability of data analysis techniques
- the ability to generalise results to the wider population of interest.

Essentially there are three aims of a questionnaire. The first is to translate the information required in the MRP into a set of questions. A questionnaire is only as good as the questions asked. The second aim is to encourage participants to participate and to complete the questions. A well-constructed questionnaire appears simple and focused, and yet will have been developed through careful preparation and pre-testing. Wording of questions should be jargon-free and designed in the language of the participant. Other key issues relate to: the use of incentives; order of questions; selection of response scales; placement of sensitive questions; cover letter; ethics; and avoiding leading questions, ambiguity and double-barrelled items. The third aim is to minimise response error. Response bias occurs when participants answer questions in a way that either deliberately or unconsciously misrepresents the truth. Deliberate falsification can manifest through: acquiescence bias, extremity bias, interviewer bias, auspices bias, and social desirability bias. Unconscious misrepresentation can occur when participants are unable to recall information, such as travel motivation (see, for example, Crompton, 1979), or simply don't know (see Research Snapshot 9.2).

Research snapshot 9.2   Avoiding uninformed responses

Even though destination image has been one of the most popular research topics in the tourism literature, there is no commonly agreed conceptualisation of the construct. As shown in Research Snapshot 9.1, the majority of studies have used structured questionnaires for measurement. There has been criticism that the way in which some researchers have selected the questionnaire scale items means a greater likelihood of some questions being irrelevant to participants (see, for example, Dann, 1996; Pearce, 1982). This then runs the risk of stimulating uninformed responses. This paper suggests that the use of a 'Don't know' (DK) option for scale questions provides participants with an alternative to skipping the question, using the scale midpoint to denote neutrality, or guessing. Of the 114 studies of destination image studies, using questionnaires, tabled by Pike (2002), none explicitly reported the use of a DK option. This paper reported that in the trial of a DK option in two destination image questionnaires. In both studies, there was a very high take-up by participants for some attributes. These results provided practical implications for the DMOs, as they highlighted information that would not have been identified without the use of the DK option.

Source: Pike, S. (2008). Destination image questionnaires: Avoiding uninformed responses. *Journal of Travel & Tourism Research*. (In press).

Causal research design • • •

Experiments can be used to analyse causal relationships between variables. Independent variables (e.g. price) are manipulated to test the effect on a dependent variable (e.g. sales). While this research approach provides the greatest degree of certainty for marketers, the complex and expensive nature of experimental designs has meant that it is the least common in the tourism marketing literature. Causal relationships are extremely difficult to prove because of the difficulty in isolating and controlling the wide range of extraneous variables in the real world, which could also impact on the dependent variable at the time of the experiment. For example, in an experiment involving the manipulation of DMO advertising spend (independent variable) to test the effect on intent to visit (dependent variable) in a target market, it would be impossible to control for extraneous variables such as competitors' advertising, terrorist acts, currency exchange rate fluctuations and so on. So at best, the research is only able to infer a causal relationship between the variables.

Sampling

The purpose of sampling is to invite participation from a portion of the population of interest. To survey the entire population requires a census, which is neither practical in most cases, nor required. Through a probability sample, where every member of the sample frame has an equal and known chance of selection, the goal of a quantitative approach is to draw a sample of participants whose characteristics closely match those of the census population. There will always be a degree of sampling error, because the data generated from a sample will by chance vary in some way from that of a census. An effective sampling plan results in data that can be generalised to the wider population of interest. Destination marketing studies commonly draw a sample from consumers in the market of interest or from visitors at the destination. The question of sample size is important, and will be dictated by issues such as: the budget, the importance of the information, statistical analyses requirements, and level of confidence. Readers will find a useful discussion on sample size determination by Baker et al. (1994).

In qualitative studies there is no rule regarding sample size (Patton, 1990). One approach is to sample until a point of data redundancy is reached. That is, the addition of any new participants will not yield any new insights. However, the research will always be interested in ensuring participants are selected purposefully, on the basis of being knowledgeable about the phenomena, having the ability to articulate, and representing a diversity of opinions.

Data collection and analysis

The data collection stage must be carefully managed to minimise potential systematic error, particularly when a team of interviewers is employed to undertake field or telephone interviews. Decisions must be made about when to collect data, as well as how to communicate with participants. The data analysis techniques selected will depend on the nature of the information required to address the MRP and therefore the MDP. There are commonly two main aims of data analysis. The first is to identify any significant differences between groups within the sample. For example, *t-tests* can be used to identify differences in perceptions held by two groups such as males and females, and *analysis of variance* (ANOVA) can be used in the same manner for more than two groups, such as by education levels. The second is to investigate relationships between variables. For example, *exploratory factor analysis* might be used to reduce a long list of attribute scales into a small subset of core themes, while *regression* can be used to identify relationships between a dependent variable and a set of independent variables.

Interpretation and presentation

Interpretation is the 'so what' stage. 'So...what does this information mean in relation to the decision-maker's problem?' This involves the use of both critical and creative thinking skills, regardless of whether the data is of a qualitative or quantitative nature. Findings need to be presented in a way that not only demonstrates the validity of the approach, but most importantly focuses on addressing the MDP and MRP.

In Chapter 1, the divide between tourism academics and practitioners was discussed, along with the call for marketing researchers to better market themselves and their work. The same challenge exists in the marketing research world in general. Marketing researchers are often left wondering why their findings are not always incorporated into marketing actions. In a 2007 Australian Market & Social Research Society seminar to address this issue, guest speaker Tiina Raikko, Consumer Insight Director for Unilever Australasia, offered these views:

- Why do we assume others will find our data as intrinsically interesting as we do?
- To engage marketers requires bringing the research to life
- Delivery is worth as much as the content
- As a marketing researcher you are useful when you know the business as well as the client, but know the customer better.

Limitations of marketing research

The opening quote in this chapter made by the worldwide CEO of Saatchi & Saatchi advertising, Kevin Roberts (see www.saatchikevin.com), provides an insight from someone in the ideas business of the difficulty in gaining an understanding of consumer thinking. Roberts is not alone in his criticism of the failure of marketing research to deliver effective consumer insights, and so it is appropriate to introduce some of the limitations of research. IMC pioneer Professor Don Schultz (2005, p. 7) offered these strong words:

> *Marketing is in trouble because marketing research is in trouble. No, make that, today marketing research is in a death spiral and its taking marketing down with it . . . . Research is supposed to present the voice of the customer. Today, it doesn't.*

Critics of current marketing research practice argue that there is an over-reliance on certain techniques that are selected on the basis of cost and familiarity rather than to gain a deeper understanding of how consumers really think. So much research is based on attitudinal data. That is, questionnaires and focus groups that provide data in the form of participants stating what they say they do and what they might do in the future. Comparatively little research generates behavioural information, analysing what people do rather than what they say they will do. The high failure rate of new products has been blamed in many cases on the reliance on flawed focus group research with a strong acquiescence bias. Such bias occurs, for example, when it is easy for participants to say they like the proposed product. This is because they are in a research situation and not a real buying situation. The failure of New Coke and Crystal Pepsi highlight how even the largest of research projects can get it wrong. Research Snapshot 9.3 heeded the call of Schultz and Schultz' (2004) call for researchers to link attitudinal and behavioural data through longitudinal studies. This research investigated the relationship between stated destination preferences and actual travel.

Research snapshot 9.3   Combining attitudinal and behavioural data

There have only been a small number of applications of consumer decision set theory to holiday destination choice, and these studies have tended to rely on a single cross-sectional snapshot of research participants' stated preferences. Very little has been reported on the relationship between stated destination preferences and actual travel. To what degree then can marketers rely on consumers' stated attitudes if there is no comparative measure of actual behaviour? This study presented a rare longitudinal examination of destination decision sets, and the first in the context of short-break holidays by car in Queensland, Australia. Two questionnaires were administered, three months apart. The first identified destination preferences while the second examined actual travel. The findings indicated a general consistency between attitude and behaviour in the short term, and support Pike's (2002) proposition that the positioning of a destination into a consumer's decision set represents a source of competitive advantage:

- In terms of unaided top of mind awareness (ToMA), participants elicited over 100 short-break destinations within driving distance of Brisbane. Brisbane residents are literally spoilt by choice of contiguous destinations.
- Participants indicated a mean of only four destinations in their short-break decision set. This has implications for those destinations not included, particularly in light of the competition mentioned in the previous point.
- There was a strong link between stated destination preferences and actual travel. Almost 75% of participants who took a short break during the study visited at least one destination from their stated decision set.
- Familiarity with preferred destinations was apparent, with 92% of participants indicated having previously visited their ToMA destination.
- Intent to visit the destination of interest was significantly higher from previous visitors than non-visitors.

A key implication for destination marketers is the recommendation to monitor decision set composition, which represents an important and practical indicator of future performance.

Source: Pike, S. (2006). Destination decision sets: A longitudinal comparison of stated destination preferences and actual travel. *Journal of Vacation Marketing. 12*(4): 319–328.

Rarely would any marketing research design be regarded as perfect. Usually, due to resource constraints such as insufficient time and/or money, every project will have limitations. It is important that such limitations are acknowledged in the final report. Case Study 9.2 describes exploratory research, which also helps to demonstrate the value of surveying non-users of a service, in addition to users. In this case, surveying non-users identified significant barriers by travellers to wine tourism in New Zealand. However, as with every exploratory research project, the research does have limitations.

Case study 9.2   Wine tourism: investigating differences between users and non-users

Abel D. Alonso, Edith Cowan University, Western Australia

The world-wide wine tourism phenomenon has gained in popularity in New Zealand as an additional activity for those travelling to rural areas, which is where most wineries are located. Wine tourism includes visiting wineries (O'Neill, Palmer, Charters & Fitz, 2001), cellar doors (Cambourne, 1998), or tasting the wine product (O'Neill, Palmer & Charters, 2002), often in combination with food offered at the winery. Some studies suggest that wine tourism provides an additional travel motivation (Macionis & Cambourne, 1998), while others see it as a critical aspect of the travel experience (Jago, Issaverdis & Graham, 2000).

Today, New Zealand has over 500 wineries (Wine Institute New Zealand, 2006), which are located in ten main wine regions. Efforts that include organising wine festivals and creating internet websites have been undertaken both nationally and regionally to enhance and market the appeal of the wine regions (see, for example, www.wine-marlborough.co.nz/). Recent international success of several New Zealand wines (Foodworks, 2006a, 2006b) has helped boost the reputation of the nation's wine industry.

While many studies focus on winery visitors, their characteristics and consumption patterns, little is known about the involvement with winery visitation among travellers in New Zealand. Recent figures about wine trail and vineyard visitation indicate modest involvement among domestic travellers, which was less than 1% in 2005 (Ministry of Tourism, 2006a), and international travellers. However, the percentage of international wine trail and vineyard visitors has increased from 1.5% in 1998 to 10% in 2006 (Ministry of Tourism, 2006b). Another area of limited knowledge is how people travelling in New Zealand view winery visitation. This dimension is particularly important to enhance the appeal of wine tourism as an alternative attraction to individuals travelling in the country.

During late-2006, exploratory research was undertaken to analyse differences in attitudes towards wine tourism by users and non-users. A total of 998 individuals travelling from the North Island to the South Island of New Zealand were invited to participate. In all, 500 responses were obtained.

Just over half (56%) of participants advised they had visited a New Zealand winery. The sample therefore provided a balance between users and non-users. The most important reasons for visiting wineries are 'to drink wines,' 'to socialise', and 'to eat.' For international non-users, 'I don't know much about New Zealand wineries,' and 'I don't know much about New Zealand wines' were clearly their main motives for not visiting wineries. In contrast, the domestic travellers' main reason was 'because I can easily buy wine/food elsewhere,' followed by 'I am not interested in winery visitation.' Interestingly, 'because I don't drink wine' was the least important reason among respondents not to visit wineries. The results show clearly that more work is required to raise the profile of wine tourism regions among both international and domestic visitors. The aspect of socialising, indicated by participants as one of their main reasons for visitation, and the peaceful/rural setting of the wineries identified in several studies (see, for example, McRae-Williams, 2004), suggest that there is much more to winery visitation than the wine/food product. Destination marketing strategies could also be implemented to educate domestic travellers and change the current views among members of this group of winery visitation as simply being an activity to buy wines or food.

Discussion question

What questions would you ask the researcher to determine possible limitations of the findings?

Further reading

Alonso, A.D., Fraser, R.A. & Cohen, D. (2007). Does age matter? How age influences the winery experience. *International Journal of Culture Tourism and Hospitality Research.* 1(2), forthcoming.
Alonso, A.D., Fraser, R.A. & Cohen, D. (2007). Investigating differences between domestic and international winery visitors in New Zealand. *International Journal of Wine Business Research*, 19(2), forthcoming.

The future of marketing research

The year: 2050. A baby is born. A small blood sample is taken with parental consent . . . and sent through to DNA screening. There the sample is tested for congenital abnormalities, future disease possibilities, criminal potential, and consumer segmentation. The results of the consumer segmentation are sent to subscriber companies around the world to be added automatically to their databases, which will predict behaviour for that person in terms of their combined demographics and DNA profile (Walkley, 2005).

The Managing Director of a leading Australian market research firm, Walkley (2005) believed current research into relationships between genetics and anti-social behaviour will lead to marketing research applications in the future. For example, identification of those with a higher propensity for being 'born loyal' will enable targeted segmentation in pursuit of brand loyalty.

While DNA based marketing research might or might not eventuate in the future, mind reading by neuroscience to test the effectiveness of advertising campaigns is already in practice. The potential of magnetic resonance imaging (MRI) technology, used by medical specialists to scan the body for diseases, to scan brainwave responses to advertising has been realised by the USA-based ideation consultancy Brighthouse. While the organisation's website (see www.thoughtsciences.com) carries endorsements by Fortune 500 companies such as Coca-Cola and in the travel sector from Delta.

Analysis of the brainwaves identifies at what points in a commercial such engagement occurs. The idea is to ensure brand imagery appears during the limited period of engagement. Clearly any technique that can achieve this will be welcomed by marketing researchers, who in the main are relying on what consumers tell them through interviews and question-naires. Alarcon (2006, p. 1) cited GAP Research's John Grono's view that researchers tend to ask consumers questions they can't answer: 'The limbic part of the brain that registers engagement and memory is non-verbal, you can't put it into words.' Neuroscience is already here and affordable for larger DMOs.

Key points

1. The marketing research process

The marketing research process involves six steps, beginning with the design of a manage-ment decision problem (MDP) and culminating in the presentation of information that will enable effective decision-making. It is important to remember that the process is cyclical rather than linear, so that the sixth step leads to the identification of a new MDP and so the process continues.

2. Exploratory, descriptive, and causal research

Depending of course on the MDP and marketing research problem (MRP), marketing research design will ideally incorporate both inductive and deductive reasoning, and therefore require a combination of qualitative and quantitative methods. The different strengths of the two approaches can provide much deeper insights into the why of buy when combined in a meaningful way.

3. Limitations of marketing research

No marketing research design will be perfect, and so it is important to develop an under-standing of limitations in terms of validity and reliability. It is important that such limitations are stated explicitly in the report.

Review questions

- Examine the extent to which your DMO is acting as an information clearing house for stakeholders.
- For the TNZ CFP, produce a research design as if you were a consultant bidding to get the contract. Due to the large scale of this project, perhaps consider a research strategy for one of the markets of interest.
- Why is it often advantageous to sample non-visitors?

Appendix 9.1   Tourism New Zealand CFP

Tourism New Zealand

Consumer Perception Research 2005

REQUEST FOR PROPOSALS (RFP)

Tourism New Zealand invites proposals to undertake consumer research in the UK, USA, Australia and Japan to further refine and enhance the positioning of the 100% Pure New Zealand global marketing campaign.

In 1998 Tourism New Zealand embarked on in-depth consumer research in Australia, USA, UK, and Japan to:

- understand the motivations of long haul travelers, and
- identify the most relevant, motivating, unique, and appropriate positioning for New Zealand as a holiday destination.

The results from this 'Foundation' research were pivotal in the initial and ongoing development of the 100% Pure New Zealand global marketing campaign launched by Tourism New Zealand in August 1999.

Framework for understanding the long-haul travel market

A key outcome of the Foundation research was the development of a framework for understanding the needs and motivations of the long haul travel market.

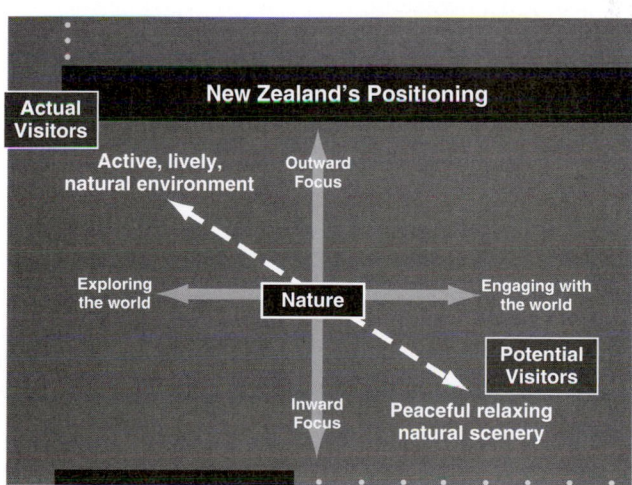

This framework aims to position long haul travellers in relation to the following questions:

- What are travellers looking for in long haul travel?
- What basic needs does the experience satisfy?

- How does New Zealand meet these needs?
- How can we use this knowledge to position New Zealand as a compelling holiday destination?

Research showed that, across all markets, *potential visitors* believed that a holiday in New Zealand delivered predominately to those seeking a quiet, relaxing holiday. In contrast, *past visitors* saw New Zealand as delivering exceedingly well to those with an energising need. Thus Tourism New Zealand needs to position New Zealand as a destination that offers an energising experience[1].

It is now six years since the Foundation research was commissioned. It is timely therefore to re-assess in-market travel dynamics and perceptions of New Zealand as a holiday destination to ensure that the 100% Pure New Zealand campaign continues to evolve, building an increasingly strong brand for New Zealand offshore.

To assess the most appropriate positioning for New Zealand in the USA, UK, Australia and Japan the research will need to:

- explore consumers' general perceptions of New Zealand, New Zealanders, and products and services of New Zealand origin
- determine how consumers perceive the personality of New Zealand
- identify icons that consumers associate with New Zealand and understand which have positive strengths that New Zealand could leverage
- identify which key messages and/or qualities would inspire consumers to think more positively about New Zealand
- examine the effect these perceptions have on New Zealand's competitive position as a tourism destination
- identify and understand the motivations of long haul travellers and Interactive Travellers®
- explore perceptions/attitudes towards travel to New Zealand
- understand the strengths and weaknesses of New Zealand's image as a destination
- identify the barriers to travel to New Zealand
- explore destination decision-making processes and opportunities for converting interest or intentions to visit New Zealand into actual travel
- identify the most relevant, motivating, unique, and appropriate positioning for New Zealand as a destination
- assess and enhance the current framework for understanding the needs and motivations of long-haul travellers.

Tourism New Zealand invites the proposer to put forward the best methodological solution for meeting the research objectives within the

---

[1] See Appendix 1 for a more comprehensive description of this framework. Individual research reports for each of the four markets included in this study can be viewed at: http://www.tourisminfo.govt.nz/cir_randd/index.cfm?fuseaction = 36

available budget. The proposed methodology will need to consider the following:

- The target audience for this research is Long-Haul Travellers or Intenders – those who have travelled long-haul in the previous twelve months OR are likely or very likely to travel to long haul destinations in the next 3 years, and who are aged 18 or over (see Appendix 2 for details).
- The 100% Pure New Zealand campaign focuses its marketing activity on a selected target group of travellers that has been identified as New Zealand's ideal visitor; namely the Interactive Traveller[2]. At least 50% of research participants will need to be Interactive Travellers®. The Interactive Traveller definition will need to match the definition used for other commissioned TNZ research. (See Appendix 2 for details.)
- Research in Japan will need to be translated and undertaken in Japanese.
- At the survey stage, certain questions such as demographics will need to be consistent with the format used in previous TNZ surveys. The successful proposer will be provided with all relevant documents and survey questions used previously in Tourism New Zealand research.
- Research design phases will require input and feedback from key Tourism New Zealand personnel. This will need to be considered when planning the project timeline.
- The proposer will need to consider in-market events such as public holidays that might effect fieldwork timetabling.

A key output of this research is the development of a 'conceptual device' or analytical framework that Tourism New Zealand can assess performance of specific campaign elements in terms of positioning, appeal, and motivational response.

Reporting:

- One full research report including an executive summary and recommendations
- Four short reports focusing on research outcomes for each of the four markets – Japan, USA, UK, Australia .
- Presentation of research highlights to key Tourism New Zealand personnel (including power point or equivalent). This will involve a minimum of two presentations, one a presentation of results and workshop on findings and the other a final presentation.
- Provision of presentation material on Tourism New Zealand templates.

Up to $400,000 NZD + GST
Proposals are due at Tourism New Zealand by 5 pm 28 January 2005.

---

[2] More detailed information about the Interactive Traveller is included in Appendix 2.

This contract must be completed by May 31st 2005 with a draft report submitted that date.

When tendering for this project we ask that you provide us with the following details:

Preferred research methodology

How the fieldwork and analysis will be undertaken detailing preferred sampling framework for qualitative and quantitative phases within the available budget.

Project plan/Timetable • • •

When research milestones will be met

Costs • • •

Costs itemised for each research phase and estimates of disbursements where applicable.

Key personnel • • •

Who will be involved in the project including references to skill base, relevant experience and qualifications.

References • • •

Evidence or examples of relevant work

Key contact • • •

Every proposal must include the name of the person to whom Tourism New Zealand may address any questions relating to the proposal.

Tourism New Zealand will be assessing proposals for this contract on the following basis:

- Evidence of an **in-depth understanding** of our requirements.
- Quality of the research design to provide a **comprehensive solution** to meeting the research objectives.
- Evidence of understanding of the **framework for understanding the needs and motivations of long-haul travellers.**
- **Prior experience** of conducting evaluation/communications research particularly in off-shore markets.
- **Quality of staff** put forward to conduct the assignment.
- Ability to supply **specialists** with relevant experience.
- **Price** and **value for money**.

Following preliminary consideration of the written proposals, Tourism New Zealand may invite one or more of the potential providers to meet with the evaluation panel to present and discuss their proposal. Proposers must provide TWO complete copies of their proposals.

For supplementary information relating to this RFP, please contact the project manager:

Vaughan Schwass
Manager – Channel Marketing and Marketing Research
Tourism New Zealand
147 Victoria street west, Auckland
PO Box 91 893, Auckland Mail Centre
Email: vaughans@tnz.govt.nz

Please make no contact in relation to this RFP with any other Tourism New Zealand employee without the authorisation of the project manager.

The lowest priced or any proposal will not necessarily be accepted. Tourism New Zealand will not be under any obligation to discuss reasons why a proposal is accepted or rejected. No proposal is deemed to have been accepted or rejected until the fact of such acceptance or rejection has been notified in writing to the proposer by Tourism New Zealand.

The requirements specified in this RFP reflect those presently known. Tourism New Zealand reserves the right to vary, in detail, the final requirements.

Proposers must ensure that the person or persons nominated to negotiate a contract have the authority to finalise details without reference to others, either in New Zealand or overseas.

In relation to this RFP and consequential negotiations, only communications from the project manager and any person authorised by the project manager will be considered as an expression of Tourism New Zealand's position.

Preference will be given to proposals that meet all the conditions of the RFP. However, in the event that no proposal can comply with this, then consideration will be given to proposers answering part of the RFP.

If, in the opinion of Tourism New Zealand, none of the proposals are acceptable, Tourism New Zealand reserves the right to enter into negotiation with one or more proposers for a satisfactory offer, or with none of the proposers.

Tourism New Zealand will not be responsible for, or pay, any expense incurred by a proposer in the preparation of their proposal or in Tourism New Zealand's evaluation of it.

The acceptance of a proposal does not create any contractual relationship between Tourism New Zealand and the proposer but represents a commitment to enter into negotiations in good faith.

All prices must be in New Zealand dollars at the time of the response and be exclusive of GST.

All submitted proposals become the property of Tourism New Zealand and will not be returned to the proposer.

General information which is not specifically requested but which proposers wish to provide is to be attached separately and clearly labelled

'Supporting Material'. Any reference in the proposal relating to this material must be specified.

All information contained in this RFP and all other information supplied by or on behalf of Tourism New Zealand to proposers will be treated as confidential, and may only be used for the purpose of preparing a proposal. This document and any copies produced with or without approval will remain the property of Tourism New Zealand and must be returned to it upon request.

Tourism New Zealand shall be entitled to rely on all statements and representations made by the proposer in response to the RFP or subsequent enquiries or correspondence whether such statements or representations are given in writing or orally.

All information submitted by proposers in their proposals that are regarded as confidential in nature, must be clearly marked 'Commercial: In Confidence'.

Tourism New Zealand would like to remind proposers that under the provisions of the Official Information Act Tourism New Zealand may be obliged to disclose certain information if a request for information is made pursuant to the Act. Tourism New Zealand will endeavour to refuse requests to release information which is commercially sensitive, but no guarantee is given that refusal to release such information will not be successfully challenged.

All proposers are required to acknowledge in their proposals that they accept the terms and conditions set forth in this Section 11. Proposals which fail to give such acknowledgement may be rejected by Tourism New Zealand.

Appendix 1   A framework of needs and motivations for understanding the long-haul travel market

Introduction

Ask a traveller about their long-haul travel experience (that is, when they've travelled more than six hours by air to reach their destination), and they'll often say this type of travel provides some of their most enjoyable and significant life experiences.

New Zealand's place in the world means we are a long-haul destination for thousands of people every year. So how can we find out whether we're providing the experience these travellers are looking for? How can we put New Zealand at the top of their list of long-haul destinations?

First, we need to define just what they're looking for – and then establish whether we can offer the experience that meets those needs.

That's what this framework aims to do. It asks questions such as:

- What are travellers looking for in long-haul travel?
- What basic needs does the experience satisfy?
- How does New Zealand meet these needs?
- How can we use this knowledge to position New Zealand as a great vacation destination?

The framework is a useful tool for New Zealand's tourism industry. Produced as part of a project for the Tourism New Zealand, it provides some valuable insights into the 'inner workings' of this unique travelling market.

Seeking discovery

All long-haul travellers describe a sense of **discovery** as a key part of their travel experience – a desire to **discover and expand their world.**

Individual travellers vary widely in how they do this, and choose destinations and experiences that meet their individual needs. Their choice may also be affected by the things they like to do at home:

- A weekend 'trail walker' may choose to backpack when they travel.
- An avid reader may travel to book fairs around the world.

However, some underlying dynamics in the market shape all travel preferences. These dynamics provide a framework for understanding the needs in the market overall.

The travel dynamics

Two key emotive forces shape long-haul travellers' decision-making in long-haul travel:

1. 'Exploration' vs 'engagement'
2. An 'outward' vs an 'inward' personal focus.

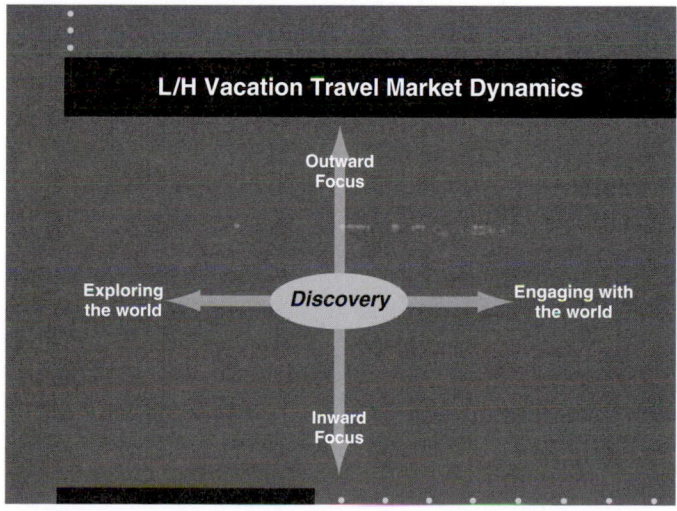

The **horizontal axis** deals with the person's relationship with the environment. It ranges from seeking to explore the world (for people who investigate or challenge their world), to seeking to engage their environment (for people who seek connection with people and/or with their natural surroundings).

The **vertical axis** deals with the traveller's personal focus on their journey.

Inwardly focused people seek a mental or emotional retreat that centres largely on their internal world. Outwardly focused people seek to connect and interact with the outside world, either physically with nature or socially with other people.

Together these two dynamics create a range of distinct needs in the long-haul market.

Travel needs and motivations

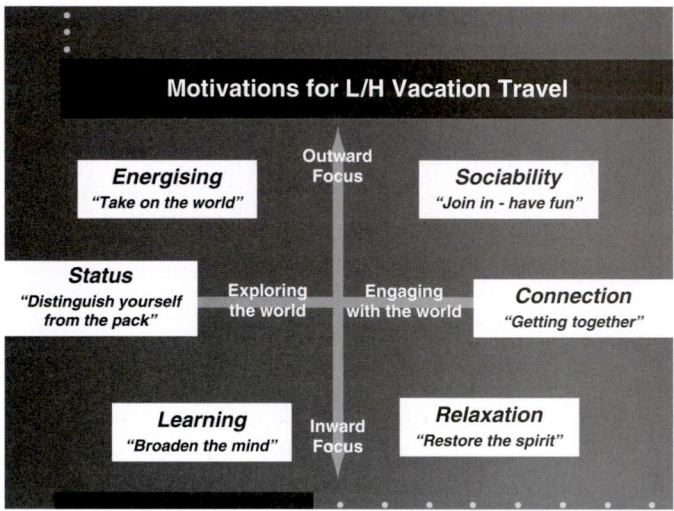

Energising – What is it?

'Energising' is about the need to experience a feeling of excitement and interaction through physical activity, experiencing oneself as a physical being. A sense of being re-energised, challenged and even exhilarated through physical activity.

> It's the feeling I get, getting to the top of a mountain I've just climbed and just standing there. A sense of accomplishment . . . it's a challenge. Climbing adds to the whole experience . . . a physical rush . . . incredible.

Who are 'energising' travellers?
Typical travellers with an energising need:

- are younger (under 40) and more physically fit than the average traveller
- are interested in outdoors activities in daily life, and may be rampers/hikers, backpackers

- use a large variety of specialist guides (*Lonely Planet, Rough Guide* etc.) as well as Internet sources such as travel sites
- like to rely on word of mouth where possible. Word-of-mouth information gives them the feeling of being insiders who discover places and experiences that are 'off the beaten track'
- see themselves as confident, energetic, adventurous and outdoorsy

Wants to get into nature, into the challenge . . . physical exhilaration.

Profile of an 'energising' traveller

'Steven' is a 27-year-old coast guard, living in New York.

Previous travel: Aruba, Barbados, Europe
Travel to New Zealand: would like to backpack New Zealand with his girlfriend.
Motivation: 'Like Christopher Columbus discovering the New World . . . Just you, thinking you are the first. Of course there have been other people like there was with Christopher Columbus then, but in your mind, in your own heart it's just you – and it's so new and real'.
Personal ideal: 'Not only accomplishment but it's a feeling like a new world conquered. Would love to bungy . . . so wild . . . incredible feeling of freedom, excitement'.

Energising – What is the ideal vacation?
Environment
A natural environment that provides the potential for release through a range of physical activities.

A place to be explored and interacted with physically.

Tracks for walking, beaches for swimming, and mountains for climbing.

Activities
Walking, tramping/hiking, climbing, river rafting, kayaking, and bicycling.

Novel activities like such as sailing and bungy jumping – but note these are not for everyone; they may be too extreme and risky for some.

The individual's physical fitness plays a part in which activities appeal.

Planning and preferred mode of travel
Travel planning can be either very involved, with plenty of research on journey detail, or more spur of the moment and allowing for a sense of freedom and excitement.

Travellers may prefer to travel independently or use a package deal, but generally find tours too restrictive.

Ideal destinations
Countries with distinctive natural environments (e.g. Nepal, South America, Australia, New Zealand) which offer the promise of the ability to interact physically with the environment.

Images that appeal to energising needs
- Images that show vibrant, exhilarating, outdoor images of physical inter-action with nature.
- Walking, bicycling, tramping/hiking, kayaking.
- Show one or two people getting into the outdoors.
- Natural images that are exhilarating and invigorating to view (e.g. majes-tic waterfalls, surf, mountains).
- Overall feeling of communications should be bold refreshing and lively (not life-threatening!).

Avoid images that are too extreme (e.g. bungy jumping) and that have relatively niche appeal. (*Note*: while pictures of 'icon' activities like 'bungy' fit well here they have the potential to alienate travellers with a less extreme approach to satisfying their energising need. Ensure eye-catching pictures of extreme adventure activities are used only in conjunction with other, less extreme activity images.)

Sociability – What is it? • • •

'Sociability' is about participating with others and having fun in a lively, outgoing and sociable environment.

Travellers with this need:

- love to share their travel experiences with others along the way
- enjoy a feeling of camaraderie or togetherness
- typically travel with a companion or group
- choose destinations that provide the potential for meeting others.

> *She just wants to have fun – not see every ruin in the world – somewhere where there is a lot of people and a lot happening . . . a feeling of excitement, energy . . . something is about to happen.*

Who are 'sociability' travellers?
Typical travellers with a sociability need:

- are younger (aged 20 to 30)
- are interested in socialising with their peers
- are not extensively travelled
- use standard sources for travel information (such as travel agent news-paper travel sections)
- see themselves as outgoing, energetic and sociable.

> *He's not married so he's out to have a good time with people his own age . . . it's all about meeting people.*

Profile of a 'sociability' traveller

'Michael' is 22 years old, a law student, and currently living in Los Angeles.

Previous travel: to Europe with family and Australia/New Zealand with a group of friends
Travel to New Zealand: a three-day package, which was a side trip from Australia. Took day tours to see local sights, and went clubbing and pubbing at night.
Motivation: 'I wanted to go on that trip . . . to party . . . some sight seeing . . . but I'm embarrassed to say it, we go out to meet girls. That was what the whole trip was about.'
Personal ideal: 'Somewhere by the beach . . . meeting people . . . the city life . . . where I could party and meet people.'

Sociability – What is the ideal vacation?
Environment
A lively, urban environment that provides the potential for socialising with locals and other travellers (ideally with people from a similar culture and age group).

Activities
Seeing the nightlife (dining out, pubs, clubbing).
   Day activities such as visiting a popular beach, recreational shopping, visiting museums, and cafés.
   Tours or cruises with other travellers of similar ages or interests.

Planning and preferred mode of travel
A more open-plan, 'free and easy' schedule, or cruises and resorts providing a 'no-planning' alternative that leaves travellers free to socialise.

Ideal destinations
Island resorts such as Greek Islands, Caribbean Islands – anywhere that offers a lively social life (Australia's cities are an excellent fit).

Images that appeal to sociability needs
- Lively images that depict social interaction against an appealing vibrant backdrop. A range of day and night, age-appropriate images (e.g. beaches and shopping during the day, dining out, pubbing or clubbing at night). People interacting in urban as well as rural settings.
- Convey lively, social and fun feelings.

Avoid images that are solitary or too rural.

Connection – What is it? • • •

'Connection' is the need to feel connected to others and at one with the environment. Travel is the opportunity to reconnect with the world – either with people (especially friends and family) or symbolically with nature.

Just somewhere where I feel whole and complete . . . a feeling of belonging, being part of everything . . .

Who are 'connection' travellers?
Typical travellers with the connection need:

- are families, couples (families may prefer short-haul travel, as it is less stressful)
- use standard sources for travel information (such as travel agent newspaper travel sections)
- see themselves as warm, friendly, relaxed, and easygoing.

She just wants to kick-back . . . get back to being a family . . . to really spend time with each other instead of two minutes over breakfast.

Profile of a 'connection' traveller

'Sherry' is a 47-year-old real estate investor, currently living in Los Angeles.
Previous travel: multiple trips to Hawaii, the Caribbean, Spain, with husband and other couples – cruising and shopping.
Travel to New Zealand: intends to backpack with her 14-year-old daughter.
Motivation: 'It's really clean, fresh and healthy . . . you know, just spending time laughing, talking, crying. It's the perfect place to really get in touch with my daughter . . . just having that bond.'
Personal ideal: 'A lot of quiet time walking and hiking together and seeing things . . . really beautiful surroundings.'

Connection – What is the ideal vacation?
Environment
A blend of urban and rural, typically an attractive town with easy access to the countryside (natural and cultural). A good range of things to do nearby.

Activities
Activities that can be enjoyed as a couple or as a family. A mixture of seeing the local nightlife (dining out, theatre) and day activities to enjoy the natural environment. Includes recreational shopping, visiting museums, light physical activities, walking, kayaking, and guided walks.

Planning and preferred mode of travel
Travel plans that allow them to take in their surroundings and enjoy who they are with, without having to rush or 'do' too many things or places.

May choose tours or package deals that allow them a hassle-free trip for themselves and their travel companions.

Ideal destinations

England and (depending on familiarity) other parts of Europe, Australia, and New Zealand.

Images that appeal to connection needs

- Images depicting a small group of people enjoying each other's company against a natural backdrop.
- Images that focus on the relationship between the people and nature. Show light, fun activities that can be enjoyed as a family or couple – walking, bicycling, and kayaking. Show one or two people enjoying the outdoors.
- Warm and friendly, conveying the connection between the people.

Avoid images that are too overtly social or too subdued.

Relaxation – What is it? • • •

'Relaxation' is the need to completely unwind and restore the spirit, taking 'time out' to forget the stresses of life. It's an essentially inward and thoughtful experience.

Travellers with this motivation seek new destinations and activities that will allow them to unwind in an unstressful and tranquil setting.

> *Nature . . . nothing but you and your surroundings . . . peaceful and relaxed . . . back to yourself again in this beautiful place.*

Who are 'relaxation' travellers?

Typical travellers with the connection need:

- are older (aged 40-plus)
- are well travelled
- use standard sources for travel information (such as travel agent newspaper travel sections)
- see themselves as mature, quiet, thoughtful and relaxed.

> *He's older, not in a rush and he likes to take his time - really relax.*

Profile of a 'relaxation' traveller

'Lisa' is a 39-year-old insurance adjuster, currently living in Los Angeles.
Previous travel: France and Germany to visit relatives.
Travel to New Zealand: two weeks to visit some New Zealand acquaintances who invited her to stay.
Motivation: 'They were so friendly . . . it was a once in a lifetime chance . . . told me how beautiful it was and I just wanted to go, how pretty it is and the restful feeling of it. When I came back I thought "Wow - I didn't know there was such a nice place on this planet".'
Personal ideal: 'Somewhere quiet and cruisey . . . subdued and relaxed.'

Relaxation – What is the ideal vacation?

Environment

A quiet but inspiring natural environment that provides real potential for relaxing and restoring the self. The culture should feel relaxed, familiar and friendly.

Activities

Activities that allow the traveller to observe the natural environment in a relaxing and non-stressful way, such as walks, cycling and bus tours to visit natural wonders. The type of activity depends on the traveller's experience, interests and fitness. Some find only the most sedate activities relaxing while others find tramping/hiking or snorkeling perfectly relaxing.

Planning and preferred mode of travel

Predictable travel – simple itineraries, package deals, or tours that really allow them to 'kick back'.

Ideal destinations

More culturally similar locations that promise spectacular natural beauty, such as Ireland, England, Scotland, Australia and New Zealand.

Other European countries (non-English speaking) that promise natural beauty (France, Sweden, etc.).

Images that appeal to relaxation needs

- Images of inspiring natural beauty – vivid and spectacular scenery that seems to invite relaxed reflection.
- One or two people – if any at all.
- A panoramic feeling that conveys a real sense of tranquility. Inspirational, breathtaking and pure feelings.

Avoid images with too many people, urban environments, or natural environments that are forbidding and do not invite or suggest relaxation.

Learning – What is it? • • •

'Learning' is about the need to understand and explore the world in an inquiring and intellectual way. Learning travellers are looking for interesting and unique locations providing a high degree of cultural difference, which they seek to explore and understand fully.

> It's that feeling of learning about a new place . . . you see yourself anew through exploring a new culture . . . it's a personal journey . . . personal growth in a way.

Who are 'learning' travellers?

Typical travellers with the learning need:

- are older (30 to 40 plus)
- are independent travellers

- are well travelled, see themselves as intelligent, thoughtful and individualistic.
- are interested in other cultures, reading, watching documentaries etc.
- use a large variety of specialist guides, including Internet sources such as chat groups and travel sites
- are happy to book their own travel directly.

She goes to places other people don't think of because she wants to understand all different people . . . wants to go everywhere.

Profile of a 'learning' traveller

'Megan' is a 32-year-old office worker, currently living in New York.
Previous travel: several trips to Europe and South America.
Travel to New Zealand: plans to visit New Zealand as a backpacker.
Motivation: 'New Zealand is just rugged beauty. The hiking there is supposed to be beautiful . . . something I want to experience for myself . . . finding out what the place and the people are like - experiencing another new culture.'
Personal ideal – 'I guess meeting the people of the land – understanding them . . . seeing the world differently and understanding more about it.'

Learning – What is the ideal vacation?
Environment

A culturally interesting environment that provides the potential for learning about new and different places. Contact with people from the local culture is important – without these travellers can find the experience dry, uninteresting and 'touristy'.

Activities

Taking part in the daily life and learning about the culture as well as the places of cultural and historical significance.

Tours that provide specialist information about the location, increasing the richness of the experience.

Activities that satisfy an interest in local architecture, cultural events such as local or international arts festivals, religious rituals, dancing.

Planning and preferred mode of travel

Detailed travel plans give these travellers a sense of competence and control.

Learning as much as they can about the culture before they go extends the travel experience into their daily life and allows them to become experts on their destination.

They prefer to travel independently, using package deals only to take advantage of a special lower price.

Ideal destinations

Exotic, mysterious destinations (different languages are no barrier for these travellers) that are culturally interesting.

Western Europe is a good starting point, then Asia, Africa, and Eastern Europe for when they gain experience.

Images that appeal to learning needs

Images that show different and interesting cultures as well as interesting and unusual natural features.

- Images should raise curiosity, be unique and compel the viewer to want to investigate.
- Overall feeling of communications should be interesting, authentic (an almost 'documentary' style) and suggest a unique experience (the only place where this happens).

Avoid images that are predictable or too 'commercial' and contrived (e.g. cultural shows obviously put on for tourists).

Status – What is it? • • •

'Status' is the need to distinguish oneself from the pack, to express one's individuality. These travellers seek a sense of sophistication and difference.

They prefer travel experiences that are individual and unique either in their luxuriousness, cultural sophistication, or intellectual significance.

> *I took an African safari and the hotel was just stunning – absolute luxury. I had heard about it and wanted to go there, it was one of the best hotels in the world ... that makes me want to go somewhere if it's going to be really special, really unique, a one of a kind.*

Who are 'status' travellers?

Typical travellers with a status need:

- are individualistic,
- are well travelled
- are interested in exotic and special destinations that not everyone travels to
- use a large variety of specialist guides or glossy travel magazines in search of unique and/or exclusive destinations
- see themselves as intelligent, discerning, individualistic, self confident and well travelled
- collect countries and experiences as badges of their status.

> *Been everywhere ... wants something special something that everyone else hasn't done already.*

Profile of a 'status' traveller

'Simon' is 59 years old and is a manager living in New York.
Previous travel: many trips to Europe, South America, Asia as an amateur photographer.
Travel to New Zealand: plans to visit New Zealand as part of a photographic trip to Australia.
Motivation: 'New Zealand specialises in beautiful waterfalls, . . . I photograph beautiful waterfalls . . . [I like to get] an appreciation of the destination, its culture.'
Personal ideal: 'It's a gorgeous place, it's got to be a very off the beaten path kind of place – it's exotic. The fact that a lot of people don't go there, it's remote.'

Status – What is the ideal vacation?
Environment
A place that is unique/exclusive and one of a kind, in:

- the environment – "the only location that has X'
- the accommodation – 'the best of this kind in the world', or
- the activities – 'the only place where you can X'.

Activities
One of a kind, trendy, exclusive, such as African safari, Peruvian mountain climbing, golfing in Scotland, skiing in New Zealand in northern summer.

Planning and preferred mode of travel
These travellers see themselves as more discerning than the average traveller – they either plan their travel themselves or allow themselves the luxury of others planning for them (cruises, tours or package deals).

Ideal destinations
Destinations that set them apart from the crowd. Either new or interesting locations such as Prague and Vietnam, or premium experiences in more traditional destinations, e.g. Paris, Rome.

Images that appeal to learning needs
- One of a kind experiences that are distinctive, unique or especially luxurious.
- Convey a sense of exclusiveness in the tone and execution.
- An air of authenticity, authority, and individuality (premium cues are only appropriate for those who seek the more luxurious side of the status need).
- Avoid images that convey destination as a conventional, everyday travel destination.

How does New Zealand meet these needs?

Two dynamics pull diagonally across the framework: the Natural axis; and the Social axis.

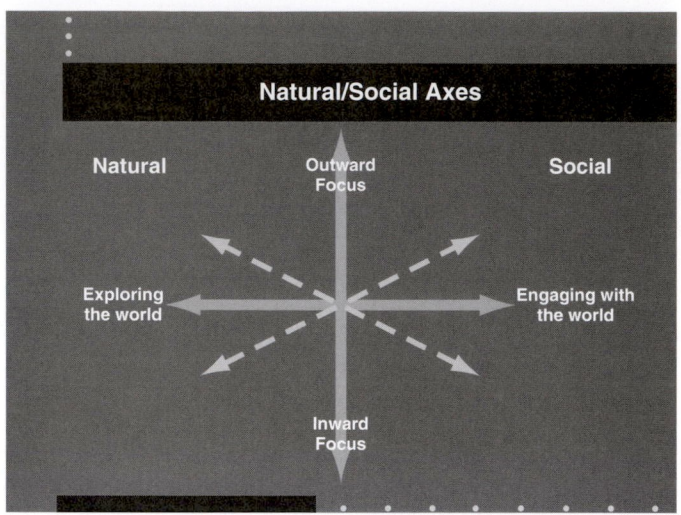

The cultural and social side of travel is covered by the **bottom left quadrant** (dealing with *a need to learn and investigate cultures*) and the **top right quadrant** (dealing with *a need to be in a sociable, outgoing and interactive context*).

The natural aspects of travel are covered by the **top left-hand quadrant** (*a need to be part of the exciting energising, enjoyment of nature*) and the **bottom right quadrant** (*a need for a more relaxed, reflective enjoyment of nature*).

Where is New Zealand in this?

Potential and actual visitors to New Zealand see New Zealand's key appeal being its natural environment – putting New Zealand strongly along the Natural rather than the Social axis.

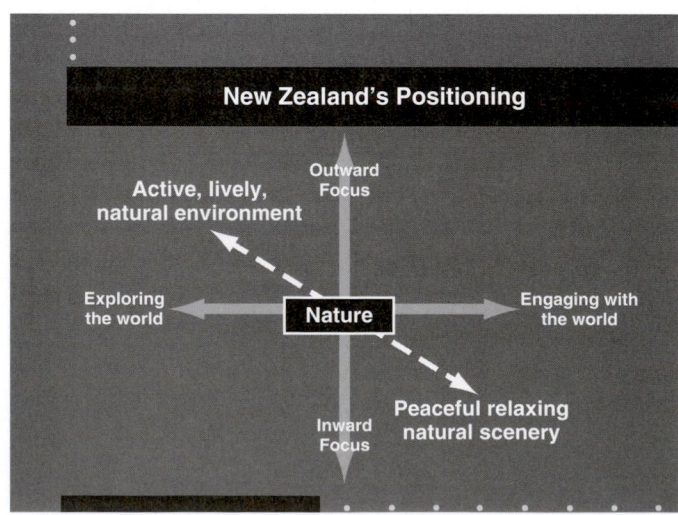

While New Zealand is well positioned to meet needs at both ends of the Natural axis, it is more important to focus on the more aspirational Energising need – focusing on Relaxation reinforces some current perceptions of New Zealand as a relatively quiet and uninteresting destination.

Perceptions of New Zealand by motivation • • •

Energising

New Zealand's distance and rugged natural beauty have strong appeal, and the country can fit the need for new and interesting outdoor destinations. However, some travellers perceive New Zealand as currently too quiet and pastoral.

> I would go there because of the nature, just to see what it is like to get lost in the wilderness down there.

Sociability

Overall, New Zealand is not an ideal fit for travellers with sociability needs, as the New Zealand experience is seen as lacking the necessary social liveliness these travellers seek.

Backpackers are a notable exception, as a social interaction through the backpacker network allows young people to meet and socialise with backpackers throughout the country.

> You don't really think of New Zealand as having a night life or many people – more quiet and relaxing.

Connection

New Zealand is seen as providing the relaxed, easy-going environment these travellers seek. However, as they enjoy group activities, they may feel there are not enough activities in the cities for a group of friends, a couple or a family.

> She's looking for something where the whole family can relax. They would be safe in New Zealand with the children but she wouldn't be sure if the kids would have enough to do. Also it's a long way to take a family and they want to do things as a family.

Relaxation

New Zealand is an ideal fit for these travellers as it is seen as providing a relaxed, scenic natural environment perfect for really kicking back and enjoying nature.

> It's a feeling of calm and serenity. He hasn't got a care in the world. Finally time to stop rushing and to smell the roses . . . to kick back and enjoy his surroundings.

Learning

New Zealand is seen as lacking a strong and different indigenous culture. Its dominantly European culture is not sufficiently exotic, mysterious or authentic for the tastes of these more independent and adventurous travellers.

> *The native culture there is pretty much gone . . . it's all just touristy stuff, so you don't really see much different.*

Status

New Zealand's unique and premium aspects can appeal to this need for 'one of a kind' or premium experiences. The exceptional natural environment coupled with factors such as off-season skiing and premium fishing, golfing, and accommodation can appeal to these very discriminating travellers.

> *I have always wanted to go skiing there in the summer time. I thought it was going to be wild to go skiing in August and July. Just really just to say to people, 'What did you do for the summer?'. I'd say, 'I went skiing.' They'd say, 'Water skiing?' I'd say, 'No, snow skiing'.*

Appendix 2 Tourism New Zealand's target market – the interactive traveller

The 100% pure campaign launched by Tourism New Zealand in August 1999 seeks to position New Zealand as a destination that offers experiences best suited to the needs of the interactive iraveller.

The interactive traveller

Our ideal visitor is defined as a regular international traveller who:

- consumes a wide range of tourism products and services
- seeks out new experiences that involve engagement and interaction with natural, social and cultural environments
- respects the environment, culture and societal values of others
- is considered a leader by his/her peers
- is not averse to planning and booking holidays directly
- uses technology to enhance their lives
- values authentic products/experiences as opposed to having a 'trend' consciousness
- is health conscious, values connection with others and places high value on authentic products and services
- enjoys outdoor activity, is sociable and seeks learning experiences.

Compared with all travellers, interactive travellers are more likely to:

- spend more time in New Zealand
- spend more per visit

- visit NZ to experience the scenery, physical activities, culture, and wildlife
- book more of their travel while in NZ
- rate their holiday experience in NZ higher
- are more likely to participate in activities
- are more satisfied with the activities they do
- are more likely to use more personal forms of transport (e.g. rental cars) and accommodation (e.g. farm stays, lodges).

Tourism New Zealand has produced a series of fliers to provide trade with an overview of how this target market is defined. These fliers can be viewed at: http://www.tourisminfo.govt.nz/cir_pub/index.cfm?fuseaction=253

Interactive traveller – standard research questions

The following are the standard questions for use in research projects to assess whether or not respondents fit the profile of an Interactive Traveller.

Section 1 • • •

Respondents will be asked if they have travelled* long haul in the previous 12 months for holiday or leisure purposes, or are likely to travel long haul in the next 3 years for holiday or leisure purposes.

Interactive travellers will agree to the first part of this question and be very likely/quite likely to travel in the next three years. An example question, for use in the UK market, follows:

Q1a

Have you travelled to a destination OUTSIDE the UK, Europe, or North Africa for holiday or leisure purposes in the last 12 months?

Q1b

In the next three years, how Likely or Unlikely are you to travel to a destination OUTSIDE the UK, Europe, or North Africa for holiday or leisure purposes?

Would you say it is:

Very likely
Quite likely
Quite unlikely
Very unlikely
Can't say

---

*(in the case of Australia, which is not a long-haul market – respondents who travel overseas)

Important notes

In the case where a respondent has actually travelled (to New Zealand), the first questions about having travelled in the previous 12 months or likelihood over the next 3 years obviously can be omitted.
Obviously 'long haul' will vary according to markets. Suggestions for the

UK, the USA and Japan follow.
UK – OUTSIDE the UK, Europe and North Africa
USA – OUTSIDE the USA, Canada, Mexico or the Caribbean
JAPAN – OUTSIDE Japan, China, Hong Kong, South Korea, Macau, Philippines, or Taiwan

Section 2 • • •

Respondents will be asked to select **one** of the following statements in response to the questions 1–5 inclusive.

(a) Strongly agree
(b) Agree
(c) Neither agree nor disagree
(d) Disagree
(e) Strongly disagree

Questions

(1) I prefer to holiday where I can see nature or be in a natural setting
(2) I'd like to holiday where I can experience the local culture
(3) I look for new experiences every day
(4) I consider myself a leader more than a follower
(5) I enjoy holidays where everything is organised for you

Interactive travellers should agree or strongly agree with questions 1–4 and disagree or strongly disagree with question 5 in this section.
    A Show Card example follows to illustrate how this could be used in face-to-face interviews.

(Show card X)

I am now going to read out some statements, please tell me whether you strongly agree, agree, neither agree nor disagree, disagree or strongly disagree with the following:

Insert Statement – xxxxxxxxxxxxxxxxxxxxx

Strongly agree
Agree
Neither agree nor disagree
Disagree
Strongly disagree
Can't say

CHAPTER 10

Destination branding

One industry after another has discovered that brand awareness, perceived quality, customer loyalty, and strong brand associations and personality are necessary to compete in the marketplace.

Aaker & Joachimsthaler (2000, p. ix)

Aims

The aims of this chapter are to enhance understanding of:

- the role and importance of destination brands
- brand identity
- consumer-based brand equity.

Perspective

Today's consumers have more product choice but less decision time than ever before. Consequently, a brand that can help simplify decisions, reduce purchase risk, create and deliver expectations is invaluable. The topic of product branding first appeared in the literature 50 years ago, but while research published in the time since provides a valuable resource for consumer goods marketers, work related to the branding of tourism destinations has been relatively sparse. This is a significant gap in the tourism and travel research fields, particularly given that a number of leading brand authors have cited the prediction that the future of marketing will be a 'battle of brands, a competition for brand dominance' (see Aaker, 1991 p. ix; de Chernatony 1993, p. 173), and that within the tourism industry destinations are emerging as the biggest brands (Morgan et al., 2002, 2004). However, it is likely that many destinations will become increasingly substitutable, if not already so, and therefore are commodities rather than brands. This chapter explores the reasons behind these assertions, with the discussion underpinned by four themes. First, the understanding that promoting product features is not sufficient to differentiate against competitors is fundamental to brand theory. Second, the already complex process of product brand development and management is intensified for destination marketers, who exert no control over the actual delivery of the brand promise. Third, and following the previous point, there has been little published research to date to guide DMOs on the long-term effectiveness of destination branding. Fourth, the view has been adopted that branding is at the very heart of marketing strategy, and so the purpose of all destination marketing activity must be to enhance the value of the brand.

The importance of brands

The first branding papers appeared in the literature during the 1950s (see, for example, Banks, 1950; Gardner & Levy, 1955). Gardner and Levy discussed stereotypes that had emerged in advertising which failed to differentiate competitive products. They espoused the importance of considering a brand as representing a personality (p. 35):

> ... a brand name is more than the label employed to differentiate among the manufacturers of a product. It is a complex symbol that represents a variety of ideas and attributes. It tells the consumers many things, not only by the way it sounds (and its literal meaning if it has one) but, more important, via the body of associations it has built up and acquired as a public object over a period of time ... The net result is a public image, a character or personality that may be more important for the overall status (and sales) of the brand than many technical facts about the product.

There is evidence to suggest branding practice was around centuries before it became an academic field. Keller (2003) cited reports about identification marks of craftsmen being found on pottery in China, Europe, and India dating as far back as 1300 BC. The evolution of brand development since the 1870s was examined by King (1970), who suggested the driving force was the cyclical balance of power in the manufacturer–distributor relationship. Branding of manufactured goods emerged during the late 19th century to counter the dominating force of wholesalers who controlled what were essentially commodity markets. Retailers purchased what was available in stock from wholesalers, who in turn dictated what manufacturers should produce. From the 1900s to the 1960s the role of the wholesaler was reduced to that of distributor, as manufacturer numbers declined to the level of oligopolies. Brands were then used to build demand for a smaller line of goods, with economies of scale leading to increased profits for manufacturers. This occurred at the expense of retailers' margins, since manufacturers controlled consumer prices. By 1970, the balance of power had shifted towards large-scale retailers, where economies of scale and their own brand labels enhanced profit levels (pp. 7–8):

> After all, many retail chains are bigger businesses than most consumer goods manufacturers; and on the whole there are more manufacturers still in most fields than the retailer really needs.

The new role for product marketers was to improve the value of their brands to the consumer as well as to the mega-retailer. King also used the term brand personality to suggest that brands held values beyond their physical and functional attributes (p. 11):

> People choose their brands as they choose their friends. You choose your friends not usually because of specific skills or physical attributes (though of course these come into it) but simply because you like them as people. It is the total person you choose, not a compendium of virtues and vices.

Following Aaker (1991, p. x), de Chernatony (1993, p. 173), and Keller (2003, pp. 39–41), there are a number of compelling reasons why branding is generating increasing awareness of the importance of brands among product and service providers: brand equity, increasing global competition, commodification, the power of retailers, sophisticated consumers, brand extensions, media cost-effectiveness, and a short-term performance orientation.

Brand equity

One of the most important impacts of branding for commercial organisations has been the increasing awareness of the balance sheet value of brands, referred to as brand equity. That is, a brand can be an asset or a liability to the firm, and as such can affect the valuation of the firm. Given the difficulty in developing new brands, there is a willingness by firms to pay a premium for the purchase of well-known brands.

Under the International Accounting Standards, the value of a brand cannot be brought to the balance sheet unless they have been acquired for financial consideration (James, 2007). This is due to the lack of an agreed framework or method for calculating brand equity. For this reason the Standards Association of Germany has launched an international working party to develop an ISO standard for brand valuation. It is expected the project will take several years.

Of the different methods available to measure intangible brand equity, *Business Week* (August, 2003) selected that used by brand consultancy Interbrand (www.interbrand.com) to calculate the value of the world's 100 top brands. Interbrand valued brand equity based on the net present value of future earning potential. The top ten brand values are shown in Table 10.1, where it can be seen that the intangible Coca-Cola brand was valued at US$70 billion. The tourism related Disney brand was ranked seventh, at US$28 billion.

The marketing budget should be regarded as an investment in consumers' associations of the brand (Keller, 2000). There is a growing view that branding lies at the core of marketing strategy, and that the purpose of the marketing programme should be to focus on developing favourable brand associations, linking the brand's attributes to consumer needs. The other motive for measuring brand equity, other than financial asset valuation, is marketing effectiveness. It is the latter, consumer-based brand equity (CBBE) which may be the most critical for organisations, since financial valuation is irrelevant if no underlying consumer-based value of the brand has been established (Keller, 1993). For destinations the concept of consumer-based destination brand equity is clearly more relevant than balance sheet values.

Table 10.1 The world's top 10 brands in 2003

Rank	2003 brand value US$ billions
1. Coca-cola	70.45
2. Microsoft	65.17
3. IBM	51.77
4. GE	42.34
5. Intel	31.11
6. Nokia	29.44
7. Disney	28.04
8. McDonald's	24.70
9. Marlboro	22.18
10. Mercedes	21.37

Source: Adapted from *Business Week*, August 2003: viewed 22/10/03 at: www.interbrand.ca/pdf/Best_Global_Brands.2003.pdf.

Increasing global competition

Competition is intensifying through the breaking down of trading barriers between nations. This and other impacts of globalisation, such as the internet, has led to a greater awareness of global competitors by both producers and consumers. Since 70% of international travellers visit only 10 countries, over 90 NTOs compete for 30% of total international arrivals (Morgan et al., 2002). The new competition phenomenon does not discriminate against famous destinations. For example, Dahles (1998, p. 56) claimed that while once competing with London and Paris to be Europe's most popular destination, Amsterdam was 'fighting for survival'. Increasing competition between traditional and emerging destinations has significant consequences for most places (Middleton, 1998, p. 153):

> The great majority will need to review and adapt their traditional organisational and marketing methods to survive and prosper in the next millennium. One can only speculate that some will be unable to make the change and will not survive as holiday destinations beyond the next decade or so.

Commodification

Commodification of products is increasing, due to the difficulty of differentiating like-products in crowded markets. As the craftsmen of a century ago would have been only too aware, product features can be quickly imitated and so do not provide a lasting source of advantage. The effect of continued commodification in markets is ultimately competition based on price (Aaker & Joachimsthaler, 2000, p. 40):

> Too many brands drift aimlessly and appear to stand for nothing in particular. They always seem to be shouting price, on sale, attached to some deal, or engaging in promiscuous channel expansion – symptoms of a lack of integrity.

An effective brand strategy can provide a means for successful differentiation. After all, in commodity categories 'something' must make a greater difference to a consumer's thinking about the competing products that offer features of a similar quality, and that something is the symbol a brand represents to the consumer (Gardner & Levy, 1955). Keller (2003) pointed to successful branding within a number of commodity categories, where product differentiation is difficult to achieve, such as water (Perrier), beer (Budweiser), cigarettes (Marlboro), soap (Ivory), pineapples (Dole), oatmeal (Quaker), and bananas (Chiquita).

The power of retailers

The power of mega retailers is increasing. Development of their own labels, access to customers, combined with their control of high-profile shelf space can be a significant barrier for small product suppliers. This power of retailers not only applies to fast-moving consumer goods in supermarkets, but equally to the distribution of tourism services through retail travel, both traditional and online.

Sophisticated consumers

Today's consumers are the most sophisticated ever to be faced by marketers. We are experienced, having been exposed to unprecedented levels of media communications, and have access to increasing sources of product information and consumer advice. In so many cases we are spoilt for choice, and we know it.

Brand extensions

Many major brands have capitalised on brand equity by extending their range of offerings across categories and segments. For example, what is a Ford, or a Cadbury or a Nike? Both managing and competing against an extensive brand portfolio hierarchy are now major challenges.

Media cost-effectiveness

Marketers are now faced with escalating media costs, often in tandem with declining advertising budgets. Also, the proliferation of new and niche media is resulting in a relative decline in the effectiveness of traditional advertising. This has led to increased interest in below-the-line promotional opportunities.

Short-term performance orientation

Marketing planning has long been driven by short-term measures of accountability. Such pressures, which may be exerted by shareholders, management and/or economic analysts, place emphasis on tactical initiatives for short-term gain rather than longer-term strategies.

Branding destinations

... we have 'somehow' failed to recognize the significance of the branding function in our efforts to increase awareness of destinations and to create the positive attitudes that are so essential to the final choice of a travel destination (Ritchie & Ritchie, 1998, p. 89).

What exactly is a destination brand? Are they 'collective hallucinations' as suggested by Professor John Urry in the keynote address to the 2003 *Taking Tourism to the Limits* conference at the University of Waikato? When considering definitions of the brand construct, it is important to consider the perspectives of both the organisation and the market. From the market perspective the commonly cited definition provided by Aaker (1991, p. 7) is pertinent to the ensuing discussion on the branding of destinations, which effectively represent 'groups of sellers':

> *A brand is a distinguishing name and/or symbol (such as a logo, trademark, or package design) intended to identify the goods or services of either one seller or a group of sellers, and to differentiate those goods from those of competitors.*

A brand must stand for something, a promise to the consumer, and so is much more than merely symbols presented to the public. It is useful to consider a brand as representing an identity for the producer and an image for the consumer. Aaker (1996) distinguished these separate components of a brand as the brand identity (internal organisation orientation), representing self-image and aspired market image, and the brand image (external market orientation) of the actual image held by consumers. The model in Figure 10.1 highlights these two distinctive components, along with a third overlapping element, which is brand positioning. It is proposed brand positioning that is the interface between brand identity and brand image, over which the DMO has some control. This chapter focuses on the development of a destination brand identity. The components of destination brand image are outlined in Chapter 11, and destination positioning is the focus of Chapter 12.

There is a lack of published research relating to tourism destination branding. This is in spite of general agreement in academia and industry that the concept of branding can be applied to destinations. In fact the topic of destination branding did not appear in the tourism literature until the late 1990s, with the first journal article by Pritchard and Morgan (1998). Gnoth (1998, pp. 758–760) suggested the special track on 'Branding Tourism Destinations' he convened at the 1997 American Marketing Science Conference, represented the first meeting of practitioners and academics on the topic.

Within a decade the first destination branding conference was staged. The initiative of Macau's Instituto De Formacao Turistica (IFT), in conjunction with Perdue University, to convene this first conference on destination

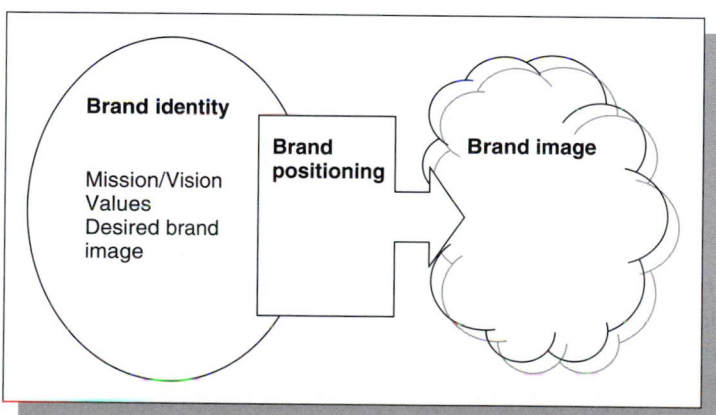

Figure 10.1
Brand identity, brand positioning and brand image

branding, was thus new territory and a test of academic interest in the topic. Ultimately, the decision was justified with around 100 delegates from 22 countries. It is hoped the conference will be staged every two years. At the time of writing the second conference was scheduled for December 2007 (see http://www.ift.edu.mo/conference/).

In the decade since Morgan and Pritchard's (1998) article, there have been relatively few published case studies applying theory to destination branding, particularly at the RTO level. However, this should be tempered by the understanding that in the general marketing and strategy literature and practice, branding has also received much less attention than the product and its functional attributes (Urde, 1999). The application of brand theory to practice is a complex and challenging process, magnified for destinations by the constraints faced by most DMOs, as discussed in Research Snapshot 10.1.

Research snapshot 10.1   Destination branding complexity

Little has been reported in the tourism literature regarding the complexity of destination branding. This paper summarised six issues that make the application of branding theory to destination a complex undertaking:

1. Destinations are far more multidimensional than consumer goods and other types of services. To be effective, positioning theory suggests reaching the minds of busy consumers requires a succinct message focusing on one or a few brand associations. Nowhere is this challenge better highlighted than in the development of a seven word slogan that encapsulates a destination's diverse and often eclectic range of natural resources, built attractions, culture, activities, amenities, and accommodation.
2. The market interests of the diverse group of active stakeholders are heterogenous. Counter to a market orientation, where products are designed to suit market needs, DMOs are forced into targeting a multiplicity of geographic markets to attract a wide range of segments for their range of products, most of which are rigid in what they can be used for. Is one slogan, such as *Idaho – great potatoes*, *tasty destinations*, or *Slovenia – the grown place of Europe*, likely to be meaningful to all market segments?
3. The politics of decision-making can render the best of theory irrelevant. The issues of who decides the brand theme, and how they are held accountable, are critical. At the level of DMO governance and decision-making, politics arises through inequality between tourism organisations. For example, Ritchie and Ritchie (1998) referred to the heavy influence of the Disney Corporation on the *Orlando Magic* destination brand.
4. There is a fine balance to be struck between community consensus and brand theory, since a top-down approach to destination brand implementation is likely to fail. Critically, DMOs lack any direct control over the actual delivery of the brand promise by the local tourism community. Without buy-in from these stakeholders the strategy will likely flail.
5. Brand loyalty, one of the cornerstones of consumer-based brand equity models, can be operationalised to some extent by measuring repeat visitation through a DMO's visitor monitor programme. Staying in touch with previous visitors is a powerful but untapped means of enhancing the destination brand, but DMOs have no access to the hundreds of thousands of visitors' contact details left at accommodation registration desks.

6. Funding is often a continuous problem for DMOs, in both scale and consistency. Even the largest DMO budgets pale in comparison to those of the major corporate brands, with which they compete for discretionary consumer spend. Since DMOs have no direct financial stake in visitor expenditure, they must continually lobby for public and private funding. A successful brand campaign leading to increased yields for local businesses does not often translate into increased revenue for the DMO.

Source: Pike, S. (2005). Tourism destination branding complexity. *Journal of Product and Brand Management*, *14*(4), 258–259.

Consumer-based brand equity

A worthwhile starting point in considering how brand theory might apply to destinations is to consider consumer-based brand equity (CBBE) models (see Aaker, 1991; Keller, 2003). CBBE comprises the following assets: brand awareness, brand associations, brand resonance, and brand loyalty.

Brand awareness

Brand awareness is the foundation of all sales activity. Consider for example the hierarchical AIDA advertising axiom, based on the hierarchy of needs proposed by Lavidge and Steiner (1961), which aims to attract attention, stimulate interest, create desire, and ultimately result in consumer action. Awareness represents the strength of the brand's presence in the mind of the target, with the goal not being to achieve general awareness, but to be remembered for the reasons intended (Aaker, 1996).

Brand associations

The aim should be to increase familiarity with the brand through repeated exposure and strong associations with the product category (Keller, 2003). Brand associations held in the mind about a product aid consumer information processing: 'A brand association is anything "linked" in memory to a brand' (Aaker, 1991, p. 109). What is most critical is that brand associations are strong, favourable, and unique, in that order (Keller, 2003).

Brand resonance

Brand resonance represents a willingness to engage with the destination. This can be viewed in terms of behaviour, such as previous visitation, or attitudinally, such as stated intent to visit in the future.

Brand loyalty

In any CBBE model, the pinnacle is brand loyalty, which is ultimately measured by repeat and referral custom. Given the increasing substitutability of destinations, the key advantages of brand loyalty for destinations include lower marketing costs, increased travel trade leverage, and word-of-mouth referrals. While a number of studies in other fields have identified correlations between customer retention and increased profits (see Aaker, 1996, p. 22), there is a dearth of literature relating to destination loyalty and switching costs (Grabler, 1997a). In an early study of repeat visitation, Gitelson and Crompton (1984) found five factors that contributed to a return to a familiar destination:

- reduced risk of an unsatisfactory experience
- knowledge that they would find their own kind of people there
- emotional or childhood attachment to experience
- opportunities to visit aspects of the destination not previously experienced
- to expose others to a previously satisfying experience.

Critical success factors

In moving towards a structure for destination brand strategy it is useful to consider potential critical success factors. In this regard Keller (2000) identified ten characteristics of the world's strongest brands, which could be used by marketers to identify strengths and weaknesses of a brand and its competitors. Unfortunately no destination brands were included in the analysis. However, Keller's brand report card does warrant consideration by destination marketers, albeit with a caveat that the level of control or influence able to be exerted by DMOs makes implementation problematic:

- **The brand excels at delivering the benefits customers truly desire.** Two implications of this for DMOs are effective marketing research and stimulating the consistency of service delivery in a myriad of service encounters over which the DMO has no control.
- **The brand stays relevant to customers.** This is a key challenge for all destinations, which evolve over time through a lifecycle. As well as staying in tune with changing consumer and travel trends, two other aspects of this are important. The first is the necessary (re)investment in product improvements to maintain and enhance the destination experience. The second is the influence of the development of new attractions and facilities by entrepreneurs, which may or may not fit the original character of the destination brand. For example, SnowWorld at Australia's Surfer's Paradise always seemed incongruent with the image of a subtropical beach resort, and yet did fit the Gold Coast's former *Coast with the most* brand theme that implied the benefit of lots to see and do.
- **The pricing strategy is based on consumers' perceptions of value.** While DMOs usually have no control over product pricing, it is possible for the DMO to institute measures to monitor perceptions of value

held by customers and non-customers in target markets. Clearly this is an important issue for DMOs, given the importance placed on value for money as an important destination attribute by travellers (see for example Baloglu & Mangaloglu, 2001).

- **The brand is properly positioned in the market by offering a distinctive value proposition.** This is challenging for DMOs given the multi-attributed nature of a destination, and the sheer number of competing places with similar offerings crowding the market place.

- **The brand is consistent.** DMOs should ensure that the delivery of all communications consistently reflects the brand's values. Politics can be a problem for destinations in this regard. For example, in the case of Valencia in Spain the public-funded DMO is required to issue new advertising contracts every year (Pritchard & Morgan, 1998, 2002). In the state of Louisiana, the Department of Culture, Recreation and Tourism is legislated to review its advertising agency account every three years (Slater, 2002). Prior to establishing a PPP-based Florida STO in 1996, any change in the politician responsible for the tourism portfolio resulted in a change of marketing strategy and slogan (see Bush, 2004). At another level is the politics of intermediaries such as airlines, travel agents and wholesalers. Vial (1997, in Morgan & Pritchard, 1998) cited the example of the *Feast for the senses* brand developed by Publicis for the Morocco Tourist Board. This was an attempt to develop an umbrella brand for use in all markets. Previously, different campaigns had been used in different markets, which had resulted in a confused image. The proposed campaign did gain the support of the tourism industry in Morocco. However, it was derailed by resistance from travel agents and tour wholesalers who viewed the campaign as promoting cultural tourism when they were in the business of catering to the need for sun and sea packages.

- **The brand portfolio and hierarchy make sense.** Hopper (2002) reported how the plethora of brands used by tourism businesses to promote London had led to a dilution of the brand designed by the London Tourist Board. In tourism there may be up to six or more levels in the destination brand family tree, as shown in Table 10.2, ranging from the country brand to local tourism businesses. The issue becomes complex

Table 10.2 Destination brand family tree

Level	Entity
1	Country brand
2	Country tourism brand
3	State tourism brands
4	Regional/macro regional brands
5	Local community brands
6	Individual tourism business brands

when considering that a major product supplier, such as Stonehenge in the south of England, Legoland in California, Sea World on Australia's Gold Coast, and Disneyland Resort Paris, might have different destination umbrella brands at the LTA, RTO, STO, and NTO levels with which they work with. A destination may be viewed as the umbrella brand, with individual products as sub-brands. Flagestad and Hope (2001) suggested that an umbrella brand for Scandinavian tourism suppliers could prove an efficient means of addressing image problems in non-Nordic markets. Such an umbrella brand can be used to endorse the credibility of the tourism sub-brands. The Australian Tourism Commission has assisted STOs such as the Western Australia Tourism Commission with brand development. Another example is the proactive role played by Tourism Queensland in developing regional brands within the state. The incentive for the RTOs is funding by Tourism Queensland to a level that can exceed the contributions of local shire councils. The concept of destination umbrella branding is related to the consumer goods strategy of applying the name of a brand to a broad range of products. The purpose is to spread positive elements of a brand's value over multiple products, through transfer phenomena such as semantic generalisation (see, for example, Mazanec & Schweiger, 1981). Potentially, the marketing efforts of each product within the brand hierarchy can flow across to other partners.

- **The brand makes use of, and coordinates, a full repertoire of marketing activities.** If it is accepted that the focus of marketing activity is to enhance consumer-based brand equity; this is a critical issue for DMOs, and one over which the organisation exerts control.
- **The brand's managers understand what the brand means to consumers.** This emphasises the importance of establishing and monitoring a focused brand positioning strategy for the destination, based on sound research to stimulate congruence between the brand identity and the brand image.
- **The brand is given proper support, and that support is sustained over the long run.** Senior management must genuinely share the belief that brand building results in a profitable competitive advantage (Aaker & Joachimsthaler, 2000). More case studies examining the long-term effectiveness of destination brands are required, particularly in terms of monitoring the long-term nature of the investment.
- **The organisation monitors the sources of brand equity.** Keller (2000) used the example of a brand audit undertaken by Disney during the 1980s, to highlight how such sources could be diluted in value. The audit found that the Disney characters, which were the main source of brand equity, were overexposed in the market through a myriad of product endorsements and licensing agreements. The serious impact of this commercialism resulted in strong negative perceptions of the brand by consumers. The Disney example highlights the value of developing a system of brand-equity management. This begins with a brand charter, detailing the philosophy of the brand and the value of branding, details of brand audits, tracking and research, and guidelines for strategies, tactics, and treatment of the brand's visual components. Within this system,

there must be effective communication between key stakeholders and marketing decision-makers.

Destination branding case studies

Case studies similar to Keller's (2000) that analyse leading destination brands to identify CSFs for DMOs will be invaluable. However, as has been stated, the number of published destination brand case studies have only emerged recently, and there a need for more case-study-based research into the long-term effectiveness of destination brand management. Relative to the number of papers published on destination image, there have been few reporting destination branding case studies. Given the recent emergence of the destination branding literature it is not surprising that the focus of cases published to date has been on brand development. With the exception of Curtis' (2001) analysis of Brand Oregon, there has been a lack of case studies examining the long-term management and effectiveness of destination brands. The case studies published to date do however provide valuable insights into the practical challenges of applying brand theory to destination brand development, particularly since most have been written by practitioners involved in the brand campaigns. Appendix 10.1 briefly summarises the contribution of six such cases:

- Brand Oregon (Curtis, 2001)
- Ohio's identity crisis (May, 2001)
- Wales' natural revival (Pride, 2002)
- Brand Western Australia (Crockett & Wood, 1999)
- War-torn central and eastern Europe (Hall, 1999)
- New Zealand's global niche (Morgan et al, 2002).

Destination brand identity development

As presented in Figure 10.1, three interrelated components of the destination brand construct are brand identity, brand position, and brand image. Brand identity has an internal focus on issues such as self-image and a vision for motivating stakeholders, while brand image represents the actual image held in the market. Brand positioning is the potential interface between the two. Destination brand identity development essentially involves four stages: (1) the appointment of a brand champion, (2) identification of the brand community, (3) a destination audit, and (4) production of a brand charter.

Brand champion

You create passion for brands first of all by example. It depends on the attitude of top management. If you are totally convinced, you become a missionary salesperson, so to speak, within the company.

This comment from a former head of marketing for Nestlé was cited by Urde (1999, p. 124), whose analysis of brand-oriented companies identified a characteristic passion for the brand. The appointment of a brand manager is an important precursor to the destination brand development. As evidenced in the case of Wales in Appendix 10.1 (see Pride, 2002), a lack of leadership can inhibit the brand's development, particularly in the initial phase. Such a role will vary depending on the size of the DMO, but will nevertheless be driven by the same principles. Branding is a complex and challenging process, and leadership, responsibility, and accountability is required. At the NTO level there have been a growing number of brand manager appointments made since the mid-1990s, such as by the Scottish Tourist Board and British Tourist Authority for example, reported by Pritchard and Morgan (1998). Clearly, the case studies written by those intimately involved with destination brand development show a passion for the cause. Such brand managers must in effect be brand champions, since 'many practitioners currently responsible for marketing destinations also regard the branding process with suspicion' (Pride, 2002, p. 110).

If the bottom-up philosophy to brand development is to be adopted it is doubtful an outsider, such as a brand consultant, will be successful in championing the process over the longer term. I am aware of the problems encountered by one RTO which delegated too much responsibility, not to mention finance, to a high-profile and articulate brand consultant, who it turned out was also commissioned by at least two competing destinations. Not surprisingly there was a strong similarity in the three destinations' brand themes. The brand champion must be seen to be part of the community. In this regard, there is in some cases a fine line walked by Brisbane-based Tourism Queensland staff who play a key role in brand development for many of the state's RTOs.

Brand community

How can we influence the trade and local authorities to support the WTB brand and the values that have been developed? (Wales Tourism Board Policy Framework Review – Competitiveness and Quality. Accessed at http://capture.wtb.lon.world.net/ 22/10/03.)

The effective development and nurturing of the destination brand will depend on the identification of a brand community. Ultimately, the destination brand community will be as important a brand communications medium as any advertising campaign, since it is they who must deliver the brand promise. Therefore it is critical that the brand identity encapsulates the values of the community, the essence of the visitor experience, as well as provide a vision to guide and motivate active stakeholders.

Any destination brand must represent local residents' sense of place... this is their home. The Oregon case in Appendix 10.1 (see Curtis, 2001) demonstrated the importance of avoiding a top-down approach by involving the local tourism industry. Research in Singapore (Henderson, 2000) suggested that the views of the host community must be taken into account (see Research Snapshot 10.2), while the Morocco experience (Vial, 1997, in Morgan & Pritchard, 1998) demonstrated the influence of travel intermediaries. There may also be a view within the community that branding of the place is not appropriate, and this needs to be ascertained. It has been asked whether selling a city to tourists is a Faustian bargain (Holcolmb, 1999, p. 69):

> *Packaging and promoting the city to tourists can destroy its soul. The city is commodified, its form and spirit remade to conform to market demand, not residents' dreams. The local state and business elites collude to remake a city in which their special interests are paramount; meanwhile, resources are diverted away from needy neighbourhoods and social services.*

This view is not often reported in the literature, perhaps due to the lack of research into the host community's views on branding 'their place'. Brand consultant Wally Olins (Olins, 2002) commented on the 'visceral animosity' of some people towards the concept of a nation as a brand. As an example Olins cited Girard's (1999, p. 241) view of the inappropriateness of a brand for France:

> *In France the idea of re-branding the country would be widely unacceptable because the popular feeling is that France is something that has a nature and a substance other than that of a corporation ... A country carries specific dignity unlike a marketed product ... In France it is unimaginable for Chirac to attempt to re-brand.*

Also important are members of the wider business community, who may not view tourism as being their core business, but who may nevertheless be indirectly involved in providing goods or services. For example, these include such diverse groups as local produce suppliers, architects, real estate agents, hairdressers, and employment agencies. A destination brand community consists therefore not only of local tourism providers but also the host population, local business community, and key travel distribution intermediaries. After all, tourism, as Gnoth (1998) reminded us, is user-defined, and the product is not controlled by any one channel power structure.

Research snapshot 10.2   The host community

Research into the perceptions of *New Asia – Singapore* by Henderson (2000), highlighted the real world challenges involved in gaining acceptance of the brand. While the development of the brand, which was launched in 1996, has been well documented (see, for example, STPB, 1996), Henderson argued that the actual impact of the branding efforts was uncertain. A small exploratory survey of local residents and English-speaking visitors revealed gaps between actual perceptions (brand image) and the intended brand values (brand identity). Concerns about place commodification were also evident. Sample limitations aside, Henderson's study insightfully highlighted the importance of consultation with the host community to ensure that what is being communicated in brand strategies is both realistic and appropriate (p. 215):

When residents are called on to live the values of the brand in pursuit of tourism goals, it would seem that marketers are in danger of assuming too much influence and a sense of balance needs to be restored. Societies cannot be engineered or places manufactured for tourist consumption without a loss of authenticity which is ultimately recognised by the visitor who will move on to seek it elsewhere.

Source: Henderson, J.C. (2000). Selling places – the new Asia Singapore brand. In Robinson, M., Evans, N., Long, P., Sharpley, R. & Swarbrooke, J. (eds), ***Management, Marketing and the Political Economy of Travel and Tourism***. Sunderland: Centre for Travel & Tourism, pp. 207–218.

A strong brand can be a unifying force for increased cooperation by all stakeholders, as observed by Curtis (2001) in the case of Oregon. Likewise, Hawes et al. (1991) found a number of USA STOs that employed a state-wide slogan as a unification mechanism. The formation of a project group that is representative of the brand community can act as a conduit between the DMO and the community, help identify stakeholder groups warranting involvement in qualitative discussions on place meaning, assist the brand manager with the development of recommendations for the DMO board, and help develop means of briefing the community on the purpose and role of the brand. Admittedly, the selection of such a representative group will always be problematic, in terms of achieving a political balance and a manageable size.

The primary role of a working group will be to develop the means for investigating (1) the host community's values and sense of place, (2) the tourism community's view of the essence of the visitor experience, and (3) the destination's tourism resources. The purpose of this stage is to identify the core values of the destination, to work towards the development of a destination brand identity.

Brand charter

It has been suggested in the chapter that the brand should be the foundation for all marketing planning. Indeed, the idea of thinking about the destination as a brand might represent a new way of thinking to many stakeholders. A brand charter can serve to motivate, remind, and guide stakeholders. Like any formal planning document, the key to readability and application is succinctness. Essential elements include, but are not limited to: a brand mission, vision, brand identity/essence statement, brand values, and guidelines for implementation and auditing. The brand mission summarises the reason for the brand's existence. For example, the following statement of Tourism Australia leaves the reader with no doubts about the importance of the brand to the organisation:

> *Brand Australia is the essence of all ATC activities. It guides the tone, design, and imagery used in all ATC communications to consumers, the travel trade and tourism industry. It forms the basis of all television, cinema, print, and online advertising as well as PR, direct mail, travel guides, internet, and trade marketing activities (ATC, 2003).*

Urde (1999, p. 126) suggested a brand vision is also required to answer the following questions: What do we want to achieve with our brand? How will the organisation realise this vision? The brand essence statement is the articulation of the brand identity. This has also been described as a brand mantra by Keller (2003), who suggested a three- to five-word statement that clearly defines the focus and boundary of the brand category, such as authentic athletic performance (Nike) and fun family entertainment (Disney). Aaker and Joachimsthaler (2000) suggested that a brand identity will usually have two to four dimensions, as well as a focused brand essence statement. They offered the example of Virgin's core identity dimensions being service quality, innovation, fun and entertainment, and value for money, while the brand essence statement is iconoclasm. The purpose of the brand essence statement and core values is to guide and motivate those within the organisation, and will not necessarily be explicit in all promotional communications. In the case of Rotorua, New Zealand, (Tourism Rotorua, 1996, p. 2) the purpose of the brand identity was fourfold:

- to reflect reality by making a compelling and believable statement about the unique qualities of the district
- to encompass all aspects of the destination by developing a theme to fit with all community and commercial applications
- to be meaningful and motivational by avoiding empty clichés and creating an idea to inspire both interest and action
- to have lasting value by remaining relevant to the aspirations of the destination for many years to come.

Examples of destination brand identities and core values from a selection of NTOs, STOs and RTOs are shown in Table 10.3.

At the risk of appearing bureaucratic, an important document for DMOs responsible for coordinating the efforts of a multiplicity of stakeholders is a brand policy manual that provides guidelines for use of symbols by the local tourism industry and intermediaries. The purpose is to ensure a consistency in application. While guidelines can be distributed in brochure form, a more cost-effective approach is the internet, such as in the case of Fraser Coast, Australia (http://tq.com.au/destinations/fraser-coast/marketing/creative-toolbox/creative-toolbox_home.cfm).

Table 10.3 Destination brand core values

Destination	Brand identity	Core brand values
Wales (Pride, 2002)	In Wales you will find a passion for life – Hwyl	Lyrical, sincere, confident, inviting, down to earth, warm
Australia (ATC, 1997, in Morgan, 2000)	Brand Australia	Youthful, energetic, optimistic, stylish, unpretentious, genuine, open, fun
New Zealand (Morgan, Pritchard & Piggott, 2002)	New Pacific freedom	Contemporary and sophisticated, innovative and creative, spirited and free
Western Australia (Crockett & Wood, 1999)	Brand Western Australia	Fresh, natural, free, spirited
Rotorua (Tourism Rotorua, 1996)	Feel the spirit Manaakitanga	Cultural diversity, stunning natural environment, awe-inspiring earth forces, sense of adventure, people, progressive community

Key points

1. The role and importance of branding

It has been suggested that the future of marketing will be a battle of the brands, and that in tourism, destinations are emerging as the world's biggest brands. The concept of branding consumer goods has attracted research interest in the marketing literature since the 1950s. In the time since, a rich resource of information has been developed to guide product marketers. However, in the tourism literature, the issue of branding destinations was not reported until the late-1990s. While interest in the field is increasing, there remains a dearth of published information to guide destination marketers. This represents a significant gap in the literature given the acknowledged importance of brands in competitive markets and the emergence of destinations as the tourism industry's biggest brands. While many aspects of brand theory have applications for DMOs, the process of branding destinations is a more complex undertaking than that for most consumer goods and services.

2. Brand identity

The purpose of a brand is to establish a distinctive and memorable identity in the marketplace that represents a source of value for the consumer. For DMOs, the value of strong consumer-based brand equity lies in the opportunity to minimise destination switching through a differentiated value proposition and increased loyalty. The fundamental challenge for DMOs is to somehow develop a brand identity that encapsulates the essence or spirit of a multi-attributed destination representative of a group of sellers as well as a host community. Such a brand identity should serve as a guiding focus for the marketing activities of the DMO and stakeholders.

3. Consumer-based brand equity

Little has been reported on the effectiveness of destination brand campaigns. A useful hierarchy for tracking effectiveness is consumer-based brand equity (CBBE). CBBE is operationalised by measuring brand awareness, associations, resonance, and loyalty.

Review questions

- To what extent does your destination's branding slogan represent your own sense of place?
- To what extent does your destination's branding slogan capture the main attractions?

Appendix 10.1   Destination branding case studies

Case 1   Brand Oregon

Oregon. Things look different here. In conjunction with the world-famous advertising agency, Wieden + Kennedy, the Oregon Tourism Commission has worked for 15 years to differentiate Oregon's travel product from its neighbours and attract visitors with this creative tagline that supports what the commission calls 'Brand Oregon' (Oregon Tourism Commission 2003–2005 Strategic Marketing Plan).

One of the most cited destination branding cases has been Curtis' (2001) candid evaluation of the evolution of Brand Oregon. Curtis wrote from the perspective of a senior research executive with the Oregon Tourism Commission (OTC). The paper provided a balanced discussion on the strengths and weaknesses of the 'Oregon – things look different here' brand campaign during the 1980s and 1990s. Impetus for the brand's development was an ailing state economy, and the approach of the campaign was to develop an umbrella brand for both tourism and economic development. Curtis observed that this proved a difficult fit and that the strength of the tourism/economic development connection fluctuated over time.

To achieve brand consistency, the tourism component of the strategy required all RTOs that received state funding to use the OTC's advertising agency. While the rationale for this approach was to achieve a consistency of promotional material, ultimately the top-down approach met resistance from the regions. However, the initiative did result in an increased awareness of the potential for cooperative marketing efforts.

Initially, the brand campaign resulted in a dramatic increase in the level of visitor enquiries, which, combined with a number of marketing awards, were regarded as positive performance indicators. More comprehensive measures were later developed to measure consumer perceptions, which ultimately are a more effective indicator of a brand's success than award ceremonies. The case provided a brief but insightful glimpse at the challenges involved in the development, implementation, and management of a state destination brand over time. The paper concluded with a summary of four key lessons learned. First, avoid a top-down approach of imposing a branding system on tourism business. Second, build on the destination's strengths and integrate newer images. Third, continually evaluate the effectiveness of the brand. Fourth, develop a long-term commitment to the strategy. Regarding the final point, at the time of writing the brand theme was still in use by the OTC, with the organisation calling for more support by other state agencies in its *2003–2005 Strategic Marketing Plan*:

Much more could be accomplished with a cohesive branding effort being adopted by all state agencies involved in promoting Oregon and state products (www.traveloregon.com/OTC.cfm, 9/10/03).

Case 2   Ohio's identity crisis

At the 2001 TTRA conference, May (2001) presented the process used to develop a new tourism brand for the state of Ohio. Previously the Ohio Division of Travel and Tourism had been successfully leveraging the advertising budget by using cooperative campaigns with industry partners. However, the partners were dominating the messages, and as a result Ohio suffered from a lack of a distinctive image in the market. As a tourism destination, Ohio had an identity crisis. The STO recognised the potential benefits of effective branding, and so a commitment was made to develop a new tourism brand that would feature in all communications.

The new brand development involved two initial research phases. Stage 1 used open-ended questions in interviews with 375 callers to the STO's free consumer enquiry line 1-800Buckeye, as well as a series of focus groups in three out-of-state markets. A key question posed in the telephone interviews was: 'How would you describe Ohio to someone who has never been here before?' The four most common responses were: 'variety of things to see/do', 'beautiful country, scenery and natural places', 'theme parks', and 'friendly people'. The purpose of the focus groups was to identify positive and negative perceptions of the state. The three key positive perceptions identified were 'amusement parks', 'a place for children', and 'shopping', while two key negative perceptions were 'rustbelt' and 'congested'. The focus groups also suggested a lack of awareness of major destination features, such as: nature, history, scenery, lots to see/do, and culture.

The second research stage involved a structured questionnaire containing a battery of 75 image attributes. This was distributed to 3800 consumers in different markets. The results identified the 'hot button' attributes desired in a holiday destination by the target audience. For these attributes, survey participants rated their perceptions of Ohio and key competitors, which were: Michigan, Pennsylvania, Indiana, Illinois, Kentucky, and West Virginia. This competitive analysis identified Ohio's key strengths and weaknesses, which are listed in the Table below:

Ohio's strengths	Ohio's weaknesses
Affordable	Scenery
Theme parks	Nature
Children enjoy	History
Close distance	

From the results, the STO identified the core challenge as being the creation of an emotive message that would overcome the weaknesses and change perceptions. A number of brand slogans, along with associated music and imagery, were developed and tested in key markets. These included:

- Ohio...Oh!
- Ohio...Where America comes to play

- Ohio, the thrill of it all
- Ohio…Where the fun never sets
- Ohio Oh WOW
- Ohio, Let Yourself Go!

The selected brand slogan, 'Ohio – so much to discover', was introduced and tested in 2000, with full implementation during 2001. The Ohio Division of Travel and Tourism claims the most frequently called state tourism free-phone hotline in the country. The call system responds to approximately 1.5 million inquiries annually (http://www.odod.state.oh.us/Travel.htm, 13/11/03). The presentation by Colleen May (May, 2001), Research Manager for the Ohio Division of Travel and Tourism, provided TTRA conference delegates with an insider's perspective of the steps involved in destination branding, and as such represented a much-needed interaction between a tourism practitioner and tourism academics.

Case 3   Wales' natural revival

> For many years that venerable and respected British oracle of information and explanation, the Encyclopaedia Britannica, essentially denied Wales' existence. Under the entry for Wales it simply stated 'for Wales please see England' (Pride, 2002, p. 109).

Another insightful practitioner perspective on destination branding was provided by Pride (2002), Director of Marketing for the Wales Tourist Board (WTB). Pride discussed the problems associated with a lack of national identity for a country that has historically been seen by the world as a suffix to England. For example, the nation has often been referred to as 'and Wales'. During the 1990s, research undertaken by the WTB and other organisations was consistently pointing to negative perceptions as a primary hindrance to the country's economic development. Tourism was one of a number of export industries affected by either negative or distorted images. Pride described the process and challenges of developing a brand strategy aimed at turning Wales' 'identity deficit' into an 'identity premium'.

Travellers from Wales' traditional markets of England's northern industrial cities had become more experienced and sophisticated in their holiday needs and expectations. They had also been increasingly drawn away to Europe's cheap sunshine destinations. These trends have forced significant structural changes in the Welsh tourism industry. Pride reported that while the tourism industry had responded with necessary high-quality accommodation and recreation facilities, the negative image remained a significant barrier to growth:

> We recognized that if we going to enhance Wales' reputation as a leisure destination, we needed a single-minded, consistent, integrated, and innovative communication strategy (Pride, 2002, p. 112).

A framework was designed to subsume a new tourism destination brand development and communication strategy under the umbrella of a new nation brand. Pride reported that the development of the country brand was the most difficult part of the entire process, primarily due to a lack of government leadership and responsibility. The intent for the tourism brand was to develop one key positioning theme, which could be adapted to suit individual markets. This was complicated by the results of extensive research by the WTB that identified significant differences in both the perceptions of Wales and the holiday needs of international and domestic travellers. Ultimately, 'natural revival' was selected as the brand positioning, based on the following qualities: unspoiled, down-to-earth, traditional values, back in time, genuine, beautiful, physical, spiritual, and hidden on England's doorstep.

A summary of the brand's implementation in the domestic and international markets, key results, and an impressive list of marketing awards are included in the paper. Pride concluded with a candid acknowledgement that the brand was still in its infancy and discussed future challenges, central to which was the real need to ensure that the brand promise is actually delivered at the destination. The case provided a rare insight into a DMO's approach to one of the core questions of this text, that is, is one position for a multi-attributed destination suitable for all markets?

Case 4   Brand Western Australia

The Western Australian Tourism Commission's (WATC) approach to branding the state was reported by the STO's CEO and brand manager (see Crockett & Wood, 1999). The authors advised the development of a new brand strategy in the 1990s which not only resulted in a successful global repositioning but also an 'entire organisational shift' (p. 276). Western Australia's landmass represents one-third of the Australian continent, a rich tourism resource with significant variations in geography and climate between different regions. In the early 1990s, WATC research found that the state lacked a meaningful identity, particularly in international travel markets. Crockett and Wood reported the development of Brand Western Australia (Brand WA), which would drive all marketing activities. The new brand was launched in 1996 and went beyond being a market repositioning campaign:

> Brand WA provided the catalyst for an entire organisational restructure within the WATC. This reflects a new corporate culture, new direction, increased accountability, performance measurement, partnerships with industry, and a clear customer focus (Crockett & Wood, 1999, p. 278).

The budget for developing and implementing an international brand strategy was limited to AUD$8.8 million over five years. The process began with the formation of a representative 'brand strategy group', to oversee the project. Significantly, Brand WA was to be a state brand, rather than only a tourism brand. Furthermore, the brand would attempt to maximise synergies with the ATC's Brand Australia. ATC representatives were therefore involved in the development of Brand WA. Other tourism partnerships established during the development phase extended to the formation of ten regional tourism organisations within the state.

The market research programme focused on consultation with end-users of the brand, as well as qualitative studies in domestic and international markets. The key questions raised were (p. 280):

- What are the attributes tourists rank as high motivators for their travel?
- What are the consumers' perceptions of Western Australia and Perth as a holiday destination?
- What do travellers imagine when they think of Western Australia and Perth?
- What are the state's major strengths and weaknesses as a holiday destination in the eyes of consumers?

While the research revealed positive perceptions of nature-based attractions, the lack of a distinctive image was also apparent. Due to limited financial resources available to address the lack of identity on a global scale, a 'Market Potential Assessment Formula' was then developed to prioritise target markets. The formula was based on the criteria of access, growth rate, market share, and synergy with ATC activity. Crockett and Wood reported the formula was used twice a year to monitor market shifts.

The market research enabled the development of a brand identity and a five-year strategy for increasing market exposure, industry partnerships, and developing new infrastructure and tourism products. The paper described many elements of the marketing mix, media campaign, regional brand extensions, and performance measures. For example, it was estimated that an initial six-week campaign in the UK resulted in 5886 visitors who spent AUD$7.3 million within the state.

Case 5   War-torn Central and Eastern Europe

Hall (1999) provided a rare analysis of the branding opportunities and challenges faced by what are predominantly fledgling destinations in post-communist Central and Eastern Europe (CEE). Tourism earnings in the region had lagged behind the rest of Europe for a number of reasons, including a short length of stay and low spending tourists from other CEE countries. Destination branding by CEE countries was constrained by lack of finance, lack of international marketing experience, and public pressure for short-term results. To illustrate the destination branding challenges faced in the region, Hall focused on Slovenia and Croatia. As new states, which were part of the former Yugoslavia, both have needed to establish national identities untainted by the conflict in the Balkans. For example, despite a long history of tourism promotion as part of Yugoslavia, post-war Slovenia faced the challenge of re-attracting previously established markets. Although Slovenia gained independence in 1991, an NTO was not established until 1996. The Slovenia Tourism Board's brand strategy was to position the destination as a western civilised country with contiguity to Austria and Italy, and away from the Balkan association. However, the destination found it difficult to achieve the numbers of visitor arrivals generated when part of the pre-war Yugoslavia federation. Hall suggested that the promotional material used to support the brand did not adequately and clearly convey a unique position for the country.

Containing most of the former Yugoslavia's coastline, Croatia was a major benefactor of tourism in the region. Following the war years it was important therefore for Croatia to establish a national tourism brand strategy that would 'convey a distinct image to clearly differentiate the country from its neighbours and reassure former markets that quality and value had been restored' (Hall, 1999, p. 234). However, Hall observed that initial branding attempts failed to differentiate the destination from others in the region. The cases demonstrate the challenges faced by war-torn countries attempting re-branding away from the former negative associations of communism and conflict. Hall concluded destination branding was poorly developed in CEE countries, and called for a more collaborative approach between private and public sectors. Although Hall found little evidence of coordination between local, regional, and national tourism interests, he admitted the issue was politically complicated (p. 235):

> This is understandable given that over much of the region there has been a desire to reduce any form of centralised planning as a reaction to the previous half-century of state socialist impositions.

The development of national brands in the 're-imaging' of former Yugoslavia has also since been discussed by Hall (2002) and Martinovic (2002).

Case 6 New Zealand's global niche

> Global competition in the world of destination marketing has never been more intense. September 11, 2001 focused the spotlight on the travel and tourism industry around the world with troubled airlines and nervous passengers creating unprecedented uncertainty ... In such a competitive environment, it is more vital than ever that those marketing a destination can make their voice heard. The 100% Pure New Zealand global marketing campaign was instigated in 1999, with the purpose of achieving this cut-through (Tourism New Zealand, 2003 – www.tourisminfo.co.nz, 22/10/03).

Morgan, Pritchard and Piggott (2002) promote a critical exploration of Tourism New Zealand's (TNZ) development of the 100% Pure New Zealand as a powerful niche travel brand. With one of the authors acknowledged as a TNZ staff member responsible for promoting the brand internationally, the case represents a much-needed destination practitioner/academic collaboration. Launched in 1999, '100 per cent Pure New Zealand' was the country's first global tourism brand. Prior to this, different campaigns had been used in different markets. New Zealand is a small, geographically disadvantaged player in the international travel market, with a relatively small NTO budget. TNZ recognised that to be more competitive on the international stage, particularly against larger neighbour Australia, required the development of a single niche brand across all markets. The vision was to position New Zealand as the world's ultimate travel destination, with a key output being to double international tourism receipts by 2005.

The focus of Morgan, Pritchard and Piggott's paper is the UK phase of the brand research and positioning implementation. Within New Zealand, significant research was undertaken in the development of the brand strategy, including surveys of local businesses, regional economists, and previous visitors. The UK research stage, which was one of a number of overseas market analyses, involved a series of 28 in-depth interviews and four focus groups. These were used primarily to identify long-haul travel motivations/needs/barriers, perceptions of New Zealand, and effective communication propositions. The paper provided a summary of UK traveller types and their needs and motivations. New Zealand was seen to appeal to a number of distinctive segments, particularly those motivated to travel for reasons of special interest or 'real travel', which was described as 'serious, adventure travel and a trip of a lifetime' (Morgan, Pritchard & Piggott, 2002, p. 344). The key perceptions held of New Zealand were: 'sense of achievement and prestige in visiting', 'adventure', 'landscape of contrasts', 'good quality wine reputation', 'friendly and welcoming', 'space and freedom', 'nature/outdoors', and 'fresh pure air'. However, major barriers to travel included: long travel distance and costs, concern that New Zealand only offered an outdoor experience, the weather, lack of things to do, and the country's conservative and serious image (p. 345):

> The branding consultants' research concluded that the outside world sees New Zealand as being full of green hills, sheep and aggressive Maori warriors, and that it is somewhat boring.

The mixed findings motivated TNZ to develop a position that focused on 'energising the traveller'. The process resulted in the brand being 'New Zealand', the brand essence 'landscape', the positioning 'New Pacific Freedom', and the global campaign slogan '100 per cent Pure New Zealand'.

During the first year the global brand campaign attracted financial support from 102 industry partners in 13 countries. This was seen as a critical success factor for an NTO with limited funding. The authors might also have added that TNZ's limited international advertising budget is also in New Zealand dollars, which is significantly discounted to all major currencies. The contribution of this case for destination marketers is the emphasis on the importance of extensive research, the need for a collaborative approach to implementation, the value of public relations and the WWW as brand promotion vehicles, and the need for a long-term commitment to the brand. In New Zealand's case the most significant long-term challenge lay in combining the brand essence 'landscape' with a globally unique point of difference.

CHAPTER 11

Destination image

Sometimes the notions people have about a brand do not even seem very sensible or relevant to those who know what the product is 'really' like. But they all contribute to the customer's deciding whether or not the brand is the one for me.

Gardner & Levy (1955, p. 35)

Aims

The aims of this chapter are to enhance understanding of:

- the role of image in destination marketing ✓
- consumer decision sets ✓
- the importance of travel context in destination image ✓ analysis.

Perspective

The images held by consumers play a significant role in travel purchase decisions, and so an understanding of the images held of the destination by consumers is important. The previous chapter introduced the concepts of brand identity, brand positioning, and brand image as distinctive components of the brand construct. These are graphically presented again Figure 11.1. Brand identity represents the values and essence of the destination community, is the self-image aspired to in the marketplace, and has an internal focus on motivating and guiding stakeholders. This chapter discusses the image component of destination branding. This represents the actual image held by consumers, which might be quite different to that intended in the brand identity. Major objectives of any marketing strategy will usually be to either create a new image, or to reinforce positive images already established in the minds of the target audience. The topic of destination image has arguably been the most prevalent in the tourism literature.

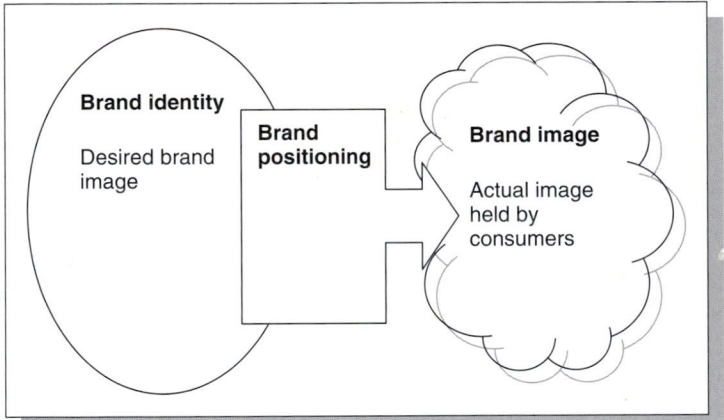

Figure 11.1
Brand identity, brand positioning and brand image

The role of image in destination marketing

At the 2000 Tourism and Travel Research Association conference in Hollywood, John Hunt used the example of three peasants breaking-in a new field, to describe the 1970s destination image research undertaken by himself, Edward Mayo and Clare Gunn. In the 30 years since their pioneering work, destination image has been one of the most prevalent topics in the tourism literature. One of my papers, for example, categorised 142 destination image studies published in the literature between 1973 and 2000 (see Pike, 2002).

Chon's (1990) review of 23 of the most frequently cited destination image studies found that the most popular themes were the role and influence of destination image in buyer behaviour and satisfaction. Indeed Hunt's (1975) view, that images held by potential travellers are so important in the destination selection process that they can affect the viability of the destination, has become axiomatic. After all, most tourism products are services rather than physical goods, and can often only compete via images. Key implications of this for destination marketers are the issues of intangibility and risk, substitutability, heterogeneity, inseparability, and perishability.

Intangibility and risk

Prior to purchase, a guitar may be played in the store, shoes can be fitted, and a car taken for a test drive. Products are tangible things that can generally be inspected, touched, trailed, and exchanged. All of our senses are available to us as we shop for products at the mall. However, the only physical evidence of a holiday destination may be in brochures, web pages, holiday snapshots, or in the media. Thus, expectations of the holiday are realisable only after purchase and actual travel (Goodall et al., 1988). It follows then that a consequence of intangibility is an increased risk in the travel purchase decision. Several types of risk may be of concern to travellers and suppliers:

- **Performance risk** Will the service perform as expected? Tourism destination performance risks include a diverse range of factors, such as poor weather, labour strikes, substandard service encounters, civil unrest, grumpy travellers, theft and other crimes, volcanic eruptions and earthquakes, fluctuating exchange rates, traffic delays, airport congestion, and terrorism. Since satisfaction with a destination will result from a series of service interactions, over which the DMO has no control, the potential for dissatisfaction is considerable.
- **Social risk** To what extent will the travel experience enhance well-being or the self-concept? Is there potential for embarrassment? There may also be a risk of stress involved when travelling in unfamiliar environments. Mansfield (1992) referred to the social stress of tourism, when motivated to travel by membership of a social reference group. For example, social risk may occur when joining a coach tour of strangers, since holidays represent interplay between merging into a group and affirming individuality (Mollo-Bouvier, 1990).
- **Physical risk** Is there potential for harm? Travellers not only assess the risk of harm at a destination, but will also consider the transport facilities and transit environments en route (see, for example, Page et al., 1994; Page & Wilks, 2004).
- **Financial risk** Does the financial investment represent value? The annual holiday is often regarded as a high involvement decision with significant household expenditure (Driscoll et al., 1994). The higher the level of involvement in the decision, the higher the perceived risk will likely be.

201

Inseparability and variability

Customers are actively involved in the delivery of a service, since production and consumption occur simultaneously. Increasingly, travellers have been seeking greater involvement in tourism products as participants rather than as passive observers (Crouch, 2000). Also, perceptions of the same destination experience may be quite different among different travellers, leading to different perceptions of value.

Perishability

Destination services are perishable, since they cannot be stored for sale later during high-demand periods. Individual businesses attempt to match capacity with projected levels of demand though measures such as yield management and sales promotions. For DMOs, this presents challenges in forecasting the impacts of seasonality, periodicity, special events, and exogenous events.

Substitutability

As has been suggested, destinations are close substitutes for others in crowded markets, since travellers have available to them a myriad of destinations that will satisfy their needs. Even taking into account price incentives, what influences a traveller to select a destination they have not previously visited? In such cases images can provide a pre-taste. Influencing these images by DMOs requires insights into the image formation process.

Image formation

While it is agreed that destination images can play an important role in travel decisions, defining destination image and understanding image formation are not so clear. A number of authors have been critical of attempts to conceptualise the construct. Certainly the range of definitions used in the tourism literature has been so great that image is becoming marketing jargon (Cossens, 1994a). It has been proposed that most destination image studies have lacked any conceptual framework (Echtner & Ritchie, 1991; Fakeye & Crompton, 1991). From a review of 15 studies between 1975 and 1990, Echtner and Ritchie suggested most definitions were vague, such as 'perceptions of an area'. Jenkins (1999) found the term destination image had been used in a number of different contexts, including for example perceptions held by individuals, stereotypes held by groups, and images projected by DMOs. Questions have been raised as to whether researchers were actually certain of the unique properties of destination image, and whether it could be accurately measured. However, this not a problem faced by destination image researchers in isolation since, in the wider marketing literature, Dobni and Zinkhan's (1990) review of brand image studies found little agreement on either the definition of the construct or on how it should be operationalised.

The mind's defence

Our minds often struggle to cope with the daily flood of advertising and other media (Ries & Trout, 1981). In this regard the explosion in destination choice and destination publicity material has only served to increase confusion among potential travellers (Gunn, 1988). A central theme within the marketing literature has been the difficulty the mind has in dealing with this increasingly busy world. However, Jacoby (1984) argued that while consumers could become overloaded with information, they would not generally allow this to occur. Instead, coping mechanisms are developed. The need for simplified processing by the mind was implicit in the definition of image proposed by Reynolds (1965, p. 69):

> *The mental construct developed by the consumer on the basis of a few selected impressions among the flood of total impressions.*

This viewpoint holds that we develop simplified images through some sort of creative filtering process. For example, we are selective about which messages attract our attention; we are selective about how we interpret and even distort information; and we are selective about which information we will retain in memory. This selective filtering is a form of perceptual defence (Moutinho, 1987). The black box of how this filtering of cognitive information occurs in the internal brain processes to produce a composite image is not yet fully understood (Stern & Krakover, 1993). The same may be said of the process of destination image formation by individuals (Baloglu & McCleary, 1999a).

Associative network memory

A number of extensive literature reviews on the topic of memory structure (see, for example, Keller, 1993; Cossens, 1994b; Cai, 2002) have found the most commonly accepted conceptualisation has been by a spreading action. This has been referred to as the associative network memory model, which sees memory as consisting as nodes and links (Anderson, 1983). A node represents stored information about a particular concept, and is part of a network of links to other nodes. Activation between nodes occurs either through the action of processing external information or when information is retrieved from memory. When a node concept is recalled, the strength of association will dictate the range of other nodes that will be activated from memory. A destination brand is conceptualised as representing a node, with which a number of associations with other node concepts are linked. Key implications of this are the level of awareness of the destination and the strength and favourability of associations with important attributes and benefits.

Another important concept for multi-attributed entities such as destinations is that of an overall or composite image (see Baloglu & McCleary,

1999a; Dichter, 1985; Gartner, 1986; MacInnis & Price, 1987; Mayo, 1973; Stern & Krakover, 1993). MacInnis and Price described imagery as a process of the representation of multisensory information in a gestalt. Discursive processing on the other hand is the cognitive elaboration of individual attributes. A key issue for destination image research is whether imagery or discursive processing is used to evaluate destinations (Echtner, 1991). In the view of Echtner and Ritchie (1991), the definitions of image used by destination researchers did not explicitly identify whether the interest was in a holistic image or in the individual attributes. My (Pike, 2002a) review of 142 destination image studies found most were using lists of attributes. Studies interested in measuring holistic impressions have included Pearce (1988), Um and Crompton (1990), and Reilly (1990).

A further dimension of destination image introduced by Echtner and Ritchie (1991) was the issue of common functional attributes versus unique and psychological features. Since most of the studies they reviewed required respondents to compare destinations across a range of common attributes, there was little opportunity to identify any attributes that may be unique to a destination. They proposed a continuum between those common functional and psychological attributes on which destinations are commonly rated and compared and more unique features, events, or auras. However, it should also be recognised that unique features may not necessarily explain a destination's competitive position if they do not offer benefits in a specified travel context.

Perception is reality

Unfortunately for the marketer, images may only have a tenuous and indirect relationship to fact (Reynolds, 1965). However, whether an individual's perceived images are correct is not as important as what the consumer actually believes to be true (Hunt 1975). This proposition continues to underpin consumer behaviour research today, often referred to as *perception is reality*. This originated from Thomas' theorem: 'What is defined or perceived by people is real in its consequences' (Thomas & Thomas, 1928, p. 572, in Patton, 2002)

Also, given a single fact, a consumer can create a detailed image of a product through simple inferences (Reynolds, 1965). One way this occurs is through 'plot value', where certain attributes are seen by an individual to go together. In this way we construct a plot from a small amount of knowledge. Knowledge of a destination's location may enable the construction of an image including likely climate and geography. For example, New Zealand's location in the South Pacific may incorrectly stimulate an image of a tropical climate. A similar phenomenon may occur through the 'halo effect', where a product that is rated highly on one attribute is then also assumed to rate highly on others. The reverse may also apply. Pizam et al. (1978) suggested a halo effect may occur at a destination where satisfaction, or dissatisfaction, of the total product is the result of an experience of one of its components.

> ## In practice
>
> One example from my own experience highlights this issue. As a destination marketer I received a handful of complaints from travellers each year, primarily relating to service encounters. One of these was from a North American visitor to Rotorua (New Zealand) who felt so strongly about their encounter that they took time to write to me after they had arrived home. During a visit to the resort's most popular visitor attraction they were handed a Fiji 20 cent coin as part of the change given at the ticket booth. When they then tried to spend that same Fiji 20 cent coin at the attraction's café they were told in no uncertain terms that foreign coins were not accepted. It is so easy for the actions of one pedantic employee to undermine a destination brand campaign, which in this case was *Full of Surprises.*

Crompton (1979a) suggested two schools of thought concerning destination image formation. Firstly, images are person-dominated. Variance will always exist as individuals have different experiences and process communications differently. On the other hand, images can be destination determined, where people form images based on experience at the destination. This implied that a destination cannot do much to create an image that is different to what it actually is. Geographers have commonly referred to images held of environments being either designative or appraisive (Stern & Krakover, 1993). The former use a cognitive categorisation of the landscape, while the latter are concerned with attitudes towards the place. These ideas are consistent with Gunn's (1988) concept of organic/induced images, which, along with cognition, affect, and conation, have been the most cited destination image formation concepts.

Organic and induced images

Gunn (1988) suggested images that were formed at two levels: organic and induced. The organic image is developed through an individual's everyday assimilation of information, which may include a wide range of mediums, from school geography readings, to mass media (editorial), to actual visitation. The induced image on the other hand is formed through the influence of tourism promotions directed by marketers, such as advertising. This usually occurs when an individual begins sourcing information for a holiday. The distinction between organic and induced images is the level of influence held by marketers. Gunn suggested destination marketers should focus on modifying the induced image since they can do little to change the organic image.

Unlike the majority of products, where information sources are mostly commercial, destination images appear to be derived from a wider range of sources (Echtner & Ritchie, 1991). They suggested therefore that Gunn's concept of organic and induced images was unique to destinations. There are two important implications of this. First, it is possible for individuals to have images of destinations that they have not previously visited. Second, since image may change after visitation (Chon, 1991; Hu & Ritchie, 1993; Hunt, 1975; Pearce, 1982a; Wee et al., 1985), it is important to separate the images held by visitors from those of non-visitors. Non-visitors will include those who would like to visit but have not yet been able to for various reasons, as well as those who have chosen not to visit. Destination image can be enhanced through travel to a destination. Milman and Pizam (1995) demonstrated how familiarity with a domestic USA destination, measured by previous visitation, led to a more positive image and increased likelihood of repeat visits. However, many studies of destination image have excluded those who have chosen not to visit (Ahmed, 1991b; Baloglu & McCleary, 1999a).

Image formation agents

Gartner (1993) proposed a typology of image formation agents with practical implications. These ranged in a continuum from overt induced advertising through to organic sources such as visitation, as shown in Table 11.1. Marketers could use such agents independently, or in some combination, depending on the marketing objectives. Due to increasing use of public relations, organic and induced images may not necessarily be mutually exclusive (Selby & Morgan, 1996), since news is more voluminous than advertising and has higher credibility (Crompton, 1979a).

Change occurs only slowly

While individual components of a destination image may fluctuate greatly over time, their effect on overall image might not be influential (Crompton,

Table 11.1 Image change agents

Image change agent	Examples
Overt induced 1	Traditional advertising
Overt induced 2	Information received from tour operators
Covert induced 1	Second-party endorsement through traditional advertising
Covert induced 2	Second-party endorsement through seemingly unbiased reports, such as newspaper articles
Autonomous	News and popular culture
Unsolicited organic	Unsolicited information received from friends
Solicited organic	Solicited information from friends
Organic	Actual visitation

1979a; Gartner, 1986). Gartner and Hunt (1987) found evidence of positive destination image change over a 13-year period, but concluded that any change only occurs slowly. Likewise, a study by the English Tourist Board (1983, in Jeffries, 2001) which analysed the impact of an advertising campaign to modify Londoners' perceptions of England's North Country over a three-year period, found only minor changes in destination image. Gartner (1993) proposed that the larger the entity the slower the image change. This supports the proposition that it is difficult to change peoples' minds, with the easier marketing communication route being to reinforce positively held images (Ries & Trout, 1981).

Cognition, affect and conation

Fishbein (1967) and Fishbein and Azjen (1975) argued for the importance of distinguishing between an individual's beliefs and attitudes. While beliefs represent information held about an object, attitude is a favourable, neutral, or unfavourable evaluation. Fishbein was concerned that both concepts were frequently subsumed under the term attitude. Instead, it was proposed that attitude comprises cognitive, affective, and conative components. *Cognition* is the sum of what is known or believed about a destination, and might be organic or induced. This knowledge may or may not have been derived from a previous visit. Cognition denotes awareness.

Affect represents an individual's feelings about an object, which may be favourable, unfavourable, or neutral (Fishbein, 1967). The number of terms used in the English language to describe affect toward a destination is in the hundreds (Russel et al., 1981). Following Russel (1980), Russel et al. factor analysed 105 common adjectives used to describe environments, and generated the affective response grid shown in Figure 11.2. Eight adjective dimensions of affect were included in the model, 45 degrees apart. The assumption was that these dimensions were not independent of each other, but represented a circumplex model of affect. The horizontal axis was arbitrarily set to represent 'pleasantness', while the vertical axis represents level of 'arousal'. In this way exciting, which is a dimension in its own right, is a combination of arousing and pleasant, while distressing is a function of arousing and unpleasant.

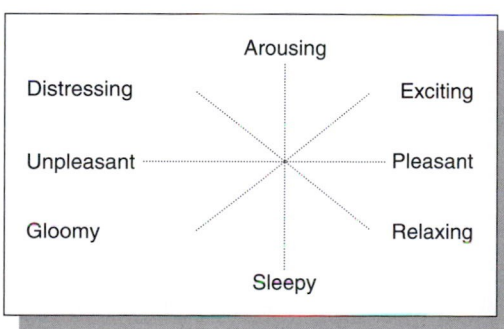

Figure 11.2
Affective response grid
Source: Adapted from
Russel, Ward & Pratt
(1981).

Using four semantic differential scales, 'pleasant/unpleasant', 'relaxing/distressing', 'arousing/sleepy' and 'exciting/gloomy', Baloglu and Brinberg (1997) demonstrated how the affective response model could be applied to destinations. They used multidimensional scaling to plot the affective positions of 11 Mediterranean destinations. Baloglu and McCleary (1999a) also reported the use of these four scales, while Baloglu and Mangaloglu (2001) used the four scales in an analysis of images held by travel intermediaries.

Russel et al. (1981) suggested that two dimensions, 'sleepy/arousing' and 'unpleasant/pleasant', could be sufficient to measure affect towards environments. Other studies have demonstrated how this can apply to travel destinations. For example, Walmsley and Jenkins' (1993) principal components analysis of repertory grid data produced the same two factor labels.

It has been suggested that affect usually becomes operational at the evaluation stage of destination selection process (Gartner, 1993). However, the evaluative image component has been overlooked in tourism (Walmsley & Young, 1998). The majority of destination image studies have focused on cognitive attributes. My analysis (Pike, 2002a) found that only 6 of the 142 published destination image papers showed an explicit interest in affective images. Only recently have destination studies studied both cognition and affect towards destinations together (see Baloglu, 1998; Baloglu & McCleary, 1999a; Dann, 1996; MacKay & Fesenmaier, 1997; Pike & Ryan, 2004). Research Snapshot 11.1 Shows the similarities in cognitive and affective images for a competitive set of destinations.

Research snapshot 11.1   Similarity in cognitive and affective images

A study of the images of a competitive set of short-break holiday destinations in New Zealand used a battery of 20 cognitive scale items and two affective semantic differential scales. Exploratory factor analyses of the cognitive scales identified quite distinctive leadership positions occupied by two of the five destinations. One destination was perceived strongly on attributes in the 'Getting away from it all' factor. The other destination rated strongly on attributes in the 'Lots to do' factor. The affective response matrix showed the first destination as leading the 'Relaxing' dimension of affect, while the second destination was perceived the most 'Exciting'. The similarity in the results of the two sets of scales was useful in describing the market positions to the management at each destination.

Source: Pike, S. & Ryan, C. (2004). Dimensions of short-break destination attractiveness – a comparison of cognitive, affective and conative perceptions. **Journal of Travel Research**, *42*(4), 333–342.

The *conative* image is analogous to behaviour since it is the intent or action component. Intent refers to the likelihood of brand purchase (Howard & Sheth, 1969). Conation may be considered as the likelihood of visiting a destination within a given time period. Woodside and Sherrell (1977) found intent to visit was higher for destinations in the evoked set, as did Thompson and Cooper (1979) and Pike (2002b). Figure 11.3 highlights how the cognition/affect/conation relationships apply in decision-making.

Figure 11.3
Cognition/affect/
conation

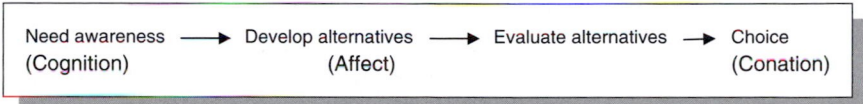

| Need awareness (Cognition) → Develop alternatives (Affect) → Evaluate alternatives → Choice (Conation) |

The process is similar to the hierarchy of effects (see Lavidge & Steiner, 1961) or AIDA model used by advertisers, where the aim is to guide a consumer through the stages of awareness, interest, desire, and action.

Myers (1992) acknowledged that the model might not always progress in this manner, since preferences might not need any cognitive antecedents. Therefore, the process could begin at any stage of the model. Manstead (1996) suggested cognition, affect, and conation towards an object would be correlated. However, this might not always be so, due to intervening or moderating variables (Fishbein, 1967). In tourism, Woodside and Lysonski (1989) suggested that preferences in the destination decision process are based on a combination of cognitive and affective associations. Baloglu and McCleary (1999a) found cognition, affect, and overall image positively influenced intent to visit a destination. Baloglu (1998) found affect influenced intent following experience at a destination.

Motivation

Arguably, motivation begins the holiday travel decision process, when a need arises that cannot be met at home (Gartner, 1993). Motives may therefore be viewed as the psychological determinants of demand (Kotler et al., 1999). Motivation in tourism is a relatively new field of study, and researchers have consistently reported a lack of understanding (see Baloglu & McCleary, 1999a; Dann, 1981; Dann et al., 1988; Fisher & Price, 1991; Mansfield, 1992; Pearce, 1982b). Tourism motivation theories have mostly been conceptual rather that empirical (Ritchie, 1996). However, the lack of theory is not unique to the tourism industry, since the issue of consumer motivation in general is not fully understood (Mansfield, 1992; Pearce, 1994):

> Since it can be justifiably claimed that these issues are not settled within the field of psychology itself, it is rather demanding to expect that they are satisfied in the context of tourist motivation (Pearce, 1994, p. 119).

Sunlust and wanderlust

One of the first attempts to explain pleasure travel motivation was Gray's (1970) concepts of wanderlust and sunlust, which subsume many of the motivation categories outlined in more recent studies. *Wanderlust* characterised the innate human need to temporarily leave familiar surroundings to experience different cultures and places. It has been suggested that apart from an innate need to explore, all other travel motivations are learnt by individuals (Mayo & Jarvis, 1981). For example, no one is born with the need for status. Therefore, an individual's travel preferences and behaviour can change during a lifetime as needs and motives are learned. *Sunlust* was described as travel for a specific purpose for benefits not available at home, such as winter sun holidays or visits to a larger city.

Push versus pull

Related to this was the work of Dann (1977) who discussed push factors to explain the link between motivation and destination choice. Motivational push factors were proposed to be a logical antecedent to the analysis of pull factors such as destination attributes. Within the push category, Dann introduced the concepts of anomie and ego-enhancement from social psychology to explain the core travel motivations. The anomic traveller seeks escape from the mundane and isolation at home to obtain opportunities for social interaction. Ego-enhancement on the other hand seeks increased self-recognition, such as opportunities to recreate oneself at a place where identity is not known, or trip-dropping at home to reinforce status.

Traveller typologies

Related to the study of tourism motivation is the work of Cohen (1972) and Plog (1974) in categorising traveller types. Cohen suggested four types of tourist roles: the organised mass tourist, the individual mass tourist, the explorer, and the drifter. While the core motives for most were variety and novelty, each group clearly differed in the level of control and predictability sought from the experience. The key variable in the typology was 'strangeness versus familiarity'. Plog introduced psychocentricity and allocentricity to travel. Psychocentrics were posited to be nervous and non-adventurous, who travel to familiar places, preferring to drive rather than fly. Allocentrics on the other hand were more confident and willing to experiment with life. These individuals would prefer new experiences such as non-touristy destinations. Both Cohen and Plog linked their concepts to the evolution of a destination's lifecycle. For example, Cohen suggested strangeness and novelty were important for travellers. Plog proposed allocentrics would be the first to visit or explore a new destination, while psychocentrics would be attracted at the maturity or even the decline stage. However, Cohen suggested mass tourism had created a paradox, where novelty was increasingly difficult to cater to as tourism had become institutionalised.

Satisfying needs

One of the problems for tourism researchers is that the motives for travel may not actually be entirely understood by travellers themselves (Crompton, 1979b, p. 421): 'The in-depth interviews caused many respondents to confront for the first time their real motives for going on a pleasure vacation.' Therefore, the reasons people give for taking holidays are not sufficient to explain motivation (Mill & Morrison, 1992). Instead, following Maslow's (1943) theory of motivation as a hierarchy of needs, Mill and Morrison argued that the key to understanding travel motivation was through the recognition of travel as a needs and wants satisfier: 'Motivation occurs when an individual wants to satisfy a need' (Mill & Morrison, 1992, p. 17). They suggested that this view of motivation is the difference between seeing the destination as a collection of attractions and seeing it as a place for satisfying needs and wants.

Gilmore (2002) suggested that holiday decisions are made on the basis of activity first, destination second, and succinctly summarised the complex field of tourism motivation into three categories: hedonism, self-improvement, and spiritual. Recognising that the needs of an individual traveller will be physical, psychological, or intellectual, Mill and Morrison linked the relationships between needs and motives referenced in the tourism literature, as shown in Table 11.2. It could be argued that the physiological and safety needs are physical, while the belonging, esteem, and self-actualisation needs are psychological. The last two categories are intellectual needs.

Table 11.2 Needs and tourism motives

Need	Motive	Tourism literature
Physiological	Relaxation	Escape, relaxation, relief of tension, sunlust, physical, mental relaxation of tension
Safety	Security	Health, recreation, keep oneself active and healthy
Belonging	Love	Family togetherness, enhancement of kinship relationships, companionship, facilitation of social interaction, maintenance of personal ties, interpersonal relations, roots, ethnic, show one's affection for family members, maintain social contacts
Esteem	Achievement, status	Convince oneself of one's achievements, show one's importance to others, prestige, social recognition, ego-enhancement, professional business, personal development, status, prestige
Self-actualisation	Be true to one's own nature	Exploration and evaluation of self, self discovery, satisfaction of inner desires
To know and understand	Knowledge	Cultural, education, wanderlust, interest in foreign areas
Aesthetics	Appreciation of beauty	Environmental, scenery

Source: Adapted from Mill & Morrison (1992, p. 20).

Consumer decision sets

When motivated to act, the individual consumer-traveller becomes a decision-maker (Mayo & Jarvis, 1981). Decisions must be made about where to go, when to go, how to get there, and what to do there. Brand decisions then essentially involve alternative brands and the buyer's own choice criteria (Howard & Sheth, 1969). Choice criteria will be associated with motives. Therefore, while a favourable image of a destination is important, it must also be aligned to the traveller's motives, to increase the likelihood of visitation (Henshall et al., 1985; Mansfield, 1992). Mill and Morrison (1992) suggested that one implication of Maslow's hierarchy of needs was that holidays targeting the satisfaction of lower-level physical and physiological needs would be treated as a necessity rather than as a luxury. Of particular interest is how travellers select a holiday destination from so many places that could ably provide satisfaction.

Consumer decision set theory offers some explanation of this most complicated aspect of consumer behaviour. Howard (1963) and Howard and Sheth (1969) introduced the evoked decision set concept to propose that the number of brands considered in any purchase decision was considerably lower than those available. The evoked set was defined as comprising only those brands the consumer will actually consider in the next purchase decision. Howard proposed that the number of brands in an individual's evoked set would remain constant at about three or four. Woodside and Sherrell (1977) were the first to investigate evoked sets of destinations in the holiday decision process. They were motivated by the proposition that the mental processes required to evaluate the features of 15 or more destinations would represent too great a task for most travellers.

The reduced set of likely alternatives that form the evoked set is part of the total set. For travellers, this total set would consist of all those destinations that may or may not be available, and which they may or may not be aware of. How many destinations must there now be on the planet? Within this total set of destinations, Woodside and Sherrell (1977) proposed the following possible overlapping subsets:

- Unavailable and unaware set
- Awareness set
- Available set
- Evoked set
- Aware and unavailable set
- Available and unaware set
- Inert set
- Inept set
- Chosen destination

Since consumers will either be aware or unaware of the existence of a product, it is from the awareness set that a purchase choice will ultimately be made (Narayana & Markin, 1975). Clearly, a destination must firstly make it into the consumer's awareness set for consideration. However, as simple and logical as this may appear, from a practical perspective this represents a significant challenge for some destinations. Lilly (1984), for example, discussed the difficulty in promoting North Staffordshire, a region with little tourism image outside its own boundaries. Likewise, strategists appointed by Papua New Guinea's NTO in 2004 found that a major barrier to the development of tourism in that country is a lack of consumer awareness about the destination (Wright, 2004).

It is important to recognise the distinction between an awareness problem and that of a negative image, since the existence of the latter denotes awareness. However, more than simply awareness of a destination is required. For example, Milman and Pizam (1995) found that awareness of a popular USA domestic destination was not necessarily a strong indicator of intent to visit. In short, other determinants of choice exist.

Due to the number of possible destinations in the awareness set, it is therefore more realistic for the marketer to determine the composition of the early consideration set. These are the destinations the consumer believes could realistically be visited within a given time period. This represents the overlap of the awareness and available sets.

Miller (1956) cited a number of studies from the consumer psychology literature to suggest that the limit to the number of stimuli people would generally be capable of processing would be around seven. Miller even linked this proposition to the use of questionnaire rating scales, where seven points had generally been considered the limit of usefulness. Woodside and Sherrell's (1977) literature review found this limit had generally been consistent in brand recall tests across product categories as diverse as cars and toothpaste.

When a consumer becomes involved in a purchase decision the early consideration set is categorised into three subsets: inert, inept, and evoked (Narayana & Markin, 1975). The inert set consists of brands for which the consumer has neither a positive nor a negative opinion. The consumer will have some awareness of the destination to stimulate initial interest and inclusion in the early consideration set, but may lack information to make a judgement. Or they may have sufficient information but see no advantage in pursuing it further at that point. The consumer is undecided about visiting these destinations within a certain time period.

The inept set consists of brands the consumer has rejected from the initial purchase consideration within some time period. Destinations in the inept set will have been rejected from the early consideration set due to negative perceptions, perhaps from comments by significant others for example.

Once the inert and inept destinations have been eliminated from the early consideration set the remaining destinations form the evoked decision set. The evoked set comprises those destinations the consumer has some likelihood of visiting within a given time period (Woodside & Sherrell, 1977). Woodside and Sherrell found that perceptions of destinations listed in the evoked set of their respondents were more favourable than for those listed in the inert and inept sets. In their study the evoked set size averaged 3.4 destinations for selection during the following twelve months. Their proposition of four plus or minus two destinations in the evoked set has been supported in other destination studies (see Thompson & Cooper, 1979; Woodside & Lysonski, 1989). Thompson and Cooper noted that no tourism study had examined the effect of travel context on evoked set size. However, my investigations of decision sets in the context of short-break holidays in New Zealand (Pike, 2002b) and Australia (Pike 2004, 2007) found a consistency in the size of the evoked decision sets with means of three to four destinations.

For consumer goods, it has been suggested that brands excluded from the evoked decision set may have a purchase probability of less than 1% (Wilson, 1981). The concept of the evoked set therefore has important implications for DMOs if it is from this set that final destination selection is made. It must be accepted that a hierarchy of destination brand saliency is formed within the evoked set of destinations, if a final selection is to be made. The higher a brand's position in a consumers mind, the higher the intent to purchase (Burke & Schoeffler, 1980; Wilson, 1981).

Top of mind awareness (ToMA)

It has been shown that top of mind awareness (ToMA), measured by unaided recall, is related to purchase preference among competing brands (Axelrod, 1968; Wilson, 1981; Woodside & Wilson, 1985). Consequently, for the destination that first comes to mind when a consumer is considering travel, ToMA must surely represent a source of advantage (Pike, 2002b).

The importance of travel context in destination image analysis

Attribute importance can vary between situations (Barich & Kotler, 1991; Crompton, 1992), as will ToMA destination preference. However, there has been limited attention to the importance of context in consumer research. In an assessment of the tourism marketing research state of the art, Ritchie (1996) proposed ten key shortcomings. Among the gaps, which Ritchie labelled the 'dark side of the universe', was travel context. Destination image studies have generally been undertaken without explicitly defining the context in which the traveller decision is being made (Hu & Ritchie, 1993).

Travel context refers to the situation or usage of the product, such as the time of year, type of trip, or geographic travel range. For example, destination brand attribute salience will likely differ between the context of a honeymoon and an end-of-season football team trip. Brand association salience therefore depends on the decision context (Keller, 1993). Golf excursions, for example, may act as both the catalyst for travel and the destination choice (Woodside, 1999). Phelps (1986) found visitors to Menorca had a low awareness of the destination they were travelling to on a package tour, since the package product was more important that the destination.

Even though it was proposed three decades ago that any list of determinant destination attributes will vary depending on situational context (see Gearing et al., 1974), only 23 of the 142 published destination image papers I analysed (Pike, 2002a) were explicit about a travel context of interest. These are highlighted in Table 11.3.

Table 11.3 Destination image papers with an explicit travel context

Author(s)	Year	Travel context
Mayo	1973	Self-drive
Anderssen & Colberg	1973	Overseas winter holiday
Dillon, Domzal & Madden	1986	Student spring break
Perdue	1986	Boating
Woodside & Carr	1988	Foreign travel
Woodside & Lysonski	1989	Foreign travel
Embacher & Buttle	1989	Summer holiday
Chon, Weaver & Kim	1991	Short break
Crompton, Fakeye & Lue	1992	Winter long stay
Javalgi, Thomas & Rao	1992	Self-drive
Hu & Ritchie	1993	Education travel
Amor et al.	1994	Sun/beach
King	1994	Sun/beach
Oppermann	1996	Convention
Go & Zhang	1997	Convention
Hudson & Shephard	1998	Snow skiing
McClellan	1998	Short break
Ritchie	1998	Bicycling
Vaughan & Edwards	1999	Overseas winter holiday
Baloglu & McCleary	1999a, 1999b	Summer holiday
Murphy	1999	Backpacking
Chacko & Fenich	2000	Convention

Key points

1. The role of image in destination marketing

Tourism marketing is generally concerned with the selling of dreams, since expectations of an intangible tourism service can only be realised after travel. The images held by consumers therefore play a critical role in their decision-making. Since tourism services can only compete via images, it is imperative marketers understand that 'perception is reality'. The brand image of the destination may or may not be quite different to the brand identity intended by the DMO. Since the first destination image studies appeared in the 1970s, the topic has become one of the most prevalent in the tourism literature. A destination's image is a repertoire of brand associations held in the mind of the consumer. These associations may be cognitive, affective, conative, or a combination of these. They may have been developed through organic sources such as previous visitation or induced sources such as advertising.

2. Consumer decision sets

Consumers are spoilt by choice of available destinations, but will only actively consider a limited number in the decision-making process. The size of the consumer's decision set of destinations will be limited to around four. The implication for DMOs examining the image of their destination is that destinations not included in a consumer's decision set will be less likely to be selected.

3. The importance of travel context in destination image analysis

Both the images held of destinations and the consumer's decision set composition will vary according to the travel context. Travel context refers to the type of travel situation, such as a romantic getaway, family camping trip, or golf weekend. A traveller will not only experience different travel contexts in the course of a lifetime, but also at different times of the year.

Review questions

- To what extent does inclusion in a consumer decision set by a destination represent a source of advantage?
- What is meant by the marketing adage, 'perception is reality', and why is this relevant to DMOs?
- Analyse the content of your DMO's advertising to determine whether the intent is to stimulate cognitive, affective, or conative brand associations.

CHAPTER 12

Market positioning

A brand position is the part of the brand identity and value proposition that is to be actively communicated to the target audience and that demonstrates an advantage over competing brands.

Aaker (1996, p. 71)

Aims

The aims of this chapter are to enhance understanding of:

- positioning as the interface between brand identity and brand image
- positioning as a source of competitive advantage
- the challenges involved in developing a narrow positioning focus for multi-attributed destinations

Perspective

Positioning should be regarded as mutually beneficial for the DMO and the consumer, since the process is underpinned by the philosophy of understanding and meeting unique consumer needs. For the organisation, the value of positioning lies in the link between the analyses of the internal and external environments. In other words, matching environment opportunities with organisation resources. Positioning can aid the DMO to cut through to the minds of consumers in markets that are crowded with the clutter of promotional messages of competing destinations and substitute products and services. However, to do so requires a narrow focus, and therefore trade-offs concerning what to leave out of the proposition. After all, a brand is 'a singular idea or concept that you own inside the mind of a prospect. It's as simple and as difficult as that' (Ries & Ries, 1998, p. 172). On the demand side, effective positioning of a brand can enable easier decision-making for the consumer. Consumers don't have time to consider the merits of all available products in a purchase decision, and will therefore appreciate a memorable and focused value proposition that appeals to their needs.

Positioning as a source of competitive advantage

Previously, a model of the destination brand construct was espoused as consisting of the concepts of brand identity, brand image, and brand positioning. This is reproduced in Figure 12.1. Chapter 10 discussed the development a brand identity, which represents the self-image or desired image, while Chapter 11 discussed brand image as representing the actual image held by consumers. The focus of this chapter is on positioning as a potential means of enhancing congruence between brand identity and brand image.

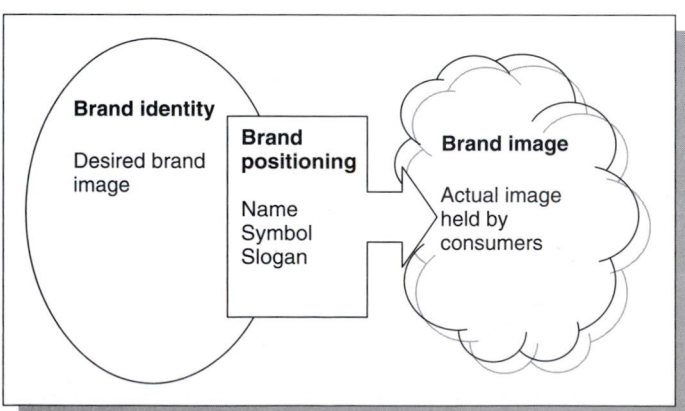

Figure 12.1
Brand identity, brand positioning and brand image

An attractive destination is one that achieves. . .

> . . . *a distinctive ToMA position, which is based on leadership in determinant attributes, in the decision sets of a significant group of travellers, who have an intent to visit within a given time period.*

From this perspective it is important to gain an understanding of what decision criteria will be used by the consumer when differentiating destinations under consideration. If a destination is perceived to be differentiated on the basis of a determinant attribute, then this is a position that should be exploited by the DMO for mutual benefit. In an ideal world the positioning campaign will be reinforcing positively held perceptions that will ease decision-making by the consumer, rather than attempt to change opinions.

Effective positioning can be a source of competitive advantage for organisations in any industry consisting of close substitutes (Porter, 1980). In most tourism markets, particularly those dominated by charter flights and package deals, competing destinations are indeed close substitutes. After all a beach is a beach isn't it? For example, the beach sunset scene in Figure 12.2 could be almost anywhere in the world.

Therefore, the successful positioning of a destination into a consumer's evoked decision set represents a source of competitive advantage over the majority of competing places (Pike, 2002b). The chapter is underpinned by Figure 12.3, which presents a proposed model of brand positioning as a potential source of competitive advantage for destinations. The model views positioning as a vehicle for influencing brand image and therefore destination attractiveness.

Figure 12.2
Beach sunset scene

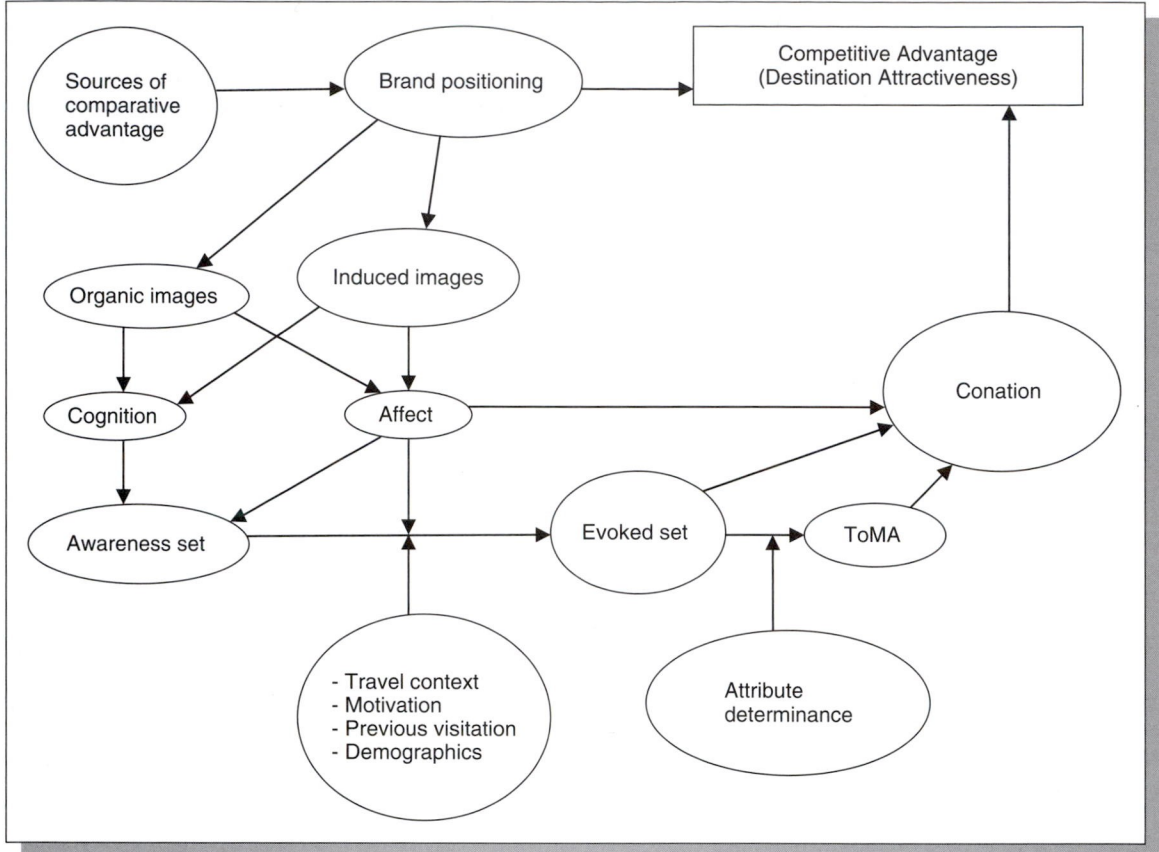

Figure 12.3 Brand positioning as a source of competitive advantage for destinations

The positioning concept

Brand positioning describes how a brand can effectively compete against a specified set of competitors in a particular market (Keller, 2003, p. 150). The concept was first introduced to the advertising community as a marketing strategy in 1969 (Trout & Ries, 1979), and has been defined as a process of 'establishing and maintaining a distinctive place in the market for an organisation and/or its individual product offerings' (Lovelock, 1991, p. 110). At the core of this quest for a distinctive place is recognition that marketing is a battle fought inside the consumer's mind (Ries & Trout, 1986, p. 169):

> *Marketing battles are not fought in the customer's office or in the supermarkets or the drugstores of America. Those are only distribution points for the merchandise whose brand selection is decided elsewhere. Marketing battles are fought in a mean and ugly place. A place that's dark and damp with much unexplored territory and deep pitfalls to trap the unwary. Marketing battles are fought inside the mind.*

Positioning theory is based on three propositions (Ries & Trout, 1986). First, we live in an over-communicated society, bombarded with information on a daily basis, at levels that are unprecedented in our history. Second, the mind has developed a defence system against the clutter. Third, the only way to cut through the clutter to the mind is through simplified and focused messages. Consequently, not selecting a positioning strategy could lead to head-on competition with stronger brands, an unwanted position with little demand, a fuzzy position where distinctive competence is unclear, or no position, where the product is unheard of (Lovelock, 1991). Porter (1980) warned that being 'stuck in the middle', with no distinctive position, was the most dangerous place to be.

Effective positioning offers the customer benefits tailored to solve a problem, in a way that is different to competitors (Chacko, 1997; DiMingo, 1988). The key construct in positioning is brand image. However, positioning requires more than an understanding of what a brand's image is in the mind of the consumer. While such studies enable an indication of satisfaction with a destination, a weakness of this approach is the inability to determine relative positioning against competing regions. Positioning requires a frame of reference with the competition, particularly in relation to those in consumers' decision sets. A position is a product's perceived performance, relative to competitors, on specific attributes (Lovelock, 1991; Wind & Robinson, 1972). Positioning studies have not been prominent in the tourism literature (Grabler, 1997b). Although positioning had featured in the economics literature as early as the 1920s (Myers, 1992), there was little mention of the construct in the marketing literature until the 1970s. Destination positioning studies have been particularly rare (Uysal et al., 2000; Heath & Wall, 1992; Yau & Chan, 1990).

Differentness ● ● ●

Ries and Trout (1986) emphasised the need for marketers to think in terms of *differentness* rather than *betterness*. This has important tourism implications, given few tourism products are unique. Differentiation is critical for destinations since they will either become places of status or commodities, with the latter leading to increased substitutability (Gilbert, 1990). Plog (2000) lamented the increasing sameness of most destinations around the world, due to the effects of globalisation. Modernity has all but destroyed the opportunity for travellers to experience different attractions (Dann, 2000). This standardisation of facilities enabled mass tourism by providing travellers with necessary familiarity:

> As a result, countries become interchangeable in the tourist's mind. Whether he is looking for good beaches, restful forests, or old cities, it becomes relatively unimportant to him where these happen to be found (Cohen, 1972, p. 172).

Effective differentiated positioning to stand out from the crowd is possible for any product (DiMingo, 1988; Moutinho, 1994). The fundamental marketing challenge faced by DMOs is to somehow match a large and diverse product range with the needs of a number of dynamic and heterogeneous markets. The desired market position, assuming one has been designed and articulated, must be presented to the market in a way that stands out from other attention-seeking messages of rival destinations and substitute products. If successful, such a position will establish the destination as top of mind in the target audience. If top of mind awareness (ToMA) is an indicator of purchase preference (Axelrod, 1968; Wilson, 1981; Woodside & Wilson, 1985), it follows that such a position in the mind offers destinations a potential source of competitive advantage (Pike & Ryan, 2004).

As discussed in Chapter 8, strategy should seek to maximise strengths, correct weaknesses, minimise threats, and maximise opportunities. Porter (1980) suggested a competitive strategy was one that positioned a business to make the most of strengths that differentiated the firm from competitors. A sustainable competitive advantage (SCA) is gained when consumers perceive a performance capability gap that endures over time (Coyne, 1986). To gain an advantage the gap must be through an attribute that represents an important buying criterion. Not all attributes that differentiate a product from competitors are actually important to the consumer, and not all important attributes are used in decision-making.

Attribute importance, salience, and determinance ● ● ●

The ideal for any product is to be perceived favourably on product attributes that are important to the target segment. Different terms have been used in the tourism literature to describe important attributes. Salience concerns the order in which features are elicited from consumers, where the most pertinent are offered first. Important attributes may be salient but not necessarily determinant (see Research Snapshot 12.1). It is essential then to identify those attributes that determine product choice, to form the basis for any positioning campaign (Lovelock, 1991; Ritchie & Zins, 1978). Myers and Alpert (1968, p. 13) offered the first definition of determinance in the marketing literature:

> *Attitudes toward features which are most closely related to preference or to actual purchase decisions are said to be determinant; the remaining features or attitudes – no matter how favourable – are not determinant.*

Research snapshot 12.1   Common determinant attribute themes

From the analysis of over 80 published destination image studies that had used lists of attributes in structured questionnaires, I summarised 18 themes (see Pike, 2003). Of these studies, 37 concluded with proposed determinant attributes or factors, which I summarised into the following 15 themes:

- Nature/scenery
- Local culture
- Price/value

- Good weather
- Infrastructure
- Friendly locals
- Safe/relaxing environment
- Lots to do
- Accommodation
- Sports activities
- Cafes/restaurants
- Historical sites
- Nightlife
- Accessibility
- Shopping

Destination market researchers can screen these themes, through focus groups and/or or personal interviews, to develop a context-specific list of attributes for use in tailored destination image surveys.

Source: Pike, S. (2003). The use of repertory grid analysis to elicit salient short-break holiday attributes. *Journal of Travel Research*, 41(3), 326–330.

To summarise, a large number of attributes may be important in a brand category. Since many competing products are likely to offer many of these features, it will be a reduced set of salient attributes used to differentiate brands. From these, only one or a few determinant attributes will be used in the final brand selection.

Positioning destinations

Few communities have developed a positioning strategy. Instead they yield to the pressure to be all things to all people, and use look-alike promotions and print brochures showing attractions ranging from historic barns to zoos – without any regard to whether these features have any drawing power (Gee & Makens, 1985, p. 29).

The destination positioning process involves seven stages.

1. Identify the target market and travel context.
2. Identify the competitive set of destinations in the target market and travel context.
3. Identify the motivation/benefits sought by previous visitors and non-visitors.
4. Identify perceptions of the strengths and weaknesses of each of the competitive set of destinations.
5. Identify opportunities for differentiated positioning.
6. Select and implement the position.
7. Monitor the performance of the positioning strategy over time.

The value proposition

The development of a proposition is arguably the greatest challenge in branding (Gilmore, 2002). Once the range of potential determinant attributes is known, a key decision must be made about which should be used as the focus of the brand positioning. While focus may be appropriate for single-product marketers, the selection of one determinant attribute by a destination marketer is usually problematic. Ries and Trout (1986) used the analogy of postcard images to sum up how a place was positioned in the mind. Another useful example is the ubiquitous roadside billboard, as shown in Figure 12.4. Clearly there is a limit to the amount of information that can be portrayed on a standard size postcard or billboard.

To stand out, and be noticed and remembered, DMOs must design a positioning strategy focused on one or few determinant attributes. Success is most likely when the range of differentiated features emphasised is small (Aaker & Shansby, 1982; Crompton, et al., 1992) and yet a destination usually comprises a diversity of features. For DMOs, this necessitates making trade-offs. After all, 'you can't stand for something if you chase after everything' (Ries, 1992, p. 7). The power of focus is due our mind's dislike of confusion (Trout & Rivkin, 1995). In an age when the information flood is increasing exponentially, the message should not try to tell the product's entire story, but rather focus on one powerful attribute, since more brand variations cause confusion. Ries (1992, p. 5) suggested that owning a word in the target's mind had become the most powerful concept in marketing. Therefore the following question should be asked: *What single idea or concept does my company (or brand) stand for in the mind of the prospect?*

In the brand literature it has been suggested that a value proposition is the promise of functional, emotional, and self-expressive benefits to

Figure 12.4
Roadside billboard

influence purchase decisions (Aaker, 1996). These are relevant to the concepts of cognitive, affect, and conative images. Functional benefits, or product attributes, by themselves do not differentiate and are easy to copy. This relates to the cognitive image or knowledge of a destination's features. Emotional benefits are the stimulation of a positive feeling. This relates to the affective image component. Self-expressive benefits strengthen the link between brand and consumer by representing symbols of our self-concept: 'A brand can thus provide a self-expressive benefit by providing a way for a person to communicate his or her self image' (Aaker, 1996, p. 99). These may include, for example, 'adventurous', 'hip', 'sophisticated', and 'successful', among others. The differences between emotional and self-expressive benefits are that self-expressive emphasises: the self rather than feelings, a public setting rather than private, future aspirations rather than memory, and the act of using the product rather than the consequence of using it. For example, the benefit of the pre- and post-brag value from visiting an exotic destination may be different to the benefit of feelings attained from being there. Following Keller (2003), three positioning deliverability criteria should be considered:

- **Is the position feasible?** For a destination this will relate to the ability of the local tourism industry and host community to deliver the promise.
- **Can the position be communicated?** In terms of developing strong, favourable, and unique associations, the efficacy of a destination's communications will depend to a large extent on whether the message is reinforcing existing positively held associations of the destination, or whether an attempt is being made to either create awareness or change opinions.
- **Is the position sustainable?** The ability of the destination to strengthen associations over time will depend on how well the position can be defended against imitating rivals.

Case Study 12.1 is a typical example of a destination faced with the challenge of differentiation in a market crowded with places offering similar attributes and benefits. In this case experiential marketing is offered as a potential opportunity to do so. Pine and Gilmore's (1989) notion of the experience economy discussed the progression of economic values from commodities to goods, to services, to experiences. Customising a good turns it into a service, and customising a service turns it into an experience. In a keynote address to the 2004 Leisure-Futures conference in Bolzano, Italy, Pine referred to experiential examples such as Japan's Ocean Dome. This is the world's largest indoor swimming pool, but in the form of an indoor beach complete with non-stickable sand. Customers pay over $300 for a family visit to the complex, which is ironically situated only 400 metres from a real beach. Other examples recommended by Pine included:

- Pike Place Fish Market in Seattle, Washington, where the actions and banter of staff is akin to a theatre experience in a fish shop
- Hotel Atlantis in Bermuda

- Othentica (see www.othentica.com), a firm specialising in creating a simulated entertainment experience for elite staff. Based on the psychological profile of participants, the simulation has something in common with the Michael Douglas movie *The Game*.

Case study 12.1   Long Lake, New York: small destinations and experiential differentiation – what to do?

Dr Richard 'Rick' M. Lagiewski, Rochester Institute of Technology, USA

Long Lake is a small town (852 inhabitants) located in the centre of the Adirondack Park in the state of New York (see http://www.longlake-ny.com/). The town is appropriately named after its 14-mile-long lake. Tourism is a major industry there, but also in the entire Adirondack Park. This has been the case since the 1950s when destinations in the Adirondack Park became easily accessible for family vacations due to the development of automobiles, a booming post-war economy, increased leisure time and income. This small town in the Adirondack Park was appealing to visitors since it offered them something different than the life in the city: private cottages, untouched nature, and numerous opportunities to enjoy the outdoors. Inevitably, however, the number of other destinations developing in the Adirondack Park that offered the same services kept increasing, and hence resulted in saturated supply.

Visitors come to Long Lake to enjoy outdoor activities (bird-watching, biking, camping, canoeing, boating, cross-country skiing, fishing, hiking, hunting, snowmobiling, star gazing) as well as concerts, craft fairs, and other events. The town's current marketing efforts are focused essentially on activities that visitors can engage in while in Long Lake. However, all the activities and events found in Long Lake can also be found in many of the other Adirondack townships. Also, most towns offer the same type of accommodation and dining options, and for that matter the same tourism infrastructure in general.

The situation can be summarised as follows: small towns (like Long Lake) in the Adirondack Park that have similar (if not the same) offering of activities, events, accommodation, and dining options (tourism product) as other lake destinations in the Adirondack Park, face the problem of commoditisation of their services. Hence, there is a need to find a way to diversify Long Lake from its competitors. Due to limited access to sources of capital, adding new physical infrastructure is not an option.

Pine and Gilmore (1999) introduced the idea that goods and services are no longer enough for differentiating and therefore advocated experiences as a form of differentiation. They explained the shift from commodities to experiences and the need to create experiences if competitors are to be differentiated from their rivals. In addition, Pine and Gilmore stated that experiences are intrinsically sensory. In other words, it does matter what one sees, hears, touches, smells, and tastes in shaping of impressions and consequently experiences. As they say (p. 59): 'The more effectively an experience engages the senses, the more memorable it will be.'

In working with Long Lake's DMO (a one-man office) the proposed idea of differentiating Long Lake through experiences is often hindered due to the persistence towards traditional marketing such as brochures. Often the concept of experiences is viewed as synonymous with a recreational activity. Again the issue is not seen as focusing on senses and emotions or feelings gained from an experience, but rather on some active participation in an outdoor activity. Also, there was still a tendency to identify and define a different physical characteristic that differentiated Long Lake from other lakes. For example, at 14 miles it was one of the longest lakes in the Adirondack Park. However, what makes this lake a unique experience in comparison to an 8-mile lake?

Discussion question

What strategies would you suggest could be used to get residents and community leaders to focus on senses, feelings, and memories that would represent the marketing vision of a vacation on Long Lake?

Further reading

Lagiewski , R. & Zekan, B. (2006). Experiential marketing of tourism destinations. *International Tourism Conference* (November). Alanya: Turkey.

Pine, J. & Gilmore, J. (1989). *The Experience Economy*. Cambridge MA: Harvard University Press.

Undertaking the seven-stage destination positioning process on a segment-by-segment basis in all markets, for different travel contexts, would present a significant and no doubt impossible challenge for DMOs. It follows that even with a wide range of attractions, some destinations may not fulfil potential opportunities (Hunt, 1975), where, due to poor decision-making, implementation and/or limited budgets, the desired image has not been achieved in the market. The following should be considered to enhance destination positioning effectiveness (Pike & Ryan, 2004, p. 341):

- An understanding of the benefits sought by the target audience, and the relative performances of the competitive set of destinations.
- Trade-offs for a focused positioning strategy based on determinant attributes.
- Implementation to 'cut-through' and stimulate intent (demand).
- The delivery and monitoring of benefits offered by the position.
- Performance measures to track effectiveness over time.
- Research to stay in touch with target audience needs.

Case Study 12.2 perhaps captures the essence of what Lagewski had in mind in Case Study 9.1.

Case study 12.2 Destination theming: Heidiland region, Switzerland

Professor Ady Milman, Ph.D., Rosen College of Hospitality Management, University of Central Florida

The continuing challenge of destinations to provide tourists with unique and memorable experiences has generated a relatively new trend of adopting theming as a strategy to enhance and develop the traditional components of the destination. This proposed orientation is not only in response to consumers' changes in tastes and preferences, but also as a marketing tool for sustaining destination competitiveness.

Successful development of a themed destination is a combination of storytelling, creative design, sound financial projections, audience analysis, and planning. Like in modern theme parks, destination theming strives to create a fantasy atmosphere that is emotionally linked to the destination. The theme is mainly communicated through visual and vocal statements, but also through other senses. In many themed destinations, theming is reflected in architecture, street furniture, signage, landscaping, costumed personnel, personal storytelling by tour guides and local residents, recreational activities, entertainment, music, food services, souvenir shops, and any other guest experiences.

One of the most remarkable examples of destination theming is Heidiland, located in the eastern part of Switzerland where Johanna Spyri wrote her well-known book *Heidi* about an unwanted orphan girl who found happiness in the Alps (Spyri, 1996). Most of Heidiland's resorts and villages are about 50–75 minutes from Zürich airport and approximately 45 minutes from Lake Constance (Swiss National Tourist Office, 2007). In the early 1990s, the Swiss Tourism Board declared the Rhine Valley in the Eastern Canton of Graubunden as Heidiland, and the region was re-dedicated in 2001 to commemorate the 100th anniversary of Spyri's death.

The Heidi story is communicated to visitors throughout the region, but particularly in the village of Oberfols, considered Heididorf or Heidi Village. In the village, visitors can visit Heidi Haus, a mid-19th century Swiss hut decorated with Heidi-era furniture, kitchen utensils, and clothes to give visitors an authentic feeling for what life in Heidi's era was really like. The village also offers souvenir shops, a small petting zoo, and a post office where visitors can send letters with the Heidi postmark (Schur, 2007). In addition, the Heidi theme is also communicated through interactive experiences, especially hiking. The Heidi Weg (Heidi Path) is a one-and-a-half-hour mountain walk that features twelve signs in several languages, each with a different excerpt from the book and an explanation of some aspect of the scenery. On top of the mountain, there is a 200-year-old cow-herder's hut where hikers can meet a character who plays Heidi's grandfather (Schur, 2007). The area also developed a brand of mineral water called Heidiland Water.

Tourism operators in Heidiland teamed together to promote the region with emphasis on healthy vacationing in an Alpine environment. Heidiland's tourism mission stresses that there is no intention of becoming a Swiss Disneyland or turning Heidiland into a giant theme park. Nevertheless, Heidi's story has provided an inspiration to develop a variety of tourist facilities, products, and activities based on the local existing natural and man-made resources.

Discussion question

Can you think of any region in the world where theming could be applied through pre-existing intellectual property? Suggest how the theme could be communicated to visitors? Brainstorm potential theming opportunities for your destination.

Further reading

Beck, E. (1997). Heidi ho! The Swiss, amid controversy, exploit the orphan. *Wall Street Journal* (Eastern Edition). October 2 1997, p. A1

Schur, Maxine (2007). Following my heart to Heidiland: Inside the landscape of a famous movie. Retrieved on 3/6/07 from: http://www.escapeartist.com/efam/43/In_Search_of_Heidiland.html

Swiss National Tourist Office (2007). Heidiland home page. Retrieved on 3/6/07 from: http://www.heidiland.ch/en/accessing_resorts.cfm

The positioning elements

When the proposition focus of the position has been determined, the elements to represent the public face of the brand must be selected. For destinations the most important positioning elements are the place name, a symbol, and a positioning slogan.

Destination names

In this competitive era, the single most important marketing decision you can make is what to name the product. The name is the hook that hangs the consumer brand on the product ladder in the prospect's mind (Ries & Trout, 1982, p. 28).

At the core of the brand is the product name (Aaker, 1991). A well chosen word can trigger meanings in the mind, and so a good brand name can begin the positioning process by communicating the major benefit of the product (Ries & Trout, 1982). However, there has been little empirical research into the contribution of the brand's name in the development of favourable brand associations (Keller, 1993), and little, if any, relating to destination names. Unlike new product developments, where an attempt can be made to select a name that enhances the positioning process through either memorability or development of associations, a destination will already have a place name, for which a history of associations has been developed (hopefully!) over time.

Tricky place names • • •

For all manner of political, economical, and practical reasons, it is usually extremely difficult to change a place name for tourism purposes, even though it might make sense to some marketers. For example, in New Zealand during a late-1980s crisis meeting that I attended between Rotorua's civic leaders and Japanese tour wholesalers, convened by the then mayor, John Keaney, to discuss the destination's ailing image in that market, one of the key outcomes was the suggestion that Rotorua change it's name to 'Kingstown'. This was a deliberate reference to Queenstown, which was the preferred New Zealand resort area for Japanese visitors. In line with Ries and Trout's (1982) view that brand names need aural qualities, Rotorua, which is an indigenous Maori name that translates as 'second lake' in English, did not appeal to the Japanese in the same way as destinations with English names such as Queenstown and Christchurch.

The 'Kingstown' suggestion was never pursued seriously beyond the meeting, for political and cultural reasons, and, I might add, was never made public. The local reaction to such a proposal does not bear thinking about!

The Rotorua problem is certainly not unique. Ries and Ries (2002) promoted the option for Guatemala to change to Guatemaya, in order to link the Mayan people and their heritage to one of a number of countries where Mayan ruins may be found. While well received by the business community in a destination struggling to differentiate, the idea is unlikely to happen. In Turkey, the Ankara Chamber of Trade president put forward a proposal to the country's Minister of Tourism to revise the destination name (www.eTurbonews.com, 1/3/07):

> *The name with which our country is known to the world, 'Turkey,'*
> *needs to be changed. This is the name of a bird in English and is used*
> *in a derogatory way to reflect the low intelligence of the bird.*

Anyway, there are places that owe much of their renown to a tricky name, such as Titicaca, Timbuktu, Popocateptl, Ouarzazate, and Gstaad (Anholt, 2002). So there are opportunities for places such as:

- Bum Bum Creek (Australia)
- Beer (England)
- Condom (France)
- Fucking (Austria)
- Hell (Norway), to name but a few!

Nevertheless, there are examples of destination name (re)creation around the world, which in some cases has been for branding reasons:

- In the Caribbean, Hog Island was changed to Paradise Island to appeal to the cruise tourism market (Ries & Trout, 1982).
- During the 1930s the Queensland beach town of Elston was renamed Surfers' Paradise.
- In 1996 the Republic of Cuervo was created by the well-known tequila brand (see Kotler, 1996) following the purchase of an island off the coast of Tortola in the Caribbean. The company unsuccessfully petitioned for country status at the United Nations, and for the admission of a volleyball team to the Olympics. Today the island is labelled CuervoNation (see www.cuervo.com).

Adding brand associations • • •

If not able or willing to officially change the name, amendments can be made to the name used to brand the destination. During 2003 the neighbouring Queensland beach towns of Bargara, Moore Park, and Woodgate all made moves to add the word beach to the destination name. The names Bargara Beach, Moore Park Beach, and Woodgate Beach clearly signal an important functional attribute for these small emerging destinations. Similarly, Florida's Lee County, home of the USA's best-known shell-collectors' haven Sanibel Island, changed the destination name to Lee Island Coast in promotions. In New Zealand's central North Island the official place name of Taupo has long been promoted by destination marketers as Lake Taupo to take advantage of the district's most noticeable natural feature (see, for example, www.laketauponz.com). Likewise, neighbouring district Ruapehu, which features the North Island's major skiing and climbing mountains, is promoted as Mount Ruapehu.

A further opportunity is that of labelling tourism macro-regions with tourism-related names. One example is Utah's promotional regions such as Dinasourland and Canyonlands. Another is Queensland's Gold Coast and Sunshine Coast. Other attempts at establishing emerging macro-regions labels within the state include:

- Fraser Coast, in reference to the world heritage listed Fraser Island
- Coral Coast, in reference to the southern starting point of the Great Barrier Reef
- Discovery Coast, in reference to Captain Cook's 1770 voyage of discovery, explicit in the name of the popular beach: The Town of 1770
- Capricorn Coast, in reference to the Tropic of Capricorn
- Tropical North Queensland.

By comparison, the names of England's macro-destination regions indicate a geographic reference point, such as South East England, and miss an opportunity to promote a travel benefit.

Destination symbols

I experienced an interesting example of how the multi-attributed nature of destinations represents a major challenge in the positioning process when as CEO of Tourism Rotorua I was presented with a request by a national television network for a graphic image of one local icon for use in the nightly weather segment. Only one image was permitted, which would be used consistently each night alongside images from other major centres. However, this high-profile opportunity proved a difficult selection due to the vested business interests in different icons by individual representatives of the RTO's board. Politics aside, symbols can enhance brand recognition and recall (Aaker, 1996) by serving as a mnemonic devise for the target (Aaker, 1991). A symbol can be a metaphor for the brand's personality, such as Marlboro's cowboy and Esso's tiger (King, 1991).

Since destination names have not usually been designed to reinforce or create associations with a product class, logos and slogans can play important roles as identifiers. A logo and/or slogan can be designed to reflect a desirable functional feature such as nature or an affective benefit such as relaxing. Aaker (1996, p. 205) suggested posing the question: 'What mental image would you like customers to have of your brand in the future?' A symbol can help to identify the brand with the product class as well as reflect the brand personality. For example, Virgin's logo, unconventional script, and rakish angle support the Virgin personality, which flaunts the rules (Aaker & Joachimsthaler, 2000). In particular, symbols that are metaphors for the brand personality are more meaningful. Ries and Ries (1998, p. 132) were critical of many efforts in this regard:

> *The power of a brand name lies in the meaning of the word in the mind. For most brands, a symbol has little or nothing to do with creating this meaning to the mind.*

Symbols can emerge from a diverse array of sources, such as a sound (Harley Davidson), architecture (Spanish adobe construction), the product's founder (KFC's Colonel Sanders), a colour (Hertz' yellow), packaging (Nivea cosmetics), script style (Cadbury chocolate), a programme (Ronald McDonald House), a character (Energizer bunny), a celebrity (Nike's Michael Jordan), or a distinctive logo (Adidas' three stripes). Ownership of such 'communication equity' represents a source of competitive advantage (Gilmore, 2002b).

For destinations, a symbol may represent well-established icons:

> *Such symbols as the Eiffel Tower, the Pyramids of Egypt, and the Great Wall of China are the kinds of unique and enduring symbols that DMOs are prepared to die for* (Ritchie & Ritchie, 1998, p. 113).

For other destinations the symbol may be a logo. In Figure 12.5 it can be seen that the London logo used in 2004 emphasised the well-known underground and taxi icons that play a prominent role in most visits to the British capital. Typically, the logo was recently changed again, as was the 2004 logo used for Brand Australia, shown in Figure 12.6, which featured the nation's favourite icon to provide instant recognition overseas (ATC, 2003). The design was developed through extensive research that identified the kangaroo as Australia's most recognisable symbol. Similarly, Florida's

Figure 12.5
London logo
Source: www.london-touristboard.com/

Figure 12.6
Brand Australia logo
Source: www.atc.net.au

Figure 12.7
Florida logo
Source: www.flausa.com

logo that was in use in 2004 has also been changed. The STO launched the new logo FLA USA in 1997, developed at a cost of US$237,000, including US$100,000 in market testing (*Marketing News*, 29/9/97). The report suggested that sunshine state tourism officials hoped the new logo, shown in Figure 12.7, would ultimately become as recognizable as the Nike swoosh. The Florida Tourism Industry Marketing Corporation (FTIMC), which changed the organisation name around the same time to Visit Florida, stated that the brand was designed for the long term.

Destination slogans

For most destinations a logo will not be sufficient to communicate a differentiated position. The addition of a slogan offers an opportunity to add more meaning to that which could be achieved by the brand name or symbol (Aaker, 1991). A slogan is a short phrase that communicates descriptive or persuasive information about a brand (Keller, 2003). Interestingly, it has been suggested that the word slogan emanates from the Gaelic term meaning 'battle cry' (Boyee & Arens, 1992, in Supphellen & Nygaardsvik, 2002). Slogans are also referred to as tag lines and strap lines.

As Sydney prepared for the 2000 Olympics, Ries and Ries (2002, pp. 153–154) proposed a new positioning slogan based on the following criteria:

- It should be a concept positioning Sydney as a world-class city alongside London, Paris, Rome, New York, and Hong Kong.
- It should be a concept that has a strong element of believability. People should say, 'Yes, Sydney is like that'.
- It should be a concept that is alliterative with the name Sydney, to enhance memorability.
- It should be a concept that is consistent with the symbol of the city, the Sydney Opera House.

They suggested only one slogan, 'Sydney, the world's most sophisticated city', which met all four criteria. At the time of writing, Sydney's actual positioning slogan was *There's no place in the world like Sydney*.

Too many destination slogans have been less than memorable (see Dann, 2000; Morgan et al., 2003; Ward & Gold, 1994). Best practice in destination promotion has been limited to a few simple slogans, such as the 1970s development of the 'I ♥ New York' campaign (Ward & Gold, 1994, p. 4):

> *The process of imitation, however, demonstrates a general paucity of creative ideas and effectively ensures that the vast majority of place promotional campaigns rarely manage to cross the threshold of ephemeral indifference.*

The slogans used during 2003 by NTOs are presented in Appendix 12.1. The approach used was to record the slogan used on the home page of each NTO's consumer website. The rationale was the assumption that since one of the basic tenets of integrated marketing communication is a consistency of message across different media, the slogan used on the DMO home page should represent the destination positioning theme. My content analysis of these slogans identified 14 positioning categories, which are listed below in order of popularity (see Pike, 2004):

- Leadership
- Discovery
- Nature
- Location
- People
- Water
- Self-expression
- Escape
- Pleasure
- Treasure
- Royal
- Vibrant
- Climate
- Culinary

Some destinations have resorted to public competitions to unearth a slogan. For example, during 2001 Tauranga District Council in New Zealand ran a competition inviting the public to design a new slogan for the district. The competition resulted in over 2500 submitted slogans (Cousins, 2001). Slogan competitions have not been limited to small destinations. Holcomb (1999), for example, reported a similar initiative by Atlanta in the USA. The obvious danger with competitions is that there may be political pressure to use the winning slogan, which may not be meaningful to the target market. Research Snapshot 12.2 provides a hierarchy for testing meaningfulness.

Research snapshot 12.2 · The USP

Unfortunately, there are few guidelines in the marketing literature for empirically testing brand slogans (Supphellen & Nygaardsvik, 2002). A useful study in the tourism literature concerning differentiation through slogans was reported by Richardson and Cohen (1993). They developed a hierarchical taxonomy of destination slogans featuring four criteria, based on Reeves' (1961) concept of a unique selling point (USP):

- The foundation of the hierarchy is that the slogan must be prepositional.
- Such propositions should be limited to one or only a few.
- The proposition(s) should sell benefits of interest to the market.
- The benefit(s) must be unique.

Richardson and Cohen categorised the slogans of 46 USA state tourism organisations. Commencing at level zero of the hierarchy, two of the state slogans examined, *Yes! Michigan!* and *Utah!*, were deemed not to be propositional. Ascending to level one of the hierarchy the slogans of six STOs featured propositions, but were no more than a plea to 'buy our product'. Examples at this level included *Discover Idaho* and *Explore Minnesota*. At level two, the proposition is equivalent to stating 'our product is good'. Of the 14 slogans at this level, examples included *Discover the spirit! North Dakota*, *The spirit of Massachusetts*, and *Vermont makes it special*. Level 3a featured nine slogans where the proposition promoted an attribute that represented a potential benefit but that almost every other state could claim. These included *Arkansas – the natural state*, *Maine – the way life should be*, and *Oregon – things look different here*. At level 3b the propositional benefit attribute used in the slogans of six states could be claimed by many states. These included *Ohio the heart of it all!*, *Oklahoma – native America*, and *Texas, like a whole other country*. At level 4a, the proposition features a unique attribute, but one that does not represent a benefit. The three states at this level were *Delaware – the first state*, *Pennsylvania – America starts here*, and *Rhode Island – America's first resort*. At level 4b, the pinnacle of the hierarchy, the slogans of only five states were considered to feature a USP:

- *Arizona – the Grand Canyon state*
- *Florida – coast to coast*
- *Louisiana – we're really cookin!*
- *South Dakota – great faces, great places*
- *Tennessee – we're playing your song*

Source: Richardson, J. & Cohen, J. (1993). State slogans: The case of the missing USP. *Journal of Travel and Tourism Marketing, 2*(2/3), 91–109.

Furthermore, a long-term and consistent brand strategy might be subject to tampering, following the appointment of new marketing managers who want to leave their personal stamp on strategies. McKercher and Ritchie (1997) cited the example of an LTA in Australia, which had four managers in six years. This led to the development of four different marketing plans, with each having a different positioning statement, resulting in marketplace confusion. Potential advantages of long-term consistency (see Research Snapshot 12.3) include enhanced consumer-based brand equity through (Pike, 2004):

- ownership of a position, such as 'Virginia is for lovers'
- ownership of an identity symbol/slogan such as 'I ♥ New York'
- assurance for local tourism businesses and travel intermediaries who invest resources in developing sub-brands that are compatible with the destination umbrella brand.

Research snapshot 12.3   Slogan durability

Analysis of the longevity of destination slogans requires access to historical data, which in the tourism literature is limited. This paper focuses on STOs in the USA and RTOs in New Zealand, for which slogans have been documented at previous points in time. USA state slogans used in 2003 were compared to those categorised by Richardson and Cohen (1993) and Pritchard (1982). It was felt that these timeframes provide an indication of the consistency of use over the short to medium term. Of the 47 slogans used in 1982, only 6 were still in use in 1993, and of the 46 slogans used in 1993, only 13 were still being used in 2003. Over a 21-year period, only six of the 1982 slogans remained in use in 2003: Arkansas, Delaware, Massachusetts, New Mexico, New York, and Virginia. The New Zealand RTO slogans used in 2003 are compared to those recorded by Pike (1998). Of the 15 slogans listed in 1998, nine of the RTOs had retained the same message over the five-year period.

Source: Pike, S. (2004). Destination brand positioning slogans – towards the development of a set of accountability criteria. *Acta Turistica*, *16*(2), 102–124.

Key points

1. Positioning as the interface between brand identity and brand image

The brand identity development approach outlined in Chapter 10 requires the effective positioning of the brand identity to achieve the desired brand image in the marketplace. Positioning is therefore the interface between the desired destination image and the actual image held by consumers. Effective positioning is mutually beneficial for DMOs and consumer-travellers.

2. Positioning as a source of competitive advantage

While consumers have an almost limitless number of destinations to choose from, they will only consider the merits of a small number in the actual decision process. A model of positioning as a source of competitive advantage for destinations was proposed; where decision set membership and top of mind awareness are key indicators of destination attractiveness and competitiveness.

3. The challenges involved in developing a narrow positioning focus for multi-attributed destinations

Effective positioning represents a source of advantage for destinations, but requires a succinct, focused, and consistent message tailored to meet the needs of target segments, to gain 'cut through' in crowded, heterogeneous, and dynamic markets. Key components of destination positioning are the brand name and symbols such as logos and slogans.

Review questions

- Why is positioning mutually beneficial for destination marketers and consumers?
- To what extent are the DMO slogans in Appendix 12.1 likely to be ephemerally indifferent?
- To what extent is your destination's slogan likely to appeal to all markets?

Appendix 12.1 NTO slogans in 2003

National Tourism Office	Theme	WWW URL
Afghanistan		No website
Albania	No slogan	www.albaniatourism.com
Algeria	No slogan	www.tourisme.dz/
American Samoa	American Samoa – America's South Pacific Paradise	www.tcsp.com/destinations/american_samoa/index.shtml
Andorra	No slogan	www.turisme.ad/
Angola	No slogan	www.angola.org/referenc/r_ttips.htm
Anguilla	Tranquillity wrapped in blue	http://anguilla-vacation.com/
Antigua	The Caribbean you've always imagined	www.antigua-barbuda.org/
Argentina	Visit Argentina the whole year	www.sectur.gov.ar/eng/menu.htm
Armenia		No web site
Aruba	Aruba is where happiness lives	www.aruba.com/
Ascension Island	No slogan	www.obsidian.co.ac
Australia	No core slogan – differs between markets	www.atc.net.au/brand.asp?sub=2OVE
Austria	Austria – holiday break away	www.austria-tourism.at/
Azerbaijan	No slogan	http://azerbaijan.tourism.az/
Bahamas	The Islands of the Bahamas – it just keeps getting better	www.bahamas.com/
Bahrain	Bahrain – island of golden smiles	www.bahraintourism.com/
Bangladesh		No website sourced
Barbados	Barbados – just beyond your imagination	http://barbados.org/
Belarus	No slogan	www.touragency.by/ru/
Belgium	Welcome to Flanders, Belgium	www.visitflanders.co.uk/index.html
Belize	Belize – mother nature's best kept secret	http://www.travelbelize.org/
Benin	No slogan	www.tourisme.gouv.bj/
Bermuda	No slogan	www.bermudatourism.com
Bhutan	No slogan	www.kingdomofbhutan.com/
Bolivia	No slogan	www.mcei.gov.bo
Bonaire	No slogan	www.infobonaire.com/index.html
Bosnia & Herzegovina	Bosnia & Herzegovina – your next adventure	www.bhtourism.ba/

National Tourism Office	Theme	WWW URL
Botswana	Make your own picture of Botswana	www.botswana-tourism.gov.bw/tourism/index_f.html
Brazil	If travelling is your passion, Brazil is your destiny	http://www.brazil.org.uk/turismo/brazilbrochure.pdf
British Virgin Islands	British Virgin Islands – nature's little secrets	www.bvitouristboard.com
Brunei	No slogan	www.visitbrunei.com
Bulgaria	Bulgaria – a treasure to discover	www.bvitouristboard.com
Burkina Faso	Burkina – land of tradition	www.mtt.gov.bf
Burundi	No slogan	www.burundi.gov.bi/tourisme.htm
Cambodia	No slogan	www.tourismcambodia.com/
Cameroon	Cameroon – toute l'Afrique dans un pays (All of Africa in one country)	www.bcenter.fr/cameroun/index.php
Canada	Canada – discover our true nature	www.travelcanada.ca
Cape Verde		No website
Cayman Islands	Could it be Cayman?	www.caymanislands.ky
Central African Republic		No website
Chad		No website
Chile	Chile – naturaleza que conmueve	www.sernatur.cl/
China	Coem say "Nihau"! ...and discover the glory of China	www.cnto.org.au
Colombia	No slogan	www.turismocolombia.com
Comoros		No website
Congo		No website
Cook Islands	Cook Islands – your recipe for true paradise	www.tcsp.com/destinations/cooks/index.shtml
Costa Rica	Costa Rica – no artificial ingredients	www.visitcostarica.com
Croatia	No slogan	www.croatia.hr
Cuba	Cuba – peaceful, safe and healthy tourism	www.cubatravel.cu/
Curacao	Curacao – in the Southern Caribbean. Real. Different.	www.curacao-tourism.com
Cyprus	Cyprus – irresistible for 9,000 years	www.cyprustourism.org/cyprus.html
Czech Republic	No slogan	www.czechtourism.com

National Tourism Office	Theme	WWW URL
Democratic Republic of Congo		No website
Denmark	No slogan	www.visitdenmark.com
Djibouti	Djibouti – terre d'echanges et de rencontres (Land of exchanges and meetings)	www.office-tourisme.dj
Dominica	Dominica – welcome to the nature island	www.dominica.dm/
Dominican Republic	Dominican Republic – experience our Caribbean	http://www.dominicanrepublic.com/Tourism/index.htm
Dubai	Dubai – the Gulf destination	www.dubaitourism.co.ae
East Timor		No web site
Ecuador	Ecuador – nature, culture, adventure and travel	www.vivecuador.com/
Egypt	Egypt – where history began and continues	www.egypttourism.org/
El Salvador	El Salvador – no hay nada como lo tuyo! (There is nothing like your own)	www.elsalvadorturismo.gob.sv/
England	Enjoy England	www.visitengland.com
Equatorial Guinea		No website
Eritrea		No website
Estonia	Estonia – positively transforming	www.visitestonia.com/
Ethiopia	Ethiopia – 13 months of sunshine	www.tourismethiopia.org/
Falkland Islands	No slogan	www.tourism.org.fk/
Faroe Islands	No slogan	www.tourist.fo/
Fiji	Fiji – the truly relaxing tropical getaway	www.bulafiji.com/
Finland	Finland – naturally	www.finland-tourism.com/
France	No slogan	www.franceguide.com
French Guiana		No website
Gabon	No slogan	www.gabontour.com/
The Gambia	The Gambia – welcome to your haven in Africa	www.visitthegambia.gm/
Georgia	No slogan	www.parliament.ge/tourism/
Germany	Germany – a country rich in experiences!	www.germany-tourism.de/

National Tourism Office	Theme	WWW URL
Ghana	No slogan	www.africaonline.com.gh/Tourism/ghana.html
Gibraltar	No slogan	www.gibraltar.gov.gi/
Greece	Greece – beyond words	www.gnto.gr/
Greenland	Greenland – out of this world	www.greenland.com
Grenada	Grenada – the spice of the Caribbean	www.grenada.org/
Guadelupe		No website
Guam	No slogan	www.visitguam.org/
Guatemala	No slogan	www.terra.com.gt/turismogt/
Guinea		No website
Guinea-Bassau		No website
Guyana	Guyana – the land of many waters	www.sdnp.org.gy/mtti/guyana.html
Haiti	No slogan	www.haititourisme.org/
Honduras	Honduras – one small country, three worlds apart	www.letsgohonduras.com/web/
Hong Kong	Hong Kong – live it, love it!	http://webserv2.discoverhongkong.com/login.html
Hungary	No slogan	www.hungarytourism.hu
Iceland	Iceland – discoveries, the whole year round	www.icetourist.is
India	Incredible India	www.tourismofindia.com
Indonesia	Indonesia – your genuine experience	www.indonesia-tourism.com/
Iran	No slogan	www.irantourism.org/
Iraq		No website
Ireland	Ireland – live a different life	www.ireland.travel.ie
Israel	No slogan	http://www.tourism.gov.il/english/default.asp
Italy	Pin Italia – che mai!	http://www.enit.it/default.asp?Lang=UK
Jamaica	Jamaica – one love	www.visitjamaica.com
Japan	Explore Japan	www.jnto.go.jp/
Jersey	Enjoyment begins with Jersey	www.jersey.com
Jordan	No slogan	www.see-jordan.com/
Kazakhstan	No slogan	www.kazsport.kz/
Kenya	Kenya – creation's most beautiful destinations, all in one country	www.magicalkenya.com

National Tourism Office	Theme	WWW URL
Kiribati	No slogan	www.tcsp.com/destinations/kiribati/index.shtml
Kuwait	No slogan	www.kuwaittourism.com
Kyrgyzstan		No website
Laos	Sabbai dee and welcome!	http://visit-laos.com/
Latvia	Latvia – the land that sings	www.latviatourism.lv
Lebanon	No slogan	www.lebanon-tourism.gov.lb
Lesotho	Welcome to the mountain Kingdom	www.lesotho.gov.ls/lstourism.htm
Liberia		No website
Libya		No website
Liechtenstein	Liechtenstein – princely moments	www.tourismus.li/
Lithuania	No slogan	www.tourism.lt/
Luxemburg	Grand Duchy of Luxemburg	www.ont.lu/
Macau	More than ever Macau is a festival	www.macautourism.gov.mo
Macedonia	No slogan	www.economy.gov.mk
Madagascar	No slogan	www.madagascar-contacts.com
Malawi	Malawi – the land of smiles and laughter	www.tourismmalawi.com/
Malaysia	Malaysia – truly Asia	http://tourism.gov.my/
Maldives	Maldives – the sunny side of life	www.visitmaldives.com.mv/
Mali	No slogan	www.tourisme.gov.ml
Malta	Malta – welcome to the heart of the Mediterranean	www.visitmalta.com
Marshall Islands		No website
Martinique	Martinique – the French Caribbean Haven	www.martinique.org
Mauritania	(No slogan)	www.mauritania.mr
Mauritius	Mauritius – an invitation to paradise	www.mauritius.net/
Mexico	The timeless experience – Mexico	www.visitmexico.com
Micronesia	Dive into the heart of exotic Micronesia	www.visit-fsm.org/
Moldova	No slogan	www.turism.md
Monaco	Monaco – an exceptional destination	www.monaco-tourisme.com
Mongolia	No slogan	www.mongoliatourism.gov.mn

National Tourism Office	Theme	WWW URL
Montenegro	Montenegro – art of nature	www.visit-montenegro.com
Monteserrat	Monsteserrat – one hundred thousand welcomes	www.visitmontserrat.com
Morocco	No slogan	www.tourism-in-morocco.com
Mozambique	Mozambique – new for you	www.mozambique.mz/
Myanmar	No slogan	www.myanmar.com/Ministry/Hotel_Tour/usefullink.htm
Namibia	Namibia – Africa's gem	www.met.gov.na/
Nepal	No slogan	www.welcomenepal.com
Netherlands	No slogan	www.holland.com/global/
Netherlands Artilles		No website
New Caledonia	Discover Caledonia – France's best kept secret	www.new-caledonia-tourism.nc/
New Zealand	100% pure NZ	www.purenz.com
Nicaragua	Nicaragua – a water paradise	www.intur.gob.ni/
Niger		No website
Nigeria	Nigeria – beauty in diversity	www.nigeriatourism.net/
Norfolk Island	Norfolk Island – paradise discovered	www.norfolkisland.com
Northern Ireland	Discover Northern Ireland	www.discovernorthernireland.com
Northern Marianas	My Marianas	www.mymarianas.com/
North Korea	No slogan	www.dprknta.com
Norway	Norway – a pure escape	http://www.visitnorway.com/foreign_offices/great_britain/
Nuie	Nuie – rock of Polynesia	www.niueisland.com/
Oman		No website
Pakistan	No slogan	www.tourism.gov.pk/
Palestine	Palestine – the Holy land	www.visit-palestine.com/
Palau	Experience the wonders of Palau	www.visit-palau.com
Panama	Panama – the path less travelled	www.visitpanama.com
Papua New Guinea		No website
Paraguay	No slogan	www.senatur.gov.py
Peru	Pack your six senses – come to Peru	www.peru.org.pe/perueng.asp
Philippines	Philippines – more than the usual	www.tourism.gov.ph/

National Tourism Office	Theme	WWW URL
Pitcairn Islands	No slogan	www.government.pn
Poland	No slogan	www.travelpoland.com/
Portugal		
Puerto Rico	Go to Puerto Rico	www.gotopuertorico.com
Qatar		No website
Reunion		No website
Romania	Romania – come as a tourist, leave as a friend	www.romaniatourism.com/
Russia	No slogan	www.russia-tourism.ru/
Rwanda		No website
Saba	Saba – the unspoiled queen…in the Dutch Caribbean	www.sabatourism.com
Samoa	Samoa – the treasured islands of the South Pacific	www.visitsamoa.us
San Marino	No slogan	www.visitsanmarino.com/
Sao Tome and Principe	Sao Tome & Principe – paradise on Earth	www.saotome.st/
Sark	No slogan	www.sark.info
Saudi Arabia	No slogan	www.sct.gov.sa/
Scotland	Live it – visit Scotland	www.visitscotland.com/
Senegal	No slogan	www.dakarville.sn/tourisme
Serbia	Serbia – three times love	www.serbia-tourism.org/
Seychelles	Seychelles – as pure as it gets	www.aspureasitgets.com
Sierra Leone		No website
Singapore	Singapore roars	www.visitsingapore.com
Slovakia	Slovakia – your choice	www.slovakiatourism.sk/
Slovenia	Slovenia – the green place of Europe	www.slovenia-tourism.si/
Solomon Islands	Solomon Islands – the treasured islands of Melanesia	www.tcsp.com/destinations/solomons/index.shtml
Somalia		No website
South Africa	Discover South Africa	www.southafrica.net/
South Korea	No slogan	www.tour2korea.com
Spain	No slogan	www.spain.info/Portal/EN
Sri Lanka	Sri Lanka – a land like no other	www.lanka.net/ctb/
St Barthelemy	No slogan	www.st-barths.com/homeeng.html

National Tourism Office	Theme	WWW URL
St Helena	Discover St Helena – emerald isle of the South Atlantic Ocean	www.sthelenatourism.com
St Kitts and Nevis	St Kitts and Nevis – two islands, one paradise	www.interknowledge.com/stkitts-nevis/
St Lucia	St Lucia – simply beautiful	www.stlucia.org/
St Maarten	St Maarten – a little European, a lot of Caribbean!	www.st-maarten.com/
St Martin	St Martin – French Caribbean	www.st-martin.org/
St Vincent and the Grenadines	St Vincent and the Grenadines – jewels of the Caribbean	www.svgtourism.com
Sudan		No website
Surinam	Surinam – the drum beat of the Amazon	www.surinam.net
Swaziland	Swaziland – the royal experience	www.mintour.gov.sz/
Sweden	No slogan	www.visit-sweden.com
Switzerland	Switzerland – get natural	www.myswitzerland.com/
Sudan		No website
Syria	No slogan	www.syriatourism.org
Tahiti	Tahiti – islands beyond the ordinary	www.tahiti-tourisme.com/
Taiwan	Taiwan – touch your heart	www.taiwan.net.tw/index.jsp
Tajikistan	Adventure on the roof of the world	www.traveltajikistan.com
Tanzania	No slogan	www.tanzania-web.com
Thailand	No slogan	www.tourismthailand.org/
Togo		No website
Tokelau Islands		No website
Tonga	The ancient Kingdom of Tonga	www.tongaholiday.com/
Trinidad & Tobago	No slogan	www.visittnt.com/
Tunisia	No slogan	www.tourismtunisia.com
Turkey	Go with the rhythm…enjoy Turkey	www.turizm.gov.tr/
Turkish Republic of Northern Cyprus	No slogan	www.trncwashdc.org/c000.html
Turkmenistan		No website
Turks & Caicos Islands	Turks & Caicos Islands – get lost	www.turksandcaicostourism.com/

National Tourism Office	Theme	WWW URL
Tuvalu	Tuvalu – timeless!	www.tcsp.com/destinations/tuvalu/index.shtml
Uganda	Uganda – the pearl of Africa	www.visituganda.com/
Ukraine	No slogan	www.tourism.gov.ua/
United Arab Emirates	No slogan	www.uae.org.ae/tourist/index.htm
United Kingdom	No slogan	www.visitbritain.com
Uruguay	Uruguay – natural	www.turismo.gub.uy/
United States of America	No slogan	www.tinet.ita.doc.gov
US Virgin Islands	US Virgin Islands – America's Caribbean	www.usvitourism.vi/en
Uzbekistan	No slogan	www.uzbektourism.uz/
Vatican City	No slogan	www.vatican.va
Vanuatu	Vanuatu – another time, another place	www.vanuatutourism.com
Venezuela	No slogan	www.turismoparatodos.org.ve
Vietnam	Vietnam – a destination for the new millennium	www.vietnamtourism.com/
Wales	Be inspired by Wales	www.visitwales.com
Wallis and Futuna	No slogan	www.wallis.co.nc/adsupwf/
West Sahara		No website
Yemen	Yemen – be ready to be astounded	http://yementourism.com/index.htm
Zambia	Zambia – the real Africa	www.zambiatourism.com/
Zimbabwe	(No slogan)	www.zimbabwetourism.co.zw

CHAPTER • • • • • **13**

Target markets

Positioning usually implies a segmentation commitment. Positioning usually means that an overt decision is being made to concentrate only on certain segments. Such an approach requires commitment and discipline because it's not easy to turn your back on potential buyers.

Aaker & Shansby (1982, p. 61)

Aims

The aims of this chapter are to enhance understanding of:

- the need to prioritise target markets
- segmentation approaches
- the challenge of market positioning in multiple target markets

Perspective

Positioning has its roots in segmentation theory. The first task in developing profitable customer relationships is the identification of target markets. The DMO marketing approach differs to the generally accepted definition of the marketing orientation as presented in general marketing theory in at least one significant way. A marketing orientation was defined in Chapter 1 as a philosophy that recognises the achievement of organisational goals that requires an understanding of the needs and wants of the target market, and then delivering satisfaction more effectively than rivals. With such an orientation, all marketing decisions are made with the customer in mind. Most DMOs have no control over the tourism services they represent, and devote relatively few resources to new product development tailored to meet identified consumer needs. Therefore, the marketing process is not one of designing products to meet market needs, but of attempting to find markets that are likely to be interested in the destination's current products and then communicating an attractive proposition. Identifying market segments that may have an interest in the destination's product range is a critical task for DMOs.

Identifying target markets

On the demand side of destination marketing, the global market of consumer-travellers is not homogenous in terms of needs (Wahab et al., 1976). Travellers from different geographic areas, socio-demographic groups, and lifestyle clusters will respond to different offers at different times, for a complex array of reasons, including the purpose of travel, individual motivation(s), time available, the time of year, and availability of other discretionary spending opportunities. Consumers will engage in different types of travel at different times of the year and their lifetime. Thousands of DMOs now compete for the attention of busy consumers through communication channels cluttered with noise from rival and substitute offerings. The greatest challenge facing DMOs is to effectively differentiate their offering at decision time.

A market orientation dictates outward-inward market-organisation thinking (Duncan, 2002). In tourism this means first anticipating travellers' needs and then developing products and services to meet these. Historically, DMOs have generally used inward-outward thinking by attempting to find markets that will be interested in a destination's existing products. While targeting products to the perceived needs of specific segments is a marketing axiom, DMOs have a broad mandate and therefore operate in mass markets with millions of consumers. Tourism demand does not represent a homogenous group of people with identical motivations (Wahab et al., 1976), and as already discussed the market interests of a destination's tourism businesses can be divergent. However, the need to focus resources then leads on to the central operational decision of tourism marketers to prioritise target markets. Positioning has its roots in segmentation theory (Haahti, 1986), and the two concepts have become inseparable in the marketing process.

Market aggregation represents an undifferentiated approach, where all consumers are treated as one, and is criticised as being a shotgun approach. At the opposite end of the continuum is total market disaggregating, where every consumer is treated individually as a separate segment. There are obvious limits as to how far this can be taken by DMOs. However, important trade customers such as inbound tour operators are an example of marketing to the needs of an identifiable individual client.

A destination's image may differ between regional markets (Hunt, 1975), between different segments (Fakeye & Crompton, 1991; Phelps, 1986), and in different travel contexts. However, DMOs seldom research the differences in the images held by different markets (Ahmed, 1996) and different travel contexts. Pechlaner and Abfalter (2002) criticised many NTOs in Europe for paying insufficient attention to the differences between markets, suggesting they were limited to using undifferentiated but cost-effective marketing, which targeted common interests and needs of all travellers. However, undertaking needs analyses on a segment-by-segment basis provides marketers with opportunities to understand the needs of target segments better than competitors (Lovelock, 1991). Research Snapshot 13.1 provides an example of this.

Research snapshot 13.1 Do you want to feel the spirit?

It has been suggested that of all the features New Zealand has to offer international visitors there is only one that is truly unique and that is the indigenous Maori people and their culture. This represents a key source of differentiation for the district of Rotorua, which has long been regarded as the country's centre of Maori culture. One-third of the local population is Maori and the district has a proud history of providing cultural experiences to travellers. Not surprisingly, the brand positioning theme launched in 1996 reflects this ... *Feel the spirit Manaakitanga*. That the theme was designed for use in all markets assumes that all markets will have an interest in Maori culture. Research into how Rotorua was positioned in the important domestic short-break market suggested strongly that Maori culture was not regarded as either a salient or determinant attribute. Rotorua has a strong position in the domestic market, but one that is based on other attributes such as 'lots do do', 'good accommodation', 'good cafes' etc. The research indicated that Rotorua should therefore consider using a different positioning theme in the domestic short-break market, to reinforce positively held perceptions.

Source: Pike, S. & Ryan, C. (2004). Dimensions of short-break destination attractiveness – a comparison of cognitive, affective and conative perceptions. *Journal of Travel Research*, 42(4), 333–342.

Positioning is based on communicating one or a few key benefits desired by the target segment. Since destinations operate in mass markets containing individuals with differing needs, can one positioning theme be adapted for use in all markets, or do the different characteristics of each market dictate a mix of distinct tailored themes as in the *think global, act local* mantra? In theory, the latter would enable separate advertising briefs to be developed that cater to the needs of different segments. However, from a practical perspective, when considering the range of segments that will be of interest to a DMO's stakeholders, both a multi-market assessment and a differentiated promotion approach appear daunting. As observed by Hooley and Saunders (1993, p. 154), an organisation taking the multiple segment approach 'may face a diseconomy in managing, supplying and promoting in a different way to each of these segments it has chosen'. Woodside (1982) also presented a warning in this regard, suggesting that it is more effective to offer one set of benefits to one significant segment.

Segmentation

Segmentation can be undertaken either by *a priori* means, where the criterion variable for dividing the market is already known, or by *posteriori* means, where no such prior knowledge exists (Calantone & Mazanec, 1991). For practical reasons many smaller DMOs will use an *a priori* approach to segmenting the global market. This is undertaken using criteria relating to easily obtainable information on geographic and demographic characteristics. For example, destinations in Central America and the Caribbean place a heavy reliance on visitors from cities in North America, while 15% of all USA arrivals are from Latin American countries (TIA, 2004, in www.restaurantnewsresource.com, 29/304). In Queensland, Australia, the largest source of visitors for each of the state's RTOs is the state capital, Brisbane.

Case Study 13.1 provides a practical example of one small destination's development of a new strategy to appeal to the growing 'silver' market.

Case study 13.1 Pimp my Nordic walking stick

Ilja Castermans-Godfried, Zuyd University, Centre of Research for Cultural Tourism, Sittard, The Netherlands

Destination marketers in the province of Limburg, which is located in the south of The Netherlands, have set two key tourism development goals. The first is to become the number two province for tourists in the Netherlands, and the second is to attract 25% more silver tourists (age 50+). In doing so, the strategy recognises the need to stimulate small and medium enterprises to be better equipped to satisfy the needs and wants of this growing target group. These experienced holidaymakers expect high quality and seek new surprising products and services from the tourism industry. Key questions asked by Limburg tourism stakeholders in the development of the strategy included: How can local hotel entrepreneurs better satisfy this demanding target segment? What innovative concepts can be developed to attract more silvers to the region?

One organisation that has responded to the DMO strategy is The Heuvelland Hotel Group (www.heuvellandhotels.nl). The group comprises 13 family hotels in South-Limburg (near

Maastricht), which started to cooperate six years ago. It was felt that the timing of the new strategy presented an ideal opportunity to further develop the alliance by introducing innovative concepts that would attract more tourists to the region and to the hotels. As part of the preparation to this project, and to obtain insight into the market in general, an analysis of the major problems that the entrepreneurs encounter in the external environment was conducted. Following this external analysis, each hotel was submitted to a hospitality audit consisting of surveys among guests in the target segment, and anonymous visits by mystery silver guests. The most important outcome of this research was that guest satisfaction was very high.

In the next stage students of the Maastricht Hotel Management School carried out a benchmark study in order to review innovative concepts within and outside the hospitality business, and to select the most appropriate concepts for the hotels. The outcomes of this project were the fuel for the final and most important part of the strategy, which was the implementation of innovative concepts by the entrepreneurs. Four promising innovative concepts were selected for implementation. The philosophy guiding selection of each was that they: (1) are new for the Heuvelland Hotels, (2) will further enhance the cooperation between the Heuvelland Hotels and other hospitality and leisure entrepreneurs, and (3) have the potential to attract more tourists to the region. At the time of writing, the concepts under development included:

- **Pimp my Nordic Walking Stick.** Artists who live in South-Limburg will be asked to pimp Nordic walking sticks in all 13 hotels. The first design, shown below, quickly attracted media publicity.

- **Heuvelland passport.** A passport distributed in conjunction with leisure enterprises in the region. The passport enables guests to obtain discounts and special activities.
- **Holiday planner.** On the portal site of the Heuvelland Hotel Group a holiday planner will be integrated.

Discussion question

What other innovative concepts would stimulate the cooperation between entrepreneurs in the hospitality and leisure sectors, and attract more silver tourists to the region?

Market portfolio models

A number of methods for measuring international markets in relative terms have been reported in the literature, such as the market potential index developed by the United States Travel Service (see Lundberg, 1990), Western Australia's market potential assessment formula (see Crockett & Wood, 1999), and the country potential generation index (CPGI) (Hudman, 1979, in Formica & Littlefield, 2000, p. 110). For example, the CPGI is expressed as:

$$CPGI = \frac{Nc/Nw}{Pc/Pw}$$

Where: Nc = the number of trips generated by the country

Nw = the number of trips generated in the world

Pc = the population of the country

Pw = population of the world

A weakness of the CPGI approach is that the model does not consider other important factors such as accessibility and per capita wealth. A more comprehensive method is multifactor portfolio modelling, which has been based on a two-dimensional matrix combining measures of market attractiveness and competitive position (see Mazanec, 1997). The matrix presents a visual tool similar to the growth-share matrix used by businesses to plot their product portfolio by market share and market growth (see, for example, Johnson & Scholes, 2002, p. 284). For destinations, market attractiveness variables considered for inclusion include market size, growth rate, seasonality effects, and price levels, while competitive position might include variables related to market share, image, and advertising budgets. Destinations and markets are rated on each variable, which are subjectively assigned a weighting since not all will be of equal importance. For processing such data Mazanec promoted the use of the IAAWIN software, which was freely available from the Vienna University of Economics and Business Administration (see www.wu-wien.ac.at). A variation of this method, using a 3×3 matrix, was reported by Henshall and Roberts (1985) in a comparative assessment of New Zealand's major markets.

Another portfolio approach, the destination-market matrix (DMM), which provides more balance between quantitative and qualitative analysis, was promoted by McKercher (1995). The DMM incorporates the destination lifecycle as well as the growth-share matrix, and displays six relationships between the destination and its markets:

- the relative importance of each market
- each market's lifecycle stage
- the age of each market in each lifecycle stage, which forms the basis of the horizontal axis
- a prediction of future performance, which forms the basis of the vertical axis
- the total number of markets attracted to the destination
- the interrelationship existing among all these markets.

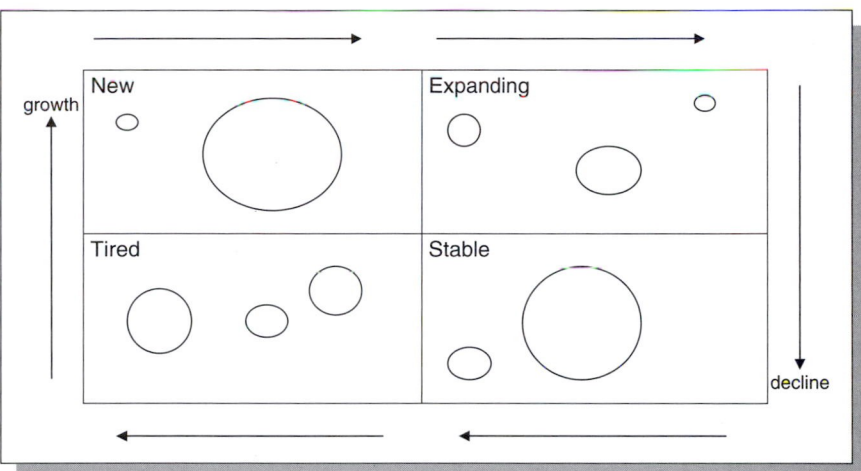

Figure 13.1
Destination-market
matrix

The four cells of the DMM, shown in Figure 13.1, represent the lifecycle stages each market would be expected to follow: 'new', 'expanding', 'stable', and 'tired'. Each circle represents a market of interest, in terms of relative size and future performance. A critical assumption of the model is that markets progress through the matrix in a clockwise direction, starting as a 'new' market in the top left-hand corner. The horizontal axis represents the age of the market in the cell. McKercher suggested that the benefits of the DMM were its flexibility, in that markets could be segmented by whatever means was most suitable to the DMO, and the ability to track the performance over time. Three Australian case studies were provided in the paper to demonstrate its effectiveness as a visual planning tool. The DMM was used by McKercher to graphically highlight unbalanced growth at the Gold Coast, the state of Victoria in decline, and balanced growth for Australia as a whole.

General utilities of market portfolio modelling techniques include aiding DMO decisions relating to promotional budget allocation for each market and enhancing understanding of the destination's relative reliance on key markets. These can then be graphically presented to stakeholders to promote or justify strategies. Often it is only with hindsight that the full implications of an over-reliance on particular markets is realised. This was particularly evident in Australia and New Zealand during the 1990s Asian economic crisis when an over-reliance on markets in the region proved a weakness of many tourism businesses. Similarly, one of the major problems in the downturn in visitors to Majorca during the 1980s was an over-reliance on the UK and German markets, which accounted for 70% of the island's visitors (Morgan, 1991). The portfolio approach can also be used by a DMO on a market-by-market basis to plot current and future attractiveness of the destination's individual products. This is useful for destinations with a diverse range of products that have differing levels of appeal for different markets. A competitive analysis of the attractiveness of other destinations' product portfolios may also be undertaken.

The *posteriori* segmentation approach usually utilises more sophisticated multivariate techniques, such as cluster analysis, to identify groups within a population that exhibit or state similar psychographic characteristics. These will involve more subjectively defined criteria such as attitudes, desired benefits, and behavioural intent. Another means is by travel purpose, including special interest groups. An almost limitless list of these include such diverse examples as: medical tourists, business meetings, incentive groups, school reunions, education field trips, bird-watchers, calligraphers, collectors, country music fans, bikers, and surfers. As examples, this section discusses three significant markets that have emerged in recent years which provide opportunities for DMOs to generate repeat visitation and destination loyalty, but which have not yet attracted significant academic research attention in may parts of the world: short breaks, gay and lesbian tourism, and family-related tourism.

Short breaks

The term *short break* is firmly entrenched in the travel industry vernacular and has regularly been the topic of articles in trade publications and in the popular press. Also, in Australia, for example, *The Sunday Mail* features a weekly travel column entitled 'Short Breaks'. However, in the tourism literature it was as recent as 1990 that Fache (1990, p. 5) referred to short breaks as a 'new form of recreation'.

Short breaks have emerged relatively recently as a significant holiday trend in Europe (Euromonitor, 1987; Fache, 1990), Australasia (Pike, 2002c, 2007) and North America (Kotler, et al., 1998; Plog, 2000). The majority of research into this travel segment has been in the UK, where the focus has been on commercial hotel packages (see, for example, Davies, 1990; Edgar, Litteljohn, Allardyce & Wanhill, 1994; Middleton & O'Brien, 1987; Teare et al., 1989; Edgar, 1997). Domestic weekend-break packages, by UK hotels, was one of a range of initiatives to counter static domestic and international visitor growth during the late-1970s. By the 1990s commercial short breaks in the UK had evolved from an off-season contribution towards fixed costs, to an all-year growth market (Edgar et al., 1994). In Europe it has been claimed that short breaks were growing at a faster rate than other holiday types Lohmann (1990, 1991) and generated the highest per day spend (Gratton, 1990). Gratton suggested that increases in the number of short breaks taken each year had reversed the decline in domestic tourism experienced in many European countries during the 1970s.

Increases in leisure time and disposable income have led to one or more shorter holidays being taken each year, which supplemented the annual holiday (Euromonitor, 1987). However, there has been little empirical investigation of the extent to which short breaks either replace or supplement the main holiday. Euromonitor also estimated that almost one-third of people took more than one such break per year, and that 40% of all holidays taken were short breaks. More recently, my own research in Australia (Pike 2004, 2007) and in New Zealand (Pike, 2002) found that participants averaged three to four short-break holidays each year. Qualitative comments from participants indicate the short break is now a psychological necessity to temporarily escape daily pressures. Fache (1994) summarised the following characteristics of short breaks:

- they do not replace annual holidays
- destinations are usually within the home country
- private cars are the main form of transport
- short breaks are taken throughout the year
- short-break takers are relatively high-spenders
- short breaks are usually a spontaneous decision

Short-break holidays lack an internationally recognised definition (Edgar, 2001). In the UK and Europe they have commonly been referred to as short holidays of up three nights (see Euromonitor, 1987; Fache, 1994; van Middelkoop, Borgers & Timmermans, 1999). However, Edgar pointed to emerging thinking that short breaks are more likely to be up to four or five nights. Intuitively, this appears reasonable given that four or five nights may or may not be considered a main holiday in many parts of the world. Although more exploratory research is needed to clarify this, I suggest that a short-break holiday is a non-business trip of between one and four nights away from the home environment.

Despite the clear significance of the short-break market, relatively few published market perceptions studies have focused on this travel context. Indeed, only two of 142 destination image papers published in the literature between 1973 and 2000 indicated an interest in short-break holidays (see Pike, 2002a). Chon et al. (1991) investigated the image of Norfolk, Virginia as a 'mini-break' destination, while McClellan (1998) analysed perceptions of Cherbourg as a potential short-break destination for French and English travellers.

In practice

Northern Tasmania Tourism offers local tourism businesses the opportunity to buy into a short-break campaign (for a copy of the prospectus see www.northerntasmania.org.au/webdata/resources/files/Short_Break_Campaign.pdf). In 2007 the $218,000 campaign ran from May to September, and promoted food, wine, heritage, culture, and Australian Football to two domestic markets: Melbourne's inner-east suburbs and Hobart's southern suburbs. Short breaks account for 18% of visitors to the region and 10% of visitor spend. Opportunities for tourism businesses to participate included:

- A display at the Tamar Valley Fine Wine and Food Festival, supported by media advertising and a letter box brochure drop.
- A display at the Melbourne and Sydney Good Food and Wine Shows, where a competition would be used to develop an e-marketing database of enquirers.

- Cooperative advertising in the *Australian Gourmet Traveller* magazine.
- Cooperative print, radio, and TV advertising.
- Inclusion in web-based suggested itineraries.
- Short-break brochure.
- Visiting journalist programme.

Gay and lesbian tourism

In the emerging field of research about gay and lesbian travellers in the tourism literature it is evident that there are mixed views about the justification for targeting this segment. On one hand, there is a stereotypical image of an affluent group with a high propensity for travel. In 2006, for example, the 11th Annual Gay & Lesbian Travel Survey in the USA (see www.communitymarketinginc.com) found that 71% of lesbians and gay men held a valid passport, and that 68% of the gay men and 57% of the lesbians surveyed travelled internationally in the previous year. On the other hand, there has been criticism from host communities and gay travellers alike, about some negative impacts on society. Hughes' (2002) literature review found a number of reasons for warranting or not warranting the targeting of gay markets by urban destinations. These are summarised in Table 13.1.

Hughes summarised the travel needs of gay men as seeking destinations that meet the usual needs of a holiday, but which also offer 'gay space', such as in pubs and clubs, as well as a lack of homophobia among residents.

Table 13.1   Targeting gay markets by urban destinations

For	Against
- the group represents a new market for existing products - they are perceived to be interested inurban tourism - general characteristics of gay men include a propensity for and frequency of travel, high travel spend, high income and education levels, an interest in culture, few family connections, and more free time	- the characteristics are not universally applicable to all gays and lesbians - segmentation by sexual orientation conceals other characteristics such as age, race, attitudes, and interests, which may have a stronger bearing on travel purchase patterns

In practice

The BTA produced a brochure entitled *Britain: You don't know the half of it* (later renamed *Britain: Inside and Out*) as part of a promotion targeting gay travellers in New York, Chicago, and Los Angeles (*Time International*, 1999, p. 28). The brochure, which touted London as the gay capital of Europe, and the seaside resorts of Brighton, Bournemouth, and Torquay as the 'queens of the south', provided details of gay pubs, clubs, hotels, shops, and bath houses. At the time the UK was attracting half a million international gay visitors annually. Spokesperson Louise Wood commented on the campaign rationale: 'We're actively targeting the pink dollar. American gays are frequent travellers, long stayers, and big spenders.' One RTB to capitalise on the BTA/Visit Britain campaign has been Marketing Manchester. Manchester features a unique gay space, hosts an annual Gayfest, and was home to the television series *Queer as Folk*. Tactics have included advertising in gay media, direct mail, representation at gay pride events, and distribution of a dedicated gay Manchester brochure. The campaign focused on emphasising the city's gay space, and provided reassurance about the community's tolerance of alternative lifestyles. In Australia, Tourism Victoria launched an international gay and lesbian tourism campaign in 2003 (www.tourismvictoria.com.au/newsletter/july_2003/story7.htm, 7/7/03). Key elements of the campaign included the Melbourne Gay and Lesbian Visitors' Guide and a newly branded gay specific website (see www.visitmelbourne.com/gaytravel).

DMOs targeting the gay market should also be prepared for criticism from the host population. Marketing Manchester's campaign has been criticised by prominent civic leaders as promoting 'sex tourism' and therefore alienating other visitors (Hughes, 2002). It was as recent as 1994 in New Zealand that the CEO of the RTO for the leading resort area Queenstown described the local council's decision to criticise a New Zealand Tourism Board (NZTB) campaign targeting the Australian gay market as 'discrimination' (*Inside Tourism*, IT487, 27/2/04, p. 8). The council passed a motion to not support any tourism promotion based on 'ethnic, race, religious, or sexual grounds'. Earlier, the country's Minister of Tourism, John Banks, stated that he was also against the NZTB's gay campaign, although he did not want to ban homosexual visitors. *Time International* (1999) reported that the new sexual openness by the British NTO was only possible following the election of the Labour government in 1997. However, Visit Britain's campaign has been slammed by some in the local gay community for a range of reasons such as welcoming gay money but not extending basic human rights like adequate policing of London's gay quarter, and stimulating 'gawping' heterosexual tourists who were creating a fishbowl effect. 'You feel like you are in a zoo' suggested one gay travel writer.

Visiting friends and relatives

Travel to visit friends and relatives (VFR) generates repeat visitors to a destination (see Gitelson & Crompton, 1984), and represents a significant component of travel patterns. With strong bonds to a destination's residents, the VRF market is generally more resilient than other segments (Godfrey & Clarke, 2000). Chon and Singh (1995) cited research by the US Travel Data Centre, which estimated almost half of leisure travel in the USA involved VFR. Clearly this presents opportunities for DMOs. For example, Stephenville in Newfoundland effectively developed a visitor market out of VFR links from marriages between USA military personnel and local women (Butler & Baum, 1999). Over 25,000 servicemen served in Newfoundland from the 1940s to 1960s. VFR tourism also offers opportunities for regions that have been characterised by high migration levels. These range from small rural areas that have experienced urban drift to countries such as Ireland, New Zealand, and Samoa, which have disproportionately large percentages of expatriates living abroad. The latter in particular enjoys seasonal influxes of visiting expatriates from the USA, Australia, and New Zealand, whose regular trips provide valuable cash injections to the fragile economy.

The VFR market also presents a number of challenges for DMOs, not the least of which is that it is not viewed positively by all in the tourism industry, and DMOs must take due care to investigate its feasibility. Critics argue that the market often ties up valuable aircraft capacity, particularly at peak holiday periods, but at the same time makes relatively little use of accommodation and tourist attractions, such as illustrated in Research Snapshot 13.3. McKercher (1996, in Bleasdale & Kwarko, 2000) described VFR tourism as an invisible activity, given the difficulty in isolating the segment within aggregated statistics.

Research snapshot 13.3   Ghana's high proportion of VFR

Bleasdale and Kwarko investigated the opportunity for Ghana to capitalise on the potential of VFR tourism. Ghana has a poorly developed image as a tourism, destination relative to competing destinations in the region such as The Gambia and South Africa. The country also suffers from the existence of health hazards such as malaria and a lack of investment capital and tourism infrastructure. In 1988 it was estimated that half of all international visitors were Ghanaian, and that many others travelling on USA or UK passports were of Ghanaian origin. Despite the high proportion of VFR travellers, their survey of Ghanaians residing in London found that very few used commercial accommodation or visited tourism attractions. They recommended therefore that the Ghana Tourist Board needed to develop proactive initiatives if the VFR segment was to contribute more to the development of the tourism industry.

Source: Bleasdale, S. & Kwarko, P. (2000) Is there a role for visiting friends and relatives in Ghana's tourism development strategy? In M. Robinson, N. Evans, P. Long, R. Sharpley, & J. Swarbrooke, (eds), *Management, Marketing and the Political Economy of Tourism* (pp. 13–22. Sunderland: Centre for Travel & Tourism.

Related to VFR is genealogy tourism or kinship tourism. Although there has been little published research to date, many destinations have the opportunity to target markets where settlers either emigrated from or emigrated to. For example, regarding the former, the *Evening News* (4/2/03, p. 14) reported on an initiative by Edinburgh tourism businesses that involved a sales mission to Canada and the USA to 'strengthen bonds of kinship' with Scotland. North America is Scotland's largest overseas market. Visit Scotland operates a dedicated website (see www.ancesteralscotland.com) under the promotional theme 'Follow in the footsteps of your ancestors … all the way home.' A report in the *National Post* (6/1/03) cited a government commissioned study in Canada that found that one-third of Canadians are interested in genealogy tourism.

In practice

Invite the World was implemented by Tourism Vancouver in 2002 to urge residents to invite friends and relatives from around the world to visit the destination. The CVB encouraged residents to send an e-postcard from tourismvancouver.com to contacts outside of Vancouver and British Columbia. In doing so, the resident was automatically entered into a weekly prize draw. The campaign ran from March to November at a cost of over C$400,000, three-quarters of which was generated from sponsors. Key results included:

- 14,098 e-postcards sent from tourismvancouver.com compared to 4122 sent over the same time period 2001; an increase of 242%
- 1,539,573 unique visits to tourismvancouver.com compared to 976,390 over the same time period 2001; an increase of 58%.
- 7966 qualified names collected by permission data capture for future e-marketing efforts.

Key points

1. The need to prioritise target markets

On the demand side of destination marketing, the global market of consumer-travellers is not homogenous in terms of needs. Travellers from different geographic areas, socio-demographic groups, and lifestyle clusters will respond to different offers at different times, for a complex array of reasons, including the purpose of travel, individual motivation(s), time available, the time of year, and availability of other discretionary spending opportunities. Consumers will engage in different types of travel at different times of the year and their lifetime. The greatest challenge facing DMOs is to effectively differentiate their offering at decision time.

2. Segmentation approaches

Market aggregation represents an undifferentiated approach, where all consumers are treated as one, and is criticised as being a shotgun approach. At the opposite end of the continuum is total market disaggregating where every consumer is treated individually as a separate segment. Segmentation can be undertaken either by *a priori* means, where the criterion variable for dividing the market is already known, or by *posteriori* means, where no such prior knowledge exists. For practical reasons many smaller DMOs will use an *a priori* approach to segmenting the global market. This is undertaken using criteria relating to easily obtainable information on geographic and demographic characteristics.

3. The challenge of market positioning in multiple target markets

While targeting products to the perceived needs of specific segments is a marketing axiom, DMOs have a broad mandate and therefore operate in mass markets with millions of consumers. The market interests of a destination's tourism businesses can be divergent. Positioning has its roots in segmentation theory, and the two concepts have become inseparable in the marketing process. A critical question for DMOs to address is whether one brand positioning theme will be meaningful in all markets of interest to stakeholders.

Review questions

- What key market segments are targeted by your DMO?
- Are separate positioning themes used for different target segments? If not, to what extent is the positioning theme relevant in each market?
- To what extent is your DMO explicitly targeting the following segments: short breaks, gay and lesbians, families?

CHAPTER 14

Marketing communications

The advertising and promotion programme is the most visible activity of a tourism board and is certain to be received with mixed reviews by the community. Criticism is likely, and board members should develop thick skins.

Gee & Makens (1985, p. 29)

Aims

The aims of this chapter are to enhance understanding of:

- integrated marketing communications (IMC)
- the potential value of visitor relationship management (VRM).

> **Perspective**
>
> There is no shortage of ways in which a destination can be promoted, and in every destination community there will be a diverse range of opinions on the tactics that should be employed. Local tourism operators' views on promotional priorities will vary for a range of reasons, including: differing levels of professional experience in marketing and tourism, vested business interests in specific types of products and target markets, access to financial resources, and their position within local industry politics. To provide a structure for stakeholders, this chapter discusses the ways in which the DMO communicates the brand position in the marketplace, based on the five tenets of integrated marketing communications (IMC). Since a key concept underpinning IMC is developing profitable relationships with targeted customers, the discussion also focuses on the largely untapped potential for visitor relationship management (VRM) by DMOs.

Integrated marketing communications

Anyone who has worked within a DMO for any length of time will almost certainly have experienced the frustration of being surrounded by many different stakeholders offering conflicting advice. Criticism can emerge at any time and from many quarters, including the media, tourism operators, travel intermediaries, government officials and elected representatives, local residents, and even other DMOs. Occasionally, the feedback is made public, such as in the criticism by local government and tourism operators in Edinburgh aimed at Visit Britain for their 'ludicrous' non-promotion of the city's famous arts festivals (see Ferguson, 2003). Critics claimed that Visit Britain advertising focused on fringe festivals instead of major attractions such as the Edinburgh International Festival and Edinburgh Military Tattoo. However, the NTO argued that given that the city is always 'booked up' during major events, advertising funds were better directed elsewhere.

Clearly, dialogue is required with the business community and host population during marketing planning, and yet the DMO must be careful to avoid the trap of trying to please everyone. The emergent shift in thinking towards destinations as brands requires a management approach that focuses on developing relationships with customers rather than simply focusing on generating sales. One such approach is integrated marketing communication (IMC), which has emerged relatively recently in the marketing literature. The first IMC texts appeared in the early 1990s (see Schultz, Tannenbaum & Lauterborn, 1993). A 2007 survey of the US Association of National Advertisers identified IMC as the highest-ranking issue for the next year (see www.ana.net). However, the topic has received little academic research attention to date in the destination marketing field, even though the issue was raised three decades ago by Wahab, Crampon & Rothfield (1976, p. 182). IMC has been defined as:

> ... a process of managing the customer relationships that drive brand value. More specifically, it is a cross-functional process from creating and nourishing profitable relationships with customers and other stakeholders by strategically controlling or influencing all messages sent to these groups and encouraging data-driven, purposeful dialogue with them (Duncan, 2002).

Inherent in this description are five important tenets that provide both opportunities and challenges for DMOs:

1. Profitable customer relationships
2. Enhancing stakeholder relationships
3. Cross-functional process
4. Stimulating purposeful dialogue with customers
5. Message synergy

Profitable customer relationships

One of the key goals in marketing is enhancing brand loyalty, which, as discussed in Chapter 10, is a critical component of consumer-based destination brand equity. The rationale for stimulating relationships with customers is that these will be more profitable over time than a series of one-off sales transactions, since the cost of reaching a continuous stream of new customers will outweigh the cost of keeping in touch with existing customers. The topics of destination loyalty, repeat visitation, and customer relationship management (CRM) have attracted relatively little research attention in the tourism literature.

The internet has impacted on the way firms interact with customers, with key issues being access, control, speed, globalisation, and automation (see Kincaid, 2003, pp. 58–59). Customers now have more access to information and therefore increased control of purchase decisions. The speed at which business happens has accelerated, and so customer expectations of how quickly transactions should take have changed. Globalisation has enabled more companies to do business outside their own country borders, enabling customers to shop around for the best deals. The people element has been removed in many transaction processes. The opportunities for, and challenges of, visitor relationship management (VRM) for DMOs are discussed in this section.

During 2006 there were strong calls from the government opposition in Bermuda for that country's NTO to move away from traditional advertising campaigns and invest more in CRM: 'We don't need to reach out to 90 million people on the eastern seaboard of the US, we need to get to them one by one' (www.travelindustryreview.com, 9/3/06). The STO for Victoria in Australia reported strong repeat visitation from some of the state's key markets (see Harris, Jago & King, 2005), such as New Zealand (over 90% repeaters), Singapore (60%), and Japan (10%). Likewise, the STO for Queensland (2006) reported 93% of visitors from New Zealand had previously visited Australia.

VRM is an important area of research given the inherent advantages of repeat visitation and the limits to the extent that relationship marketing may be used by DMOs of destinations that host hundreds of thousands of visitors. Periodic destination marketing newsletter *Eclipse* devoted a special issue to CRM for destinations. *Eclipse* found only one NTO in 2003 that employed a specialist CRM senior executive.

Relationship marketing is the attempt to establish a long-term bond with the customer. This presents challenges for DMOs. Not the least of which is the difficulty in obtaining quality customer data from service providers over which they have no direct control. In 2002, for example, incoming BTA CEO Tom Wright announced a major customer relationship management strategy that would aim for 6 million active database records by 2006 (Marketing, 7/11/02).

In practice

In highlighting the limited degree of destination relationship marketing in practice, Fyall et al. (2003) reported two case studies. The first, Project Stockholm, is an example of an introductory attempt to engender more loyalty towards a destination, albeit without loyalty-building tools. The project is a cooperative initiative by the Stockholm RTO, Scandic Hotels, and SAS airlines, specifically targeting European weekend tourists. A benefit card was designed for the project, offering added value in the form of free local transport and discounts at shops and restaurants. The second was the Club Program developed to reward repeat visits to Barbados. The programme boasted 1700 members who had visited the island at least 25 times. Rewards have included luncheons hosted by the Barbados Tourism Authority and unofficial ambassador status. One of the key problems for DMOs highlighted by Fyall, Callod and Edwards (p. 654) was the expense of retaining single visitors in comparison to the predominant transactional marketing activities:

> *What thus appears sound in theory and operational in practice, particularly as a weapon to achieve sustainable competitive advantage in the marketplace, is likely to remain in its implementation infancy for destinations for some time.*

Although the internet offers so many communication advantages, Research Snapshot 14.1 provides a rare insight into the extent to which RTOs are engaging in VRM. More research is required to assist destination marketers address the issue of how to initiate meaningful dialogue, at the right time, with the hundreds of thousands of potential repeat visitors, with whom they do not have direct contact.

Research snapshot 14.1   How do we target repeat visitors?

We are all spoilt by choice of available destinations, and so it is likely many places are substitutable. Therefore, successfully differentiating a destination at the time a travel decision is being made is arguably the greatest challenge faced by DMOs. Underpinned by the proposition that communicating with previous visitors will be a more efficient use of resources than traditional advertising, this paper reports an exploratory investigation into the extent to which regional tourism organisations (RTO) in Queensland, Australia, are encouraging repeat visitors from their largest market. Destination marketers face a unique set of challenges and impediments, relative to marketers of other products and services. The research highlights some of the issues that will inhibit VRM development by these RTOs for some time to come. A mixture of personal, paired, and group interviews were conducted with 17 management staff at 11 RTOs, focusing on two questions:

- To what extent is your organisation able to track repeat visitors?
- To what extent is your organisation attempting to keep in touch with visitors, to stimulate repeat visitation?

Key findings were:

- an inability to track repeat visitation
- little targeting of repeat visitation through communication with previous visitors
- the assumption that major accommodation operators were engaged in VRM
- acknowledgement of the need for a destination-level VRM system in the future.

While there was a general recognition of the potential for visitor relationship management (VRM), none of the RTOs had yet been able to develop a formal approach to stay in touch with previous visitors.

Source: Pike, S. (2007). Repeat visitors – An exploratory investigation of RTO responses. **Journal of Travel & Tourism Research**, Spring, 1–13.

From a review of the CRM literature, it is suggested DMOs seeking to engage in relationship marketing should consider the following:

- **The selection of customers who offer maximum yield**. Selection criteria, which may prove problematic for a DMO due to data collection constraints, include frequency and volume of visits, spending patterns, and probability of future visitation.
- **Ensuring high quality service encounters**. This requires the marketing concept to extend to the entire destination. As with service standards, the DMO is reliant on the organisational cultures of the destination's many individual businesses. Initiatives include cooperative destination networks, visitor surveys, improving employee satisfaction, and a quality grading system such as Qualmark (see www.qualmark.co.nz). Almost 75% of tourism suppliers at New Zealand's 2004 TRENZ travel exchange were Qualmark accredited (*Inside Tourism*, IT490, 18/3/04).

- **Providing added value to selected customers**. The DMO must stimulate cooperative efforts to monitor and provide sources of value. For example, during off-season periods, communication could be made with previous domestic visitors offering bundled packages, at an advertising cost saving to the destination and a price saving to the traveller.
- **Developing a philosophy of nurturing long-term mutually beneficial relationships**. Clearly, however, the benefits of the relationship for the destination must outweigh the costs.

Enhancing stakeholder relationships/Cross-functional process

The responsibilities of destination brand management should not rest solely with the DMO. One of the greatest marketing challenges faced by DMOs, certainly in the implementation of IMC, is stimulating a coordinated approach among all those stakeholders who have a vested interest in, and will come into contact with, the target visitors. Ideally, what is required is an understanding by all stakeholders of what the brand identity is, what the brand image is, and what the brand positioning strategy is. The more that stakeholders have an understanding of the rational behind the brand strategy, the more effectively they will be able to integrate their own marketing and customer interactions. Clearly, it is too much to expect all stakeholders to do so, and yet in theory the approach represents a powerful opportunity to enhance the destination brand.

There are essentially three main reasons for DMOs coordinating a *cooperate to compete* approach among tourism operators. The first has been driven out of necessity to stretch the promotional budget. DMOs and tourism operators have recognised the value in pooling limited financial resources to create a bigger bang in the market place. The second major driver in developing a cooperative destination marketing approach has been a greater awareness that the traveller's experience of a destination can be marred by one bad service encounter. So, it makes little long-term sense for a small group of large visitor attractions to work on marketing and quality issues independently, if the mass of remaining small businesses become the weak link in the visitor's destination experience by failing to deliver. Thirdly, it has only been relatively recently that the concept of brand synergy has become the third key rationale for a destination's cooperative marketing approach.

In practice

Northern Tasmania Development, the RTO for Launceston and Northern Tasmania in Australia, provides an impressive online prospectus for tourism businesses (see http://www.northerntasmania.org.au). The 2007/08 prospectus set out the entire year's marketing programme, with indications of where tourism businesses could buy into six major campaigns: Big Tour campaign, Short Tour campaign, Short Breaks campaign, VFR campaign, What's On in Tasmania, and Flinders Island campaign. The prospectus includes copies of the television commercials as well as brochure specifications.

Purposeful dialogue

Anholt (2002, p. 53) likened marketing to chatting someone up in a crowded bar:

> *In effect, you walk up to somebody you have never met, and have a few seconds in which to convince them you are worth getting to know better, and to win the chance of a longer conversation. Often a joke will do the trick, but if the bar is in Finland or Iraq (unlikely), where making strangers laugh is both difficult and unwelcome, a different opening gambit might be preferable. Either way, there are few countries and few people who will fall in love with a stranger who kicks off the conversation with a long list of his natural advantages, impressive family tree and key historical achievement.*

All marcom should be about purposeful dialogue with the target market. Marcom is the marketing element over which the DMO is able to exert the most control, and is therefore the focus of DMO activities. The purpose of marcom should be to enhance brand associations and market position, with the communication objective being to inform, persuade, or remind consumers about the destination. DMOs use promotion to either pull consumers to the destination or push them through travel intermediaries. In the competitive markets in which DMOs operate, innovative promotional ideas can very quickly be adopted by rival destinations, and so there tends to be a commonality of DMO activity.

Message synergy

The WTO (1999a) estimated that the breakdown of promotional budgets for NTOs was: advertising (47.1%), public relations (11.5%), promotional activities (28.9%), public information (3.7%), research (3.5%), and 'other' (5.2%). More recently, a survey of 10 NTOs by Dore and Crouch (2003) also found that consumer advertising (35%) represented the largest item in the promotional budget. This was followed by personal selling to the trade (23%), publicity and public relations (17%), trade advertising (12%), direct marketing (7%), sales promotion partnerships (5%), and personal selling to consumers (1%). IMC does not use any different marcom (marketing communication) tools. Ideally, the five key promotional tools of advertising, public relations, direct marketing, sales promotions, and personal selling should be integrated to provide a consistency of message.

Advertising

Advertising is paid non-personal promotion of ideas or products by an identifiable sponsor (Kotler et al., 1998). The role of advertising is to stimulate the desired images of the brand in the mind of the consumer in such a way that leads to action. There are four generally accepted stages in the design and implementation of any advertising campaign:

1. Setting the objectives, which include those relating to sales targets and communication purpose.
2. Budget allocation decisions, for which methods include the affordable approach, % of sales, competitive parity, and objective and task.
3. Message decisions, including both the content of the messages and the type of medium
4. Campaign evaluation, including the communication impact and resultant sales.

Of these, it is arguably the message decisions that are most problematic for DMOs. Ward and Gold (1994) suggested that many destination advertising efforts lacked professionalism. In particular they pointed to a tendency towards wordiness in advertisements, which is better suited to direct mail communications, as well as a lack of identification of a USP. These criticisms reflect one of the themes of this text, which is the difficulty in promoting multi-attributed places to a dynamic and multidimensional marketplace. The purpose of all DMO advertising should be to enhance consumer-based brand equity. The segmentation and positioning strategy should therefore guide all message decisions. Ideally, advertising should be targeted and have a clear focus and point of differentiation. However, politics and substitutability combine to constrain the marketers of destinations. Morgan (2000, p. 345) cited this comment from an interview with the editor of *Advertising Age*:

> *When you look at the ads ... you can see transcripts of the arguments at the tourist boards ... the membership of which all wanted their own interests served ... you can see the destruction of the advertising message as a result of the politics.*

In practice

An example of a DMO viral campaign is that of Tourism Queensland in 2007, which was started by a government press release by the Minister of Tourism. The consumer receives an email that has been provided by a friend who has seen the campaign website (www.whereelse.com.au). The friend is invited to enter a competition by clicking on a link embedded in the email. When entering the competition the consumer is asked to subscribe the STO's e-newsletter, and to provide the email addresses of five friends. Each email address elicited gives the participant an additional entry in the holiday draw.

Brochures

The first destination travel guides were printed in France in 1552 (Sigaux, 1966). Since the establishment of the first DMOs, brochures have been a common form of destination advertising. Jeffries (2001, p. 72) suggested this may have been as much to do with providing tangible evidence to the local tourism industry of 'fair' exposure:

> It may be the projection of a political and administrative entity and only coincidentally meaningful from the consumers' point of view, offering too much information in some respects and not enough in others.

In the past, the production and distribution of the annual destination brochure has been the most important and expensive item in the promotional budget of many RTOs (Pritchard & Morgan, 1995). Pritchard and Morgan cited research by the ETB that estimated that only 5% of domestic trips in the UK used a travel agent. Without the influence of such intermediaries the role of the brochure has traditionally been important.

A key decision in the design of a destination brochure is its purpose, of which there are two main categories. The first role is to attract visitors to the destination. The design focus is on developing the image of the destination, and the brochure usually has the style and quality of a magazine, often with no advertising content. Distribution is external to the destination since brochures are expensive to produce, and will often be the primary sales aids used to service travel exhibitions and direct consumer enquiries. The second role is a 'visitors guide' designed as a directory of facilities and attractions to aid trip planning. This provides an opportunity for local advertisers to pick up a share of business from travellers at the destination. Distribution may take place both externally, such as in ticket wallets, and locally through the VIC and accommodation outlets. Often, for smaller RTOs the purpose will be to achieve both functions with one brochure due to a lack of funds and reliance on advertising revenue.

In practice

Visitor guides that are reliant on advertising are often controlled by private sector interests, saving the RTO time and money. However, in other cases ownership by the RTO can raise valuable promotional funds. For example, we used this approach at Tourism Rotorua during the 1990s to raise over $100,000 annually to fund a television advertising campaign. The visitors guide then became the official destination brochure, used to service campaign responses, which made it easier for local operators to prioritise the multitude of advertising opportunities presented to them. The initiative also enabled the RTO to demonstrate to council funders the direct financial contribution of the private sector towards destination marketing. As was discussed in Chapter 2, generating such financial contributions is otherwise problematic, particularly for generic destination image advertising. This was not without political ramifications however, as one of the private sector destination guides went out of business as a result. The guide was produced by an elected local government official, who sat on the committee to which we reported.

There has been little published research about the role and effectiveness of brochures in traveller decision-making. Clearly more research is required; particularly given that this traditional form of information dissemination has been under threat since the arrival of the internet in 1996. A survey by Wicks and Shuett (1991) of tourism brochure producers in the USA, which included CVBs, found the majority reported that the sales aid was produced without any specific target market in mind. Likewise, Alford (1998) cited research commissioned by the English Tourist Board, which found that consumers were most likely to be influenced by the type of holiday or activity, whereas RTBs were promoting regions or towns. RTBs generally still produced the regional brochure as if trying to be all things to all people. Pritchard and Morgan's (1995) content analysis of destination image promotion brochures used by local authorities in Wales identified the following key features:

- An eye-catching image on the front cover designed to attract attention.
- A single graphic device on the front cover, such as a logo or symbol, intended to reinforce a campaign theme.
- Identifying symbols within the brochure to reinforce the presence of unique destination features.
- Multidimensional images to reflect the multi-attributed nature of the destination. The study identified 2000 images in 28 brochures, of which 70% were of scenery.
- An average 54%–46% ratio of images versus information.

Pritchard and Morgan's (1995) main criticisms of the Welsh brochures included a general lack of identifying a distinctively Welsh identity and a lack of images of people. They also found that most destinations were using similar images. An interesting example of this recently occurred in Australia. Morley and Stolz (2003, p. 3) reported the embarrassment of Gold Coast Tourism Bureau officials after the discovery that the destination had been inadvertently using a Sunshine Coast beach scene in 100,000 copies of the Gold Coast's 2003 *Holiday Guide*. In reference to the ensuing national television coverage of the faux pas, the Sunshine Coast's RTO chairman responded: 'We appreciate all the publicity we can get.'

In practice

Davidson and Rogers (2006, p. 119) cited the innovative practice of the Glasgow City Marketing Bureau (www.seaglasgow.com) which prints visitor guides on a daily basis, with a printed 'best before' date: 'The premise for doing so is that DMOs own nothing but information: if they provide out-of-date information via their brochures, this compromises their services.' Similarly, during 2007, Northern Tasmania Development, in Australia, introduced customised downloadable brochures from their website (see www.northerntasmania.info).

Websites

According to a Travel Industry Association of America study, there were around 64 million American online travel planners using the internet in 2002 (TIA, press release, 12/12/02). This represented a dramatic increase over 1997, when an estimated 12 million Americans were planning and researching travel options online. 42% of TIA respondents indicated they did all or most of their travel planning online, up from 29% who did so in 2001.

Watson (2006) cited research from Carleton University in Canada, which estimated that internet users only take one-twentieth of a second to decide if they like the look of a website. Speaking at the 2006 British Travel Fair, E-consultancy training director Craig Hanna suggested that the majority of travel sites were 'atrocious' and lose business because they are difficult to navigate (www.travelmole.com, 6/3/06). Hanna cited research showing 67% of users click off pages because they encountered difficulties. Research Snapshot 14.3 provides some insights into what travel consumers want online.

Research snapshot 14.3   Destination websites – learning what consumers want

During 2005, USA-based Strategic Marketing & Research Inc completed an investigation of consumers' internet travel planning, and in doing so evaluated a number of state and regional DMO websites. A mix of quantitative and qualitative methods were used, including observation of web usage. Key results included:

- 61% of travellers 'always or often' used the internet in travel planning
- relatively few travellers visited destination sites
- most popular sites used were accommodation brands and travel brands such as Travelocity and Expedia

The research concluded that DMOs had not established a role for their websites. DMO sites were not regarded by travellers as being either the official source or sufficiently comprehensive. Recommended success factors for destination sites included:

- uncluttered homepage, as presented by Massachusetts
- clear directions to users, as provided by Missouri
- easy to navigate, as developed by Texas
- divided by types of trips rather than by geography, as achieved by Arizona
- place important information on the left-hand side, as the right-hand side and bottom are frequently overlooked
- suggested itineraries, as provided by Connecticut
- provide links to accommodation and attractions.

Source: Miller, D. (2005). Destination websites – Learning what consumers want. Presentation at the Travel & Tourism Research Association Conference, New Orleans.

In spite of the increasing access to information technologies (IT), such as the internet, DMOs often struggle to keep up with the rapid advances in IT and their implications for marketing. In summarising a workshop coordinated by the National Laboratory for Tourism and eCommerce for tourism and IT leaders to address this challenge, Gretzel et al. (2000, p. 154) argued that future success of DMOs was related to a change in approach rather than technology itself. That is, DMOs must learn to proactively adapt to change to enhance organisational viability:

> *Most of the problems organisations face today when designing and implementing online strategies stem from trying to fit everything into existing structures and models. It is suggested that DMOs need to redefine their nature of business and the underlying models and processes . . . Since the Web is ever-evolving and new challenges occur 'at the speed of thought', these changes should be directed toward increasing the organisational flexibility and openness to change.*

The workshop developed a number of principles for the development of web strategies by DMOs:

- A combination of online and offline advertising is most effective in utilising the potential of the internet.
- A website should not be viewed as a standalone advertising tool.
- Banners and cross-advertising should be used to control web traffic.
- The most important points of entry for users searching for tourism information are portals.
- A consistent advertising message across different media creates synergy between online and offline strategies.
- Internet marketing strategies should be based on personalisation, experience, involvement, and permission.

> ## In practice
>
> In 2007, Tourism Australia relaunched its Australia.com website as part of a strategy that places digital at the heart of the DMO's global push (see Livesly, 2007). The new site, which took over a year to develop, has been designed as a central gateway for travellers. The joint initiative between the NTO and eight STOs is the first of its kind where visitors are able to access information from STOs. An overlay map of Australia has been added to each STO site, so that visitors can move backwards and forwards between NTO and STO sites with ease. Due to the level of negotiation required to get the NTO and STOs working together, the site designer admitted it was 'the project nobody thought would happen'.

A key advantage of the internet for DMOs is the ability to develop sites specifically to cater for different segments. This partly overcomes the problem in destination branding of designing and communicating one destination brand for all markets. Niche advertising in traditional media can direct the target to the branded site. Examples include:

- The Finland Tourist Board's family website (see www.finland-family.com/eng/).
- Tourism Victoria's gay and lesbian site (see www.visitmelbourne.com/gaytravel).
- Tourism Australia's working holiday site (see www.work.australia.com).
- Visit Scotland's ancestral tourism site (see www.ancestralscotlant.com).

The domain name ● ● ●

It could be argued that online branding essentially begins with domain names, which have become a digital market akin to real estate. The proliferation of domain name registrations has been such that by 2000 all three-letter combinations, as well as 98% of English words, had already been registered (Keller, 2003). Intuitively, acquisition of the destination domain name, such as NewZealand.com, appears a wise move. However, Tourism New Zealand's purchase of the domain for NZ$1 million caused a political stir during 2003. Government opposition tourism spokeswoman Pansy Wong, a former director of the NTO, labelled the purchase rash, embarrassing, and made without a prior cost-benefit feasibility study. TNZ CEO George Hickton responded that the purchase was timely given the prediction by www.wordlingo.com that domain names would increase in value tenfold during the next decade. Hickton claimed that domain names were the most logical starting point for potential travellers seeking information about a destination, pointing to a claim by www.lee-online.com that 65% of all users type the URL into their browser, either by guesswork or memory. Minister of Tourism Mark Burton argued the move

Table 14.1 Non-travel-related destination domains

www.canada.com	Canwest Global Communications Corporation
www.brazil.com	Business portal
www.germany.com	Parked site
www.nigeria.com	Community and business portal
www.zimbabwe.com	News site
www.ireland.com	The Irish Times

was a 'sound investment' as a portal for tourism and business interests, and suggested the South African government offered $US10 million for SouthAfrica.com while Korea.com sold for US$5 million (*Inside Tourism*, IT448, p.1).

In this regard, one regional city in New Zealand was forced to pay NZ$100,000 to a porn site for the city's domain name. Other examples of destination domain names, belonging to a DMO or a private sector travel company, include: Australia.com, France.com, Italy.com, Fiji.com, and Scotland.com. However, as shown in Table 14.1 some major destination domains remain owned by non-tourism interests at the time of writing. Since 2004 a number of sites that were business portals are now travel related. These include, for example, www.usa.com, www.japan.com, www.brazil.com and www.wales.com.

Many consumers use major search engines such as Google, Yahoo, and MSN in the early stages of an online information search, and then click through the top listed search results. It has been suggested that almost 75% of online travel purchases begin with a search using a search engine (see Jarvis, 2006). Not everyone gets their online search right. Picture the surprise of a young British couple who boarded a flight for Sydney, as shown on their online air tickets, only to eventually arrive at the wrong destination (Montgomery, 2002). The couple thought they had purchased tickets to their dream destination, Sydney in Australia, but ended up in Sydney, Canada, 'a sleepy one-horse town in Nova Scotia with a population of 26,000'. Wade (2006) proposed five ways to optimise a website's search ranking:

1. **Target market analysis** A website's traffic patterns can be studied using software such as Webtrends, Urchin, Index Tools, or Clicktracks. Analysis of the most popular pages, which search engines deliver traffic, how long visitors stay on pages, and so forth can improve understanding of what visitors are looking for.
2. **Keyword research** Identify the keywords and phrases being used by the target audience. Again, software such as Alexa, Google, and Wordtracker(R) is available to analyse usage patterns of each term. The goal is to find terms that are frequently searched, but have low competition from competing sites.

3. **High-quality content with optimised writing** Write for the reader first, then rewrite by including the keywords. Incorporate keywords in the title, subheadings, as well as content, while keeping the text readable.
4. **Link building campaigns** Since search engines use links to determine site relevance, develop links with popular sites.
5. **Fresh content via news releases, articles and blogs** A site's ranking improves if content is freshened. News releases to reputable wire services will see distribution of the story to major search engine news systems. Also, hyperlinking keywords will increase the number of links to the site and therefore potentially higher search placement.

Yahoo! Search Marketing Regional Managing Director Craig Wax (2006) suggested that since keywords are the lifeblood of a search campaign, select 50 or more, based on the three stages of a buying cycle: research, shop, buy. Yahoo's keyword selector tool provides monthly data on popular keywords (see http://inventory.overture.com/d/searchinventory/suggestion/).

Note: The International Federation for IT and Travel & Tourism (IFITT) promotes international discussion about information technologies in the tourism sector (www.ifitt.org). IFITT introduced the first scientific journal in this field (*Journal of Information Technology & Tourism*) and coordinates the annual ENTER academic conference (for reviews of the topics contained in the conference proceedings see Pike 2005, 2007, 2007).

Key points

1. Integrated marketing communication (IMC)

A market orientation is an outward-inward market-organisation approach, dictating marketing decisions that are concerned with designing products to meet the unmet needs of target consumers. However, most destination marketing has been limited to an inward-outward approach. DMOs are constrained by having no control over product development and must therefore focus on finding markets for existing products. IMC represents a relatively new approach to marketing. Key tenets of IMC are the development of profitable customer relationships, a cross-functional process, purposeful dialogue with customers, effective relationships with stakeholders, and synergy of messages. IMC represents the way forward for DMOs confronted by significant changes in the destination marketing paradigm.

2. The potential value of VRM

The purpose of all marcom is to enhance consumer-based brand equity. However, there has been relatively little research published in the tourism literature dealing with the potential of visitor relationship management (VRM). VRM represents an opportunity to gain marcom efficiencies by staying in contact with previous visitors who have the propensity for repeat visits. The core challenge inhibiting VRM adoption by most DMOs is that the destination marketer rarely comes into contact with actual visitors. Most visitor records are held by local accommodation houses.

Review questions

- In your own words, summarise the concept of IMC. What are the key challenges faced by DMOs in implementing IMC?
- What are the potential benefits for your DMO to engage in VRM? What practical steps could your RTO undertake to engage in VRM?

Distribution

Aims

The aims of this chapter are to enhance understanding of:

- tourism distribution
- travel trade events

Perspective

For marketers in general, distribution refers to the physical supply of goods from the place of manufacture through various channels to the point of sale. This is usually a complex process involving the logistics of supply chain management as well as demand management. In service marketing however, distribution does not involve the physical transportation of a tangible product. The concepts of immovability and inseparability generally mean the destination product is consumed at the place of production and the tourism provider and the consumer must be present for the service to be delivered. The closest function to physical distribution is the means by which a DMO delivers destination tourism information to consumers. A destination visitor guide for example, which is ultimately a form of marcom, must somehow be distributed to the trade and consumers. Also, in terms of the traditional 4 Ps, distribution can be viewed as the place of tourism consumption, which includes the destination itself. Key issues are location, accessibility and perceived distance.

Tourism distribution

In terms of delivering a product to the point of sale, distribution refers to the tourism reservation mechanism. Distribution channel intermediaries for tourism services include tour wholesalers, travel agencies, and airlines. Intermediaries often represent the most effective means of reaching travellers, but at the same time can be one of the highest operating costs. Commission to intermediaries represents the distribution cost.

Apart from operating local VICs, most DMOs leave reservation systems to the private sector. DMOs have moved away from operating a wholesale business, to focus efforts on marketing. One exception to this is Tourism Northern Territory in Australia (see www.holidaysnt.com/specials). Operating a wholesale business has political implications relating to the selection of businesses included in the packages.

In practice

The Australian Tourism Data warehouse (www.atdw.com.au) is a trade site designed to provide intermediaries with access to product and destination information from a single source in a common format. On the supply side, database provides all tourism businesses with cost-effective online distribution.

Increasingly, DMOs are providing links to special offers from constituent tour operators, as in the case of:

- Tourism Ireland's new web site launched in 2006 (see www.discoverireland.com)
- Tourism New Zealand (see www.newzealand.com)
- Northern Tasmania Development (see www.northerntasmania.info).

In practice

In Scotland the NTO licensed a private operator to use the name VisitScotland.com for a travel booking site. The company posted a loss of over £2 million in 2004, when bed and breakfast operators boycotted the site. The operators refused to pay a 10% commission, as they were under the impression that the site was owned by the NTO, to which they already paid memberships levies (see www.travelmole.com, 23/9/04).

Joint ventures

Few people are better qualified to discuss the tangled web of DMO/intermediary relationships that Owen Eagles, Managing Director of ANZCRO (www.anzcro.com.au), a travel wholesaler with offices in Australia, New Zealand, England, and the USA. With 28 years DMO experience working for New Zealand's NTO in Australia, New Zealand, and the USA, and 12 years at ANZCRO, Eagles understands only too well the dynamics of the relationship between DMOs and those within the tourism distribution system:

> It's a real mess, and not well understood by all the players themselves who end up protecting their jobs with populist decisions promoting apparent success through a scenario of smoke and mirrors.

As will be discussed in Chapter 19, it is very difficult to quantify the return on investment for DMO initiatives. Eagles argues that one way to do so is through joint venture (JV) projects between DMOs and intermediaries; a scenario where investment return can ultimately be measured by bookings. Such a JV between ANZCRO and NTO, three RTOs, and four travel agency chains is an example of effectively steering through the politics to achieve a vertically integrated joint venture (JV). The JV is summarised in Case Study 15.1, while Eagles' views on the positives and negatives of such JV projects is shown in Table 15.1.

Table 15.1 Positives and negatives of DMO/intermediary JVs

Positives	Negatives
• Ability to measure results – through the origin and timing of sales	• Negotiating the clutter available to the consumer at travel agent outlet (often overcome with educational incentives and productivity rewards).
• Ability to budget for and control costs	
• Ability to choose appropriate supplier constituents who contribute towards the marketing programme with special product offers (very measurable by their unique and coded nature) and cash	• Choosing the right wholesaler and suppliers – both should have a working relationship in place
• Choice of a wholesaler whose distribution system is clear and concise – e.g. one that may have preferred relationships with 2500 retail travel agents in Australia	• Managing the compromises necessary with a number of project partners, particularly in the production of visual material
• Ability to leverage the campaign by increasing resources with contributions from suppliers, and airline, wholesaler, and travel agent chain	• Maintaining the destination product offer over a substantial period of time, say three years, so that it has time to become established
	• The accusation, by suppliers not selected, that the DMO is biased and unfairly leaning towards those suppliers chosen for the product offer

Case study 15.1 'Autumn Escape'. A JV campaign between an NTO, three RTOs, a travel wholesaler, and four retail travel agency chains

Chris Gowing, Team Leader Marketing, ANZCRO, and Owen Eagles, Managing Director, ANZCRO

ANZCRO is a leading wholesaler of New Zealand self-drive products in the Australian market. The company recognises the importance of creating JVs with New Zealand regions as a way of increasing market exposure for products. Similarly, the RTOs recognise that promotion in another country is expensive, and unless it is tied to a saleable package, advertising would be limited to awareness building. Australians have a high awareness of New Zealand, which is their most popular international destination. Australia is the largest source of visitors for New Zealand. However, the average Australian's knowledge about what New Zealand offers travellers is limited. New Zealand is predominantly a self-drive touring destination, and itinerary planning can be one of the most complex for travel agents, in comparison to selling a stay-put resort-style holiday in Bali or Fiji. Unfortunately, in many travel agencies the New Zealand sales role is often seen as being similar to domestic travel and so responsibility is in the hands of junior staff who lack in-depth product knowledge. ANZCRO recognises the importance and influence of the retail travel agent in selling self-drive, and so places emphasis on supporting agents, and not selling direct to the public.

This case outlines one of a series of seasonal JVs undertaken with New Zealand RTOs during the past three years. In this case, the partners included the NTO Tourism New Zealand and three RTOs in New Zealand's South Island: Queenstown, Dunedin, and

Christchurch/Canterbury. The impetus for linking with the NTO in the 2007 JVs was that the major RTOs committed all the JV funding in Australia to Tourism New Zealand's high-profile 'What's on in New Zealand' television and newspaper campaign promoting travel in the autumn season. The NTO JV campaign left wholesalers like ANZCRO bereft of opportunities to work with cash-strapped RTOs. Previously, in conjunction with the RTOs, ANZCRO distributed the RTO JV packages to Australian travel agents in over 200,000 brochures. ANZCRO believes strongly that the hard copy collateral is important, given the hands-on nature of planning self-drive itineraries in New Zealand. Many RTOs would naturally like to participate in JVs with ANZCRO but simply don't have the money. Politically this can be difficult, since ANZCRO sells New Zealand-wide products.

TV advertising on the Australian networks referred viewers to a Tourism New Zealand website promoting, in this case, ANZCRO's autumn travel packages to Queenstown, Dunedin, and Christchurch/Canterbury with four Australian retail travel agent chains. To support the retail agents, ANZCRO, for example, sponsored a page in the travel catalogue of Flight Centres. Flight Centres is one of Australia's largest travel agency chains, and distributes over 300,000 copies of the travel catalogue each month. ANCRO's month-long participation in the campaign's performance was monitored through the company's reservation call centre. Web traffic data was also provided by Tourism New Zealand.

Discussion questions

- A significant issue raised in the case is that of RTO politics concerning which local operators are included in the packages promoted. Since the majority of businesses can't be included in these packages, and therefore not attract sales, the potential for criticism is strong. How could the RTO be absolved from this responsibility and therefore not be seen to favour some local businesses over others?
- Why does ANZCRO believe so strongly in the use of traditional travel brochures to support new media campaigns?

Travel trade events

Arguably the most effective means of stimulating meaningful dialogue with customers is personal selling. Trade shows provide an opportunity to use personal selling to launch new products, services, brands, and facilities. DMOs with small budgets tend to favour such push strategies as they cost less than consumer advertising (Pearce et al., 1998). Opportunities include trade exhibitions such as ITB in Berlin (www.itb-berlin.com), and special interest travel trade exhibitions such as International Travel Expo Hong Kong.

In practice

ITB Berlin the world's largest travel and tourism exhibition started in 1966. With an overall display area of 150,000 square metres, the 2006 event attracted 10,856 exhibitors (www.travelwirenews.com, 10/3/06). Even at this size, space is so tight that an increasing number of displays feature two storeys.

The WTO maintains a calendar of major travel trade events (see www.unwto.org/calendar/index.php?t=99&), which is ever expanding. For example, China, the emerging powerhouse of world tourism, opened its first World Travel Fair (WTF) in February 2004 (News@PATA, 25/2/04). Likewise, the first Turkish inbound travel exhibition took place in 2004 (www.travelmole.com, 25/3/04). The first travel exhibition in Eastern Africa took place in Arusha, Tanzania, in 2006 (www.travelwirenews.com, 22/3/06).

Since the 1990s, DMO participation at travel trade events has shifted from awareness building towards cooperative promotions with stakeholder tourism businesses. In this role the DMO underwrites the often substantial cost of the display space and onsells participation space to constituent tourism businesses. The cooperative funding approach enables the DMO to stretch resources further, while controlling message synergy. The tourism businesses would otherwise find the participation cost prohibitive. Often, at the larger international events, the NTO will be supported by STOs and RTOs rather than individual businesses.

Tourism exchanges

Tourism exchanges are similar in concept to speed dating, as depicted in Figure 15.1. The local product supplier hires booth space to gain access to international travel intermediaries in the form of short meetings of around 15 minutes. Logistically, it is possible for the supplier to schedule appointments with only a small number of buyers during a two-day event. Suppliers must therefore be targeted in their appointment preferences, and take advantage of social networking opportunities to meet other contacts they were unable to schedule appointments with. Commonly, the NTO

Figure 15.1
A booth at a travel exchange. Photo courtesy of Trish May, May Communications.

invites key international buyers to the destination for a 2–3 day meeting, and offers pre- and post-familiarisation tours. Considerable organisation is required, along with sponsorship by airlines and other tourism businesses.

Tourism exchange meetings are increasingly seen as an effective means of reaching key travel decisions by providing tourism suppliers with individual meetings with a limited number of retailers and wholesalers selected by the NTO and major airlines. The trade representatives are generally flown to the destination for the meetings with suppliers and then offered familiarisation tours. Examples include:

- Arab World Travel & Tourism Exchange (see www.awtte.com)
- Australian Tourism Exchange (see www.tradeevents.australia.com)
- The British Travel Trade Fair (www.britishtraveltradefair.com), which attracts 300 exhibitors and 3000 domestic and international buyers.
- International Pow Wow, USA (see www.powwowonline.com), for which the 2005 event was expected to generate over $3 billion in travel bookings in the following three years (www.travelwirenews.com, 17/5/05).
- South Pacific Tourism Exchange (see www.tcsp.com)
- Tourism Rendevouz New Zealand (TRENZ) (see www.nztia.co.nz/Tianz-Events/TRENZ.asp)
- PATA Travel Mart (see www.PATA.org)
- China Outbound Travel & Tourism Market (see www.cottm.com), which is the only dedicated outbound travel exchange in China

---

In practice

When the 2002 Australian Tourism Exchange was held in Brisbane over 2500 hotel rooms were used by 2000 tourism suppliers, 80 international and domestic media, and 670 travel buyers from 50 countries (Cameron, 2002). According to the ATC managing director, it was estimated that the A$8 million cost of the event would generate up to A$2 billion in trade for Australia: 'This event delivers more export earnings and business than any other in Australia.' The importance of the event led to the development of industry briefing seminars by Tourism Queensland and the ATC. The 2007 Australian Tourism Exchange was expected to generate more than $10 million in spend by delegates for the host state Queensland, as well as the ongoing business development value. The Queensland state government committed $1.5 million to the event. (Wade, 2006). Operators were also able to access information from the seminars online in the form of PowerPoint slides with voice reproduction (http://www.tq.com.au/ate., 20/4/03).

The increasing numbers of international tourism exchanges is forcing competition for the limited numbers of key travel decision-makers. Unfortunately, in 2004 this competition led to the cancellation of the South Pacific Tourism Exchange, as shown in Figure 15.2.

Figure 15.2
South Pacific Tourism
Exchange cancellation.
Source: http://www.tcsp.
com/public/spte2004.
shtml, 25/03/04.

South Pacific Tourism Exchange 2004 – CANCELLED

The SPTO regrets to advise all interested Buyers and Sellers that due to a shortfall in the number of targeted Buyers and Sellers, we have now decided to cancel the event. The cancellation is largely attributable to its similarity and closeness to other tradeshows and tourism exchanges being held in the region at the same time (including ATE, TRENZ, and BFTE, where similar Buyers and Sellers are attending. We particularly wish to thank all who expressed their interest and support for SPTE. We apologise for any inconvenience caused to you.

    If you have any questions or require further information, please feel free to contact us using our Contact Form.

In practice

Tourism Australia coordinates participation of local tourism suppliers at 30 global trade events annually (see www.tradeevents. australia.com).

Trade education

In an effort to improve distribution effectiveness, many NTOs have established formal training programmes for selected travel agents in key markets. The most common initiative involves the accreditation of specialist agents. In the USA, for example, where there are over 30,000 travel agents, the NTO can direct consumer advertising responses to the specialist agent nearest the enquirers' post-code area. The NTO has the benefit of knowing that the specialist agent has the resources to service the enquiry, the agent benefits from the lead generation, and the risk of uncertainty is alleviated for the consumer. At the 2007 Tourism Australia Market Briefings, it was suggested the there had been a 40% conversion rate from enquiry to booking at USA Aussie Speicialists. In New Zealand, 1700 out of 3000 agents were members of the programme. Examples of specialist destination agent programmes include:

- Tourism Ireland's Shamrock Club (www.shamrockclub.net)
- Tourism Australia's Aussie Specialists (www.tourism.australia.com).
- Tourism New Zealand's KEA (Kiwi expert agents) club.

Other methods of training include familiarisation (also referred to as famils and educationals) tours to the destination and educational roadshow seminars. However, the latter is losing favour with time-poor agents. For example, the chair of the Association of National Tourism Office Representatives (ANTOR) in the UK observed that the there is very little interest from agents in destination roadshows (www.travelmole, 8/6/05):

ANTOR members accept that the day of the travel agent roadshow is probably dying on its feet. Agents have made it pretty clear they are not interested.

Key points

1. Tourism distribution

The distribution (place) element of the marketing mix is vastly different for marketers of tourism services than for consumer goods. Tourism distribution traditionally concerns the development and communication of package offerings through travel trade intermediaries such as tour wholesalers, airlines, and travel agents. Key approaches used by DMOs to educate intermediaries about package opportunities include travel exchanges, travel expos, and training programmes.

2. Travel trade events

Arguably the most effective means of stimulating meaningful dialogue with customers is personal selling. Trade shows provide an opportunity to use personal selling to launch new products, services, brands, and facilities. DMOs with small budgets tend to favour such push strategies as they cost less than consumer advertising. Opportunities include trade exhibitions, special interest travel trade exhibitions, tourism exchanges, and trade education seminars.

Review questions

- Why have DMOs generally moved away from operating wholesale and/or retail travel services?
- Design a two-day familiarisation visit to your destination for travel trade intermediaries. What are your objectives? What product trade-offs have you made that may upset those businesses not involved?

CHAPTER 16

Public relations

Advertising is what you pay for . . . editorial is what you pray for!

Trout & Rivkin (1995)

Aims

The aims of this chapter are to enhance understanding of:

- managing relationships with stakeholders
- the advantages of media publicity as a communication medium
- DMO publicity initiatives.

Perspective

For destinations, publicity represents market exposure, which might be favourable or unfavourable. A wit once suggested that any publicity is good publicity unless it is an obituary. In this philosophy the concern is not about what is being said about you but whether you are being talked about at all. Publicity can occur from many sources, with which the DMO may or may not have had any control, involvement, or even knowledge. The cost-effectiveness and relatively high credibility of media editorial coverage are attractive to destination marketers with limited resources. However, it is important to recognise that publicity is not the only aspect of public relations (PR). PR is more than publicity-seeking, in that it represents a concerted effort to develop favourable impressions of a destination. This involves both the generation of positive publicity by the DMO as well as the stimulation of positive relations between internal and external stakeholders. Since DMOs are essentially in the business of communication, the process of communication management should not be left to chance.

Communications management

Since DMOs are essentially in the business of communication, the process of communications management, otherwise known as public relations (PR), should not be left to chance. Barry (2002, p. 2) defined PR as:

> *The process of managing how, when, and in what way you communicate, so that you may ultimately influence the behaviour, attitude, and perceptions of those important to you.*

Inherent in this description is the notion of stakeholders, in addition to consumers in target markets, who are important to the organisation. PR covers a wide spectrum of functions, including:

- achieving positive editorial media coverage
- engaging the public
- active management of communications
- application of strategy and creativity in reputation management
- networking with potential clients at seminars, exhibitions, and events
- wining and dining important customers

While PR is a communication process, publicity is a communication medium. Publics represent stakeholders. A stakeholder is anyone who can impact on or be impacted by the organisation. Some stakeholders will be quite active, while others are passive. The latter might only become

Table 16.1 PR hierarchy

Function	Philosophy
Press agentry	Striving for media publicity
Public information	Disseminating objective but positive information only
One-way asymmetrical	Utilising research to design messages that will stimulate stakeholders to behave the way the organisation desires
Two-way symmetrical	Using research and open communication to enhance relationships, where both the organisation and publics can be convinced of the need for change

active over a topical issue, or never at all. Academic models of PR use the hierarchy shown in Table 16.1. Effective PR then requires the organisation to (1) monitor stakeholders' perceptions, (2) reinforce the brand identity, and (3) be prepared to adjust to change.

Tourism has been relatively slow to adopt PR (Seaton, 1994). PR may be viewed as a two-pronged approach to communication management for DMOs. On one hand, the focus of most PR initiatives by DMOs will be attempting to generate editorial media publicity for the destination. Accordingly, the chapter does focus on this aspect of PR. On the other hand, there is a need to manage relations with stakeholders, who represent a much broader group than consumers in target markets. An important first step is prioritising groups of stakeholders, and identifying opportunities for dialogue. Seaton (1994) listed 20 common groups of tourism stakeholders. Particularly active stakeholders include:

- politicians and government policy-makers
- the host community, including local residents, taxpayers, and other industries

Political lobbying

Political lobbying is important for DMOs at all levels for two primary reasons, both of which have the wider tourism community interests at heart. The first is securing long-term funding security (see Research Snapshot 16.1), and the second is influencing policies that have the potential to impact on tourism development and destination competitiveness.

Research snapshot 16.1   Tourism as a re-election vehicle for politicians

Pritchard (1982) reported an interesting PR initiative by Wisconsin's STO. For the constituency of every government representative, the STO had its research department prepare a breakdown of the number of tourism businesses, tourism employees, tourism tax revenue, and the total value of tourism to the area. The STO then sent this information to each legislator to improve the case for tourism marketing funding. This initiative resulted in 240 press releases being generated by the legislators to their local media around the state. The end results were twofold. The first was an increased public awareness of the value of tourism, and the second was an increased awareness of tourism as a re-election vehicle for legislators.

Source: Pritchard, G. (1982). Tourism promotion: Big business for the states. *HRA Quarterly, 23*(2), 48–57.

McGehee et al. (2006) undertook a comparative analysis of the attitudes of state legislators in North Carolina (USA) towards tourism in 1990 and 2003. They found that while legislators viewed tourism more positively in 2003, their knowledge of it remained limited. This aspect was disappointing given the extent to which the STO had employed lobbying strategies. In the limited research related to such lobbying, McGehee et al. pointed to White's (1991) study that analysed four types of lobbying commonly used by non-profit organisations:

- Constituency-based lobbying, where initiatives include forming coalitions with other organisations and stimulating influential constituents to lobby.
- Classic direct techniques of lobbying, which include asking government officials to express an opinion on an issue, serving on advisory committees, and alerting legislators to the effect of a particular bill.
- Electronic lobbying by email.
- Schmoozing techniques of lobbying, which involve providing favours for political officials, filing lawsuits, attempts to influence public appointments, and making contributions to political campaigns.

It was suggested that the most effective technique was the constituency-based one. McGehee et al. (2006) concluded that while the North Carolina STO was employing classic direct techniques as well as constituency-based initiatives, a more aggressive approach was required.

Host community relations

The tourism industry should be seen as being part of the local community, and not some separate entity. Open and ongoing communication needs to take place between the DMO and the host community, for a number of reasons. Examples of inclusiveness include:

- The destination brand should encapsulate local residents' sense of place, and so their views need to be canvassed at the brand identity development phase. Part of being a good neighbour is about understanding their situation.
- Residents need to be made aware of new tourism-related product and infrastructure developments as early as possible in the process.
- Residents interact with visitors in a variety of situations such as at gas stations, supermarkets, and beaches. Support for tourism will hopefully manifest itself in friendly encounters.
- Local taxpayers should be aware of the purpose of DMO funding by government in terms of the social and economic benefits for the community.
- Residents and other business sectors should have a forum for communicating tourism-related problems at an early stage.

In practice

From the onset of my tenure as CEO of Tourism Rotorua, it became glaringly obvious that local pride levels were appallingly low. The destination at the time was suffering an image crisis in the marketplace, and the negative media publicity had as much negative effect in the local community as it did in major tourism markets. Out of necessity, our team developed a local tourism awareness programme with two primary aims. The first was to help enhance local pride in the district, and the second was to increase awareness of the value of the tourism industry to the local economy. The campaign included:

- a district-wide open day of local tourism attractions – local residents had the opportunity to visit over 40 attractions free of charge during the day
- distribution of a *Good Host Kit* to all local households (see Figure 16.1) – the kit contained a passport of year-long special offers for locals who were hosting visitors – a copy of the *Rotorua Visitors Guide*, a calendar of events, and a fact file on tourism's contribution to the local economy
- a local media campaign including radio and print advertising and press releases
- he start of weekly tourism awareness columns in two newspapers and weekly spots on two radio stations
- research to benchmark and later track community perceptions of tourism.

Figure 16.1
Good Host Kit

DMOs therefore need to consider initiatives involving communication forums and research to track community acceptance of visitors. In terms of developing a community relations programme, the Centre for Regional Tourism Research in Australia developed an excellent kit for RTOs during 2000 (see Rosemann, Prosser, Hunt & Benecke, 2000). The authors highlighted common challenges in communicating tourism benefits to a community:

- A lack of leadership to take responsibility for this role
- Limited time and funds
- Lack of specific data
- Negative community perceptions
- Media attention towards negative impacts
- The time lag between implementation of tourism policies and resultant impact.

The kit provided suggested tactics, along with cases from practice around Australia. A brief selection of examples is shown in Table 16.2.

Local tourism operators

The underlying purpose of the DMO is not always obvious to some members of the host community, including some local tourism operators. In my experience many have been surprised to learn that the purpose, from the government funder perspective at least, is to enhance the economic prosperity of the district, usually with a focus on direct, indirect, and induced job creation. Rather, many have assumed that the DMO was there only to serve local tourism operators, which is the case in a minority of member-based associations that do not receive government funding. Clearly, there is a difference, but if the tourism community hasn't been informed, it is dangerous to assume they will automatically understand. The DMO should therefore initiate regular measures to identify the extent to which the community understands the organisation's purpose

Table 16.2 Communicating the benefits of tourism to the host community

Tactics	Examples
Community initiatives • Information expos • Programmes to engage the visitor interest in local culture • Targeting visiting friends and relatives (VRF) tourism • Encourage locals to experience local tours • Provide residents with familiarisations of businesses indirectly involved in tourism • Reduced admission prices for locals accompanying visitors • Local attraction loyalty cards • Encourage community involvement in the visitor information centre • Voluntary ambassador programmes • Direct mail initiatives • Regular visits to local services clubs • Visits to high schools	The small island state of Tasmania developed a 'Tourism awareness week' to overcome misconceptions and complacency in the community. Initiatives included an advertising campaign, a positioning slogan ('tourism means jobs') and logo targeting key opinion leaders, emails to businesses, news releases, and a question in parliament for the Tourism Minister about activities to boost tourism. The initial campaign won a 1999 Pacific Asia Travel Association (PATA) Gold Award. Similar campaigns have been organised in New South Wales and the Australian Capital Territory.
Business initiatives • Promote information availability as a community resource • Service award programmes • Create a membership level for businesses indirectly involved in tourism	Members of the Capricorn Tourism & Development organisation were encouraged to stamp their cheque payments with 'It was only possible to pay this account because of tourism.' Recipients are also encouraged to join the organisation.
Local government initiatives • Lobby local government elected representatives • Educate local government	The Country Victoria Tourism Council produces two booklets for local governments in the state: 'Why should local government invest in tourism' and 'Local government and tourism: the partnerships'.
Media initiatives • Build strong media relationships • Find ways to make tourism newsworthy • Host media open days • Regular press releases and newspaper column • Invite media to local tourism meetings	Townsville Enterprise Limited developed a range of activities including: weekly staff meetings to develop story ideas, two newspaper columns sponsored by media members, an annual briefing for all media, and a two-weekly newsflash. Over $100,000 in airtime and space has been provided by media sponsors annually.
Research initiatives • Engage in local research fund by local government • Publish tourism statistics regularly • Survey tourism dependent workers to feed back to the community	

and role. To enhance credibility in the community, Gartrell (1994, p. 281) recommended a strategy of consistently using messages that repeat key terms: 'Telling the bureau's story may seem mundane or repetitious, but the message must be stated again and again.' Examples of key repetitive terms include those related to 'economic development' and 'tax benefits'.

Local business also need to be briefed on DMO strategies, such as the brand identity, and on tactics such as joint venture promotional opportunities. Again, a forum for two-way participative communication is necessary so that (1) opportunities are maximised, and (2) potential problems are handled before the issue is brought to the attention of the media. Initiatives include market briefings, networking functions, an annual conference, newsletters, and annual report. A dedicated website for members can also be used effectively to disseminate information and seek feedback.

Media relations

Journalists rely on interesting story angles, but they don't spend their lives waiting for us to call. For most tourism organisations, the balance of power in the journalist/PR relationship will be with the former. DMOs need a proactive approach to developing relations with local media. Such relationships develop through a mix of positive human traits such as trust, honesty, perseverance, humour, reliability, and consistency. Further, the relationship is not one-way only. That is, it is not always about sending story ideas to the journalist. There may be times when the journalist contacts the DMO for comment, possibly about a crisis the organisation might be facing. Clearly, the DMO needs to be prepared to handle such a cold call. One 'no comment' about a tricky situation might jeopardise how the same media will react to the DMO's next story release. Barry (2002, pp. 42–45) promoted the three Ws of media relations:

- **Why is what we have to say of interest?** Is it news? It is the job of the communicator to ensure the needs of the journalist are met. Is it relevant to their audience?
- **When is their deadline for accepting information?** Expecting the media to revolve around the communicator's timetable is arrogant.
- **What format does the media require?** The journalist's preference will dictate whether your message is actually noticed.

Handling negative publicity

Images held of a destination may be either positive or negative, although in reality will usually consist of both. Effective corrective marketing is difficult, and it has been suggested that once a negative image has become established, marketing activities will not be able to reverse it (Ahmed, 1991a). In the case of Ireland, Ehemann (1977) found an overwhelmingly negative image portrayed in both the hard news and general media. Ehemann was interested in the evaluative vocabulary used in the media about a destination, and the nature of the image that might be developed by an individual with no direct experience of a destination. A number of case studies concerning this issue have been reported in the tourism literature:

- Bramwell and Rawding (1996) reported on the challenges involved in attempting to change the negative image of Bradford, an English industrial city.
- In Wales, Selby and Morgan (1996) found that even after considerable redevelopments, Barry Island still had an image of being dirty and tatty. This may have reflected the organic perceptions held prior to the redevelopment.
- Similarly, Amor, Calabug, Abellan and Montfort (1994) reported that the image held of Benidorm remained negative, despite consumer and trade awareness of attempts to change it.
- Meler and Ruzic (1999), discussing the negative image of post-war Croatia, suggested that one or a few negative attributes could stimulate the creation of a negative image of a destination.

At a local community level, negative media issues can relate to a diverse range of issues such as: crime against visitors, natural disasters, DMO funding, impacts of tourism growth, controversial building developments. As will be discussed in Chapter 18, the DMO should not leave a response to chance. Recovery from a disaster or negative issue requires planning.

Effective media relations is one of the most important aspect of a destination recovery response, since negative reporting in the mass media can affect the viability of a destination. The media has a propensity for relaying 'bad news' rather than positive coverage of a destination's recovery. Beirman (2003a, pp. 25–26) advised DMO media managers that they should be prepared for the following questions:

- What is being done to assist victims?
- What is the extent of the damage/casualties?
- What is being dome to reduce, minimise, or eliminate future risks?
- What can the government/destination authorities do to guarantee safety?
- Why did this event occur in the first place?
- Who is to blame?
- How long will the crisis last?

During a serious crisis all international marketing should cease, given that these will be worthless if consumers are bombarded with negative news images on their televisions (Mansfield, 1999). The focus of communications at this stage should be on providing accurate information dissemination. Strengthening of relations with the media will be necessary to generate greater positive publicity, since misinformation is one of the greatest challenges to tourism.

Quarantelli (1996, in Faulkner, 1999) observed four key characteristics in the role of the media in USA disasters. Interestingly, the first has been a lack of disaster preparedness planning by the mass media. Second, tensions have emerged between local media and national media over disaster ownership. Third, the media have tended to selectively report activities of organisations with which they have an established relationship. Fourth, television has been prone to perpetuate disaster myths.

In practice

Misinformation in the USA about the 2001 outbreak of foot and mouth disease in the UK led to perceptions that the disease was a human condition, and that all of England was 'closed'. One of the greatest communication challenges was maintaining a positive outlook in destination promotion, while simultaneously promoting the negative impacts to government (Hopper, 2002. p. 83):

Frisby (2002) provided a detailed first-hand account of the PR activities undertaken by the BTA during the foot and mouth outbreak. Initiatives undertaken during the crisis included: media releases, fortnightly newsletters, sponsored overseas media visits, video news releases and background tapes, and development of a media extranet. At the peak of the outbreak the BTA's call centre in New York received an average of 700 calls each day about the crisis. Frisby (p. 90) claimed that media misinformation was such that enquiries included, for example, 'Should we bring our own food?' and 'Can we travel around safely?' At the height of the outbreak, the London Tourism Board was conducting around six broadcast interviews a week with media, which were focused heavily on the negative.

On a much smaller scale, comedian John Cleese caused great offence in Palmerston North in 2006, when he labelled the city 'the suicide capital of New Zealand' (NZPA, 2006). Cleese suggested 'if you want to kill yourself but lack the courage to, I think a visit to Palmerston North will do the trick'. The city increased exposure to the issue by developing a 'Passionate about Palmerston North' competition in New Zealand and Australia, which invited people to write about why they would like to visit. Palmerston North claimed to have had the last laugh by naming a local rubbish tip after Cleese.

However, attempts to place a positive spin on events led former magazine editor Warwick Roger to offer this reflection of the PR industry:

> *Journalists, for the most part, still work in the interests of the public. PR and advertising people . . . operate only in the interests of money and bullshit (Inside Tourism, p. 246).*

Case Study 16.1 discusses the political implications of a major event that attracts significant government support, but which has attracted negative publicity.

Case study 16.1 'Schoolies' week on Queensland's Gold Coast

Dr Noel Scott, School of Tourism, University of Queensland

'Schoolies' week is a major annual tourism phenomenon in Australia involving students who have completed Year 12, the final year at high school (see www.schooliesweek.gov.au). Each year in November (traditionally a low season for Gold Coast tourism), some 30,000 such students travel to the Gold Coast to spend a week's holidays with their friends. 'Schoolies' week began when local students staying in their parents' Gold Coast beach houses held a series of parties around 1975–1978. 'Schoolies' subsequently became popular as a 'rite of passage' with increasing numbers of students attending and using commercial apartments and hotels. After 1991, a commercial company, Breakfree Holidays, began to advertise 'Schoolies' accommodation packages to interstate school leavers.

In 1995, 'Schoolies' week received significant negative publicity due to a civil disturbance in the main street, purportedly caused by drunken 'Schoolies'. Following this, the Gold Coast City Council (GCCC) became much more active in the planning and management of 'Schoolies' week. In 1996, the GCCC provided entertainment for 'Schoolies' week and in 1997 a GCCC 'Schoolies' week officer was appointed. Thereafter, 'Schoolies' week has been increasingly organised, with an official media spokesman provided by the GCCC and numerous innovations introduced to reduce harmful behaviour by 'Schoolies'. In 2001, 'Schoolies' week was estimated to be worth $12.5 million in direct expenditure. Similar celebrations have begun to be organised in several other locations around Australia.

Today, 'Schoolies' week is a 10-day-long festival supported by 500 volunteers, with a significant presence by both the police and private security, partly to avoid violence and public drunkenness, and partly to reduce predatory sexual behaviour by older males. The state Education, Health, and Police departments provide educational material about 'Schoolies' week in schools, and evening entertainment is provided on the beach.

The Gold Coast 'Schoolies' festival is hugely successful for the commercial companies who sell accommodation to the 'Schoolies', but costs the local and state governments millions of dollars. As the 'Schoolies' week festival takes place primarily on public land, such as the beach and streets of the Gold Coast, there is currently little possibility of recouping this money. Local businesses such as fine-dining restaurants, retail shops, and tourist attractions do little business from 'Schoolies', who spend on accommodation, food, and alcohol, and little else. The local community finds 'Schoolies' an imposition although accept that it is 'part of the Gold Coast scene'. The Destination Marketing Organisation (Gold Coast Tourism) is not significantly involved in the organisation of the 'Schoolies' week festival.

Discussion question

As the managing director of Gold Coast Tourism, a local journalist has asked your opinion of 'Schoolies' week for a story she is preparing. What are you going to tell her?

Further reading

Scott, N. (2006). Management of tourism: Conformation to whose standards? In B. Prideaux, G. Moscardo & E. Laws (eds), *Managing Tourism and Hospitality Services: Theory and International Applications*. Wallingford: CABI.

Importantly, remember there is no obligation for the media to use your story ideas. As discussed in Chapter 3, at the 2005 Tourism & Travel Research Association conference in New Orleans (just prior to Hurricane Katrina), keynote speaker Peter Greenberg, well known to Americans as 'the travel detective' on one of the national television networks, challenged the audience with the same question he poses to destination promoters who lobby him to film a segment at their place: 'Tell me what experience you offer me that I cant find anywhere else.'

Publicity

There has been a lack of research reported in the literature on the use of publicity as a promotional tool by DMOs (Dore & Crouch, 2003). However, undertaking campaigns to generate publicity is the most visible aspect of PR. Editorial media coverage offers DMOs two key benefits. Firstly, publicity campaigns are far more economical and cost-effective than paid advertising. Secondly, news generally has higher credibility than paid advertising. Trout (1995) suggested that six times as many people read an average news article as read the average advertisement. Trout attributed this to editors being better communicators than advertising agencies. Consumer suspicion about paid advertising is not a new phenomenon, as evidenced by the view of Wahab et al. (1976, p. 73) three decades ago:

> To obtain a buying decision means overcoming the buyer's resistance to yet one more sales message. There are so many, and life has taught him that they promise so much more than they achieve, that the buyer acquires a built-in suspicion and hostility, which we know as sales resistance.

The publicity programme should integrate the brand messages being used in other marketing communications. To do so requires similar planning with clear objectives, target audience, message proposition, and tactics. A DMO's publicity programme commonly focuses on the following tactics:

- Visiting journalists programme
- Capitalising on movies, television, and literary figures
- Capitalising on icons.

Visiting journalists programme

In a survey of the publicity practice of 10 NTOs from Europe, Africa, and Asia/Pacific, Dore and Crouch (2003) found that the largest budget item within the PR budget was the visiting journalists programme (VJP). This is also often referred to as a visiting media programme (VMP). While the PR allocation was the third highest in the promotional budget, behind advertising and personal selling, it was rated as the highest in importance by NTO respondents due to the cost-effectiveness. Key problems with VJPs identified by NTOs include: limited funds and staff resources, lack of industry support, short notice arrival of media, quality control of ensuing publicity, and results not meeting expectations.

While much publicity about places occurs in the general news and entertainment media without the influence of DMOs or the travel industry, travel writers are a primary target of DMO PR managers. For example, in 2003 the Canadian Tourism Commission (CTC) launched a website specifically for travel media (see www.gomediacanada.com). The site contains travel stories, CTC media releases, links to the tourism industry, information on media tours, market research results, and a photo/video library.

Courtenay (2005) cited research estimating that around one-third of travellers stated the travel media influenced their travel plans. Travel articles in newspaper and magazine travel columns are commonly positive about destinations, given the writer has usually been sponsored by the DMO, airline, accommodation, and attractions. For this reason, Lundburg (1990) reported that travel writers from the *New York Times*, *Wall Street Journal*, and *Washington Post* were not permitted to accept 'freebies'. While other newspapers, such as the *Los Angeles Times* and *Dallas News*, also did not allow staff to travel free, stories could be purchased from freelance writers who may have done so. However, many travel writers tell it as they find it, so hosting the media is not without some risk.

In practice

Travelwriters.com (www.travelwriters.com) is an example of one of the many resources available to current and aspiring travel writers, and provides advice for PR agents, DMOs, and tourism operators, such as: a writer database, travel publications directory, and press release forum. A community of 10,000+ professional travel writers, Travelwriters.com, is based on a simple principle: to connect top-tier travel writers with editors, PR agencies, tourism professionals, CVBs, and tour operators, nurturing the important link that so heavily influences the travel media.

Media database

An essential element of any publicity programme is a database of travel writers and other news media. For larger DMOs such databases are becoming more sophisticated, and capture individual journalists' previous articles, travel preferences, and personal information. The Society of American Travel Writers (www.satw.org) was established 50 years ago as a professional association to raise standards in the travel writers profession. The British Guild of Travel Writers (see www.bgtw.metronet.co.uk) was established in 1960. The Guild's 220 mostly freelance members contribute to 38 national and provincial daily newspapers, 56 magazines, 86 general interest publications, 37 trade journals, 42 in-flight magazines, and travel guidebooks.

> **In practice**
>
> To more effectively assist journalists, the Orlando/Orange County CVB developed a Journalist VIP Passport (Courtenay, 2005). CVB members offer pre-qualified journalists complimentary services, accommodation, and meals. The passports permit visiting journalists to plan flexible itineraries, to which the CVB can tailor specific information and other items to fit a particular story angle.

David Hickie, head of Gadfly Media and publisher of *Luxury Travel* magazine suggested that wealthy travellers don't have the time or desire to scour the internet (Cincotta, 2006). Hickie argued that luxury travellers want all the work done for them, and prefer the credibility of glossy magazines over internet content: 'Most of what you'll find online is just what the hotel or resort has written about itself.' Cincotta provided similar sentiments by publishers of *Gourmet Traveller*, *Travel & Leisure*, and *Cruise*, who argued that such publications are trusted and authoritative sources of information for discerning travellers. Sandra Hook, publisher of *Vogue Entertaining & Travel*, argued that magazines' point of difference is an obvious one:

> *Magazines provide inspiration with their editorial and pictorial coverage of destinations. Readers are presented with new destinations and travel opportunities. The net basically provides up-to-date information on destinations that the potential traveller has already selected.*

> **In practice**
>
> One small Australian LTA with a small limited budget that has been successful in attracting national publicity for a destination is Queensland's Burnett Shire Council. The Burnett Shire is the headquarters for the Coral Coast region (www.coralcoast.org), which is a small coastal community located 350 kilometres north of Brisbane, the state capital. The region is classified as an 'emerging' destination by Tourism Queensland, and the local council provides a relatively modest financial allocation to destination promotion. However, council staff, who have other roles but work part-time on tourism initiatives, have been very proactive in terms of targeting high-profile media, and coordinating industry support for the visits through their work with a Tourism Industry Advisory Committee (TIAC).
>
> In October 2003 the shire hosted the weather segment of Australia's leading national breakfast television programme. Presenter Sami Lucas broadcast a series of 12 five-minute segments live from Bargara Beach, Moore Park Beach, and Bundaberg over three days. Equivalent advertising value of the airtime was estimated at A$600,000.

The total cost of hosting the film crew was approximately A$20,000, of which almost all was provided by tourism industry sponsorship. The previous year the council successfully hosted the television programme *Destinations*, which produced a half-hour segment on the Coral Coast's attractions. The cost of hosting the programme was A$17,000, which was shared between council and local tourism interests. In a local media release (6/2/03), Mayor Ray Duffy enthused:

> This is an exciting time for Council and the Coral Coast. Through this programme we have the potential to reach over 4 million viewers nationally.

The *Destinations* programme was credited locally as being a major force in the 'discovery' of the Coral Coast as a new tourism destination by Australians, and coincided with the council's million-dollar redevelopment of the Bargara Beach foreshore. The months following these events represented a new era of tourism development in the area by interstate property developers and investors. The council used the programme to launch a brief television advertising campaign promoting the region. These examples help to demonstrate how significant national publicity can be for a small destination without a large advertising budget. The examples also demonstrate how PR can be cost-effective for a small destination community through council coordination and in-kind contributions spread between industry in the form of accommodation, rental cars, and meals.

Resource library

It is good practice for DMOs to maintain a resource library to service the needs of the media and trade. Resources typically include photos, brand imagery, and video clips of local attractions. These are useful, for example, for travel writers who are not equipped to replicate professional images that may have been obtained in perfect weather conditions and by special means such as a helicopter. Limited time, resources, and inclement weather can inhibit the travel writer's ability to record suitable images during a brief visit. In recent years resource libraries have become digital. In 2002, for example, the Canadian Tourism Commission launched a photo CD, which contained 100 images as well as links to a searchable database on a website with over 800 photos (see www.canadatourism.com). The images are free to use in publicity for Canada, within guidelines on the conditions of use included with the CD. In New Zealand, Tourism Rotorua outsources the image bank to an organisation specialising in the online management of brand image integrity:

> The storage, maintenance and effective distribution of brand standards and brand identity artwork is often complex, repetitive, slow and expensive, especially when distributing internationally. Incorrect

> *artwork can be used or corners cut as lead times evaporate. These lapses can jeopardise the success of a brand. The arrival of the internet as a reliable communications tool has made obsolete the traditional hard copy manual, bromides, couriered disks, etc. (www.e-see.com/marketing/aboutesee2.htm, 29/3/04).*

Requests for destination imagery by media and tourism operators, including photos and brand logos, are vetted to ensure appropriate representation.

Movies, television programmes and literary figures

As well as opportunities in the general and travel media, readers will be aware of television programmes that have generated publicity in various parts of the world for destinations such as in the cases of *Coronation Street* and *Queer as Folk* (Manchester), *Sea Change* (Australia, see Beeton, 2001), *Neighbours* (Australia), *Bergerac* (Jersey, see Tooke & Baker, 1996), and *Cheers* (Boston) to name but a few. Movie- and television-induced tourism is not a new phenomenon. Davidson and Maitland (1997) reported how the West Yorkshire village of Holmfirth became a tourism destination overnight in 1972 following the airing of the BBC TV series *The Last of the Summer Wine*. Similarly, Bradford made use of its television and film history to promote short-break packages based on *Wuthering Heights*, *Emmerdale Farm*, and *The Last of the Summer Wine* (Buckley & Witt, 1985). Voase (2002) cited research indicating that the main reason for visiting Austria for three out of every four international visitors was the film *The Sound of Music*. A year after the 1977 movie *Close Encounters of the Third Kind* was released, the level of visitors to the Devil's Tower National Monument increased by 74% (Riley & Van Doren, 1992). Other examples of movie-induced tourism discussed by Riley and Van Doren included: *Deliverance* (Rayburn County, Georgia), *Dances with Wolves* (Fort Hayes, Kansas), *Thelma and Louise* (Arches National Monument, Georgia), *Field of Dreams* (Iowa), *The Piano* (New Zealand), *Steel Magnolias* (Natchitoches, Louisiana), and *Crocodile Dundee* (Australia).

Many DMOs have been proactive in maximising movie and television exposure. Petersburg in Virginia took advantage of the 2003 release of the movie *Cold Mountain* to promote tours of the Battle of the Crater scene of the 1864 civil war, which is relived in the opening scenes of the movie (Bergman, 2004). The New Zealand government allocated a special fund of $10.4 million in 2001/2002 and NZ$4.4 million in 2002/2003 towards promotion of the *Lord of the Rings* trilogy (Foreman, 2003). The state of North Carolina provides a website discussing the importance of the movie industry (see www.ncinformation.com/nc_movie_industry.htm). Since 1980, North Carolina has attracted over 600 feature films. A number of case studies of movie-induced tourism have been reported in the tourism literature, including: Nottingham and *Robin Hood – Prince of Thieves* (see Holloway & Robinson, 1995), New Zealand and the

Lord of the Rings trilogy (see Croy, 2004), Australia and *Ned Kelly* (see Frost, 2003).

While there is evidence that movies do increase visitors to the location (Tooke & Baker, 1996), movie-induced tourism does have its critics. For example, the director of *Natural History New Zealand*, a documentary owned by Fox Television Studios, described the tourism focus on *Lord of the Rings* as 'tacky': '. . . it's just extraordinary to listen to boring little people trying to quantify it in value (to) tourism. It is sickening' (*Inside Tourism*, IT488, 5/3/04). There has also been criticism in Wales that it was the landscape there that country inspired Tolkein's Middle Earth, and not New Zealand. In examining the tourism impact of the Australian TV series *Sea Change* on the seaside village of Barwon, Beeton (2001) lamented a change in the visitor mix, which may have long-term impacts on the destination's traditional holiday market. DMOs interested in this emerging area of research will find a rich resource of examples of the positive and negative impacts of film locations in the papers of Riley and Van Doren (1992), Tooke and Baker (1996), and Riley et al. (1998).

Stein (2006) suggested that a large part of the success of the controversial film *Borat* was inadvertently created by the government of Kazakhstan by firstly threatening legal action and then taking out an unsuccessful four-page tourism ad in the *New York Times*.

Movies and intellectual property ● ● ●

While the *Lord of the Rings* movie trilogy generated enormous publicity for New Zealand, there was initial resistance from the producers to permit Tourism New Zealand to promote areas where filming took place. Producers were reluctant to have Middle Earth associated with New Zealand for fear of damaging the first film's mystery. Ultimately, Tourism New Zealand was able to demonstrate that an association between New Zealand and the movies would be beneficial. Tourism New Zealand was required to seek the producers' permission before any aspect of the movie could be used in promotions.

Literary figures ● ● ●

The topic of literary tourism is not widely reported in the academic literature, even though there is evidence of novels as promotional tools dating back to the 19th century. For example, *The Mystery of a Hansom Cab* by Fergus Hume is said to have attracted many tourists to Melbourne, Australia, where the murder-mystery was set (Richardson, 1999). There exists a tourism industry based on visits to the areas where famous literary figures once lived. This is particularly evident in the UK, where the NTO actively promotes sites that offer a glimpse of the lives of Britain's authors, playwrights, and poets (see www.visitbritain.com). Examples of regional destinations that are laying claims as the home of Britain's finest wordsmiths include (Brace, 2007):

- Thomas Hardy's Wessex
- Emily Bronte's West Yorkshire (www.brontecountry.info)
- William Shakespeare's Stratford-upon-Avon (www.shakespeare-country.co.uk)
- Jane Austen's Hampshire
- William Wordsworth's Lake District (www.lake-district.gov.uk)
- Charles Dickens' London (www.hiddenlondon.com)

Theme parks also take advantage of literary figures. May 2007 saw the opening of Dickens World in the UK, themed around the life, times, and books of the author, and there was an announcement that Universal Studios and Warner Brothers were to develop a *Harry Potter* theme park in Orlando, Florida, based on the writings of author J.K. Rowling.

Capitalising on icons

Another popular form of publicity for destinations is the stimulation of 'big things'. One of the most spectacular of these, and possibly from the only-in America category, (see Schofield comment, 2002) is the eight-storey office building that is built in the shape of a basket, the headquarters of the Longaberger Basket Company. Icon development is particularly popular in small towns, where eye-catching roadside icons can become 'must see' photo opportunities for some travellers. Morley (2003) reported on the proposal in Augathella, 660 kilometres west of Queensland's state capital Brisbane, to build a giant monument in honour of the prolific meat ant. The Augathella and District Tourist and Progress Association proposed the idea after the town of 430 residents was bypassed by the Matilda Highway. Some Australian examples are shown in Table 16.3. In 2007, five of the icons were featured in a special set of Australian postage stamps, entitled *Big Things*.

Other initiatives

Other DMO initiatives that fall under the label publicity include:

- stimulation of the use of locations in corporate brochures, such as by Canada in Porsche's magazine (*Marketing Magazine*, 17/3/03).
- contra prizes for game shows
- contra prizes for consumer goods retail competitions
- sponsorship of media competitions
- encouraging department stores to use destination themes
- public 'film' evenings
- use of celebrities as tourism ambassadors, such as the Tourism Australia's use of world surfing champion Lane Beachley, model Megan Gale, and swimmer Ian Thorpe. Maison France used actor Woody Allen

Table 16.3 Examples of Australian small town icons

Icon	Town
The Big Apple	Stanthorpe
The Big Avocado	Byron Bay
The Big Banana	Coffs Harbour
The Big Cheese	Bega
The Big Cow	Nambour
The Big Guitar	Tamworth
The Big Lobster	Kingston
The Big Merino	Gouldburn
The Big Oyster	Taree
The Big Peanut	North Tolga
The Big Pineapple	Nambour
The Big Pie	Yatala
The Big Prawn	Ballina

in the trade promotion video *Lets Fall in Love Again*. The Queen and royal family participated in the promotion of British Tourism Day 2003 (www.travelmole.com, 10/6/03).

Key points

1. Managing relationships with stakeholders

Public relations is more than publicity-seeking, in that it represents a concerted effort to develop favourable impressions of a destination. This involves both the generation of positive publicity by the DMO as well as the stimulation of positive relations between internal and external stakeholders. Since DMOs are essentially in the business of communication, the process of communication management should not be left to chance.

2. Advantages of media publicity as a communications medium

Editorial media exposure holds a number of advantages for destination marketers, in relation to above-the-line advertising. In particular, the medium is cost-effective and has higher credibility. Establishing an open working relationship with general news media and travel writers is critical.

3. DMO publicity initiatives

As well as stimulating media editorial through media releases and visiting media programmes, other popular approaches include stimulating publicity based on the locations of movies, television and literary figures.

Review questions

- Imagine you have been asked by a television network to provide a photo of an icon that best represents your local destination. This photo will be used, alongside those from other centres, briefly during the evening weather update. Explain why. Share your views with others and gauge the level of agreement.
- Brainstorm ideas for a release to the general media. Select one idea and prepare a release.

CHAPTER 17

Meetings marketing

Man is, above all, a gregarious animal, and there can be no doubt that the need to gather regularly with others who share a common interest is one of the most human of all activities.

Davidson & Rogers (2006, p. 3)

Aims

The aims of this chapter are to enhance understanding of:

- the potential to attract meetings, incentive groups, conventions, and exhibitions
- the specialised nature of convention bureaus
- the importance of a destination's promotional appeal.

Perspective

Travel for the purpose of meetings, incentive programmes, conventions, and exhibitions (MICE) has emerged as one of the fastest growing and most resilient travel segments for destinations worldwide. The market provides most DMOs with opportunities to enhance occupancy and attendance at a wide range of local businesses, often during off-peak periods. Recognition of the value of the MICE market has seen an increasing number of DMOs develop convention bureaus to enhance competitiveness. While there has been relatively little published research into convention destination attractiveness, it seems clear that in addition to meeting facilities, a critical factor is the promotional appeal of the destination to delegates. DMOs and CVBs use a range of promotional activities to enhance perceptions of the destination in the minds of influential convention planners responsible for destination selection.

Meetings, incentives, conferences, exhibitions (MICE)

Business works best in real time, real touch networks. Meeting face to face remains the ultimate way to plug into a business network.

Queensland Business Acumen, May, 2007

The need to meet in person to discuss common interests has been a major part of human activity since ancient times (see Fenich, 2005). Since the first CVB was formed over a century ago there has been recognition by destinations of the value of the meetings market, which today encapsulates meetings, incentive travel, conferences/conventions, and exhibitions/expositions (MICE). The term 'meeting' is used to describe a multiplicity of business and social events. For example, Fenich listed 47 synonyms, ranging from 'buzz session' to 'congress'. For the purpose of this chapter, the definitions of the key forms of meetings of interest to destination marketers are those proposed in the Convention Industry Council's Accepted Practises Exchange (APEX – see www.conventionindustry.org/glossary/). These are shown in Table 17.1. APEX is an initiative that aims to unite the meetings industry in the development and eventual implementation of voluntary standards, which will be called accepted practices.

The most common form of meeting is corporate events such as annual general meetings, sales meetings, staff training retreats, product launches, and incentive trips (Davidson & Rogers, 2006). Other buyers of destination meeting services are associations, the public sector, and SMERFs, the name given to social, military, religious, and fraternal groups. The characteristics of these major segments as summarised by Davidson and Rogers are listed in Table 17.2.

Table 17.1   Key meetings industry definitions

Term	Definition
Meeting	An event where the primary activity of the attendees is to attend educational sessions, participate in meetings/discussions, socialise, or attend other organised events. There is no exhibit component to this event.
Incentive travel	A travel reward given by companies to employees to stimulate productivity.
Convention	An event where the primary activity of the attendees is to attend educational sessions, participate in meetings/discussions, socialise, or attend other organised events. There is a secondary exhibit component.
Exhibition	(1) An event at which products and services are displayed. The primary activity of attendees is visiting exhibits on the show floor. These events focus primarily on business-to-business (B2B) relationships. (2) Display of products or promotional material for the purposes of public relations, sales and/or marketing.
Trade show	An exhibition of products and/or services held for members of a common or related industry. Not open to the general public.
Public show	An exhibition that is open to the public, usually requiring an entrance fee.

Table 17.2   Characteristics of major segments

Corporate	Association	Government	SMERF
The process of deciding to hold events is relatively straightforward. But the actual corporate meeting buyer may be difficult to identify within the initiator's organisation: secretaries, personal assistants, marketing executives, directors	The process of choosing a destination can be prolonged. A committee is usually involved in the choosing of the destination; and the organisers may be volunteers from the association's membership.	Considerable variety in terms of length of event and budgets available. However, budgets are usually scrutinised, since public money is being used. High security measures are indispensable:	Price sensitive regarding accommodation rates and venue rates; but more recession-proof than corporate meetings. Held by organisations that are run by volunteers – so the task of identifying them can be challenging.

(Continued)

309

Table 17.2 (Continued)

Corporate	Association	Government	SMERF
of training, and many others may book corporate events. Attendance is usually required of company employees. Lead times can be short. A higher budget per delegate. Venues used: hotels, management training centres, unusual venues. Delegates' partners are rarely invited, except in the case of incentive trips.	Attendance is voluntary. A lower budget per delegate, since for some attendees, prices is a sensitive issue and they may be paying their own costs. Venues used: conference centres, civic and academic venues. Delegates' partners frequently attend.	these meetings are frequently accompanied by demonstrations and disruptions.	Frequently held over weekends and in off-peak periods. Often held in second-tier cities, using simple accommodation and facilities. Attended by delegates who bring their spouses/families and are likely to extend their trips, for leisure purposes.

Since the majority of meetings involve less than 1000 delegates, most tourism destinations are able to cater to the market (Abbey & Link, 1994, in Oppermann, 1996b). The meetings market is generally more resilient than holiday segments, and also offers the destination the opportunity to build additional business during the off-peak periods. The value of the meetings market is certainly considerable. For example, in the USA the Convention Industry Council estimated the 2004 value of the meetings market to exceed US$122 billion. In Australia the sector generates over A$7 billion in direct spending (Weaver & Lawton, 2006).

There is evidence to suggest that the impact of electronic meeting mediums, such as teleconferencing, has not made a significant impact on the growth of the meetings sector. Future Watch 2007, an annual survey of the meetings industry undertaken by Meetings Professionals International, found that virtual meetings was not a major component of participants' activities. Nevertheless, Tress and Sacks (2004, in Davidson & Rogers, 2006) warned of the emerging over-supply of conference facilities, particularly in the USA. An increasing number of convention centres are becoming white elephants. They cited the example of one centre, which after a US$75 million expansion in 2003, attracted only 23 conferences in 2004.

Incentive travel

Incentive travel programmes were introduced by corporations as a means to motivate staff to achieve targets. Such targets are related to business objectives, and commonly involve sales increases or cost reductions. Rewards might include individual travel, but commonly involve large groups. In addition to the achievement of the corporate objectives, other benefits to the organisation of incentive travel include (Witt & Gammon, 1994):

- opportunities for networking and communication between staff and management
- opportunities for social interaction between those working independently, such as sales reps and dealers, conveys a sense of belonging
- generating enthusiasm
- fostering loyalty to the company and retaining top performers.

Two characteristics of the incentive travel market that have particular appeal to DMOs are: (1) this type of travel usually takes place in groups, and often very large groups, such as the 10,000 Japanese door-to-door bra saleswomen hosted by Sydney, Australia; (2) the tailored nature of reward packages tend to generate a higher than average yield.

Incentive travel planning is a specialised craft, and destinations targeting this segment need to carefully consider the resources required. Itineraries are custom-made to suit the needs of the group, and tend to be creative in terms of venues and activities. Witt and Gammon (1994) suggested that only destinations at the mature stage of the lifecycle need apply, since there needs to be a well-developed infrastructure, good accessibility, and a sufficient mix of attractions. They cited this account by an incentive travel specialist of a function at the Rose Garden in Thailand (p. 20):

> The Rose Garden is just outside Bangkok and it is a fairytale place. The participants walk in and there is an elephant show to greet them. There is a demonstration of various arts and crafts going on during cocktails. There is a circular area by the river where the buffet is set up and different foods from all the different regions of Thailand are laid out. There is a boat on the river that is lit up with an orchestra playing with singers. This is followed by a full show – Thai dancing, boxing, etc. At the end, everyone joins in a ceremony with candles and goes down to the river and puts their candles into it. Thousands of candles floating in the river – it is quite pretty. All the little Thai children come out to say goodnight to everybody. Everyone is in tears because the children are so sweet.

For the incentive to appeal to staff, the itinerary needs to be attractive, and the destination needs to be well known to staff and have brag value. Travel time to the destination is also important, given that incentive group travel is commonly in the form of a short break. Promotion is clearly very targeted, usually involving personal selling to incentive travel specialists who are contracted by the corporation.

Convention bureaus

The meetings market brings together a diversity of businesses such as hotels, convention centres, transport operators, attractions, caterers, conference planners, and entertainers. The complex web of relationships necessitates coordination at the destination level. However, not all DMOs operate a convention bureau, due to the specialised nature of operations and investment required. For example, in Queensland Australia, only six of the state's 14 RTOs have a convention bureau.

As discussed in Chapter 3, the convention and visitor bureau (CVB) concept originated in Detroit (USA) in 1896, from a suggestion by a local journalist to promote the city as a convention destination. The USA was also to develop the first purpose-built convention centre, during the 1960s (Davidson & Rogers, 2006).

In Mexico the first CVBs were established in the late-1960s and early-1970s, to service visitors attracted to the 1968 Olympics and 1970 Football World Cup (Cerda, 2005). The first was established in Guadalajara in 1969. However, it was not until the 1980s that government provided funding for the CVBs. Cerda reported over 40 CVBs were established during the late-1990s and early-2000s. The first UK CVBs were formed in the 1980s (see Rogers, 2005). Interestingly, the first national CVBs were not established until 1973 (Germany) and 1974 (Finland).

Most CVBs in the USA have membership programmes, even with government room tax funding. Many DMOs are reliant on member subscriptions for funding, which can be a double-edged sword. On one hand more members generate increased funding, while on the other hand they generate more responsibility in providing benefits. After all, 'most CVBs don't want members unless they can help that member to secure business' (Walters, 2005, p. 163). So membership should make sense, and Walters provides a useful guide to membership development, retention, and dismissal. The major benefits of CVB membership promoted by Walters (pp. 169–170) are:

- member events (mixers, annual dinner, marketing updates)
- convention and meeting planner sales leads
- group tour or motor coach sales leads
- convention service sales leads (after a meeting is booked, the planner may be looking for caterers, audiovisual services, speakers etc.)
- listings in publications and on a bureau's website
- ability to place brochures in a visitor centre
- referrals from a visitor centre
- discounts on health insurance, shipping, or long-distance calling
- ability to advertise in the CVB's publications or on its website
- ability to participate in bureau sponsored co-op ads
- ability to participate in bureau-led sales missions or trade shows
- chance to host news media and travel writers
- ability to participate in bureau familiarisation show and events
- chance to expose one's business to other bureau members
- membership plaque of window decal showing membership status
- bureau publications in quantity, usually at no charge

- complimentary links from a bureau's website
- subscription to the bureau's newsletter and other insider information
- benefit from the bureau's lobbying efforts or access to elected officials
- access to and ability to influence the bureau's marketing plan.

Professional bodies

In 1914 the International Association of Convention Bureaus, later to become the International Association of Convention & Visitor Bureaus in 1974 (IACVB), and now known as Destination Marketing Association International (DMAI), was formed with 28 members. According to Rob Stern, DMAI Director of Information Services, by the end of 2006 there were 1412 CVBs in the USA. From a meetings marketing perspective, membership benefits of DMAI include (see www.iacvb.org):

- Destinations Showcase. In the USA, the only trade show purposefully designed for destination exhibitors is the DMAI's annual Destination Showcase. An average of 70% of meeting planners in attendance walk the floor with a request for proposals (RFP) in hand. These attendees on average plan 11 meetings a year, including one outside the USA (see www.destinationsshowcaseonline.com).
- Meeting Industry Network. An online database of over 32,000 past and future meetings by over 16,000 organisations.
- Lead generation. DMAI provides online RFP distribution by meeting planners.
- Meeting Industry Almanac. Convention bureaus can reach over 30,000 meetings professionals in the annual Meeting Industry Forecast.

There is an abundance of resources now available on the meetings market that are able to be accessed through professional bodies. A selection of leading organisations is listed in Table 17.3.

Table 17.3 Professional meetings organisations

Organisation	URL
Destination Marketing Association International	www.iacvb.org
Meeting Professionals International	http://www.mpiweb.org
Union of International Associations	www.uia.org/
International Congress and Convention Association	www.iccaworld.com/
Meetings Industry Association of Australia	www.meetingsevents.com.au
Meetings Industry Association of the UK	www.mia-uk.org

(Continued)

Table 17.3 (Continued)

Organisation	URL
Trade Show Exhibitors Association	www.tsea.org
Joint Meetings Industry Council	www.themeetingsindustry.org
International Association of Exposition Managers	www.iaem.org
International Association of Fairs and Expositions	www.fairsandexpos.com
Convention Liaison Council	www.conventionindustry.org
Professional Convention Management Association	www.pcma.org
Society of Incentive Travel Executives	www.site-intl.org
International Association of Professional Congress Organisers	www.iapco.org
Convention Industry Council	www.conventionindustry.org
Association of British Professional Conference Organisers	www.abpco.org

Importance of destination's promotional appeal

The promotional activities for convention bureaus are still based on the marketing orientation of matching available resources with environment opportunities. The convention bureau is engaged in targeting appropriate buyers with a value proposition. It is just as important to monitor how the destination is perceived by meeting planners as it is by travellers. Oppermann (1996) identified a paucity of published research into convention destination images with which to guide destination marketers. Research Snapshot 17.1 highlights the importance of investigating the destination's strengths and weaknesses, relative to competing places, in the minds of convention planners.

Research snapshot 17.1   Convention destination image analysis

Oppermann (1996) lamented the lack of published research into convention destination images, despite the size and rapid growth of the market. He chose to gain insights into how 30 North American cities were perceived as convention destinations from the perspective of association meeting planners. Association conferences are reasonably flexible in terms of destination selection, and association planners are akin to tour operators who are involved in selecting a destination and on-selling to members. Planners are only too aware that potential delegates usually have a selection of conferences on offer each year, and the choice of destination plays a role in decision-making. The study targeted members of the Professional Convention Management Association. In the sample, 79% of participants indicated that their responsibilities included selection of the conference destination.

The results provided rankings of the importance of 15 convention destination attributes, along with how each of the 30 destinations was perceived on each attribute. This approach enabled an understanding of how each destination is positioned relative to competing places. Two further implications were noted. First, the association convention planners differed in their destination selection criteria in terms of attribute importance. Second, previous experience with a destination emerged as a crucial factor in destination image.

Source: Oppermann, M. (1996). Convention destination images: analysis of association meeting planners' perceptions. *Tourism Management, 17*(3), 175–182.

Image is important in the meetings market as conventions are usually held at places that are 'exciting', because they will attract more delegates. However, Chacko and Fenich (2000) lamented the lack of research into what makes an attractive convention destination. Their content analysis of 12 previous studies enabled a synthesis of important convention destination attributes. They identified 12 such attributes for use in their survey of convention planners' perceptions of seven destinations. Regression analysis identified 'promotional appeal' as a significant predictor for overall convention destination attractiveness for most of the cities in the study. The most critical factor, they concluded, was the convention planner's ability to sell the destination to potential delegates. The activities undertaken by the Sydney CVB (see Harris, Jago & King, 2005, pp. 31–32) typify the ideal by convention bureaus in general:

- sales calls, direct mail, telemarketing, and lobbying those responsible for the destination location
- conducting site inspections for those responsible in deciding the destination location
- PR activities to position the destination as a world-class meetings destination
- preparation and presentation of bid documents
- general destination promotional activities
- production of marketing collateral to support the bid process
- assisting development of promotional strategies to increase delegate attendance
- coordinating marketing research.

Results obtained by the CVB during 2001/2002 highlight the return on marketing investment in this sector. By primarily directing marketing efforts towards attracting an international meeting, the CVB was successful in winning 32 events, with an estimated 30,000 participants, for a total value of $143 million to the city (Harris, Jago & King, 2005).

In practice

Gold Coast Tourism, Australia, engaged a local corporate meetings, incentives, and events planning company, SquareOne Events (www.squareoneevents.com), to stage an event spectacular welcoming 275 senior corporate executives to the destination. The event was used to launch the inaugural Business Insights 2007, which promotes the destination as a business destination. The RTO's brief to the organiser was to create an event with a 'wow' factor that enhanced the destination's Very GC brand positioning. The venue for the occasion was a dome pavilion erected on the sand at the beach. The interior was carpeted, air-conditioned, and decked-out with leather lounges. Creative lighting and a swing-music band was used to create a supper club feel. The dome's clear walls provided ocean views.

Source: *Queensland Business Acumen* magazine (May, 2007, p. 62).

Cooperative alliances

DMOs understand that relatively few conferences will return to the same destination every year. National association conferences commonly circulate around a country in a cyclical manner. Consider the location of the Tourism & Travel Research Association conference in recent years, for example: Hollywood, California (2000), Washington DC (2001), Fort Myers, Florida (2002), St Louis, Missouri (2003), Montreal, Canada (2004), New Orleans, Louisiana (2005), Dublin, Ireland (2006), Las Vegas, Nevada (2007).

Like the Olympic Games, it is possible to secure a return conference, after a period of time. Some DMOs therefore see merit of forming alliances with other destinations. Key rational include the sharing of resources and a greater presence in the market. For example, imagine an association conference that in the USA alternates between the west coast, east coast, and mid-west. If a member of the alliance on the west coast has successfully hosted the association's conference this year, a member on the east coast seeking to bid the following year can obtain insights into the bid process critical success factors for that particular association. This is mutually beneficial for the association and the DMO alliance.

In practice

The BestCities Global Alliance (www.bestcities.net) was the first international alliance of convention bureaus, with eight partners in five continents: Cape Town, Copenhaagen, Dubai, Edinburgh, Melbourne, San Juan, Singapore, and Vancouver. The alliance promotes the following advantages to conference organisers:

- *Global access* – one email or phone call provides access to the most professional convention bureaus and attractive destinations in the world.
- *Innovative bid proposals* – our members work with local industry suppliers,public sectors, and your organisation to ensure that all your requirements are met.
- *Expert advice* – careful, expert advice on all aspects of planning a meeting at the chosen destination.
- *Quality assurance* – all member bureaus have undergone a rigorous inspection and approval process and are continuously monitored by client evaluations.
- *Client forums* – platform for peer-to-peer networking and discussion of topics related to managing international organisations and planning their meetings.

Destination planners

Davidson and Rogers (2006), who write extensively in this field, recommend that one of the most sophisticated conference destination guides is that of the Madrid Convention Bureau www.munimadrid.es/congresos. Tourism Toronto claimed that the launch of its new digital destination planner in 2005 was the first of its kind in North America (www.travelindustrywire.com, 26/4/05). Designed for meeting professionals and tour operators, the planner is in the form of a CD-ROM. Once installed on a user's desktop, Digital Toronto provides links to a product and services directory that is updated monthly (see www.tourismtoronto.com).

Responding to RFPs

The CVB or DMO is seen as an impartial information source for meeting professionals. When a meeting planner, organisation, or association contacts the CVB, the office acts as a facilitator of tailored information on available facilities. The CVB in turn manages a leads process for members to bid for the business. This can extend to social and entertainment services, in addition to meeting space and accommodation. For example, the Las Vegas CVB sent out 3000 leads to local businesses during 2003 (Cortez, 2004).

> **In practice**
>
> An interview with an executive from the Sydney CVB identified the following general steps in the meeting bidding process (Harris, Jago & King, 2005, p. 33):
>
> - Identify meetings with the potential to be hosted by the destination, and encourage local associations and firms to bid for their organisation's conference.
> - Obtain the bid criteria from the association.
> - Seek clarification on the bidding process, and work with the local association to develop a bid document.
> - Involve a professional meeting planner in the budget development.
> - Conduct a site inspection.
> - Lodge the bid, and undertake destination promotional activities.
> - For successful bids, engage in promotional activity aimed at potential delegates.

Local support

As evidenced in the summary of the bid process by the Sydney CVB, encouraging local organisations to bid for conferences is a major part of conference marketing. Examples of best practice by CVBs in this regard include (Davidson & Rogers, 2006):

- Spokane Area CVB www.visitspokane.com
- Cardiff Convention Bureau www.cardiffconferencebureau.co.uk
- Aberdeen Convention Bureau www.aberdeenconferences.com
- Melbourne Exhibition and Convention Centre www.mecc.com.au and www.mcvb.com.au

> **In practice**
>
> Between 60,000 and 70,000 meetings are organised in the city of Brussels, Belgium, every year. The events attract an estimated 7 million participants, who spend on average €320. This US$4 billion in annual spending supports 22,000 jobs. Brussels Meeting Week (see www.brusselsmeetingsweek.be) is an initiative to enhance local community perceptions of the value of the meetings industry. In 2006 the initiative won the International Federation of Associations' Profile & Power Award. In 2007 the week of activities was organised to coincide with the staging of the 2007 European Meetings Industry Fair.

Key points

1. The potential to attract MICE

Travel for the purpose of meetings, incentive programmes, conventions, and exhibitions (MICE) has emerged as one of the fastest growing and most resilient travel segments for destinations worldwide. The market provides most DMOs with opportunities to enhance occupancy and attendance at a wide range of local businesses, often during off-peak periods.

2. The specialised nature of convention bureaus

Recognition of the value of the MICE market has seen an increasing number of DMOs develop convention bureaus to enhance competitiveness.

3. The importance of a destination's promotional appeal

While there has been relatively little published research into convention destination attractiveness, it seems clear that in addition to meeting facilities, a critical factor is the promotional appeal of the destination to delegates. DMOs and CVBs use a range of promotional activities to enhance perceptions of the destination in the minds of influential convention planners responsible for destination selection.

Review questions

- Explain why promotional appeal is such an important aspect of a MICE destination.
- How important is the MICE market to your destination? Examine the extent to which your DMO is targeting segments in this market.

CHAPTER 18

Disasters and crises

Good management can avoid crises to some degree, but must equally incorporate strategies for coping with the unexpected event over which the organisation has little control.

Faulkner (1999, p.7)

Aims

The aims of this chapter are to enhance understanding of:

- the difference between a disaster and a crisis
- the potential impact of government and non-government travel advisories
- DMO responses to disasters.

Disaster or crisis?

Bali was one of Australia's most popular overseas destinations until the October 2002 terrorism bombing of a tourist precinct left the destination in a state of crisis, from which it has still not fully recovered, due in part to a further terrorist bombing in 2005. It is important to note the distinction between the terms disaster and crisis. Faulkner (1999) suggested that a crisis was representative of a self-inflicted situation caused by such problems as inept management practices or the inability to adapt to a changing environment. A disaster on the other hand is a sudden catastrophic change over which the organisation has little or no control. From this perspective a crisis could be considered as occurring during the period between when a natural or man-made disaster strikes a destination and recovery is achieved. The degree of internal crisis caused by the external disaster (see Figure 18.1) will vary between organisations, depending on the nature of the event, and management's preparedness, availability of resources, and ability to react.

Although a destination in crisis is not a modern phenomenon, the field of study has only emerged recently in the tourism literature. As David Beirman stated in the opening line of his text *Restoring Destinations in Crisis*: 'No tourism destination is immune from crisis' (2003, p. xiii). It could be expected that preparing contingency plans for crises would be an important element of any DMO planning. However, it is rare for such a topic to dominate much meeting time among stakeholders until disaster strikes. Observations of publicly available strategic plans for NTOs and STOs also

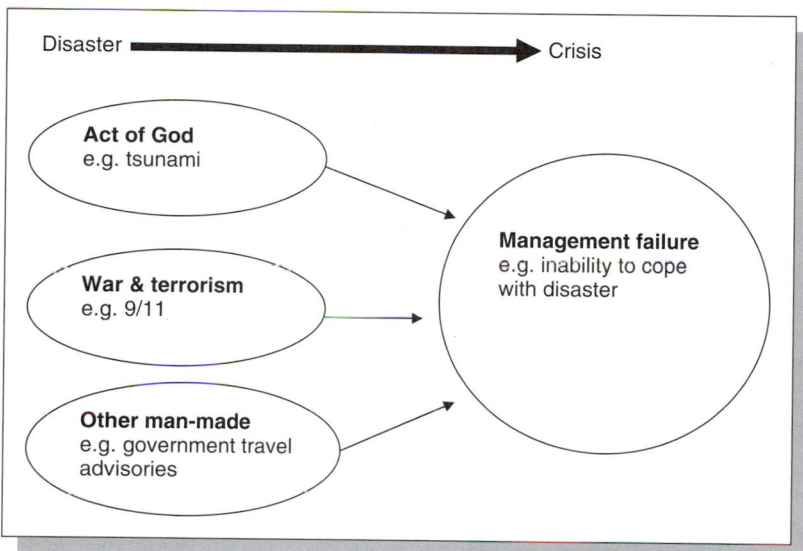

Figure 18.1
Disaster or crisis

indicate that contingency planning for many has not been a priority until recently. For example, PATA (1991, in Litvin & Alderson, 2003) noted that the majority of its members, including NTOs, did not include crisis management in strategic planning, despite an average estimation that they stood a 40% chance of facing a crisis.

In practise

William Hanbury provided a first-hand account of what it is like to be in the hot seat at the time of a disaster without a contingency plan (see Hanbury, 2005). He had been in the position of CEO of the Washington DC Convention & Tourism Corporation (WCTC) for only five months at the time of the 9/11 attacks. The WCTC was not organised to deal with even a minor disaster at the time, let alone the largest economic crisis to face the USA capital. Having been formed only five months previously, following the under-performance of the previous DMO, the WCTC was in the midst of major restructuring. The new DMO had no disaster response plan. Hanbury described how the team responded to ultimately manage the situation, and outlined a summary of lessons learned.

In the quest for increased visitors and spending, which is how a DMO is ultimately judged, crisis planning may be viewed as a luxury of time if a disaster hasn't actually occurred nearby to stimulate discussion. I am aware of one RTO that had regularly ignored pleas from the local civil defence coordinator to consider contingency plans in what is a recognised earthquake zone. The coordinator's concern was that all entrances to the destination were via bridges, which risk collapse in a significant quake. This would severely impact on the ability to evacuate visitors. The rationale for contingency planning was that a major earthquake is highly likely to strike the destination at some unknown time in the future – maybe not for 10,000 years, but maybe next week. The approaches literally fell on deaf ears at the RTO. To be fair to the tourism industry however, until recently there has also been an absence of any case studies in the literature to guide such DMO disaster planning.

Some disasters may be of a short-term nature, such as the 1996 massacre of 35 tourists by a lone gunman at Port Arthur in Tasmania, Australia, and the 1992 Hurricane Andrew in Florida. Others might be long term, such as the political ban on USA citizens visiting Cuba. The ban was imposed by President J.F. Kennedy in 1963, but was later lapsed by President Carter, and then re-imposed by President Reagan in 1982 (www.travelmole.com, 27/10/03). The Middle East is a region that has suffered from ongoing acts of war and terrorism. Mansfield (1999) outlined six major cycles of tourism decline and recovery in Israel due to different security situations since 1967. As a result, Israel has suffered the prevailing image of a high risk destination. The cycles were caused by:

- the Six Day War in 1967
- the 1973 Yom Kippur war between Israel, Egypt and Syria
- the 1981 intensification of the Palestine Liberation Organisation's attacks
- the late-1980s double cycle of international and domestic terror
- the 1990–91 Gulf War
- the terrorised peace cycle of the 1990s.

Unfortunately, from his analysis of these events, Mansfield concluded that once each crisis had ended and recovery in visitor arrivals was evident, neither the government nor tourism industry planned for a future crisis event. This is evident in Case Study 18.1, which examines Israel's marketing recovery efforts between 2001 and 2006.

Case study 18.1   Israel tourism's marketing recovery 2001—July 2006

Dr David Beirman, Director of Struan & Associates Tourism Crisis and Recovery Specialists, Australia

International tourism arrivals to Israel reached a peak during 2000, which was the year of Christianity's bimillennium. During that year 2.67 million tourists arrived in Israel. At the end of September 2000 the Palestinian Intifada broke out, resulting in an immediate decline of tourism arrivals to Israel. Much of the decline was based on a fear amongst potential travellers of terrorism, and an overwhelming perception that Israel was a risky and dangerous destination. In fact during the height of the Intifada between 2000 and 2004, a total of four tourists were killed as a direct consequence of political violence. The steep decline in tourism arrivals reached its nadir in 2002, when only 864,000 tourists arrived in the country.

The Israeli Ministry of Tourism and its representative offices around the world undertook a major recovery campaign which resulted in tourism numbers beginning to recover in 2003 to 1.03 million, growing to 1.5 million in 2004, and reaching 1.9 million in 2005. Until the outbreak of border conflict on the Lebanese frontier in July 2006 Israel tourism growth for the first half of 2006 was a further 25%. The key strategic foundation for rebuilding tourism to Israel, which was developed in January 2001, centred on stratifying the market into three key segments:

- Stalwarts – Travellers with high commitment and high affiliation.
- Waverers – Travellers with modest commitment and high affiliation.
- Discretionary – Travellers with low commitment and low affiliation

During the first phase of recovery in 2001–2004, most marketing activity was focused on the stalwart market, which comprised of Jews, Christian Zionists, and business travellers, with many solidarity groups being encouraged and formed. During 2004–2005 there was a focus on the waverer market, which comprised Christian pilgrims and other groups in Europe, North America, East Asia, and Australasia with a high level of affiliation. By 2005 there was a switch in emphasis to attract the discretionary (vacation market) through partnerships with tour wholesalers and airlines, which resumed flights and tour programmes in Israel.

The basic strategy was to build a staircase of confidence in Israel as a safe and attractive tourist destination. This was aided by a reduction in the intensity of political violence from 2004 to July 2006. During the recovery phase Israel hosted many travel agents, travel writers, religious leaders, and high-profile celebrities who readily provided positive testimonials which were publicised by Israel's government tourism offices in targeted consumer and trade media campaigns in their respective markets.

By the beginning of 2006 the Israeli Ministry of Tourism undertook a more aggressive marketing campaign to attract a growing range of tourists in all key source markets. The recovery came to an abrupt end with the outbreak of military conflict on the Israel–Lebanon border in July 2006, but since the end of this conflict in August 2006 the Israeli Ministry of Tourism immediately utilised a similar approach to recommence recovery.

Note: Dr David Bierman was Director of the Israel Government Tourism Office (Australasia and South West Pacific) from 1994 to 2006, and was directly involved in the strategy discussed in this case.

Discussion question

How does the employment of a market recovery based on market stratification build the staircase of confidence in restoring tourism to a destination that has suffered perceptual damage due to a crisis event?

Further reading

Beirman, D. (2003). *Restoring Tourism Destinations in Crisis*. Sydney: Allen and Unwin.

Like Israel, Northern Ireland tourism has suffered a negative image from terrorism over three decades. However, Leslie (1999) found the even though the associated negative publicity of the 1970s had decreased considerably, Northern Ireland had become increasingly substitutable as a destination for UK travellers. O'Neill and McKenna (1994) found by comparison that in the 1990s, visitor numbers to Northern Ireland had merely re-established the 1960s 'pre-trouble' levels, whereas volumes in Great Britain and the Republic of Ireland had increased by over 50%.

Uncertainty

Tourism destinations have always been, and will continue to be, at risk to exogenous events. Such *wildcard* events, have been described by Hall (2005) as being low probability but high impact. Arguably, the greatest impact of these on the tourism industry is uncertainty:

- Uncertainty of travellers to risk personal safety on what is after all a discretionary activity. During periods of insecurity, consumers can choose either to travel somewhere perceived to safe or delay travel plans. For example, Hopper (2002) reported that within hours of the 9/11 strikes in the USA, hotels in London were receiving cancellations from all over the world. In France, visitors from the USA declined by an estimated 90% in the month immediately following September 11, 2001.
- Uncertainty of investors and small business owners to invest or reinvest in repairs, maintenance, upgrades, or new developments.
- Uncertainty of tourism staff on the future of their career. This even extends to tourism degree and diploma courses, which can suffer from concerns held by prospective students and parents.

Resilience

On a global basis the tourism industry has historically proven to be resilient, with remarkably quick recoveries following major crises. For example, IATA CEO Giovanni Bisignani suggested that following the 1991 Gulf War, a year when tourism arrivals only increased by 1%, growth in 1992 was 8% (www.travelmole.com, 26/3/03). Even with the events of 9/11, international arrivals exceeded 700 million for the first time in 2002, representing an increase of 3% over 2001 and 19 million more than 'Millennium year' (WTO media release, 27/1/03).

War and terrorism

In 1997, an unlucky 58 overseas visitors and 4 Egyptians were gunned down outside one of Egypt's most famous temples in Luxor. The attack cost Egypt's tourism industry US$2 billion in lost earnings (Edgell, 1999). One year after the 2002 Bali bombings, a United Nations report estimated the unemployment rate to be up by almost one-third and that street vendors' sales were down by 50% (www.eturbonews.com, 14/10/03). The ILO (2003) estimated the total loss of jobs in world tourism at over 11 million following the terrorist attacks of 9/11, representing a loss of one in every seven jobs in tourism and travel. The CEO of the International

Air Transport Association (IATA), Giovanni Bisignani, predicted that the 2003 war in Iraq would cost the global airline industry US$10 billion in losses, on top of the US$30 billion in losses following September 11, 2001 (www.travelmole.com, 26/3/03). At the time, a survey by the Tourism Association of America estimated that over 70% of Americans were not interested in travelling overseas (www.travelmole.com, 15/4/03).

Events such as these have increased the global profile of the link between terrorism and tourism. Terrorists have recognised the symbolism of tourism and the vulnerability of tourists. Unfortunately, the issue is one that is likely to confront the tourism industry for generations. It therefore behoves DMOs to consider contingencies for the effects of such events in their own region and in other parts of the world.

The emerging literature on destinations in crisis contains a number of case studies that will be of value. For example, in 1999 the *Journal of Travel Research* published a special issue on tourism crises caused by war, terrorism, and crime (Vol. 38/1). The guest editors advised that the 11 published articles represented a cross-section of those presented at the 1997 War, Terrorism: Times of Crisis and Recovery conference held in Dubrovnik, Croatia. The conference was the second, following a meeting in Sweden in 1995, to focus on the relationship between tourism, security, and safety. The first tourism crisis text, by Beirman (2003a), examined the crises and responses of 11 case studies. A special volume on the topic by the *Journal of Travel & Tourism Marketing* generated a further 12 papers. The diverse range of tourism disaster and crisis issues addressed in Bierman's (2003a) text and the journal special issues are listed in Table 18.1. At the

Table 18.1   *Disaster and crisis papers*

Journal of Travel Research, 1999, Vol. 38 (1)	Journal of Travel & Tourism Marketing, 2006, Vol. 19 (2/3)	Bierman (2003a)
Classification of crime and violence at destinations (Pizam)	Crisis management: A suggested typology (Laws & Prideaux)	USA and 9/11
Managing the effects of terrorism (Sönmez, Apostolopoulos & Tarlow)	Crisis management in winter alpine sports resorts: The 1999 avalanche disaster in Tyrol (Peters & Pikkemaat)	Egypt's terrorist attacks against tourists, 1990–98
New Orleans tourism and crime (Dimanche & Lepetic)	Quantifying the effects of tourism crises: An application to Scotland (Eugenio-Martin, Sinclair, & Yeoman)	Israel and the Palestinian uprising, 2000–02
Tourism potential of the peace dividend (Butler & Baum)	Sri Lanka's civil war, 1995–2001
Management and recovery of tourism in Israel (Mansfield)	Tourism and the impact of the foot and mouth epidemic in the UK (Leslie & Black)	Fiji's political coups of 1987 and 2000
		Turkey's Izmit earthquake, 1999

(Continued)

Table 18.1 (Continued)

Journal of Travel Research, 1999, Vol. 38 (1)	Journal of Travel & Tourism Marketing, 2006, Vol. 19 (2/3)	Bierman (2003a)
The Northern Ireland situation (Leslie)	The impact of foot and mouth disease on a peripheral tourism area (Irvine & Anderson)	Britain's foot and mouth disease, 2001
Lessons of rebuilding tourism in the Philippines, Sri Lanka and Pakistan (Richter)	Canadian seasonality and domestic travel patters: Regularities and dislocations as a result of the events of 9/11 (Smith & Carmichael)	South Africa's crime wave, 1994–2000
Dark tourism (Lennon & Foley)		Australia's Port Arthur massacre, 1996
Political instability, war, and tourism in Cyprus (Ionnides & Apostolopoulos)	The significance of crisis communication in the aftermath of 9/11 (Fall & Massey)	Croatia and the Yugoslavia war, 1991–1995
The role of tourism in the aftermath of violence (Anson)	Crisis management strategies of hotel managers (Yu, Stafford & Amoo)	Philippines' multiple crises, 1990–2001
USA policy on traveller safety and security (Smith)	Privation as a stimulus to travel demand? (McKercher & Pine)	
	Japanese tourism and the SARS epidemic of 2003 (Cooper)	
	Tourism industry employee work stress: A present and future crisis (Ross)	
	Tourism crises and disasters: Enhancing understanding of system effects (Scott & Laws)	

time of writing, a 2007 *Journal of Travel & Tourism Marketing* special issue on tourism crises was in press.

Natural disasters

The Federal Emergency Management Agency (FEMA) listed over 50 declared natural disasters that occurred in the USA during 2003. The FEMA website (see www.fema.org) provides a valuable resource on disaster management, including education and training information. The range of other natural disasters to impact on destinations have included:

- The 2006 tropical cyclone Larry, which caused an estimated half-a-billion dollars damage in North Queensland, Australia.
- The 2005 Hurricane Katrina that devastated New Orleans, USA.

- The 2004 Boxing Day tsunami, which directly affected 11 countries. Appendix 18.1 provides a summary of lessons from the disaster, as written by someone involved, just a week after the event.
- In 2003 Bermuda's worst hurricane for 80 years struck the destination, forcing the tourism industry to virtually shut down due electricity failures and road closures (www.travelmole.com, 8/9/03).
- During 2003, overseas visitors were injured by a 15-minute tornado in Costa Blanca (www.travelmole.com, 8/9/03).
- The 2003 bushfires in northeast Victoria, Australia, which devastated over 1.1 million hectares.
- The 2002 outbreak of foot and mouth disease in the UK highlighted how other destinations can suffer from a disaster in another country. For example, one politician from the Republic of Ireland labelled Britain as the 'leper of Europe' for the negative image being tagged to the wider region (Frisby, 2002). Ironically, it was London, an urban destination with minimal farming activity and no incidence of foot and mouth, which experienced the greatest negative economic impact of the foot and mouth disease (Hopper, 2002).
- The 1999 Izmit eruption in Turkey (see Beirman, 2003a).
- The 1995 Kobe earthquake.
- The 1993 Sydney bushfires (see Christine, 1995).
- Hurricane Andrew hit Florida in 1992 and forced the closure of Miami Beach for a week (Portorff & Neal, 1994).
- The Philippine's 1991 Mt Pinatubo eruption.
- Hurricane Gilbert in Cancun, Mexico, during 1988.
- The 1982 Mt Usu eruption in Japan (see Hirose, 1992, in Faulkner, 1999).
- In the winter of 1981–82, Florida's STO was forced to spend US$600,000 on an emergency three-week advertising campaign to counter negative media publicity about a brief and unseasonal cold spell (Pritchard, 1982).

SARS-induced panic

During the first half of 2003, Severe Acute Respiratory Syndrome (SARS) caused panic in the travel industry worldwide. SARS was estimated to have affected over 8000 people and was responsible for over 800 deaths (Manning, 2003). China was the worst affected, with the emerging destination giant experiencing its first decline in international visitor arrivals in 2003 (www.eturbonews.com, 7/8/03). Other than the loss of life, the most significant aspect of the SARS outbreak to impact on the tourism industry was the mass-media coverage. A March 2003 press release by PATA called for 'accurate, restrained and sensible travel advice and media reporting' of SARS (patanews@pata.th.com, 17/3/03). PATA urged all those reporting to be geographically specific and avoid alarmist statements. The following day in an e-mail to the TRINET online tourism research community, Professor Bob McKercher of the Hong Kong Polytechnic University lamented how the global media frenzy was feeding perceptions of a 'disaster':

> *While the health scare is no doubt of concern, we must keep a proper perspective on it. The local and global media is in something of a feeding frenzy. As a resident of HK, it is worrying, but remember that, out of a population of 7 million, only 100 people have fallen ill, so far.*

McKercher (2003) later introduced the term SIP (SARS induced panic) to the tourism lexicon, arguing strongly that SIP was a greater threat to tourism than SARS. A KPMG report estimated that Toronto's tourism industry lost C$190 million in the first two months of SARS (McClelland, 2003).

Man-made disasters

In addition to acts of God, destinations are at the mercy of man-made disasters such as travel advisories and others that are representative of management failures such as an economic crisis, violence, anti-social visitors, and poor planning.

Travel advisories

All national governments have a responsibility to provide an advisory service for their citizens, identifying potentially risky destinations. Most countries provide regularly updated travel advisories on government websites, and the implications for the DMOs of these countries are significant in terms of the damage to the image of their destination and the necessary recovery marketing efforts. The extent to which promotional efforts are negated by government travel advisories is a contentious issue. It is important to consider that the negative images created by publicity surrounding a disaster can last far longer than any physical destruction to infrastructure or tourism facilities.

During 2003 the travel advisory website of the UK Foreign and Commonwealth Office (see www.fco.gov.uk/travel) provided citizens with a list of some of the major terrorist attacks that had occurred around the world during the previous 18 months. These are shown in Table 18.2. In 2007 the same site advised against all travel for any reason to parts of 25 countries.

The extent to which travel advisories contributed to the loss of jobs in different parts of the world following 9/11 is debatable. However, government travel advisories have been regarded as extremely controversial in many quarters for their significant role in exacerbating negative economic impacts, particularly on poorer nations. Rarely is a travel advisory posted about western industrial countries. For example, few countries issued advisories against visiting the USA after 9/11, or the United Kingdom during the 2002 foot and mouth outbreak. Unfortunately, most advisories

Table 18.2   Global terrorist attacks during 2002–2003

A suicide car bomb against a synagogue in Djerba, Tunisia, in April 2002 that killed 18 European tourists and local Tunisians

A suicide attack against a bus in Karachi carrying French engineers in May 2002

A series of ETA bombings during the summer of 2002 in resorts on the Costa Blanca and the Costa del Sol and other cities in Spain

The bombs in Bali in October 2002 that killed over 200 tourists and local Indonesians

The attacks in Mombassa in November 2002 that killed 17 Kenyans and Israelis

The shooting of three American medical charity workers in Yemen in December 2002

An attack on a hotel nightclub in Colombia on 17 February 2003

A British national was shot and killed in Saudi Arabia on 20 February 2003

A campaign of terrorist bombings in March and April 2003 in the Philippines and Indonesia, including attacks on an airport and a ferry terminal in the southern Philippines and at Jakarta airport

Al Qa'ida were almost certainly responsible for the suicide bombings in Riyadh on 12 May that targeted the homes of westerners, including British citizens, living in the kingdom (Saudi Arabia)

Over 40 people were killed in a series of suicide attacks in Casablanca on 16 May, including at a hotel and restaurant used by westerners

There were suicide bomb attacks in Istanbul on 15 November and further attacks on 20 November, which were on British-related targets: the British Consulate General and the HQ of HSBC in Turkey

are issued against less developed countries that can ill-afford the resultant tourism downturn. Philippine Tourism Secretary and PATA Associate Chairman Richard Gordon suggested that travel advisories reward the terrorists (Alcantara, 2003):

> *It is really a cover-your-behind memo issued by a foreign bureaucrat. Jobs have been lost and it's time issuing countries take responsibility for their actions.*

Opanga (2003) strongly suggested that travel advisories from the UK and USA governments were responsible for the collapse of tourism in Kenya:

> *The irony is, it is Kenyans, not Americans or Israelis , who have borne the brunt of terrorist attacks on Americans and Israelis.*

Jordan Tourism's worldwide director reacted strongly to a 2003 travel advisory of the UK Foreign and Commonwealth Office (FCO) recommending against travel to the country, claiming misperceptions of what was a safe country:

> *Whenever there is trouble in the Middle East we expect the FCO to issue a statement that inevitably includes Jordan…but for us it is business as usual. Jordan is a safe country.*

In practise

Beirman (2003b) reported on a recovery seminar in Kenya during 2003, which was convened by the Kenyan Association of Tour Operators to 'establish what was required to alter the negative travel advisories which had crippled Kenyan tourism during the first half of 2003'. Beirman questioned the motives for the continuation of travel advisories by the USA and Australian governments that warned of an 'imminent terrorism attack', even though this had not materialised after six months. Kenya's minister of tourism visited the UK in mid-2003 in a failed attempt to urge the government to change the travel advisory (www.travelmole.com, 6/6/03).

In response to member states' concerns about the nature of government travel advisories, PATA established a website in 2003 to disseminate 'impartial' advice for travellers (see www.travelwithpata.com). PATA recommended to travellers that the best advice regarding travel advisories was to use a wide range of sources. However, travel advisories are also announced by organisations other than governments:

- The World Health Organization issued SARS travel advisories for a number of destinations in 2003, including parts of China, Toronto, Hong Kong, and Taiwan.
- Universities now provide travel advisories for students and staff.
- Public pressure groups can also exert pressure on private tour companies. Australian environmental groups have been urging tourists to boycott travel to Tasmania, in a protest against the felling of native forests there (www.travelmole.com, 23/3/04). Leading UK tour operator Abercrombie and Kent reportedly bowed to pressure from pressure groups and agreed to stop promoting tours to Burma (www.travelmole.com, 29/7/03).
- Travel warnings may also come from terrorist groups. For example, a report in the UK's *Independent* newspaper cited the Basque separatist terror group ETA as warning foreign travellers not to visit Spain in 2003 (www.travelmole.com, 4/8/03):

> *In 2003 ETA will once again strike hard against the Spanish tourist industry and it cannot guarantee that anyone who enters the war zone will not be injured.*

Economic crisis

During 2001, Turkey experienced one of the country's worst economic crises, initiated through an argument between the President and the Prime Minister (see Okumus & Karamustafa, 2005). Neither the government nor the tourism industry had in place any plans to manage such an event. This resulted in ad hoc responses, and did not result in any shift towards planning for future disasters in Turkey.

One of the most recent significant man-made disasters to impact negatively on the tourism industry was the 1997/1998 Asian economic crisis. Heavy and, some would argue, reckless, short-term borrowing by banks and businesses in the region for investments in real estate and the share market were poorly managed (Henderson, 2002). Consequently, the withdrawal of capital and loss of confidence in the region's financial sector created a domino effect through national economies, which at one point created fears of a collapse of the world economy. Prior to the economic crisis, the Asia-Pacific region was experiencing the world's fastest growth in international visitor arrivals. As a result of the boom in intra-regional travel within the Asia-Pacific region many businesses and destinations became over-exposed to markets within the region, and paid the price when the crisis emerged.

Violence

In 1996 at a popular tourism attraction in Tasmania, Australia, a lone gunman killed 35 people, including domestic and overseas tourists. During October 2003 there was violent rioting in the streets in the leading Jamaican destination of Montego Bay (www.eturbonews.com, 28/10/03). A month earlier, the tranquil Maldives was hit by rioting that led to late-night curfews (www.travelmole.com, 23/9/03). Arguably, violent crimes such as these are representative of the failure by government to manage security.

Excessive crime and unruly behaviour can affect the image of a destination, and crime against visitors has led to negative reputations for many urban destinations around the world. For example, violent crimes in Miami and Orlando reached such a level in 1993 that they caused a decrease in visitor arrivals to the entire state (Pizam, 1999). Dimanche and Lepetic (1999) provided a case study of the impact of crime levels on tourism in New Orleans, where the murder rate was eight times the national average and five times that of New York. In 1997 the New Orleans CVB hired an outside consultant to develop a marketing plan to address the negative crime image of the city. However, Dimanche and Lepetic found that while the tourism industry in the city was under siege from a high-crime rate, there was a lack of concern among the tourism community, due to no noticeable drop in revenues. They strongly urged operators to heed the warning signals before the situation became a crisis.

Anti-social visitors

Ironically, the source of a crime problem at a destination can often be the visitors to the area. For example, business in the Greek Island of Faliraki was estimated to be down by almost one-third in 2003 as a result of anti-social behaviour by visitors (www.travelmole.com, 21/7/03). Travel-Mole.com was citing a report in the *Daily Telegraph*, which suggested that British tourists in particular were responsible for the high levels of bad behaviour that included sexual assaults, drunkenness, and lewdness. Initiatives introduced by authorities to counter the resultant 'image problem' included extra police on the beat, and a requirement for tour operators to provide police with details of planned pub crawls.

Poor planning

Poor planning can also eventually lead to a crisis phase for a destination, such as in the case of Rotorua, New Zealand, during the 1980s and 1990s, as outlined in Case Study 6.1 in Chapter 6 and Case Study 18.2 below. Other examples of destinations in decline or stagnation that have been discussed in the literature have included Hamm in Germany (Buckley & Witt, 1985), Majorca (Morgan, 1991), Cleveland, USA (Rubel, 1996), Canada (Go, 1987), Bermuda (Conlin, 1995), Amsterdam (Dahles, 1998), Gold Coast, Australia (Faulkner, 2002), Atlantic City and Coney Island, USA (Cross & Walton, 2005).

Case study 18.2   Blackpool's next 'resort cycle' stage: Rejuvenation or decline?

John Clarke, Liverpool JMU

Blackpool in England (www.blackppoltourism.com) is often seen as the world's first and biggest working-class holiday resort. The destination grew up in the 19th century, and in the hundred years from 1870 to 1970 its massive and rapid expansion made Blackpool virtually synonymous with the popular English seaside destination.

The destination's growth coincided with the coming of the railways and the development of northern industrial towns, whose 'wakes' weeks released the cotton hands and other industrial workers for brief intervals of 'fresh air and fun'. Through this period Blackpool dominated people's images of what a seaside holiday was like. It's entertainments attracted top stars, the famous Illuminations lighting extravaganza extended the summer season into autumn, and the Golden Mile and Pleasure Beach provided the attractions of side-shows, amusements, and fairgrounds to the mix. Walton (1998) estimated that visitor figures rose from 7000 per season to 58,371 between 1871 and 1911. By the 1930s, visitor numbers were averaging 7 million a year, and in the 1950s and 1960s these numbers were sustained.

In the second half of the 20th century, however, Blackpool began to experience two related transformations, due to social, economic, and demographic forces that were reshaping the British mass-holiday market. The first was the switch in visitors from 'long-stay' holidaymakers, who stayed in hotels or boarding houses for a week or a fortnight, to short visits by people who came for the weekend. Many others increasingly visited the Pleasure Beach or drove along the promenade during the Illuminations without staying overnight at all. At the same time, research showed clearly that the profile of Blackpool's visitors was rapidly ageing; the people who came, mostly the un-affluent working class, were from an older generation who had 'always gone to Blackpool'. Their children and grandchildren were not following suit. This worrying pattern seems to fit the model of the resort-cycle outlined by Goodall (1992), with many people identifying the changes in the last quarter of the twentieth century as representing the fifth stage of 'stagnation', or even the sixth stage of 'decline'.

However, as Walton (1998) pointed out, Blackpool had survived as a major leisure destination for so long because of its ability to innovate and change. The famous tower, the three piers, the annual Illuminations, and the Pleasure Beach were all evidence that the resort was able to adapt its attractions to what people wanted.

In the early years of the new millennium it appeared that a new opportunity had opened up for Blackpool to renew its attractiveness. The British government undertook to reform UK gambling laws in ways that would make it possible for casinos to operate without the restrictions created by the need to be a member to be able to play. A significant proposal was to site one Super-Casino in Britain, with towns and cities invited to bid for the licence. For Blackpool this seemed promising, particularly given the destination's existing accommodation and infrastructure. At a more cynical level, many argued that Blackpool already had a reputation as a place with a high transient population, relatively high crime rates, and the free availability of what were seen as 'tacky' leisure activities. People talked of Blackpool as the British answer to Atlantic City, the US seaside town that is the location of a major gambling industry. Blackpool assembled a bid despite the objections of some residents who feared the social and environmental consequences, and its local politicians were very optimistic. Blackpool's bid was for…

> …a 24-hour casino with around 70 gaming tables and 2500 slot machines. There would be a 500-room hotel to accommodate the expected influx of visitors. Councillors say the development would kick-start regeneration of the area, allowing increased funding for the tram network and renovation of the famous seafront (Guardian Unlimited, 2007).

In January 2007 the government's decision was to locate the Super-Casino in the city of Manchester. The leaders of the Blackpool bid were devastated. A common response was that the decision meant that there was no future for the town other than the long-predicted decline. Steve Weaver, the local council's chief executive, said: 'The future of the town now looks far more uncertain – no easy answers' (Ward, Carter & Topping, 2007).

Discussion question

Imagine you are a member of a working party set up by Blackpool's local council to advise it on ways of coping with decline after the Super-Casino failure. Recognising the socio-economic changes in the British holiday market, how else could Blackpool market its assets of recognisability, plentiful accommodation, a range of pubs, theatres, amusement arcades, and the most popular 'free entry' funfair in the UK?

> **Further reading**
>
> Goodall, B. (1992). Coastal resorts; Development and redevelopment. *Built Environment*, *18*, 5–11.
> Walton, J. K. (1998). *Blackpool*. Edinburgh: Edinburgh University Press.
> Walton, J. K. (2000). *The British Seaside –Holidays and Resorts in the Twentieth Century*. Manchester: Manchester University Press.

Other examples of man-made disasters impacting on the tourism industry include:

- The 2002 collapse of Australia's major domestic air carrier Ansett Airlines.
- Pacific nuclear testing in the South Pacific in 1995 (see Elliott, 1997).
- Labour strikes such as those by Australian airline pilots in 1989–90 (see Lavery, 1992) and USA air-traffic controllers in 1981.
- The 1989 *Exxon Valdez* oil spill at Prince William Sound, Alaska.
- The 1989 political uprising in Tiananmen Square, China (see Gartner & Shen, 1992; Roehl, 1990).
- The 1970s global oil crisis. The impact in New Zealand was so significant that the government ordered the closure of petrol stations on Sundays. Another initiative that impacted on tourism was the introduction carless day stickers, where every car was forced to carry a sticker indicating one day of the week when it could not be used.
- The nationalisation of Mexico's oil industry in the 1930s caused an immediate decline in self-drive tourists from the USA (Berger, 2006).

DMO responses to disasters

> *The intensity of the moment during a crisis is clearly not the time to commence such planning*
>
> *(Litvin & Alderson, 2003, p. 189).*

Any destination thrown into a crisis situation will be forced to implement recovery strategies to avoid or minimise a crisis situation in the future. Since no destination is immune to disasters, it surely behoves the DMO to develop some form of strategy, in conjunction with civic authorities, in advance of an admittedly unknown exogenous event. Research Snapshot 18.2 highlights the difficulty in not having a plan for a 'surprise crisis'. However, until recently there have been few resources available to advise DMOs. While some guidelines have been developed for recovery from natural disasters there has been little published on crisis management strategies following acts of terrorism (Sönmez et al., 1999). Clearly the purpose of a crisis management plan is to be prepared. A plan should guide the DMO at a time when distress and panic are likely. Sönmez et al. suggested that a guidebook can include: roles and responsibilities, action checklists, a directory of contacts, and media guidelines such as sample press kits and what to do/not do at media conferences.

In practice

Following a recommendation of the PATA Bali Tourism Recovery Taskforce, PATA created a crisis manual for member governments (see PATA, 2003). The manual provides a checklist of critical tasks to be undertaken during a crisis, as well as a directory of crisis specialists.

Research Snapshot 18.2   Katherine's 1998 Australia Day flood

Faulkner and Vikulov (2001) examined the role of a tourism disaster management plan in the case of the 1998 Australia Day flood at Katherine. Located in the Northern Territory, in Australia's tropical north, Katherine receives heavy rainfall that is a routine of the wet season. However, the 1998 flood was the worst in the town's history, inundating half of the homes, all of the CBD, and most tourism businesses. This natural disaster challenged the survival of the local tourism industry, and occurred so quickly that the Katherine Regional Tourism Association (KRTA) was involved in a 'surprise crisis' with a very limited decision time (p. 343):

> The urgency of the disaster situation means that operators and the RTA did not have the luxury of reflecting on the most appropriate action to take. Nor was there time to engage in the consultations necessary to produce a fully coordinated response.

Faulkner and Vikulov found that despite the possibility of a '100-year flood' no tourism operators had disaster management plans, other than regulatory evacuation plans. Following the recovery period, the KRTA proceeded to develop a destination disaster management plan in conjunction with emergency service organisations. Concurrently, the RTO also decided to be more proactive in enhancing disaster awareness among local operators. The downside however was that as a result of directing resources to these efforts the KRTA's ability to continue strategic marketing planning was restricted.

Source: Faulkner, B. & Vikulov, S. (2001). Katherine, washed out one day, back on track the next: A post-mortem of a tourism disaster. Tourism Management, 22(4), 331–344.

Resources

While ensuring the safety of visitors and rebuilding infrastructure and tourism facilities will be paramount, these activities are beyond the scope of the vast majority of DMOs. This section is therefore limited to discussing the marketing aspects of recovery from disasters. One RTO that did have a crisis plan on September 11, 2001, was Charleston in South Carolina (Litvin & Alderson, 2003). The first meeting of the Charleston Area Convention

& Visitors Bureau (CACVB) crisis team took place on the afternoon of September 11. However, the CACVB plan immediately proved to be of limited value as all scenarios were based on local events such as hurricanes and floods. There was no scenario for an incident 500 miles away.

Clearly, a DMO's ability to respond effectively will depend on the level of resources available. Depending on the scale of the crisis, this will likely require strong lobbying by DMOs for government intervention. Examples include:

- Following the events of 9/11 the Southern Governors' Association adopted a resolution that endorsed six points, involving federally funded advertising, tax credits, policy development, and passenger security screening (Kubiak, 2002, p. 19).
- In 2002, the British government announced a £40 million marketing package to reverse the estimated £2 billion drop in tourism revenue from the foot and mouth outbreak (Kleinman & Bashford, 2002).
- In response to the 1989–90 pilot's strike in Australia, which resulted in a decrease of over 100,000 international visitor arrivals, the Australian federal government provided an additional 'Recovery Plan' fund of A$18.5 million to the NTO (Lavery, 1992).
- In 2003, Hong Kong Tourism Board Executive Director Clara Chong announced funding of HK$400 million for a series of special events to repair the post-SARS image of Hong Kong (www.eturbonews.com, 19/8/03).
- The Indonesian government allocated $44.6 million for a global campaign to lure visitors back to Bali following the October 2002 bombings (Osborne, 2003).
- At the height of the SARS publicity the Canadian federal government pledged an additional C$15.5 million to promote Toronto and Canada as safe destinations (www.eturbonews.com, 17/6/03).
- The Florida state government provided US$20 million for tourism advertising following 9/11 (Word, 2003). This stimulated a further $25 million in private-sector funding (Bush, 2004).
- The *Financial Times* reported that the Thailand government took the unusual step of promising US$100,000 to any tourist catching SARS while visiting the country (www.travelmole.com, 21/5/03). Authorities made the offer due to concern over the April arrival figures which were down by almost half, even though Thailand had been declared a SARS-free zone. The initiative followed a $US100,000 SARS-free guarantee by Thai Airways.

Not all DMOs are fortunate to receive extra funding following a disaster. For example, as discussed in Chapter 5, destinations reliant on a bed tax for revenue generation, such as North American CVBs like Las Vegas, face a decline in budget when bed nights are down. During the Asian economic crisis, the Indonesian Tourist Promotion Board was forced to close important overseas offices in Frankfurt, London, Los Angeles, Singapore, Taipei, and Tokyo, as a result of a lack of funding and huge debts (Henderson,

2002). The CEO of the British Incoming Tour Operators Association criticised the British government for failing to adequately support the tourism industry during the foot and mouth crisis (www.travelmole.com, 13/3/03). The criticism was fuelled by reports that the tourism industry received £20 million in additional funds while facing a loss of £5 billion, and yet the agricultural sector received compensation payments of £1 billion.

Successful tactics implemented by DMOs in following disasters have included:

- a disaster management taskforce
- scenario building
- public relaions
- autsourcing expertise
- cooperative campaigns
- travel trade familiarisations
- providing support for local businesses
- stimulating discounts and adding value
- market concentration

Disaster management taskforce

The purpose of a management taskforce is to minimise the level of guess-work during a disaster. The DMO is in an ideal situation to coordinate immediate and ongoing marketing responses, working closely with any damage response entity to ensure consistency of messages.

DMOs at all levels may form a taskforce that fits within the existing governance structure. Meetings need not have the same frequency as other panels, but should draw on expertise from relevant fields, such as civil defence, public health, and infrastructure. Sönmez, Apostolopoulos and Tarlow (1999) suggested organising teams within the taskforce with different responsibilities, such as: public relations, promotion, information coordination, and fundraising. Other initiatives worth considering, particularly in high-risk areas, include:

- working cooperatively with neighbouring destinations
- communicating the current contingency plan to industry
- providing annual workshops for DMO staff and industry on crisis management and scenario building

In most cases a taskforce is instigated following the disaster. For example, the PATA Bali Recovery Taskforce was established immediately following the October 2002 bombings to assist Indonesia. Within a week of the 2001 outbreak of foot and mouth disease in the UK, the BTA had set up its Immediate Action Group (Frisby, 2002). Two weeks after 9/11, the London Tourist Board (LTB) established the London Tourism Recovery Group (London Tourist Board, 2001, in Hopper, 2002).

The first role of the taskforce is to assess the situation for impact on visitor arrivals. Primary impact concerns will be the level of visitation decrease (visitor numbers, nights, spend) and for what period of time. The second role is to respond as quickly as possible, initially focusing on information dispersal in a manner that fosters a sense of trust in the DMO by the media and travelling public. This may be necessary to clearly demarcate where the problem is, particularly if a number of areas have been unaffected. For example, Florida has a coastline of over 1000 miles, and Hurricane Andrew in 1992 only affected 10 miles of beaches (Portorff & Neal, 1994). Portoff and Neal cited a UK newspaper headline that read 'Hurricane Bearing Down on Disney Beaches', and yet the distance between Orlando and the affected beaches was over 200 miles.

Scenario building

Disasters, whether natural or man-made, are rarely predictable. If destinations are to prepare contingency plans for possible disasters, it is important to look forward as well as backwards, with the caveat that history is no predictor of the future. While it would be futile to attempt to predict the future (Drucker, 1995), what can be valuable is the use of scenarios. Scenario building attempts to construct views of possible futures, in an effort to better plan for uncertainty (see Schwartz, 1992; Johnson & Scholes, 2002). Strategic choices can be made based on how the different scenarios might unfold. In theory, this then offers the relative security of being prepared for, to varying degrees, whatever type of scenario happens. Scenarios should be seen as carefully constructed plots, rather than predictions. When attempting to envision the future, assumptions must be made for each scenario. Since the assumptions are the key elements in determining the basis for each plot, the number should be kept to a minimum, to reduce complexity. For each scenario, a number of questions can be developed, including:

- What might lead to success or a speedy recovery where others may fail?
- What might happen to current customers?
- What might happen to future suppliers?
- What type of businesses will fare best/worst?
- What are the most important activities that need to be addressed first?
- Where should marketing resources be directed?

In practice

During 2005 a media 'frenzy' developed over the threat of Avian Flu spreading from Asia to Europe in the form of a pandemic. Visit Scotland undertook scenario planning for such an eventuality. Page et. al. (2006) provide a rare insight into the scenario building exercise from the perspective of a DMO. The case is an example of best practice in the tourism industry, both in terms of the planning process and the sharing of information with other NTOs.

Public relations

Clearly, the media play an important role in communicating the impacts of disasters to the public. Therefore public relations initiatives are a critical component in any disaster response strategy. This issue was addressed in Chapter 16.

Outsourcing expertise

Few DMOs are likely to have the resources to employ a permanent disaster management specialist, and few DMO staff are likely to have been trained in crisis management. Depending on the level of disaster/crisis, such a specialist might need to be outsourced to work with the taskforce. In 2003 the London Tourist Board took the step of offering a three-month contract for a marketer to focus on encouraging Londoners to spend more in their own city during the war in Iraq (*Marketing*, 6/3/03). The temporary position reported to a committee formed by the LTB, the Greater London Authority, and the London Development Agency.

Likewise, outsourcing of PR specialists may be needed to temporarily coordinate public information dissemination. For example, at the RTO level, the Katherine Regional Tourism Association employed a journalist to work with the media following the 1998 Australia Day flood (Faulkner & Vikulov, 2001). At the NTO level, during the 2001 UK outbreak of foot and mouth disease the BTA contracted a global PR agency to minimise the negative perceptions of Britain overseas (Frisby, 2002). However, BTA PR director Frisby candidly acknowledged a post-crisis recommendation to not outsource to a global agency in the future (p. 99):

> *Although the appointed agency performed well in the initial rebuttal phase, after six weeks it became clear that a lack of product knowledge meant that enormous inputs of time and expertise were required in order to continue to produce results.*

Coordinating cooperative campaigns

Key advantages of a coordinated marketing response include (Mansfield, 1999): economies of scale, consistency of image-related messages, more effective assessment of performance, reduced infighting between different tourism sector groups, and positive signals for the travel industry and target markets. Regarding the last point, during the 2001 UK foot and mouth disease outbreak a feature of the BTA's response was working closely with national and regional tourist boards and key government departments, in an effort to minimise negative media coverage and to provide reassurance to the public (Frisby, 2002).

The events of 9/11 enabled the CACVB to successfully implement cooperative packages, which it had previously been unable to stimulate in more settled times (Litvin & Alderson, 2003). Similarly, Hopper (2002) reported that one of the key lessons learned by the London Tourism Board in the wake of 9/11 was the need for effective dialogue with tourism operators.

Hopper suggested a legacy of the improved public–private sector relationship established during the crisis has become a model for future marketing of the destination.

Travel trade familiarisation visits

Trade familiarisation visits are also an important function coordinated by DMOs. Following the 2003 terrorism attacks in Turkey, the Balkan Federation of Travel and Tourist Agencies Associations planned such initiatives to develop solidarity with intermediaries in the region. On the assumption that negative images of Turkey would affect tourism to nearby member countries, the federation planned familiarisation visits to Istanbul for leading world tourism authorities during 2004 (www.eturbonews.com, 25/11/03). Hosting large groups of travel industry personnel on familiarisations by the Turkish Ministry of Tourism was a major reason for that country's rapid recovery following the 1999 Izmit earthquake (Beirman, 2003a).

Supporting local tourism businesses

Mansfield (1999) suggested that governments in high-risk areas should provide financial incentives for tourism investors, given the probability of future losses. A number of cases in the literature have reported initiatives to support local tourism operators during a crisis:

- In China, post-SARS initiatives included visa exemptions for some nationalities (www.eturbonews.com, 7/8/03).
- VAT was reduced from 13% to 3% on hotels in Jordan during the 2003 war in Iraq (www.travelmole.com, 9/6/03).
- The Israel Ministry of Tourism has provided subsidies for tourism operators marketing the destination (Beirman, 2002).
- Following 9/11, the CACVB enlisted an online booking company to conduct workshops for local tourism businesses (Litvin & Alderson, 2003).
- During the 2001 UK outbreak of foot and mouth disease, the BTA used the organisation's website to update industry with information and advice (Frisby, 2002).
- In 2006 the Australian government invited businesses affected by tropical cyclone Larry to apply for financial assistance.

Stimulating discounts and adding value

The introduction of special deals has been a regular component of Israel's post-crisis recovery programmes (Beirman, 2002). Beirman (2003a) cited the examples of Delta Airlines, which provided 10,000 free seats to New York following 9/11, and Insight Vacations, which provided a one-week package in Egypt for US$1 as a value add-on to its European tour product following the 1997 Luxor massacre. During the 2001 UK outbreak of foot and mouth disease, the BTA used the organisation's trade website to ask operators to provide details of special deals, details of which were used in media releases and publicised on the organisation's consumer website (Frisby, 2002). Following 9/11, one of the recovery initiatives of the London mayor was a £500,000 contribution towards free and discounted tickets to the city's theatres.

Market concentration

As highlighted in Case Study 19.1, one of the most important crisis decisions concerns trade-offs about which markets to focus recovery efforts. During the Asian economic crisis the Singapore Tourism Board concentrated on markets unaffected by the economic downturn (Henderson, 2002). During the UK foot and mouth disease outbreak in 2001 the BTA focused attention on 11 key markets (Frisby, 2002). On the correct assumption that Americans would be reluctant to fly in the short term following September 11, the CACVB focused attention on cities within a 10-hour drive (Litvin & Alderson, 2003). All scheduled advertising was pulled immediately and replaced with a new campaign featuring the tagline: 'A short drive down the road, a million miles away'.

During the foot and mouth disease outbreak in the UK, the London Tourism Board (LTB) directed attention towards the domestic market (Hopper, 2002). The LTB particularly focused on promoting domestic short breaks to the capital. However, by February 2002, the Pacific Asia Travel Association (PATA) had stated concern at the trend towards stronger domestic promotion in many PATA countries (PATA, 2002). The concern was due to the potential for discouraging outbound travel, resulting in lower inbound arrivals within the region, which would further impact on airline profitability.

Dark tourism

At first you might wonder why a section on dark tourism should be included in a chapter on disasters and crises. Well, there is a dark side to image marketing, where some travellers are attracted to the negative images of places that have suffered disasters (Ahmed, 1991c). This phenomenon has been labelled *dark tourism* (see, for example, Lennon & Foley, 2000) and *thano tourism* (see Seaton, 1996), where tourists visit scenes of death and disaster for reasons of remembrance, education, or entertainment. In 2005, the level of academic interest in the topic led to the launch of a dark tourism website www.dark-tourism.org.uk, with the goal to become the 'one-stop shop' for researchers and students interested in accessing information on the topic.

That so many travellers are attracted to scenes of disaster is perhaps representative of our innate sense of curiosity, which in part manifests in our desire for travel to explore, rather than a purely morbid inclination. An example of the latter however was the report of 'ghoulish Aussie tourists flocking to the jail housing convicted drug smugglers Schapelle Corby and the Bali Nine' (Wockner & Weston, 2006, p. 9). The Indonesian jail was becoming a must-see for some 'jail tourists', wanting a glimpse of the 10 infamous young Australians, some of whom are on death row.

Alternatively, the visit might represent a pilgrimage or merely a photo opportunity. In some cases curiosity might be immediate to view the devastation. Incredibly, shortly after the war in Iraq in 2003, UK travellers were signing up for tours of the country. A report in the *Daily Express* cited bookings by travellers to a tour organised by Hinterland Travel to 'see what has happened to the country' (www.travelmole.com, 6/8/03).

In other cases a sustained curiosity is developed. For example, the site of the 1985 air crash in which 256 members of the US 101st Airborne Division were killed remains one of the most popular visitor attractions in Gander, Canada (see Butler & Baum, 1999). In Rotorua, New Zealand, disaster struck in June 1886 when Mount Tarawera erupted, destroying three Maori villages with the loss of 150 lives and obliterating the fledgling destinations' most notable tourism attraction at the time, the Pink and White Terraces. This was a devastating blow for tourism (Stafford, 1986), only 40 years after the first tourist arrivals. However, within two years Rotorua's annual visitor arrivals were higher than pre-eruption levels (Reggett, 1972). Part of the continued interest in Rotorua was the eruption aftermath and new volcanic craters, which remain attractions today. The city of San Francisco marked the 100th anniversary of the 1906 earthquake with a series of events and promotions. Similarly, the city of Napier in New Zealand strongly promotes its art-deco architecture, which was a result of rebuilding after a devastating earthquake in 1931.

The diversity of other examples of sites of death or disaster attracting visitors include:

- Alma tunnel in Paris where Princess Diana was killed in 1997
- Robin Island, near Cape Town in South Africa, where Nelson Mandela was jailed
- The site of Pompeii in Italy
- World War II death camps in Poland
- The site of US President John F. Kennedy's assassination
- Holocaust Memorial Museum, USA
- Lenin's tomb in Moscow
- The house in Winchester, England, where Jane Austin died
- Hawaii's USS *Arizona* memorial
- New York's Ground Zero
- Elvis Presley's gravesite in Memphis
- World War II prisoner-of-war camps, such as Colditz Castle, Germany
- USA's civil war Petersburg National Battlefield
- Auschwitz-Birkenau Memorial and Museum, Poland
- Turkey's World War I battlefield at ANZAC Cove, Gallipoli
- Peace Memorial Park in Hiroshima, Japan
- Nanjing Massacre Memorial, China

Visits to sites of death is not a modern phenomenon (Seaton, 1996). There have been suggestions that the World War of 1914–1918 was the start of the modern dark tourism era, due to the introduction of movie cinemas around the same time. The popularity of sites of death and disaster has demonstrated there can also be a positive effect of such events. Admittedly, with some moral dilemmas DMOs should (sensitively) be alert to new marketing opportunities.

In practise

In 2005, the government of Phnom Pehn in Cambodia signed a deal with Japanese entrepreneurs to manage the Cheung Ek Memorial, which proved contentious with some local residents (Cripps, 2005). The 'killing fields' genocide memorial houses a tower of an estimated 8000 human skulls, some of the estimated 3 million victims who died at the hands of former dictator Pol Pot's Khmer Rouge. Cripps cited relatives who suggested victims were being 'sold for profit'. However, the local mayor argued that the decision was justified since most package tours feature the memorial as a regular stop:

> This project will benefit our country's tourism as some tourists do not just want to visit our historic temples. They also what to see with their own eyes the past violence of the 'Killing Fields'.

Key points

1. Disaster or crisis?

No destination is immune to disaster. Every DMO should consider the possibility of a disaster at some stage in the future. Disasters can be man-made or acts of God. They can be short term or long term. Almost all will be unpredictable and beyond the control of the DMO. The level of preparedness for a disaster at a destination will determine the extent to which a management crisis manifests.

2. Travel advisories

All national governments have a responsibility to provide an advisory service for their citizens, identifying potentially risky destinations. Most countries provide regularly updated travel advisories on government websites, and the implications for the DMOs of these countries are significant in terms of the damage to the image of their destination and the necessary recovery-marketing efforts. The extent to which promotional efforts are negated by government travel advisories is a contentious issue. It is important to consider that the negative images created by publicity surrounding a disaster can last far longer than any physical destruction to infrastructure or tourism facilities.

3. DMO responses

Since a state of crisis can affect the viability of the destination, DMOs have a responsibility to prepare disaster response plans. The level of such planning has until recently been very low. However, the recent increase in acts of war and terrorism has forced more destinations to act. The topic of destination crisis management is an emerging research field within the tourism literature. A number of case studies have been reported in recent years, and provide a valuable resource for DMOs considering contingency planning. Key activities that DMOs should consider include: the formation of a permanent disaster taskforce, scenario building and risk analysis, coordinated marketing responses, market concentration, outsourcing of media relations, and initiatives to support local businesses.

Review questions

- Discuss the extent to which your DMO has a disaster response strategy published in the public domain.
- Has your destination ever been affected by a disaster? Analyse the effectiveness of the recovery strategy.
- What are the potential risks to your destination that could lead to a disaster and crisis in the future?
- What travel advisories are currently in place by your government? To what extent do you agree with these warnings?
- Why have DMOs in general been slow to develop a disaster response strategy?

Appendix 18.1 10 lessons learned from the South Asia tsunami of 26 December 2004

Sálvano Briceño, Director, Inter-agency Secretariat of the International Strategy for Disaster Reduction

1. We are all vulnerable to natural disasters

The tsunami affected a total of 50 countries, of which 11 were directly affected. An additional 39 developed countries were indirectly affected by losing nationals who were present in the region, either tourists or expatriates.

2. Coastal zones and small islands are often densely populated areas that increase people's risk and vulnerability

Nearly 3 billion people, or almost half the world population, live in coastal zones which in many cases are prone to hazards including tropical cyclones, floods, storms, and tsunamis. Often coastal populations are dependent on the sea for their livelihoods and do not have the choice to live elsewhere. Small island countries such as the Nicobar and Andaman islands are barely a few metres above sea level, which means that evacuation to higher land is almost impossible.

3. Public awareness and education are essential to protecting people and property

In Thailand more than 1800 people were saved because a tribal chief recognised there was something wrong and decided to evacuate his people up to the hills. A 10-year-old girl from England saved 100 tourists on a beach in Phuket after alerting her mother of the imminent tidal wave and prompting a speedy evacuation to safety. She recognised the signs after learning about tsunamis in her geography class. In Japan, Hawaii, and Cuba children know from an early age what to do if tropical storms, cyclones or earthquakes strike.

4. Early warning saves lives

In Kenya, thousands of people were immediately evacuated in Mombassa because they were alerted to the wave making its way across the Indian Ocean. While the appropriate technology to detect seismic activity already exists, a failure in communication meant that the relevant authorities and local communities were caught unaware by the tsunami.

5. Countries need to work together at the regional and international levels ahead of time, instead of waiting until disaster strikes and then to respond

There is a need for countries in the Indian Ocean to develop a regional early warning system that focuses on tsunamis. The tsunami highlighted that other regions at risk have no regional early warning in place, such as the Caribbean and countries along the Mediterranean coastline, and need to have one as quickly as possible.

6. Reducing risk depends on communication and information exchange between the scientific community and politicians

The disaster showed that in the absence of an open dialogue, valuable information and research from technical sectors is redundant. We need to strengthen the link between scientific institutions and national and local authorities that need to react to avoid human, economic, and social losses from disasters.

7. Develop and enforce building codes in areas where earthquakes and tsunamis are common

The damage to buildings was huge, and could have been reduced if building codes and retrofitting measures had been taken. After the Bangladeshi flood in the 1970s, government decided to build all the key buildings with two or more storeys. In the Maldives, a lot of people who escaped went up to the top floor. Clearly, the further away you are from the sea the safer you are, and so new legislations may need to be considered for the construction of hotels and tourist sites in coastal zones.

8. Humanitarian aid needs to invest more in prevention and go beyond food, medicine, and immediate needs

Donor funds need to think about the longer-term and include prevention in aid packages. If we are able to collect 3 billion dollars in two weeks we should be able to spend 10% of it in prevention. We are trapped in a reactive rather than proactive development trajectory.

9. International, regional, and national organisations should work better together and be better coordinated

Coordination is an essential element of disaster prevention, mitigation, preparedness, and response by the entire UN system, governments, and non-governmental organisations. Efforts need to be made to promote complementarity and avoid duplication. Governments need to demonstrate their political will and commitment to disaster risk reduction through concrete measures.

10. The media have a social responsibility to promote prevention

Journalists need to be sensitised and maintain an ongoing focus on prevention aspects of disasters. We must remind ourselves of the disasters happening on an almost daily basis around the world, such as locusts in western Africa and drought.

Source: http://www.reliefweb.int (7/1/05)

CHAPTER 19

Performance metrics

In boom times, tourist bodies typically take the credit for increased visitation and infrastructure development, while, in downturns, the same bodies blame the lack of government funding and seek increases to budgets.

Craik (1991, p. 24)

Aims

The aims of this chapter are to enhance understanding of:

- the challenge of quantifying a DMO's contribution to destination competitiveness
- measures of DMO effectiveness
- the measurement of consumer-based brand equity.

> **Perspective**
>
> It is fitting to conclude by considering the effectiveness of DMOs. Do they generate an appropriate return for the millions spent on promotion? What is an appropriate return on investment? it actually possible to quantify the contribution of DMO efforts towards destination competitiveness over the short term? Are such quantifiable short-run measures appropriate for DMOs? Should there not be a lasting legacy of effects of DMO efforts over time, in the quest for destination competitiveness, such as enhancement of destination image and the nurturing of fledgling tourism businesses? Instead of receiving income from sales, many DMOs rely predominantly on grants provided by government, and are not therefore accountable to shareholders in the same manner as a commercial enterprise. Destination marketers find themselves accountable to a board of directors, tourism sector groups, local taxpayers, and government. The effectiveness of DMOs therefore needs to be evaluated based on a combination of indicators relating to market performance and organisation performance.

DMO effectiveness measurement

Monitoring DMO effectiveness is a necessary but challenging undertaking, particularly in terms of destination competitiveness. Currently there is no model to quantify the relationship between the work of DMOs over time and overall destination competitiveness. Reflect for a moment on the visitors who are in London, for example, at the time you are reading this. To what extent are they likely to be there as a result of induced initiatives by the former NTOs, the current NTO Visit Britain, the RTB Visit London, airlines, tour wholesalers, or individual tourism businesses? To what extent are they there as a result of their own organic attitude development through word-of-mouth referrals, movies, media news, or school geography lessons? If visitor arrivals are up or down this year, to what extent can this be attributed to the DMO, relative to exogenous factors such as interest rates, hallmark events, or disasters? DMOs will certainly claim credit when things go well. For example, Visit Florida celebrated 10 years of operation in 2006 with the following results achieved since 1996: visitor numbers up 78%, visitor spending and tourism taxes up 51%, tourism jobs up 18% (www.travelindustryreview.com, 1/3/06).

Consider also the destination you are likely to travel to next. To what extent are you able to recall what initially stimulated your interest, and what role the DMO has played in shaping your image of the destination and intent to visit? One of the most challenging and least reported aspects of destination marketing is that of measuring performance. The extent to which DMOs are able to monitor the effectiveness of their activities is a key destination marketing management function, not only for improving future promotional efforts but also for accountability, funding purposes, and in some cases their very survival as an entity.

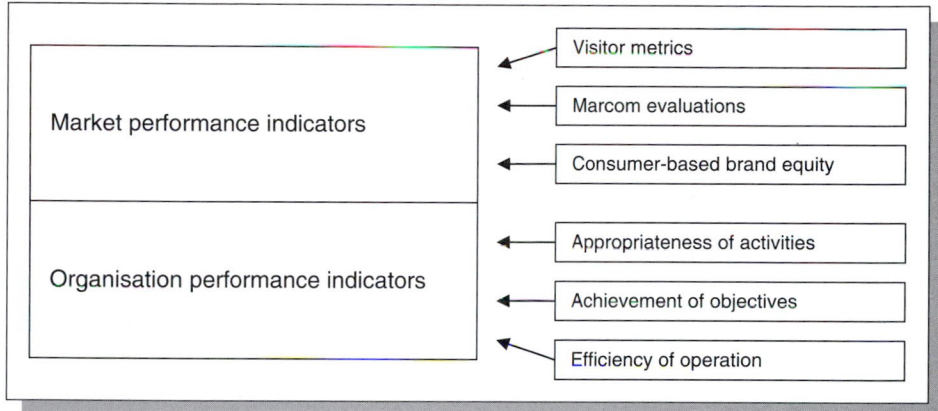

Figure 19.1
DMO
effectiveness

Celebrating success is important for public agencies such as DMOs, to enhance their credibility in the minds of stakeholders. However, readers should also be aware of the complexities in measurement when interpreting any such claims. The problem is of course that the DMO never knows the long-term effect of campaigns on future visitor arrivals, and of course those travellers who purchased travel independent of the campaign sponsors. A number of studies highlight the lack of market research undertaken to monitor the outcome of destination marketing objectives in Australia (see Prosser, 200; Carson, Beattie & Gove, 2003), North America (Sheehan & Ritchie, 1997; Masberg, 1999), and Europe (Dolnicar & Schoesser, 2003).

The problem of measuring performance is not unique to destination marketing. For example, the topic of brand metrics is also rare in the services marketing literature (Kim, Kim & An, 2003). Australian Marketing Institute (AMI) President Roger James (2005, p. 29) lamented the lack of mainstream media coverage about the marketing effectiveness of corporate Australia: 'We see many examples of outstanding strategic marketing, yet few boards receive comprehensive information about marketing performance.' At the time of writing, the AMI was working on the establishment of a metrics toolkit for marketers (see www.ami.org.au).

The two main categories of indicators to address in the evaluation of DMO effectiveness as shown in Figure 19.1 are evaluations of (1) market performance, and (2) organisation effectiveness.

Market performance

The theme of the 2004 Travel & Tourism Research Association (TTRA) conference was 'Measuring the tourism experience: When experience rules, what is the metric of success?' (see www.ttra.com). Performance metrics is a topical issue, and in the tourism literature has appeared relatively recently, particularly for DMOs. For example, Sheehan and Ritchie's (1997) literature review found very little interest in DMO market performance measures, while Faulkner (1997) suggested that most evaluations reported had been ad hoc. From a survey of local government tourism offices in

Australia's state of Victoria, Carson et al. (2003) suggested that up to one-third of shire councils lacked a system of performance monitoring for tourism objectives. In the USA as recently as the 1990s the issue was reported as being problematic. Pizam (1990) cited research indicating that only a minority of STOs actually bothered to evaluate the effectiveness of their promotions. Likewise, Hawes et al. (1991) found that only 7 of 37 STOs used measurable objectives and performance measures. In an examination of the Italian NTO's promotional plans, Formica and Littlefield (2000, p. 113) discovered that the entire section on evaluation of the plan was missing: 'Instead, spurious correlations often led to subjective evaluations of promotional performances.' Sheehan and Ritchie's (1997, p. 113) survey of CVBs identified the following as the most significant barriers to measuring non-financial performance:

- subjectivity of measures, and the difficulty in proving their importance to sceptics
- the lack of ability to measure tourism activity
- lack of research funds
- consistency in the collection or reporting of data
- lack of cooperation from partners

This section discusses three categories of market performance: visitor monitor programmes, marcom evaluations, and consumer-based brand equity (CBBE). It is likely that CBBE will become more widely adopted in the future, since the concept represents a bridge between past promotional efforts and future market performance.

Visitor metrics

Even though it is difficult to quantify the DMO contribution to visitor metrics, common destination performance measures have included visitor numbers, average length of stay, spending, and market share. The most common method for capturing these metrics is through a visitor monitor programme. Other concepts being tested include tourism satellite accounts for NTOs and employment multipliers and yield for STOs and RTOs. For more details on such economics of destinations, the reader is referred to Vanhove (2005).

Visitor monitor programmes • • •

Counting the number of visitor arrivals has long been a measure of the health of a destination's tourism industry. Most NTOs today have access to international visitor arrivals data through collection by immigration officials at arrival gateways. However, the collection of visitor data is more difficult for STOs and RTOs. It was as recent as 2000, in a keynote address at the TTRA conference in Hollywood, that the director of the Los Angeles CVB asked delegates for assistance in developing a valid method for tracking visitor flows to the region. At that time the CVB did not have an accurate measure of visitation, which impeded marketing performance evaluation.

The emergence of visitor monitor programmes has provided STOs and RTOs with a vehicle for tracking arrivals, but has occurred only recently for most DMOs. Indeed, there are still many RTOs that do not operate a visitor monitor and rely on data captured in NTO or STO intercept surveys. Many countries, such as Australia for example, still lack a national standard of regional visitor monitors. To guide Australian RTOs on regional data collection methods, the Centre for Regional Tourism Research has established a website (see www.regionaltourism.com.au). One of the aims of the project is to progress the development of a national standard in data collection and reporting. A range of resources is available to RTOs, including case studies, as indicated in Figure 19.2.

Similarly, to foster the development of global standards in tourism data collection the WTO (1995) produced a manual for the collection of tourism statistics by NTOs. The manual provides a comprehensive guide to a range of data issues, including: visitor surveys, measuring outbound tourism, measuring domestic tourism, describing tourism supply, and measuring economic costs and benefits of tourism.

centre for
REGIONAL TOURISM
research

Southern Cross
University

Figure 19.2 Centre for Regional Tourism Research is a resource available to RTOs

> The availability of local level data about tourism markets and business performance has consistently been identified as a critical issue for the development of Australia's regional tourism industries. The Centre for Regional Tourism Research has commenced a programme to identify the need for local level tourism data, and develop standards and protocols which will help tourism managers collect, analyse, and use locally collected data. This web site has been developed as a companion to a national series of workshops on collecting and managing regional tourism data. It attempts to summarise the principles behind good data collection, and provide some insights into the sorts of regional collections currently available, and the lessons in resource management learnt in those collections. Any comments on the nature of this web site, and its usefulness to managers considering or undertaking local data collection would be most welcome. It is also possible to arrange for a data workshop in your region.
>
> This site provides information about what regional tourism data can be about, and how it might be used in managing destinations. It examines existing sources of regional tourism data and the quality of those sources. It provides a framework (BAD) for helping you decide whether to use existing data sources or collect your own. It illustrates management principles through a number of case studies of regional

data collections. It highlights the resource management issues involved in collecting and maintaining locally collected data, and identifies some strategies for dealing with these issues. It also points to a small number of resources which might assist you further.

As part of the research project, the Centre is seeking case studies of local level data collections from across regional Australia. If you have a case study from your region, please send an email with your contact details and a brief description of the data collection to dcarson@scu.edu.au .

One country that has developed a national standard for regional tourism statistics is New Zealand, which has been operating a commercial accommodation monitor (CAM) since the late-1990s. Coordinated by central government (see www.statisticsnz.govt.nz), the CAM requires all commercial accommodation providers to participate. Statistics New Zealand publishes monthly data on capacity, occupancy rates, visitor nights, length of stay, and employee numbers. Among the benefits of a national standard visitor monitor is the ability for regions to undertake market-share analysis. RTOs have access to month-on-month CAM data for all regions. This enables benchmarking of performance by each RTO in comparison to previous points in time, and relative to competing regions. Also, accommodation operators are able to compare their visitor mix, length of stay, and occupancy rate with the local and national averages.

Arguably easier to implement in a small country, the New Zealand CAM evolved out of a desire to establish a national standard at a time when RTOs were developing their own measurement instruments. The first regional visitor monitor was developed by the Queenstown Promotion Board in 1990. After analysing the Queenstown programme, I established the country's second monitor six months later in Rotorua. One notable addition was a monthly survey of local households to provide a measure of visitors staying privately with friends or relatives. The monitor was not without its teething problems. For example, a national newspaper cartoonist poked fun at our office after the market research firm engaged to coordinate the data collection made a major calculation error. The error was only picked up after the results had been published. The cartoon, which appeared in the *New Zealand Herald* (10/2/95), highlights the high-profile nature of DMO performance measurement. Many aspects of the national CAM are based on the Queenstown and Rotorua models.

Critics of visitor monitor programmes argue they are flawed, due to a reliance on individual accommodation operators completing the monthly forms accurately and honestly. A key issue in the development of visitor monitors is gaining the confidence of accommodation operators; convincing them their individual data will be pooled and not accessible by a third party. In the Rotorua case it took months of sometimes heated debate with accommodation representatives to gain acceptance of the need for, and benefits of, a visitor monitor. The end result was a tracking system that became a key element of the RTO's reporting to the local government, which funded destination marketing. Clearly, however, visitor monitor results should only be promoted as an indicator of destination competitiveness, and not, for the reasons indicated in the chapter introduction, used as a singular measure of DMO effectiveness.

Marcom evaluations

Some aspects of destination marketing require long-term and subjective measures of effectiveness. Other aspects are more readily measured objectively and in the short term as is discussed in Case Study 19.1. The case summarises a joint venture campaign that sought, in the words of the organiser, 'to get results the old-fashioned way'. The case clearly demonstrates how it is possible to track the effectiveness of such a joint venture destination promotion.

Case study 19.1 'Priscilla, Queen of the Desert'...getting sales the old fashioned way

Owen Eagles, Managing Director, ANZCRO

During the early 1990s, one of New Zealand's NTO strategies was a joint-venture fund to stimulate cooperative destination marketing offshore. The concept was to match private sector contributions dollar for dollar in campaigns that would produce measurable sales. At the time, ANZCRO (www.anzcro.com.au) was starting out as a new wholesaler of New Zealand travel arrangements in the Australian market. One of the defining moments in the development of ANZCRO into a business that today generates over $75 million annual turnover worldwide was securing $250,000 in joint-venture funding from the NTO. As you will see, this was a very hands-on initiative, and so once the JV was approved the NTO did not play an active role. The plan was to target a sector of the Australian market that ANZCRO argued had been a missed opportunity for New Zealand country people. Australia is such a large country that destination marketers had tended to focus their efforts on city people. This case describes what might be considered an old-fashioned approach to destination marketing, but also one that provided a measurable return to the NTO, ANZCRO, and other partners.

At the time, travel patterns in New Zealand were moving away from coach-touring holidays to self-drive by rental car or motor home. Coach-tour companies disappeared and new entrepreneurs emerged. ANZCRO's mission was to become the leading wholesaler of self-drive products for Australian travel agents. The opportunity to target rural Australia was too costly for one emerging firm like ANZCRO to undertake, and so the joint-venture funding was sought to develop a cooperative approach between the NTO and ANZCRO, with the additional support of car rental, motor home, and accommodation operators at various stages. The argument for targeting rural Australia was built on the following mix of research and assumptions:

- Extensive residential postcode analyses of Australian visitor arrivals at New Zealand's international airports indicated a significant proportion from outside the main Australian cities.
- Australia's farming communities have a strong awareness of New Zealand, through a history of agricultural links.
- NTO and travel company sales reps rarely called on country travel agents.

- Rural travel agents are loyal to travel operators who do make the effort to service them.
- Country people usually have to travel long distances for their holidays, and so the length of holiday tends to be longer and more seasonal.

In comparison to many of today's electronic promotions, this joint-venture strategy was to undertake an old-fashioned sales mission to talk to country people face to face. Central to the campaign was the purchase and renovation of a bus (as shown below), which was fitted with: a kitchen that would be used to prepare breakfast for travel agents, luxury Volvo seats, a television screen for showing NTO videos, and an office for ANZCRO representatives to meet with prospective travellers. The roadshow would visit country towns in the states of Queensland, New South Wales, South Australia, and Victoria in a series of two-week bursts over 12 months. This was a very hands-on mission. Group members, who included a Maori cultural troupe as well as the travel representatives, travelled long distances on the coach, and had to assemble/disassemble displays at each stop. To save expenses the group stayed in camping grounds, and became experts at barbeque cooking!

Before each stop, ANZCRO contacted the local council for main street parking permission, let the local media know what was going to happen, and sent out a message to local travel agents. The schedule was gruelling, which was why two weeks was the limit for each trip. The team would park the coach in the best profile spot in the main shopping street by 5 a.m. and set up the street displays. Travel agents were given a breakfast presentation at 7 a.m., and then briefed on how they would benefit from the campaign. The rest of the day was devoted to providing Maori concerts and old-fashioned spruiking to passers-by about New Zealand travel options. At night the Maori troupe would often perform at local clubs.

A feature of the mission was that performance measurement could be tracked though a simple quote form that was printed in triplicate. ANZCRO would provide interested locals with a personalised suggested drive itinerary of New Zealand and provide a written quote for transport, accommodation, and sightseeing on the spot. One copy of the quote was given to the consumer, one kept on file by ANZCRO, and the third given to the consumer's recommended travel agent. Since the itinerary had been prepared and the quote provided, all the agent had to then do was make a phone call to the consumer to convert a sale.

The rural travel agents loved it because they were being under-serviced by the industry at large. The costs of servicing regional Australia are enormous. The agents never saw reps…they never saw campaigns…no other destination was out there at all. While the actual sales information remains commercially sensitive, it would be an understatement to say the campaign was a winner. In fact the roadshow was so successful, that after the 12-month NTO joint venture ended, the private sector partners continued the initiative for a further 12 months. The number of bookings that could be directly traced to the mission far exceeded expectations.

Discussion questions

- In addition to the direct tracking of bookings made, what other results could have occurred as a result of the sales mission?
- What barriers prevent other organisations from undertaking such an 'old-fashioned' method of reaching consumers?
- What do you consider the main advantages and disadvantages of such a DMO joint-venture fund?

Note: For readers not familiar with 'Priscilla, Queen of the Desert', this is a well known Australian movie about a dance troupe's adventurous travels to country towns by bus.

Advertising • • •

Slater (2002, p. 155) cited the Louisiana cabinet secretary to the Department of Culture, Recreation and Tourism: 'The more money we spend, the more visitors we get.' However, the relationship between advertising and sales has yet to be established in the marketing literature (see Schultz & Schultz, 2004). A central problem is the difficulty in controlling for the range of extraneous variables over which the DMO has no control but which will be in play at the time of the advertising. Hughes (2002, p. 158) discussed the difficulties in measuring the effectiveness of Manchester's gay tourism advertising campaign:

> The campaign is ongoing and its success since 1999 has been difficult to assess given that, for obvious reasons, no record is kept of the number of gay and lesbian tourists, and even if there was it would be difficult to attribute any increase to any one cause.

A number of studies have concluded that the link between destination advertising and tourist receipts was tenuous (see, for example, Faulkner, 1997, p. 27). McWilliams and Crompton's (1997) study of the impact of advertising on low involvement travel decisions estimated that only 24%

of leisure travellers over a two-year period requested travel literature. Nevertheless, there have been many claims over the years about the success of DMO advertising campaigns:

- It has been suggested the 'I [add love symbol] New York' promotion was so successful that it generated an increase of almost 12% in tourism receipts over the previous year (Holcolm, 1999). Between 1977 and 1981 the US$32 million campaign was estimated to have generated at least eight times that amount in additional tax revenues and US$2 billion in extra tourism revenue for the state (Pritchard, 1982).
- It was estimated that an initial six-week campaign in the UK, which launched Western Australia's new destination brand, resulted in 5886 visitors who spent A$7.3 million within the state (Crockett & Wood, 1999).
- The April 28th (2003) internet newsletter of the Colorado Tourism Office reported results of a 2002 advertising effectiveness study designed to measure the return on investment for tourism advertising (www.colorado.com). The report claimed that 1.86 million visitors, who spent US$522 million, visited Colorado as a 'direct result' of the STO's US$2.5 million advertising campaign. On this basis it was claimed that every advertising dollar generated US$205 in visitor spending and US$12.74 in tax revenue.
- Hopper (2002) reported the results of the London Tourist Board's £720,000 foot and mouth outbreak recovery strategy, which included 202,000 views of the campaign web page and 7290 bed nights.

In addressing the question of whether destination advertising increases sales, Woodside (1990) found no published research in the tourism literature other than conversion studies. A conversion study estimates how many enquiries from advertising are converted to visitors, and what the characteristics are of the converted visitors. To do so involves surveying a sample of consumers who have responded to a DMO promotion during the year. A number of authors have been critical of tourism conversion studies. For example, Faulkner's (1997) literature review identified a number of common methodological deficiencies in their application, of which two of the most significant were:

- improper sampling techniques, and a failure to not take sampling error into account when interpreting results
- not considering non-response bias, since those who visit a destination are more likely to respond to a survey.

Other difficulties identified in McWilliams and Crompton's (1997) literature review included:

- respondent problems in recalling expenditure at the destination
- problems of measuring without considering the stage of the decision process
- failure to take into account advertising by competitors
- a lack of focus on programme objectives.

While acknowledging that advertising conversion studies will capture some respondents who had already made a decision to visit the destination prior to requesting the information package, Perdue and Pitegoff (1990) proposed four major benefits for DMOs:

- the ability to monitor changes that result from advertising campaigns over time
- the ability to assess how well the advertising is reaching the target segment
- the opportunity to assess the quality of the information package and its contribution to visitor satisfaction
- the opportunity to undertake pre- and post-campaign surveys.

Woodside (1990) proposed that the most effective means of examining the relationship between advertising and sales is through field experiments. Separate groups can be exposed to different advertising in what are termed split-run techniques. A famous example of this approach used by Bud-wieser Beer in the USA was reported by Ackoff and Emshoff (1975, in Keller, 2003). The experiment, which tested seven advertising levels, ranging from no advertising at all through to +200% advertising spend, ran for a full year. Interestingly, the 'no advertising' market achieved the same level of sales as the 'same level of advertising', and the -50% advertising achieved an increase in sales. The researchers concluded strong brands do not require the same level of advertising as lesser known or liked brands. Readers should be careful with this! An example of a destination application of an experimental design is summarised in Research Snapshot 19.1.

Research Snapshot 19.1   Using an experimental design to test advertising impact

An example of a split-market variation used to analyse destination advertising was reported by Schoenbachler et al. (1995) in an analysis of the effectiveness of an advertising campaign run by a USA STO. They used three geographic markets, two of which were exposed to the same advertising, while a control group received no advertising. Following the advertising campaign, a mail questionnaire was sent to 3000 consumers in each of the three markets to measure unaided recall, awareness of destination features, image, and intent to visit. It was found that intent to visit and awareness of destination features was much higher in the two test markets compared to the control group that received no advertising.

Source: Schoenbachler, C., di Benetto, A., Gordon, G.L. & Kaminski, P.F. (1995). Destination advertising: Assessing effectiveness with the split-run technique. *Journal of Travel & Tourism Marketing*, 4(2), 1–21.

Publicity • • •

PR performance measurement is also problematic. For example, Barry (2002) reported the finding of a survey of UK PR consultants, where one in five revealed they did not believe the success of their PR efforts could be measured. In acknowledging this difficulty, Trout (1995) argued that most PR activities are not positioning strategies. Rather they are 'name in the press' tactics, which are measured in the same way you measure chopped liver – by the pound! Trout argued that content seemed to be largely irrelevant. Weight is all that counts.

DMOs have tended to focus on this publicity aspect of PR measurement. Equivalent advertising value (EAV) has been a popular means for DMOs to monitor the results of their media activities, in the absence of more comprehensive approaches. EAV is a simplistic measure of the amount of advertising dollars required to purchase the equivalent amount of air time or column centimetre generated by the PR initiative. As an example, for 1996–97 the Australian Tourist Commission reported EAV in excess of A\$675 million (ATC, 1998, in Dore & Crouch, 2003). Similarly, measuring EAV has been an important aspect of marketing for the Colorado Tourism Office, which has suffered from a lack of state-government funding. For the year ending June 2003, the STO claimed EAV of US\$22 million through the placement of 1172 media clips.

While EAV can be a useful public-relations tool in a DMO's efforts to enhance credibility among stakeholders, there are a number of problems that should be factored into reporting:

- EAV figures do not provide any indication of who actually read the article or viewed the screening, and more importantly how many were part of the DMO's target segment(s).
- The old adage 'any publicity is good publicity' should be considered in terms of how the publicity reinforced brand associations.
- Not all media articles included in EAV figures can be directly attributed to DMO initiatives.
- There can be a significant time lag between organising and hosting a media visit and subsequent publication, which can skew reporting of year-on-year activities and results.

Qualitative analyses are also required. As the corporate press officer for the BTA, Frisby (2002, p. 98) indicated that the results of the NTO's PR campaign during the foot and mouth outbreak included: 600 articles and broadcast features, 151,000 square centimetres of print, and 2700 seconds of broadcast coverage of Britain as a tourism destination. While Frisby calculated that the overall result represented '216 million positive opportunities to see' worth £1.9 million, he also advised that the results were measured using both qualitative and quantitative assessment of media coverage:

> *The media evaluation system measures individual items of overseas print and broadcast coverage, incorporating the type of publication, content, story angle, audience and readership and impact – scoring each. Other information is also recorded to develop data and aid customer relationship management with individual journalists.*

Barry (2002) suggested that the golden rule is about knowing where you started from. What is the current position, and what is the publicity campaign objective?

Travel trade events • • •

Travel trade events can be difficult to evaluate. The success of familiarisation tours of a destination by intermediaries could be assessed in terms of image improvement and bookings. However, it has been suggested that formal evaluations of these initiatives have not generally been conducted by DMOs (Perdue & Pitegoff, 1990). Likewise, monitoring the effectiveness of participation at travel exhibitions has proven difficult and time-consuming, and as a result often neglected by DMOs. At one level the influence of travel show interaction on actual travel is difficult to measure. At another level, it is even difficult at consumer shows to screen genuine enquirers from brochure collectors, and identify those with a propensity to visit the destination. However, most consumer exhibitions now charge admission fees, which does provide an element of screening compared to setting up a display in a shopping mall. DMOs often distribute coupons, for which the redemption rate can be measured, or attempt to collect database listings through competitions. Pizam (1990) reported that USA STOs had generally used 'rough' measures of travel show effectiveness. The most common methods included: numbers of enquiries, numbers of contacts, amount of literature distributed, staff evaluations, conversion studies, number of group bookings, and surveys.

Consumer-based brand equity (CBBE)

The power of a brand lies in the minds of consumers (Keller, 2003, p. 59).

Generally, there has been a tendency in tourism marketing to focus on short-run measures of marcom effectiveness. This is a reflection of the short-term focus that pervades many boardrooms. Relatively few current DMO decision-makers are likely to still be in office in ten years time, since the high profile and political nature of DMOs management inhibits long periods in governance and senior management. While short-run performance indicators are important, they should also be supplemented with indicators addressing a longer-term view of sustainable destination competitiveness.

An emerging concept for monitoring market perceptions is the model of CBBE, which was presented in Chapter 10. CBBE measurement is based on the premise of developing an understanding of how marketing initiatives are impacting on consumer learning and recall of brand information. However, given the time-consuming, costly and more subjective nature of market research, it is perhaps not surprising that this has been a relatively new activity for DMOs at state and regional levels. For example, in evaluating the initial effects of the Brand Oregon campaign, Curtis (2001, p. 76) lamented the lack of perceptions research:

> In terms of evaluation of the initial campaign, the Tourism Commission essentially took account of two factors; first, the number of visitor enquiries received, and, second, the number of awards won from the advertising industry for the campaign. Unfortunately, no consumer evaluation of the image campaign nor a critical analysis of the campaign's effectiveness was ever conducted.

In Chapter 10, Aaker's (1991) model of CBBE was introduced as comprising brand awareness, brand associations, brand resonance, and brand loyalty. CBBE can be viewed as a bridge between previous marcom and future performance. Research Snapshot 19.2 shows how the model was operationalised to benchmark an emerging destination's CBBE at the launch of a new brand positioning campaign in 2003. At the time of writing, the results of a repeat study in 2007 were being analysed to determine any changes in CBBE after four years of the brand campaign.

Destination awareness

The first goal of marcom is to enhance awareness of the brand. However, as discussed in Chapter 11, measuring the number of destinations in a consumer's awareness set is likely to be prohibitive and indeed pointless given the sheer number of destinations consumers are likely to be aware of. Awareness in itself is not therefore an indicator of attitude. What is important is understanding where the destination lies within the hierarchy of awareness levels, which range from non-awareness to an intent to visit. Of particular interest are the issues of top of mind awareness (ToMA), decision set composition, and behavioural intent. I have used this approach in a number of short-break destination positioning studies (see, for examplee, Pike, 2002b). ToMA was operationalised using an unaided question. Fishbein and Ajzen (1975) proposed that any question exploring the relationship between attitude and behaviour must include the following:

- The behaviour, which for the study was a holiday.
- The target object at which the behaviour is directed, which were domestic destinations.
- The situation in which the behaviour is to be performed, which was self-drive short breaks.
- The time at which the behaviour is to be performed, which was within the next 12 months.

The question designed to incorporate all four points was: Of all the short-break holiday destinations that are available for you to visit in the next 12 months, if you were driving, which destination first comes to mind? The destination named is representative of ToMA at that point in time.

Following this, the decision set composition was addressed by asking respondents to list the names of any other destinations they would also probably consider. Some researchers (see, for example, Woodside & Carr, 1988) have prompted respondents to mention at least three destinations. Such a prompt can however limit respondents' thinking. Identification of the decision set composition is important in understanding the competitive set of destinations, which is critical in positioning analysis.

Destination brand associations ● ● ●

An important area of market research for DMOs is investigating the congruency between brand identity and brand image. This is a measure of how successfully the positioning strategy has enhanced the desired destination brand associations over a given period of time. As previously discussed, what is most critical is that brand associations are strong, favourable, and unique, in that order (Keller, 2003). A range of qualitative and quantitative techniques are available to measure these. My review of 142 destination image studies provided a categorisation of approaches used in measuring the strength and favourability of associations (Pike, 2002a).

Destination brand resonance ● ● ●

Resonance relates to the level of engagement with the brand. For destinations, there are two important variables: previous visitation and intent to visit in the future. For example, Tourism New Zealand reported research indicating the success of its *100% Pure NZ* global campaign (*Inside Tourism*, IT454, 10/6/03, pp. 1–2). The research in the USA, UK, and Japan focused on interactive travellers, described as 'TNZ's target market of high-spending, environmentally and socially aware travellers.' The report cited CEO George Hickton as describing key success indicators as being the extent to which respondents in the target market expressed a desire to visit New Zealand. In each market the number of respondents indicating such intent had increased since a previous survey in 2000.

However, it must be acknowledged that without a longitudinal research component any stated intent to visit cannot be regarded as an accurate indicator of future behaviour. As previously indicated, little has been published in the tourism literature concerning the relationship between stated intent and actual travel. More longitudinal designs could be used to monitor the relationship between stated intent and actual travel.

Destination loyalty ● ● ●

Word of mouth referrals and repeat visitation are the ultimate measure of a consumer's loyalty towards a destination. Milman and Pizam (1995) demonstrated how familiarity with a domestic USA destination, measured by previous visitation, led to a more positive image and increased likelihood of repeat visits. While repeat purchase behaviour was introduced in the marketing literature during the 1940s (Howard & Sheth, 1969), little research has been undertaken in the area of destination loyalty (Oppermann, 1999). Accurately measuring this is likely to be beyond the capacity of most regional visitor monitors. Instead, approaches to collecting information range from intercept surveys of visitors at the destination (see, for example, Gitelson & Crompton, 1984; Gyte & Phelps, 1989; Oppermann, 1996b; Pyo et al., 1998) to mail surveys that captured previous visitors and non-visitors (see Fakeye & Crompton, 1991; Crompton et al., 1992; Pike, 2002b). Such studies can be useful in identifying the demographic characteristics, influences, motivations, as well as the behavioural patterns such as expenditure and length of stay, of those most likely to have the propensity for repeat visits. This can in turn inform more targeted promotional efforts, which are likely to be more cost-efficient than attempts to attract first-time visitors (see, for example, Reid & Reid, 1993).

Research Snapshot 19.2   CBBE for an emerging destination

In Queensland, Australia, there are 14 tourism regions officially recognised and supported by the state tourism organisation (STO), Tourism Queensland (see www.tq.com.au). The STO provides financial and human resources to each RTO for the development of destination brands. In recent years most RTOs have developed new brand campaigns for use in the Brisbane market. Brisbane, the state capital, is the most important market in terms of visitor arrivals for numerous contiguous destinations in Queensland and northern New South Wales. The paper focuses on Bundaberg and the Coral Coast(http://www.queenslandholidays.com.au/destinations/bundaberg-coral-coast-and-country/ index.cfm), which has been categorised by the STO as an 'emerging destination'.

During 2002, exploratory research undertaken by Tourism Queensland found that while Bundaberg had strong name recognition in the Brisbane market as the home of Bundaberg Rum and Bundaberg Ginger Ale, the region lacked a clear identity as a holiday destination. Consumer focus groups suggested that three key barriers to visiting the region were the perception there was 'nothing to do', the driving distance, and lack of nightlife, restaurants, cafes, and shopping (Tourism Queensland, 2003). In response to these findings, a new destination brand was launched in February 2003. The new brand positioning theme was *Take time to Discover Bundaberg, Coral Isles and Country*. The objectives of the new brand were (1) to raise awareness of the destination, (2) to stimulate increased interest in and visitation to the region, and (3) to educate the market about things to do.

To benchmark CBBE for the destination at the time of the brand launch, a longitudinal design was used. Two mail surveys were distributed, three months apart. The first used questions to analyse participants' short-break preferences, while the second examined actual travel. The results provide measures of brand salience, brand associations, and brand resonance for a competitive set of destinations in their most important market, in the context of short breaks by car.

For the Coral Coast, the results indicated that the destination held weak CBBE in its most important market at the time of the launch of a new brand campaign. While the hierarchy of brand salience, brand associations, and brand resonance did not provide a single measure of CBBE, the structure of the results does provide indicators, related to the brand campaign objectives, for which the effectiveness of future promotional activity can be evaluated. The results clearly highlight the challenge facing the destination in what is a crowded and competitive market.

Note: At the time of writing, data from a follow-up survey undertaken during 2007 was undergoing analysis. The purpose of the 2007 study was to measure the extent to which the brand campaign during the previous four years had been successful. Early indications were that, in relation to the brand objectives, the level of CBBE had not improved.

Source: Pike, S. (2007). Consumer-based brand equity for destinations: Practical DMO performance measures. *Journal of Travel & Tourism Marketing*, 22(1).

Organisational performance

> *Good management starts with good measurement*
>
> *(Aaker, 1996, p. 316).*

Organisation performance evaluation is concerned with the degree to which an entity has achieved its objectives, the appropriateness of those objectives, and the efficiency of implementation. Akehurst et al. (1993, p. 59) found the main performance indicators for European NTOs to be:

- the amount of activity of the NTO, such as the number of trade fairs attended
- promotion cost per tourist or per additional tourist, or per dollar of expenditure
- grants per job created.

An independent marketing audit is recommended as a systematic process for evaluating marketing practice. An audit would be expected to examine the following (Hooley et al., 1993):

- marketing environment audit – to assess changes in the macro and operating environments
- strategy audit – to assess the appropriateness and clarity of corporate and marketing objectives and the appropriateness of the resource allocation
- analysis of the structure, efficiency, and interface efficiency of the marketing department
- analysis of marketing systems such as information system, planning system, and control system
- cost-effectiveness analysis
- analysis of marketing mix

Elliott (1997, p. 12–14) proposed the following questions to address organisational efficiency:

- Have objectives been achieved for the lowest cost?
- Have resources been used efficiently?
- Has the return on public investment been reasonable?

Heath and Wall (1992, p. 185) offered the following questions:

- Is the mission of the DMO for the region clearly stated in market-oriented terms? Is the mission feasible in terms of the region's opportunities and resources? Is the mission cognizant of tourist, environmental, business, and community interests in a balanced way?
- Are the various goals for the region clearly stated, communicated to, and understood by the major tourism businesses in the region?
- Are the goals appropriate, given the region's competitive position, resources, and opportunities?
- Is information available for the review of progress toward objectives, and are the reviews conducted on a regular basis?

Stakeholder perceptions

Such internal audits might not be sufficient for DMOs, given the range of active stakeholders. Monitoring stakeholder perceptions or organisation performance should also be considered, as was the case in Research Snapshot 19.3.

Research Snapshot 19.3   Using IPA to monitor perceptions of DMO performance

Evans and Chon (1989) trialled the applicability of importance-performance analysis (IPA) in the formulation and evaluation of tourism policy at two USA destinations. The first destination was at the 'maturity' stage, and had a number of community conflicts regarding tourism policy. The second destination was classified 'immature', in that the small rural community did not have an established tourism industry and was exploring the possibility of developing tourism. IPA requires participants to firstly rate the importance of a series of attributes and then to rate the performance of the destination of interest across the same range of attributes.

In addition to the tourism policy research objectives, local business operators at the 'mature' destination were surveyed in relation to the perceived performance of the local DMO:

- Did members of the business community feel that the DMO was performing well?
- Was the DMO mission clear?

The results indicated that the DMO was not perceived to be performing well in relation to community expectations. Also, the mission was not clear for most participants. The IPA results were helpful to the DMO in resolving a community conflict and in clarifying the organisation's mission. Evans and Chon recommended that the DMO repeat the IPA each year to monitor the business community's perceptions of performance.

Source: Evans, M. R. & Chon, K. (1989). Formulating and evaluating tourism policy using importance-performance analysis. *Hospitality Education & Research*, *13*(2), 203–213.

Tourism Vancouver management have long recognised the need to report performance tracking to stakeholders. The CVB introduced monthly tracking of around 70 measures, and quarterly reporting to the industry was introduced in 1993 (Vallee, 2005). These include an investment effectiveness index that analyses the accomplishment of goals against investments.

Destination marketing awards – the chance to celebrate success!

Successful destination marketers are usually hard-working, creative, and highly competitive, and so enjoy the recognition of their peers. For example, in a media release distributed in October 2005, Tourism Australia Managing Director Scott Morrison welcomed news that the destination had been awarded 'cool brand' status in the annual Cool Brand Leaders list in the UK:

> We are thrilled that the Brand Council in the UK has named Australia as one of the world's Cool Brand Leaders, especially as this is the first time that a country has been included on its annual list.

One of the academic reviewers of my previous text criticised having a section on destination marketing awards. However, anyone with any practical marketing experience will appreciate that awards represent rare tangible (albeit subjective) recognition, such as in the 'best stand award' shown in Figure 19.3. For example, over 2500 people attended the 2007 Australian Tourism Awards ceremony. Examples of prestigious destination marketing awards include:

- The 2006 National Council of Destination Organizations (USA) awards were presented to the Alexandria Convention and Visitors Association (Virginia), the Alaska Travel Industry Association, and the Finger Lakes Visitors Connection (New York).
- The 2006 ICCA marketing award went to Glasgow City Marketing Bureau.
- The 2006 National Council of State Tourism Directors (USA) award for best overall state tourism marketing program went to Virginia Tourism Corporation.
- The 2006 Australian Tourism award for destination marketing went to Destination Noosa.

Figure 19.3
Best stand award at the
Singapore Travel Expo

In practise

At the 53rd annual PATA conference in 2004, Tourism New Zealand was awarded the Grand Award for Marketing, for reversing a declining share in major tourism markets during the 1990s. Under the heading 'TNZ 100% Pure Champion', PATA (http://patanet.org/archives/news@pata/17mar04.htm#3) summarised the 100% Pure New Zealand campaign success factors as:

- Pre-planning research showed that of those international travellers who recognised New Zealand as a potential destination, 87% never intended to visit – the problem was branding and proposition.
- TNZ defined its target market as 'interactive travellers', constituting about 4% of the international holiday travel market.
- '100% Pure New Zealand' branded New Zealand's natural beauty and indigenous culture by portraying warm welcomes, interactive experiences, freedom of movement, and 'being at one with the way the world should be'.
- The campaign's promotional media and materials were consistent, creative, and of high quality, the two highlights being the PATA Gold Award-winning website www.newzealand.com and poster.
- TNZ had successfully captured its target market, contributed to a significant increase in visitor arrivals, and helped New Zealand tourism recover from recent global crises much faster than its competitors .

Key points

1 The challenge of quantifying the DMO contribution to destination competitiveness

Isolating and quantifying a DMO's contribution to destination competitiveness is currently an impossible task. Ultimately, the success of a destination will be as a result of a combination of factors, many of which will be exogenous to the DMO. Examples include the global economy, hallmark events, government visa policies, the weather, disasters, and the marketing activities of others. DMOs at all levels should be wary of staking claims to overall credit for the success of a tourism season, in exactly the same way that they should not accept sole responsibility for a poor industry performance.

2 Measures of DMO effectiveness

There are three dimensions in modelling measures of DMO effectiveness. The first two are internal organisation measures: the appropriateness of activities and the efficiency of the plan in relation to stakeholder expectations. The third, and more challenging task, is that of measuring the effectiveness of marcom. With the exception of advertising conversion studies there has been relatively little published about measuring the success of DMO marcom.

3 Measuring consumer-based brand equity

The reliance on short-run return on investment measures of effectiveness misses the DMO's full contribution to destination competitiveness. Efforts should also be made to model and measure consumer-based destination brand equity. This requires market research to estimate levels of destination awareness, brand associations, perceived value, and destination loyalty.

Review questions

- Why is it so difficult to quantify a DMO's contribution to destination competitiveness?
- What range of measures are reported by your DMO to monitor market performance?
- What range of measures are reported by your DMO to monitor organisation performance?
- How is your DMO capturing visitor metrics such as arrivals, length of stay, spend, and repeat visitation? What limitations can you identify in the data collection?

References

Aaker, D. A. (1991). *Managing Brand Equity*. New York: Free Press.

Aaker, D. A. (1996). *Building Strong Brands*. New York: Free Press.

Aaker, D. A. & Joachimsthaler, E. (2000). *Brand Leadership*. New York: Free Press.

Aaker, D. A., Kumar, V., Day, G.S., Lawley, M. & Stewart, D. (2007). *Marketing Research: The Second Pacific Rim Edition*. Milton, Qld: Wiley.

Aaker, D. A. & Shansby, J. G. (1982). Positioning your product. *Business Horizons*, May/June, 56–62.

Agarwal, S. (1997). The resort cycle and seaside tourism: An assessment of its applicability and validity. *Tourism Management*, 18(2), 65–73.

Aguilo, E., Riera, A. & Rossello, J. (2005). The short-term price effect of a tourist tax through a dynamic demand model. The case of the Balearic Islands. *Tourism Management*, 26, 359–365.

Ahmed, Z. U. (1991). The influence of the components of a state's tourist image on product positioning strategy. *Tourism Management*, December, 331–340.

Ahmed, Z. U. (1991a). Marketing your community: Correcting a negative image. *Cornell HRA Quarterly*, February, 24–27.

Ahmed, Z. U. (1991b). The dark side of image marketing. *The Tourist Review*, 4, 36–37.

Ahmed, Z. U. (1996). The need for the identification of the constituents of a destination's tourist image: A promotion segmentation perspective. *Journal of Professional Services Marketing*, 14(1), 37–60.

Ahmed, Z. & Krohn, F. B. (1990). Reversing the United States' declining competitiveness in the marketing of international tourism: A perspective on future policy. *Journal of Travel Research*, 29(2), 23–29.

Akehurst, G., Bland, N. & Nevin, M. (1993). Tourism policies in the European Community member states. *International Journal of Hospitality Management*, 12(1), 33–66.

Alarcon, C. (2006). Brainwave or bull? *B & T*, 56(2556), P. 1, 4.

Alcantara, N. (2003). Travel advisories reward terrorists, says Gordon. www.eturbonews.com, 24/10/03.

Alford, P. (1998). Positioning the destination product: Can regional tourist boards learn from private sector practice? *Journal of Travel & Tourism Marketing*, 7(2), 53–68.

Amor, F., Calabug, C., Abellan, J. & Montfort. (1994). Barriers found in repositioning a Mediterranean 'sun and beach' product: The Valencian case. In A. V. Seaton et al. (eds), *Tourism the State of the Art*. Chichester, England: John Wiley & Sons.

Aron, C. S. (1999). *Working at Play: A History of Vacations in the United States*. New York: Oxford University Press.

Ashworth, G. & Goodall, B. (1990a). *Marketing Tourism Places*. New York: Routledge.

Ashworth, G. & Goodall, B. (1990b). Tourist images: Marketing considerations. In B. Goodall & G. Ashworth (eds), *Marketing in the Tourism Industry: The Promotion of Destination Regions* (pp. 213–238). London: Routledge:

Ashworth, G. J. & Voogd, H. (1990a). *Selling the City: Marketing Approaches in Public Sector Urban Planning*. London: Belhaven Press.

Ashworth, G.J. & Voogd, H. (1990b). Can places be sold for tourism? In G. Ashworth & B. Goodall (eds), *Marketing Tourism Places* (pp. 1–16). New York: Routledge. ATC. (2003). http://www.atc.net.au/brand.asp. Accessed 20 December.

Ateljevic, I. (1998). Circuits of Tourism: (Re)Producing the Place of Rotorua, New Zealand. Unpublished PhD thesis. University of Auckland.

Ateljevic, I. & Doorne, S. (2000). Local government and tourism development: Issues and constraints of public sector entrepreneurship. *New Zealand Geographer*. 56(2), 25–31.

Australian Department of Industry, Tourism and Resources. (2001). *Destination Competitiveness: Development of a Model with Application to Australia and the Republic of Korea*. Canberra: Industry Tourism Resources Division. Available on-line at: http://www.industry.gov.au/library/content_library/DestCompetitiveRpt.pdf

Axelrod, J. N. (1968). Attitude measures that predict purchase. *Journal of Advertising Research, 8*(1), 3–17.

Baker, K. G., Hozier Jr, G. C., & Rogers, R. D. (1994). Marketing research theory and methodology and the tourism industry: A nontechnical discussion. *Journal of Travel Research*, Winter, 3–7.

Banks, S. (1950). The relationship between preference and purchase of brands. *Journal of Marketing, 15* (Oct), 145–157.

Baloglu, S. (1997). The relationship between destination images and sociodemographic and trip characteristics of international travellers. *Journal of Vacation Marketing, 3*(3), 221–233.

Baloglu, S. (1998). An empirical investigation of attitude theory for tourist destinations: A comparison of visitors and nonvisitors. *Journal of Hospitality & Tourism Research, 22*(3), 211–224.

Baloglu, S. & Brinberg, D. (1997). Affective images of tourism destinations. *Journal of Travel Research*, Spring, 11–15.

Baloglu, S. & Mangaloglu, M. (2001). Tourism destination images of Turkey, Egypt, Greece, and Italy as perceived by US-based tour operators and travel agents. *Tourism Management, 22*, 1–9.

Baloglu, S. & McCleary, K. W. (1999a). A model of destination image. *Annals of Tourism Research, 26*(4), 868–897.

Baloglu, S. & McCleary, K. W. (1999b). US international pleasure travelers' images of four Mediterranean destination: A comparison of visitors and nonvisitors. *Journal of Travel Research. 38* (November), 144–152.

Barich, H., & Kotler, P. (1991). A framework for marketing image management. *Sloan Management Review*, 32(2): 94-104.

Barnett, G. (2006). Government apathy could 'wipe millions' off tourism earnings.www.travelmole.com. 1 March.

Barney, J. (1991). Firm resources and sustained competitive advantage. *Journal of Management. 17*(1), 99–120.

Barney, J. (1996). *Gaining and Sustaining Competitive Advantage*. Reading, Massachusetts: Addison-Wesley.

Barrett, R. (2006). Where else but in… *The Courier-Mail*, 9–10 December, 3.

Beirman, D. (2002). Marketing of tourism destinations during a prolonged crisis: Israel and the Middle East. *Journal of Vacation Marketing, 8*(2), 167–176.

Beirman, D. (2003a). *Restoring Destinations in Crisis*. Crows Nest, NSW: Allen & Unwin.

Beirman, D. (2003b). Kenyan tourism's recovery. www.eturbonews. 1 October.

Belk, R. W. (1975). Situational variables and consumer behavior. *Journal of Consumer Research*, 2, December, 157–164.

Beeton, S. (2001). Smiling for the camera: The influence of film audiences on a budget tourism destination. *Tourism, Culture & Communication*, 3, 15–25.

Beeton, S. (2001). Cyclops and sirens: Demarketing as a proactive response to negative consequences of one-eyed competitive market. *TTRA Conference*. Florida.

Benfield, R. W. (2001). 'Turning back the hordes': Demarketing as a means of managing mass tourism. *TTRA Conference*. Florida.

Berger, D. (2006). *The Development of Mexico's Tourism Industry – Pyramids by Day, Martinis by Night*. New York: Palgrave MacMillan.

Bergman, J. (2004). A peek into hell's pit. *The Sunday Mail*, Brisbane, 22 February, 6.

Black, J. (1992). *The British Abroad: The Grand Tour in the Eighteenth Century*. New York: St Martin's Press.

Blalock, C. (2000). Slow, steady approach might win funds for tourism promotion. *Hotel & Motel Management*, 215(11), 10.

Bleasedale, S. & Kwarko, P. (2000). Is there a role for visiting friends and relatives in Ghana's tourism development strategy? In M. Robinson, N. Evans, P. Long, R. Sharpley & J. Swarbrooke (eds), *Management, Marketing and the Political Economy of Tourism* (pp. 13–22). Sunderland: The Centre for Travel & Tourism.

Bojanic, D. C. (1991). The use of advertising in managing destination image. *Tourism Management*, December, 352–355.

Bolson, F. (2005). Alliances. In R. Harrill (ed.), *Fundamentals of Destination Management and Marketing* (pp. 219–228). Washington: IACVB.

Bonham, C., Fujii, E., Mi, E. & Mak, J. (1991). The impact of the hotel room tax: An interrupt time series approach. *National Tax Journal*, 45(4), 433–441.

Bonham, C.S. & Gangnes, B. (1996). Intervention analysis with cointegrated time series: The case of Hawaii hotel room tax. *Applied Economics*, 28, 1281–1293.

Bonham, C. & Mak, J. (1996). Private versus public financing of state destination promotion. *Journal of Travel Research*, Fall, 3–10.

Bowes, S. (1990). The role of the tourist board. In B. Goodal & G. Ashworth (eds), *Marketing in the Tourist Industry: The Promotion of Destination Regions*. London: Routledge.

Brace, M. (2007). In the footsteps of literary greats. *The Sunday Mail*, Escape, 12–13. Nune 3rd.

Bramwell, B. & Rawding, L. (1996). Tourism marketing images of industrial cities. *Annals of Tourism Research*, 23(1), 201–221.

Bramwell, B. & Sharman, A. (1999). Collaboration in tourism policymaking. *Annals of Tourism Research*, 26(2), 392–415.

Brewton, C. & Witham, G. (1998). United States tourism policy: Alive, but not well. *Cornell Hotel and Restaurant Administration Quarterly*, July, 50–59.

Britton, R. A. (1979). The image of the Third World in tourism marketing. *Annals of Tourism Research*, July–Sept, 318–329.

Bronner, F. & de Hoog, R. (1985). A recipe for mixing decision ingredients. *European Research*, July, 109–115.

Brown, B. J. H. (1985). Personal perception and community speculation: A British resort in the 19th century. *Annals of Tourism Research*, 1, 355–369.

Brown, D. (1995). *Inventing New England: Regional Tourism in the Nineteenth Century*. Washington, DC: Smithsonian Institution Press.

Buck, R. C. (1978). Towards a synthesis in tourism theory. *Annals of Tourism Research*, 5(1), 110–111.

Buckley, P. J. & Witt, S. F. (1985). Tourism in difficult areas: Case studies of Bradford, Bristol, Glasgow and Hamm. *Tourism Management*, September, 205–213.

Bueno, A. P. (1999). Competitiveness in the tourist industry and the role of the Spanish public administrations. *Turizam*. 47(4), 316–331.

Buhalis, D. (2000). Marketing the competitive destination of the future. *Tourism Management*, 21(1), 97–116.

Buhalis, D. & Cooper, C. (1998). Conference report: The future of traditional tourist destinations. *Progress in Tourism and Hospitality Research*, 4, 85–88.

Bull, A. (1995). *The Economics of Travel & Tourism*. Melbourne: Longman.

Burke, W. L. & Schoeffler, S. (1980). *Brand Awareness as a Tool for Profitability*. The Strategic Planning Institute. Boston: Cahners.

Burton, M. L. & Nerlove, S. B. (1976). Balanced designs for triads tests: Two examples from English. *Social Science Research*. 5, 247–267.

Bush, J. E. (2004). The story of a public/private tourism marketing partnership. In B. Dickenson & A. Vladimir (eds), *The Complete 21st Century Travel & Hospitality Marketing Handbook* (pp. 121–127). Upper Saddle River, NJ: Pearson.

Butler, R. W. (1980). The concept of a tourist area cycle of evolution: Implications for management of resources. *Canadian Geographer*, 24(1), 5–12.

Butler, R. W. & Baum, T. (1999). The tourism potential of the peace dividend. *Journal of Travel Research*, 38, 24–29.

Cai, L. A. (2002). Cooperative branding for rural destinations. *Annals of Tourism Research*, 29(3), 720–742.

Cambourne, B. (1998). Wine tourism in the Canberra District. In J. Carlsen & R. Dowling (eds), *Wine Tourism: Perfect Partners*. Proceedings of the First Australian Wine Tourism Conference, Margaret River, 1998.

Carley, C. (2005). Product development. In R. Harril (ed.), *Fundamentals of Destination Management and Marketing*. Lansing: Michigan: Education Institute of the American Hotel & Lodging Association.

Carroll, P. (1991). Policy issues and tourism. In P. Carroll, K. Donohue, M. McGovern & J. McMillen (eds), *Tourism in Australia* (pp.20–43). Sydney: Harcourt Brace Jovanovich.

Carson, D., Beattie, S. & Gove, B. (2003). Tourism management capacity of local government – An analysis of Victorian local government. In R. W. Braithwaite & R. L. Braithwaite (eds), *Riding the Wave of Tourism and Hospitality Research*. Proceedings of the Council of Australian University Tourism and Hospitality Education Conference. Coffs Harbour: Southern Cross University, Lismore. CD-ROM.

Cerda, E. L. (2005). Destination management in Mexico. In R. Harrill (ed.), *Fundamentals of Destination Management and Marketing* (pp. 259–272). Washington: IACVB..

Chacko, H. E. (1997). Positioning a tourism destination to gain a competitive edge. *Asia Pacific Journal of Tourism Research*, 1(2), 69–75.

Chacko, H. E. & Fenich, G.G. (2000). Determining the importance of US convention destination attributes. *Journal of Vacation Marketing*, 6(3), 211–220.

Chamberlain, J. (1992). On the tourism trail: A nice little earner, but what about the cost? *North & South,*. September, 88–97.

Chon, K. (1990). The role of destination image in tourism: A review and discussion. *The Tourist Review*, 45(2), 2–9.

Chon, K. (1990b). Traveler destination image modification process and its marketing implications. *Developments in Marketing Science*, 13, 480–482.

Chon, K. (1991). Tourism destination image: Marketing implications. *Tourism Management*, March, 68–72.

Chon, K., Weaver, P. A. & Kim, C. Y. (1991). Marketing your community: image analysis in Norfolk. *Cornell HRA Quarterly*, February, 31–36.

Choy, D. L. J. (1992). Lifecycle models for Pacific Island destinations. *Journal of Travel Research*, Winter, 26–31.

Choy, D. J. L. (1993) Alternative roles of national tourism organizations. *Tourism Management*, 14(5), 357–365.

Christine, B. (1995). Disaster management: lessons learned. *Risk Management*, October, 19–34.

Chu, R. K. S. & Choi, T. (2000). An importance-performance analysis of hotel selection factors in the Hong Kong hotel industry: A comparison of business and leisure travellers. *Tourism Management*, 21, 363–377.

Cincotta, K. (2006). Web content, glossy editorial: A happy co-existence. *B & T*, 31 March, 15.

Cohen, E. (1972). Toward a sociology of international tourism. *Social Research*, 39, 164–182.

Cohen, E. (1979). Rethinking the sociology of tourism. *Annals of Tourism Research*, Jan/Mar, 18–35.

Collier, A. (1997). *Principles of Tourism – A New Zealand Perspective* (4th edn). Auckland: Addison Wesley Longman.

Collins, J. C. & Porras, J. I (1997). *Built to Last*. New York: HarperCollins.

Conlin, M. V. (1995) Rejuvenation planning for island tourism: the Bermuda example. In M. V. Conlin & T. Baum (eds), *Island Tourism: Management Principles and Practice*. Chichester: John Wiley & Sons.

Cooper, C. (1994). The destination lifecycle: An update. In A. V.Seaton (ed.), *Tourism the State of the Art* (pp. 340–346). Chichester, UK: John Wiley & Sons.

Cortez, M. J. (2004). Las vegas: To brand the new destination. In B. Dickenson & A. Vladimir (eds), *The Complete 21st Century Travel & Hospitality Marketing Handbook* (pp. 159–167). Upper Saddle River, NJ: Pearson.

Cossens, J. (1994). Destination image: Another fat marketing word? *Tourism Down Under Research Conference Proceedings*. Palmerston North: Massey University.

Cousins, J. (2001). 2500 slogans vie for prize. *Bay of Plenty Times*. Tauranga. p. 1.

Coventry, N. (1998). *Inside Tourism*. 205, April 24.

Coventry, N. (2001). *Inside Tourism*. 352, May 03.

Coventry, N. (2006). *Inside Tourism*. 621, 1 December .

Coyne, K. P. (1986). Sustainable competitive advantage: What it is, what it isn't. *Business Horizons*, January–February, 54–61.

Craik, J. (1991). *Government Promotion of Tourism: The Role of the Queensland Tourist and Travel Corporation*. Brisbane: The Centre for Australian Public Sector Management, Griffith University.

Cripps, K. (2005). Cambodia's mass grave site privatized. www.travelwirenews.com. 12 April.

Crockett, S. R. & Wood, L. J. (1999). Brand Western Australia: A totally integrated approach to destination branding. *Journal of Vacation Marketing*, 5(3), 276–289.

Crompton, J. L. (1979a). Motivations for pleasure vacation. *Annals of Tourism Research*, Oct–Dec, 408–424.

Crompton, J. L. (1979b). An assessment of the image of Mexico as a vacation destination and the influence of geographical location upon that image. *Journal of Travel Research*, Spring, 18–23.

Crompton, J. (1992). Structure of vacation destination choice sets. *Annals of Tourism Research*, 19 , 420–434.

Crompton, J. L. & Duray, N. A. (1985). An investigation of the relative efficacy of four alternative approaches to importance-performance analysis. *Academy of Marketing Science*, 13(4), 69–80.

Crompton, J. L., Fakeye, P. C. & Lue, C. (1992). Positioning: The example of the Lower Rio Grande Valley in the winter long-stay destination market. *Journal of Travel Research*, Fall, 20–26.

Cross, G. S. & Walton, J. K. (2005). *The Playful Crowd – Pleasure Places in the Twentieth Century*. New York: Columbia University Press.

Crouch, G.I. (2000). Services research in destination marketing: A retrospective appraisal. *International Journal of Hospitality & Tourism Administration*, 1(2), 65–85.

Crouch, G. I. & Ritchie, J. R. B. (1999). Tourism, competitiveness, and societal prosperity. *Journal of Business Research*, 44, 137–152.

Croy, G. (2004). The Lord of the Rings, Middle Earth, New Zealand and tourism. Presentation. 14th International Research Conference of the Council for Australian University Tourism and Hospitality Education. Brisbane: University of Queensland.

Cruise, K. R. & Sewell, K. W. (2000). Promoting self-awareness and role elaboration: Using repertory grids to facilitate theatrical character development. *Journal of Constructivist Psychology*, 13, 231–248.

Curtis, J. (2001). Branding a state: The evolution of Brand Oregon. *Journal of Vacation Marketing*, 7(1), 75–81.

Cushman, G. (1990). Tourism in New Zealand. (1990). *World Leisure and Recreation*, 32(1), 12–16.

Dadgostar, B. & Isotalo, R. M. (1992). Factors affecting time spent by near-home tourists in city destinations. *Journal of Travel Research*, 31(2), 34.

Dadgostar, B. & Isotalo, R. M. (1995). Content of city destination image for near-home tourists. *Journal of Hospitality & Leisure Marketing*, 3(2), 25–34.

Dahles, H. (1998). Redefining Amsterdam as a tourist destination. *Annals of Tourism Research*, 25(1), 55–69.

D'Amore, L. J. (1988). Tourism – The world's peace industry. *Business Quarterly*, 52(3), 78–81.

d'Hauteserre, A-M. (2000). Lessons in managed destination competitiveness: The case of Foxwoods Casino Resort. *Tourism Management*, 21(1), 23–32.

Dann, G. M. S. (1977). Anomie, ego-enhancement and tourism. *Annals of Tourism Research*, March/April, 184–194.

Dann, G. M. S. (1981). Tourist motivation: An appraisal. *Annals of Tourism Research*, 8(2), 187–219.

Dann, G. M. S. (1996). Tourists' images of a destination: An alternative analysis. *Journal of Travel & Tourism Marketing*, 5(1/2), 41–55.

Dann, G. M. S. (1996b). The people of tourist brochures. In T. Selwyn (ed.), *The Tourist Image: Myths and Myth Making in Tourism*. West Sussex: John Wiley & Sons.

Dann, G. M. S. (2000). Differentiating destination in the language of tourism: Harmless hype or promotional irresponsibility. *Tourism Recreation Research*, 25(2), 63–72.

Dascalu, R. (1997). Romania plans reparations for nationalised hotels. *Reuters*, August 11.

Davidson, R. & Maitland, R. (1997). *Tourism Destinations*. London: Hodder & Stoughton.

Davidson, J. & Spearritt, P. (2000). *Holiday Business – Tourism in Australia Since 1870*. Carlton South, Vic: Melbourne University Press.

Davidson, R. & Rogers, T. (2006). *Marketing Destinations & Venues for Conferences, Conventions and Business Events*. Oxford: Elsevier.

Davies, B. (1990). The economics of short breaks. *International Journal of Hospitality Management*, 9(2), 103–109.

Day, G. S. & Wensley, R. (1988). Assessing advantage: A framework for diagnosing competitive superiority. *Journal of Marketing, 52*(April), 1–20.

de Chernatony, L. (1993). Categorizing brands: Evolutionary processes underpinned by two key dimensions. *Journal of Marketing* Management, *9*, 173≠188.

de Haan, T., Ashworth, G. & Stabler, M. (1990). The tourist destination as product: The case of Languedoc. In G. Ashworth & B. Goodall (eds), *Marketing Tourism Places* (pp. 156–169). New York: Routledge.

d'Hauteserre, A-M. (2000). Lessons in managed destination competitiveness: The case of Foxwoods Casino Resort. *Tourism Management, 21*(1). 23–32.

Dichter, E. (1985). What's in an image. *The Journal of Consumer Marketing, 2*(1), 75–81.

Dillon, W. R., Domzal,, T. & Madden, T. J. (1986). Evaluating alternative product positioning strategies. *Journal of Advertising Research*, Aug–Sept, 29–35.

Dimanche, F. & Lepetic, A. (1999). New Orleans tourism and crime: A case study. *Journal of Travel Research, 38*, 19–23.

Dimanche, F. & Moody, M. (1998). Perceptions of destination image: A study of Latin American intermediary travel buyers. *Tourism Analysis, 3*, 173–180.

DiMingo, E. (1988). The fine art of positioning. *Journal of Business Strategy*, March/April, 34–38.

Dobni, D. & Zinkhan, G. M. (1990). In search of brand image: A foundation analysis. *Advances in Consumer Research, 17*, 110–119.

Doering, T. R. (1979). Geographical aspects of state travel marketing in the USA. *Annals of Tourism Research*, July–Sept, 307–317.

Dolnicar, S., Grabler, K. & Mazanec, J. A. (1999a). A tale of three cities: Perceptual charting for analysing destination images. In A. G. Woodside, G. I. Crouch, J. A. Mazanec, M. Oppermann. & M. Y. Sakai (eds), *Consumer Psychology of Tourism, Hospitality and Leisure*. Wallingford: CABI.

Dolnicar, S., Grabler, K. & Mazanec, J. A. (1999b). Analyzing destination images: A perceptual charting approach. *Journal of Travel & Tourism Marketing, 8*(4), 43–57.

Dolnicar, S. & Schoesser, C. M. (2003). Market research in Austrian NTO and RTOs: Is the research homework done before spending millions? In R. W. Braithwaite & R. L. Braithwaite (eds), *Riding the Wave of Tourism and Hospitality Research*. Proceedings of the Council of Australian University Tourism and Hospitality Education Conference. Coffs Harbour: Southern Cross University. CD-ROM.

Donnelly, F. (2005). Branding the brain. *The Courier-Mail*, November 5–6, p. 31.

Donnelly, M. P. & Vaske, J. J. (1997). Factors affecting membership in a tourism promotion authority. *Journal of Travel Research*, Spring, 50–55.

Dore, L. & Crouch, G. I. (2003). Promoting destinations: An exploratory study of publicity programmes used by national tourism organizations. *Journal of Vacation Marketing , 9*(2), 137–151

Doxey, G. V. (1975). A causation theory of visitor-resident irritants. *Proceedings of the Travel and Tourism Research Association's 6th Annual Conference*. San Diego, CA.

Dredge, D. (2001). Local government tourism planning and policy-making in New South Wales: Institutional development and historical legacies. *Current Issues in Tourism, 4*(2/4), 355–380.

Driscoll, A., Lawson, R. & Niven, B. (1994). Measuring tourists' destination perceptions. *Annals of Tourism Research, 21*(3), 499–511.

Drucker, P. (1995). *Managing in a Time of Great Change*. Oxford: Butterworth-Heinemann.

D'Silva, C. & Bharadwaj, M. (2004). The sleeping giant – India wakes up to the tourism challenge. *Executive Report*, July, pp. 5–7.

Duncan, T. (2002).*IMC: Using Advertising and Promotion to Build Brands.*? Place: McGraw-Hill.

Dwyer, L., Livaic, Z. & Mellor, R. (2003). Competitiveness of Australia as a tourist destination. *Journal of Hospitality and Tourism Management*, 10(1), 60–78.

Dwyer, L. Forsyth, P. & Rao, P. (1999). Tourism price competitiveness and journey purpose. *Tourism*, 47(4), 283–299.

Dwyer, L., Forsyth, P. & Rao, P. (2000). The price competitiveness of travel and tourism: A comparison of 19 destinations. *Tourism Management*, 21(1), 9–22.

Echtner, C. M. & Ritchie, J. R. B. (1991). The meaning and measurement of destination image. *Journal of Tourism Studies*, 2(2), 2–12.

Echtner, C. M. & Ritchie, J. R. B. (1993). The measurement of destination image: An empirical assessment. *Journal of Travel Research*, 31(3), 3–13.

Edgar, D. A., Litteljohn, D. L., Allardyce, M. L. & Wanhill, S. (1994). Commercial short-break holiday breaks – The relationship between market structure, competitive advantage and performance. In A. V. Seaton (ed.), *Tourism the State of the Art*. Chichester: John Wiley & Sons.

Edgell, D. L. (1999). *Tourism Policy: The Next Millennium*. Champaign, Ill: Sagamore.

Edlin, (1999). Too much tax to tourism? *Management*, May, 60.

Ehemann, J. (1977). What kind of place is Ireland? An image perceived through the American media. *Journal of Travel Research*, 16, 28–30.

Elliott, J. (1997). *Tourism – Politics and Public Sector Management*. London: Routledge

English ? (2000). Government intervention in tourism: Case study of an English seaside resort. In M. Robinson, N. Evans, P. Long, R. Sharpley & J. Swarbrooke (eds), *Management, Marketing and the Political Economy of Travel and Tourism* (pp. 86–101). Sunderland: The Centre for Travel and Tourism.

Enright, M. J. & Newton, J. (2005). Determinants of tourism destination competitiveness in Asia Pacific: Comprehensiveness and universality. *Journal of Travel Research*, 43, 339–350.

Enright, M. J. & Newton, J. (2006). Tourism destination competitiveness: A quantitative approach. *Tourism Management*, 25, 777–788.

Ermen, D. & Gnoth, J. (2006). A reclassification of tourism industries to identify the focal actors. In M. Kozak & L. Andreu (eds), *Progress in Tourism Marketing*. Oxford: Elsevier.

Evans, M. R. & Chon, K. (1989). Formulating and evaluating tourism policy using importance-performance analysis. *Hospitality Education & Research*, 13(2), 203–213.

Fache, W. (ed) (1990). *Shortbreak holidays*. Rotterdam: Center Parcs.

Fache, W. (1990b). Holiday villages for the four seasons of the year and the four seasons of life. In W. Fache (ed.), *Shortbreak holidays*. Rotterdam: Center Parcs.

Fache, W. (1994). Short break holidays. In S. Witt & L. Moutinho (eds), *Tourism Marketing and Management Handbook* (2nd edn) (pp. 459–467). Hertfordshire: Prentice Hall International.

Fakeye, P. C. & Crompton, J. L. (1991). Image differences between prospective, first time, and repeat visitors to the Lower Rio Grande Valley. *Journal of Travel Research*, 30, 10–16.

Faulkner, B. (1997). A model for evaluation of national tourism destination marketing programs. *Journal of Travel Research*, Winter, 23–32.

Faulkner, B. (1999). *Tourism Disasters: Towards a Generic Model*. CRC Tourism Work-in-Progress Report Series: Report 6.

Faulkner, B. (2002). *Rejuvenating a Maturing Destination – The Case of the Gold Coast*. Altona, Vic: Common Ground Publishing.

Faulkner, B., Oppermann, M. & Fredline, E. (1999). Destination competitiveness: An exploratory examination of South Australia's core attractions. *Journal of Vacation Marketing*, 5(2), 125–139.

Faulkner, B. & Vikulov, S. (2001). Katherine, washed out one day, back on track the next: A post-mortem of a tourism disaster. *Tourism Management, 22*(4), 331–344.

Fayos-Solá, E. (2002). Golbalization, tourism policy and tourism education. *Acta Turistica, 14* (1), 5–12.

Fenich, G. G. (2005). *Meetings, Expositions, Events and Conventions – An Introduction to the Industry*. Upper Saddle River, NJ: Pearson.

Ferguson, B. (2003). Tourism chiefs under fire for festivals snub. *Evening* News, Edinburgh, 15 August.

Ferrario, F. F. (1979a). The evaluation of tourism resources: An applied methodology. Part 1. *Journal of Travel Research*, Winter, 18–22.

Ferrario, F. F. (1979b). The evaluation of tourism resources: An applied methodology. Part 2. *Journal of Travel Research*, Spring, 18–22.

Fishbein, M. & Ajzen, I. (1975). *Belief, Attitude, Intention and Behavior: An Introduction to Theory and Research*. Philippines: Addison-Wesley.

Flagstaff, A. & Hope, C.A. (2001). "Scandinavian winter"; antecedents, concepts and empirical observations underlying a destination umbrella branding model. *Tourism Review, 56*(1/2), 5–12.

Foodworks (2006a). Spy Valley wins accolade in Japan. Retrieved January 8th, 2007 from http://www.foodworks.co.nz/news/newsprevious.htm

Foodwoks (2006b). Lowburn Ferry pinot noir wins in Austria. Retrieved January 8th, 2007 from http://www.foodworks.co.nz/news/newsprevious.htm

Formica, S. & Littlefield, J. (2000). National tourism organizations: A promotional plans framework. *Journal of Hospitality & Leisure Marketing, 7*(1), 103–119.

Foreman, M. (2003). Tourism chomping through old grants. *The Independent*. 17 July.

Forsyte Research. (2000). Topline results of the 1999 domestic tourism study. New Zealand Tourism Conference. Wellington.

Foster, J. J. (1998). *Data Analysis – Using SPSS for Windows*. London: Sage.

Frewer, L. J., Howard, C. & Shepherd, R. (1998). Understanding public attitudes to technology. *Journal of Risk Research, 1*(3). 221–235.

Frisby, E. (2002). Communicating in a crisis: The British Tourist Authority's responses to the foot-an-mouth outbreak and 11th September, 2001. *Journal of Vacation Marketing, 9*(1), 89–100

Frost, W. (2003). Bravehearted Ned Kelly – Destination image and historic films. Taking Tourism to the Limits – An International Interdisciplinary Conference in the Waikato. University of Waikato.

Galbraith, J. R. & Lawler, E. E. (1993). *Organizing for the Future*. San Fransisco: Jossey-Bass.

Gardner, B. B., & Levy, S. J. (1955). The product and the brand. *Harvard Business Review*, March–April, 33–39.

Gartner, W. C. (1986). Temporal influences on image change. *Annals of Tourism Research, 13*, 635–644.

Gartner, W. C. (1989). Tourism image: Attribute measurement of state tourism products using multidimensional scaling techniques. *Journal of Travel Research*, Fall, 16–20.

Gartner, W. C. (1993). Image information process. *Journal of Travel & Tourism Marketing, 2*(2/3), 191–215.

Gartner, W. C. (1996*). Tourism Development – Principles, Processes, and Policies*. New York: John Wiley & Sons

Gartner, W. C. & Bachri, T. (1994). Tour operators' role in the tourism distribution system: An Indonesian case study. *Journal of International Consumer Marketing, 6*(3/4), 161–179.

Gartner, W. C. & Hunt, J. D. (1987). An analysis of state image change over a twelve-year period (1971–1983). *Journal of Travel Research*, Fall, 15–19.

Gartner, W. C. & Shen, J. (1992). The impact of Tiananmen Square on China's tourism image. *Journal of Travel Research*, Spring, 47–52.

Gartrell, R. B. (1992). Convention and visitor bureau: Current issues in management and marketing. *Journal of Travel & Tourism Marketing*, 1(2), 71–78.

Gartrell, R. B. (1994). *Destination Marketing for Convention and Visitor Bureaus*. Dubuque, Iowa: Kendall/Hunt Publishing Company.

Gatty, B. & Blalock, C. (1997). New organization brings new energy to marketing the US. *Hotel & Motel Management*, 17 (17 Feb).

Gearing, C. E., Swart, W. W. & Var, T. (1974). Establishing a measure of touristic attractiveness. *Journal of Travel Research*, 12(4), 1–8.

Gee, C. Y. & Makens, J. C. (1985). The tourism board: Doing it right. *The Cornell Quarterly*, 26(3), 25–33.

Getz, d., Anderson, D. & Sheehan, L. (1998). Roles, issues, and strategies for convention and visitors' bureaux in destination planning and product development: A survey of Canadian bureaux. *Tourism Management*, 19(4), 331–340.

Gilbert, D. (1990). Strategic marketing planning for national tourism. *The Tourist Review*. 1: 18-27.

Glaesser, D. (2003). *Crisis Management in the Tourism Industry*. New York: Butterworth-Heniemann.

Glenn, J. C. (1989). *FutureMmind: Artificial Intelligence*. Place?Acropolis.

Gnoth, G. (1998). Branding tourism destinations. Conference report. *Annals of Tourism Research*, 25(3), 758–760.

Go, F. (1987). Selling Canada. *Travel & Tourism Analyst*, December, 17–29.

Go, F. M. & Govers, R. (2000). Integrated quality management for tourist destinations: A European perspective on achieving competitiveness. *Tourism Management*, 21(1), 79–88.

Go, F. & Zhang, W. (1997). Applying importance-performance analysis to Beijing as an international meeting destination. *Journal of Travel Research*, Spring, 42–49.

Godfrey, K. & Clarke, J. (2000). *The Tourism Development Handbook*. London: Continuum.

Goeldner, R. C., Ritchie, J. R. B. & McIntosh, R. W. (2000). *Tourism: Principles, Practises, Philosophies* (8th edn). New York: Publisher?.

Goh, K. L. & Fairgray, D. (1999). *New Zealand Domestic Tourism Forecasts: 1999–2005*. Takapuna: McDermott Fairgray.

Gold, J. R. & Ward, S. V. (1994). *Place Promotion*. Chichester: John Wiley & Sons.

Goodall, B. & Ashworth, G. (eds) (1990). *Marketing in the Tourism Industry: The Promotion of Destination Regions*. London: Routledge.

Goodall, B., Radburn, M. & Stabler, M. (1988). *Market Opportunity Sets for Tourism*. Reading: University of Reading.

Goodrich, J. N. (1978). The relationship between preferences for and perceptions of vacation destinations: Application of a choice model. *Journal of Travel Research*, Fall, 8–13.

Grabler, K. (1997a). Perceptual mapping and positioning of tourist cities. In J. A. Mazanec (ed.), *International City Tourism* (pp. 101–113). London: Pinter.

Grabler, K. (1997b). The managerial perspective. In J. A. Mazanec (ed.), *International City Tourism* (pp. 147–166). London: Pinter.

Grabler, K. (1997c). Cities and the destination life cycle. In J. A. Mazanec (ed.), *International City Tourism* (pp. 54–71). London: Pinter.

Grabler, K. (1997d). The city travellers' view. In J. A. Mazanec (ed.), *International City Tourism* (pp. 167–184). London: Pinter.

Gray, H. P. (1970). *International Travel – International Trade*. Lexington, Massachusetts: Heath Lexington Books.

Greenwood, J. (1993). Business interest groups in tourism governance. *Tourism Management*, 14(5), 335–348.

Gregory, R. (1987). *The Oxford Companion to the Mind*. Oxford: Oxford University Press.

Gretzel, U., Fesenmaier, D. R., Formica, S. & O'Leary, J. T. (2006). Searching for the future: Challenges faced by destination marketing organizations. *Journal of Travel Research*, 45, 116–126.

Guardian Unlimited. (2007). The supercasin contenders. January 30. Press Association accessed at http://business.guardian.co.uk/story/0,,2001910,00.html accessed 20/3/2007.

Gunn, C. (1988). *Vacationscape: Designing Tourist Regions* (2nd edn). Austin: Bureau of Business Research, University of Texas.

Gunn, C. (1994). *Tourism Planning: Basics, Concepts, Cases* (3rd edn). London: Taylor and Francis.

Hall, C. M. (1998). *Introduction to Tourism: Development, Dimensions and Issues* (3rd edn). Sydney: Pearson Education Australia.

Hall, C. M. (1999). Rethinking collaboration and partnership: A public policy perspective. *Journal of Sustainable Tourism*, 7(3/4), 274–289.

Hall. C. M. (2005). The future of tourism research. In B. W. Ritchie, P. Burns & C. Palmer (eds), *Tourism Research Methods – Integrating Theory with Practise*. Wallingford, Oxfordshire: CABI Publishing.

Hall, D. (1999). Destination branding, niche marketing and national image projection in Central and Eastern Europe. *Journal of Vacation Marketing*, 5(3), 227–237.

Hall, D. (2002). Brand development, tourism and national identity: The re- imaging of former Yugoslavia. *Journal of Brand Management*, 9(4/5), 323–334.

Hamel, G. & Prahalad, C. K. (1989). Strategic intent. *Harvard Business Review*, May–June, 63–76.

Handy, C. (1994). *The Empty Raincoat: Making Sense of the Future*. New York: Random House.

Hanbury, W. A. (2005). Case study in crisis management: Management lessons learned from 9/11 and its aftermath. In R. Harrill (ed.), *Fundamentals of Destination Management and Marketing* (pp. 99–108). Washington DC: IACVB.

Harrill, R. (2005). *Fundamentals of Destination Management and Marketing*. Washington, DC: IACVB.

Harris, R., Jago, L. & King, B. (2005). *Case Studies in Tourism & Hospitality Marketing*. Frenchs Forest, NSW: Pearson.

Hashimoto, A. (2002). Tourism and sociocultural development issues. In R. Sharpley & D. Telfer (eds), *Tourism and Development: Concepts and Issues* (pp. 202–230). Clevedon: Channel View Publications.

Hashimoto, A. & Telfer, D. J. (2001). Tourism distribution channels in Canada. In D. Buhalis, & E. Laws (eds), *Communication Issues in NTO Distribution Strategies* (pp. 243–258). London: Continuum.

Hayes, T. (2006). How did they bloody well do that? *B&T*, 7 April, 14.

Hazbun, W. (2000). Enclave orientalism: The state, tourism, and the politics of post-national development in the Arab world. In M. Robinson, N. Evans, P. Long, R. Sharpley & J. Swarbrooke (eds), *Management, Marketing and the Political Economy of Travel and Tourism* (pp. 191–205). Sunderland: The Centre for Travel & Tourism.

Heath, E. (1999). Key trends and challenges in destination marketing: The need for a new paradigm. *Tourism Destination Marketing – Gaining the Competitive Edge*. Proceedings of the conference of the European Travel & Tourism Research Association. Dublin: TTRA European Chapter, 174–196.

Heath, E. (2003). Towards a model to enhance destination competitiveness: A South African perspective. CAUTHE Conference. Coffs Harbour: Southern Cross University.

Heath, E. & Wall, G. (1992). *Marketing Tourism Destinations: A Strategic Planning Approach*. New York: John Wiley & Sons.

Henderson, J. C. (2000). Selling places: The new Asia-Singapore brand. In M. Robinson, N. Evans, P. Long, R. Sharpley & J. Swarbrooke (eds), *Management, Marketing and the Political Economy of Travel and* Tourism (pp. 207–218). Sunderland: The Centre for Travel & Tourism.

Henderson, J. (2002). Managing a tourism crisis in Southeast Asia: The role of national tourism organizations. *International Journal of Hospitality & Tourism Administration*, 3(1), 85–105.

Henshall, B. D., Roberts, R. & Leighton, A. (1985). Flt-drive tourists: Motivation and destination choice factors. *Journal of Travel Research*, Winter, 23–27.

Hiemstra, S. J. & Ismail, J. A. (1992). Analysis of room taxes levied on the lodging industry. *Journal of Travel Research*, 31(1), 42–49.

Hiemstra, S. J. & Ismail, J. A. (1993). Incidence of the impacts of room taxes on the lodging industry. *Journal of Travel Research*, 31(4), 22–26.

Holcolm, B. (1999). Marketing cities for tourism. In D. R. Judd. & S. S. Fainstein (eds), *The Tourist City* (pp. 54–70). Newhaven: Yale University Press.

Hollingshead, K. (2001). Policy in paradise: The history of incremental politics in the tourism of island-state Fiji. *Tourism*, 49(4), 327–348.

Holloway, J. C. (1994). *The Business of Tourism*. Harlow, Essex: Longman.

Holloway, J. C. & Robinson, C. (1995). *Marketing for Tourism* (3rd edn). Harlow, Essex: Addison Wesley Longman.

Hooley, G. J. & Saunders, J. (1993). *Competitive Positioning: The Key to Market Success*. Hertfordshire: Prentice Hall International.

Hoover (2003). Industry execs appointed to new tourism board. www.bizjournals.com. 11 August.

Hopper, P. (2002). Marketing London in a difficult climate. *Journal of Vacation Marketing*, 9(1), 81–88.

Horn, C., Fairweather, J. R. & Simmons, D. C. (2000). *Evolving Community Response to Tourism and Change in Rotorua*. Rotorua Case Study Report No. 14. Christchurch: Lincoln University.

Howard, J. A. & Sheth, J. N. (1969). *The Theory of Buyer Behavior*. New York: John Wiley & Sons.

Howie, F. (2003). *Managing the Tourist Destination*. London: Continuum.

Hu, Y. & Ritchie, J. R. B. (1993). Measuring destination attractiveness: A contextual approach. *Journal of Travel Research*, 32(2), 25–34.

Hudson, S. & Shephard, G. W. H. (1998). Measuring service quality at tourist destinations: An application of importance – performance analysis to an alpine ski resort. *Journal of Travel & Tourism Marketing*, 7(3), 61–77.

Hughes, H. L. (2002). Marketing gay tourism in Manchester: New market for urban tourism or destruction of 'gay space'? *Journal of Vacation Marketing*, 9(2), 152–163

Hunt, J. D. (1975). Image as a factor in tourism development. *Journal of Travel Research*, Winter, 1–7.

Inkson, K. & Kolb, D. (1998). *Management*. Auckland: Addison Wesley Longman.

Ioannides, D. (2003). The economics of tourism in host communities. In S. Singh, T. J. Timothy & R. K. Dowling (eds), *Tourism in Destination Communities* (pp. 35–54). Oxford: CABI Publishing.

Jacoby, J. (1978). Consumer research: A state of the art review. *Journal of Marketing*, 42(April), 87–96.

Jacoby, J. (1984). Perspectives on information overload. *Journal of Consumer Research*, 10, 432–435.

Jago, L. K., Issaverdis, J. P. & Graham, D. (2000). The wine tourist: What's in a name? In E. Michael (ed.), *Proceedings of the 2000 CAUTHE National Research Conference in Victoria, Australia, 2000* (pp. 64–71).

Jafari, J. (1984). Industry, academe and the national tourist organizations. *Tourism Management*, 5(2), 155–156.

Jafari, J. (1993). Anchoring tourism projects on a scientific foundation. In R. R. Bar-On & M. Even-Zahav (eds), *The First International Conference on Investments and Financing in the Tourism Industry Conference Proceedings*. Jerusalem: Israel Ministry of Tourism.

James, R. (2007). Brand valuation – A global initiative. *Professional Marketing*, June–July, 9.

Jankowicz, A. D. (1987). Whatever became of George Kelly? Applications and implications. *American Psychologist*, 42(5), 481–487.

Jankowicz, A. Z. D. & Cooper, K. (1982). The use of focussed repertory grids in counselling. *British Journal of Guidance and Counselling*, 10(2), 136–150.

Jarvis, G. (2006). Online sales rise rapidly. *Travel Industry Wire*. www.travelindustrywire.com/news. 21/2/06.

Jefferson, A. (1991). Market product relationships. In L. J. Lickorish (ed.), *Developing Tourism Destinations: Policies and Perspectives* (pp. 1–57). Harlow, Essex: Longman.

Jeffries, D. (1989). Selling Britain – A case for privatisation? *Travel & Tourism Analyst*, 1, 69–81.

Jeffries, D. (2002). *Governments and Tourism*. Oxford: Butterworth-Heinemann.

Jenkins, C. L. (1991). Development strategies. In L. J. Lickorish (ed.), *Developing Tourism Destinations: Policies and Perspectives* (pp. 59–118). Harlow, Essex, Longman.

Jenkins, J. (1995). A comparative study of tourist organisations in Australia and Canada. *Australia-Canada Studies*, 13(1), 73–108.

Jenkins, J. (2000). The dynamics of regional tourism organisations in New South Wales, Australia: History, structures and operations. *Current Issues in Tourism*, 3(3), 175–203.

Jenkins, O. H. (1999). Understanding and measuring tourist destination images. *International Journal of Tourism Research*, 1, 1–15.

Jennings, G. (2001). *Tourism Research*. Milton, Qld: Wiley.

Johnson, G. & Scholes, K. (2002). *Exploring Corporate Strategy* (6th edn). Harlow, Essex: Pearson Education.

Jones, S. (2006). New domain attracts 16,000 registrations. *Travel Mole*. www.travelmole.com, 15/3/06.

Kearsley, G. W, Coughlan, D. P. & Ritchie, B. W. (1998). *Images of New Zealand Holiday Destinations: An International and Domestic Perspective*. Dunedin: University of Otago Centre for Tourism.

Keller, K. L. (1993). Conceptualizing, measuring, and managing customer-based brand equity. *Journal of Marketing*, 57(January), 1–22.

Keller, K. L. (2003). *Strategic Brand Management*. Upper Saddle River, NJ: Prentice Hall.

Keller, P. (1998). Destination marketing: Strategic questions. In P. Keller (ed.), *Destination Marketing – Reports of the 48th AIEST Congress, Marakech*, 9–22.

Keller, P. (2000). Destination marketing: Strategic areas of inquiry. In M. Manente & M. Cerato (eds), *From Destination to Destination Marketing and Management* (pp. 29–44). Venice: CISET.

Kelly, G. A. (1955). *The Psychology of Personal Constructs*. New York: Norton.

Kelly, G. A. (1970a). A brief introduction to personal construct theory. In D. Bannister (ed.), *Perspectives in Personal Construct Theory*. London: Academic Press.

Kelly, I. & Nankervis, K. (2001). *Visitor Destinations*. Milton, Qld: John Wiley & Sons.

Kennedy, P. (1993). *Preparing for the Twenty-First Century*. London: HarperCollins.

Kerr, B. & Wood, R. C. (2000). Tourism policy and politics in a devolved Scotland. In M. Robinson, N. Evans, P. Long, R. Sharpley & J. Swarbrooke (eds), *Management, Marketing and the Political Economy of Travel and Tourism* (pp. 284–296). Sunderland: The Centre for Travel & Tourism.

Kim, H., Kim, W. G. & An, J. A. (2003). The effect of consumer-based brand equity on firms' financial performance. *The Journal of Consumer Marketing*, 20(4/5), 335–351.

Kim, S., Crompton, J. L. & Botha, C. (2000). Responding to competition: A strategy for Sun/Lost City, South Africa. *Tourism Management*, 21(1), 33–41.

Kincaid, J. W. (2003). *Customer Relationship Management*. Upper Saddle River, NJ: Prentice Hall.

King, S. (1970). Development of the brand. *Advertising Quarterly*, Summer, 6–14.

King, S. (1991). Brand-building in the 1990s. *Journal of Marketing Management*, 7, 3–13.

Kleinman, M. & Bashford, S. (2002). BTA set for 40m blitz to tempt back tourists. *Marketing*, Feb 28, 6.

Kolb, B. N. (2006). *Tourism Marketing for Cities and Towns – Using Branding and Events to Attract Tourists*. Oxford: Elsevier.

Kolb, D. A., Rubin, I. M. & Osland, J. S. (1995). *Organizational Behavior – An Experiential Approach*. Englewood Cliffs, NJ: Prentice Hall.

Kotler, P., Bowen, J. & Makens, J. (1999). *Marketing for Hospitality and Tourism* (2nd edn). Upper Saddle River, N.J: Prentice-Hall.

Kotler, P., Haider, D. H. & Rein, I. (1993). *Marketing Places*. New York: Free Press.

Kotler, P., Adam, S., Brown, L. & Armstrong, G. (2003). *Principles of Marketing*. (2nd edn). Sydney: Prentice Hall.

Kozak, M. (2002). Destination benchmarking. *Annals of Tourism Research*, 29(2), 497–519.

Kubiak, G. D. (2002). Travel & tourism: Export of tomorrow. *Spectrum: The Journal of State Government*, Spring, 18–20.

La Page, W. F. (1995). Case studies of partnerships in action. *Journal of Park and Recreation Administration*, 13(4), 61–74.

Lasser, C. (2000). Implementing destination-structures: Experiences with Swiss cases. In M. Manete & M. Cerato (eds), *From Destination to Destination Marketing and Management* (pp. 111–126). Venice: CISET.

Lathrop, J. (2005). Board governance. In R. Harrill (ed.), *Fundamentals of Destination Management and Marketing* (pp. 191–218). Washington: IACVB.

Lavery, P. (1990). *Travel and Tourism*. Huntington, UK: ELM Publications.

Lavery, P. (1992). The financing and organisation of national tourist offices. *EIU Travel & Tourism Analyst*, 4, 84–101.

Lavidge, R. E. & Steiner, G. A. (1961). A model for predictive measurements of advertising effectiveness. *Journal of Marketing*, 25, 59–62.

Law, C. M. (1993). *Urban Tourism – Attracting Visitors to Large Cities*. London: Mansell.

Laws. E. (1995). *Tourist Destination Management*. London: Routledge.

Lavery, P. (1990). *Travel and Tourism*. Huntington, UK: ELM Publications.

Lavery, P. (1992). The financing and organisation of national tourist offices. *EIU Travel & Tourism Analyst, 4*, 84–101.

Leiper, N. (1979). The framework of tourism. *Annals of Tourism Research*, Oct–Dec, 390–407.

Leiper, N. (1995). *Tourism Management*. Collingwood, Vic: TAFE Publications.

Lennon, J. & Foley, M. (2000). *Dark Tourism – The Attraction of Death and Disaster*. London: Continuum.

Lennon, J. J., Smith, H., Cockerell, N. & Trew, J. (2006). *Benchmarking National Tourism Organisations and Agencies – Understanding Best Practice*. Oxford: Elsevier.

Leong, S. M. & Tan, C. T. (1992). Assessing national competitive superiority: An importance-performance matrix approach. *Marketing Intelligence & Planning, 10*(1), 42–48.

Leslie, D. (1999). Terrorism and tourism: The Northern Ireland situation – a look behind the veil of certainty. *Journal of Travel Research, 38*, 37–40.

Levy, L. H. & Dugan, R. D. (1956). A factorial study of personal constructs. *Journal of Consulting Psychology, 20*(1), 53–57.

Lickorish, L. J. (1992). *Developing Tourism Destinations: Policies and Perspectives*. Harlow, Essex: Longman.

Lilly, T. (1984). From industry to leisure in The Potteries. *Tourism Management, 5*(2), 136–138.

Litvin, S. W. & Alderson, L. L. (2003). How Charleston got her groove back: A convention and visitors bureau's response to 9/11. *Journal of Vacation Marketing, 9*(2), 188–197.

Livesly, J. (2007). Tourism Australia in global inline push. *B & T Magazine, 57*(2613), 1.

Lohmann, M. (1990). Evolution of shortbreak holidays in Western Europe. In W. Fache (ed.), *Shortbreak Holidays*. Rotterdam: Center Parcs.

Lohmann, M. (1991). Evolution of shortbreak holidays. *The Tourist Review, 46*(2), 14–23.

Lohmann, M. & Kaim, E. (1999). Weather and holiday destination preferences, image, attitude and experience. *The Tourist Review, 2*, 54–64.

Long, J. (1994). Local authority tourism strategies: A British appraisal. *The Journal of Tourism Studies, 5*(2), 17–23.

MacCannell, D. (1976). *The Tourist*. New York: Shocken Books.

MacInnes, D. J. & Price, L. L. (1987). The role of imagery in information processing: Review and extensions. *Journal of Consumer Research, 13*, 473–491.

Macionis, N. & Cambourne, B. (1998). Wine and food tourism in the Australian capital territory: Exploring the links. *International Journal of Wine Marketing, 10*(3), 5–16.

MacKay, K. J. & Fesenmaier, D. R. (1997). Pictorial element of destination in image formation. *Annals of Tourism Research, 24*(3), 537–565.

MacKay, K. J. & Fesenmaier, D. R. (2000). An exploration of cross-cultural destination image assessment. *Journal of Travel Research, 38*(May), 417–423.

Mak, J. (1988). Taxing hotel room rentals in the US. *Journal of Travel Research, 26*(1), 10–15.

Mak, J. & Nishimura, E. (1979). The economics of a hotel room tax. *Journal of Travel Research, 17*(1), 2–6.

Malhotra, N., Hall, J., Shaw, M. & Oppenheim, P. (2006). *Marketing Research: An Applied Orientation* (3rd edn). Sydney: Pearson.

Manning, A. (2003). WHO lifts last SARS travel warning. www.eTurboNews.com 25 July.

Mansfield, Y. (1992). From motivation to actual travel. *Annals of Tourism Research*, *19*, 399–419.

Mansfield, Y. (1999). Cycles of war, terror, and peace: Determinants and management of crisis and recovery of the Israeli tourism industry. *Journal of Travel Research*, *38*, 30–36.

March, R. (2003). A marketing-oriented model of national competitiveness in tourism. CAUTHE Conference. Coffs Harbour: Southern Cross University.

Marks, J. A. (2004). Convention and visitors bureaus. In B. Dickenson & A. Vladimir (eds), *The Complete 21st Century Travel & Hospitality Marketing Handbook* (pp. 139–146). Upper Saddle River, NJ: Pearson.

Martilla, J. A. & James, J. C. (1977). Importance-performance analysis. *Journal of Marketing*, January, 77–79.

Masberg, B. A. (1999). What is the priority of research in the marketing and promotional efforts of convention and visitors bureaus in the United States? *Journal of Travel & Tourism Marketing*, *8*(2), 29–40.

Maslow, A. H. (1943). A theory of human motivation. *Psychological Review*, *50*, 370–396.

Matejka, J. K. (1973). Critical factors in vacation area selection. *Arkansas Business and Economic Review*, *6*, 17–19.

May, C. (2001). From direct response to image with qualitative and quantitative research. Presentation at the 32nd annual conference of the Travel & Tourism Research Association. Fort Myers, FL.

Mayo, E. J. (1973). Regional images and regional travel behaviour. *The Travel Research Association 4th Annual Proceedings*. Idaho.

Mayo, E. J. & Jarvis, L. P. (1981). *The Psychology of Leisure Travel*. Massachusetts: CBI Publishing Company.

McClelland, C. (2003). Toronto tourism loses $190 million, says report. www.eTurboNews. com. 18 June.

McDonnell, I. & Darcy, S. (1998). Tourism precincts: A factor in Bali's rise and Fiji's fall from favour – An Australian perspective. *Journal of Vacation Marketing*, *4*(4), 353–367.

McGehee, N. G., Meng, F. & Tepanon, Y. (2006). Understanding legislators and their perceptions of the tourism industry: The case of North Carolina, USA, 1990 and 2003. *Tourism Management*, *27*(2), 684–694.

McKercher, B. (1995). The destination-market matrix: A tourism market portfolio analysis model. *Journal of Travel & Tourism Marketing*, *4*(2), 23–40.

McKercher, B. (2003). SIP (SARS induced panic) a greater threat to tourism than SARS (Severe Acute Respiratory Syndrome). *e-Review of Tourism Research (eRTR)*, *1*(1), www.ertr.tamu.edu.

McKercher, B. & Ritchie, M. (1997). The third tier of public sector tourism: A profile of local government tourism officers in Australia. *Journal of Travel Research*, *36*(1), 66–72.

McMillan, E. (2005). Financial management. In R. Harrill (ed.), *Fundamentals of Destination Management and Marketing*. Washington, DC: IACVB.

McMurray, A. J., Pace, R. W. & Scott, D. (2004). *Research: A Commonsense Approach*. Southbank, Vic: Thompson.

McWilliams, E. G. & Crompton, J. L. (1997). An expanded framework for measuring the effectiveness of destination advertising. *Tourism Management*, *18*(3), 127–137.

Medlik, S. & Middleton, V. T. C. (1973). The tourist product and its marketing implications. *International Tourism Quarterly*, 3,28–35.

Meethan, K. (2002). Selling the difference: Tourism marketing in Devon and Cornwall, South-west England. In R. Voase (ed.), *Tourism in Western Europe: A collection of Case Histories* (pp. 23–42). Oxford: CABI publishing.

Meler, M. & Ruzic, D. (1999). Marketing identity of the tourist product of the Republic of Croatia. *Tourism Management, 20*, 635–643.

Melian-Gonzalez, A. & Garcia-Falcon, J. M. (2003). Competitive potential of tourism in destinations. *Annals of Tourism Research, 30*(3), 720–740.

Mihali, T. (2000). Environmental management of a tourist destination: A factor of tourism competitiveness. *Tourism Management, 21*(1), 65–78.

Mill, R. C. & Morrison, A. M. (1986). *The Tourism System: An Introductory Text*. Englewood Cliffs, NJ: Prentice Hall.

Mill, R. C. & Morrison, A. M. (1992). *The Tourism System: An Introductory Text* (2nd edn). Englewood Cliffs, NJ: Prentice Hall

Mill, R. C. & Morrison, A. M. (2002). *The Tourism System*. Dubuque, Iowa: Kendal/Hunt.

Miller, A. (2003). Leicester promotions: Destination management for maximising tourist potential. In N. Evans, D. Campbell & G. Stonehouse (2003), *Strategic Management for Travel and Tourism* (pp. 358–361). Oxford: Butterworth-Heinemann.

Milman, A. & Pizam, A. (1995). The role of awareness and familiarity with a destination: The central Florida case. *Journal of Travel Research, 33* (3), 21–27.

Mollo-Bouvier, S. (1990). Short-break holidays: Where are the children? In W. Fache (ed), *Shortbreak Holidays*. Rotterdam: Center Parcs.

Montgomery, S. (2002). Tourists' dream holiday short of expectations. *The Courier-Mail*, Brisbane, 6 August, 3.

Moore, K., Fairweather, J. R. & Simmons, D. G (2000). *Visitors to Rotorua: Characteristics, Activities and Decision-making*. Rotorua Case Study Report No. 12. Lincoln University.

Morgan, M. (1991). Dressing up to survive – Marketing Majorca anew. *Tourism Management*, March, 15–20.

Morgan, N. (2006). Destination marketing organisations (book review). *Tourism Management, 27*, 533–545.

Morgan, N., Pritchard, A. & Pride, R. (2002). *Destination Branding – Creating the Unique Destination Proposition*. Oxford: Butterworth-Heinemann.

Morgan, N., Pritchard, A. & Pride, R. (2004). *Destination Branding – Creating the Unique Destination Proposition* (2nd edn). Oxford: Butterworth-Heinemann.

Morley, P. (2003). Tiny town hope statue will be the ant's pants. *The Sunday Mail*, Brisbane, 6 April, 19.

Morley, P. & Stolz, G. (2003). Gold Coast blunders by promoting wrong beach. *The Courier Mail*, Brisbane, 3.

Morrison, A. M., Braunlich, C. G., Kamaruddin, N. & Cai, L. A. (1995). National tourist offices in North America: An analysis. *Tourism Management, 16*(8), 605–617.

Morrison, A. M., Bruen, S. M. & Anderson, D.J. (1998). Convention and visitor bureaus in the USA: A profile of bureaus, bureau executives, and budgets. *Journal of Travel & Tourism Marketing, 7*(1), 1–19.

Murphy, P., Pritchard, M. P. & Smith, B. (2000). The destination product and its impact on traveller perceptions. *Tourism Management, 21*(1), 43–52.

Myers, J. H. & Alpert, M. I. (1977). Semantic confusion in attitude research. *Advances in Consumer Research, 4*, 106–110.

Myers, J. H. (1992). Positioning products/services in attitude space. *Marketing Research*, March, 46–51.

Myers, J. H. & Alpert, M. I. (1968). Determinant buying attitudes: Meaning and measurement. *Journal of Marketing, 32*(October), 13–20.

Naisbitt, J. (1994). *Global Paradox*. William Morrow.

National Tour Association. (2003). Company information. Retrieved on March 30, 2003: http://ntaonline.com

Nguyen, M. (2006). Industry snaps. *B&T*, *56*(27 Jan), 1, 4.

Nicholas, C.L. (2004). New York City and Company. In B. Dickenson & A. Vladimir (eds), *The Complete 21st Century Travel & Hospitality Marketing Handbook* (pp. 147–153). Upper Saddle River, NJ: Pearson.

Nickerson, N. P. & Moisey, R. N. (1999). Branding a state from features to positioning: Making it simple? *Journal of Vacation Marketing*, *5*(3), 217–226.

Nykiel, R. A. & Jascolt, E. (1998). *Marketing Your City, USA*. New York: Haworth Hospitality Press.

NZPA. (2006). City fights Cleese's fawlty claims. *The Courier-Mail*, 22 March, 40.

NZTB. (1992). *A Review of Rotorua's Tourism Infrastructure*. Wellington: Policy, Planning and Investment Division, New Zealand Tourism Board. July.

NZTPD. (1976). *75 Years of Tourism*. Wellington: New Zealand Tourist & Publicity Department.

O'Halloran, R. M. (1992). Tourism management profiles: Implications for tourism Education. *FIU Hospitality Review*, *10*(1), 83–91.

Okumus, F. & Karamustafa, K. (2005). Impact of an economic crisis – Evidence from Turkey. *Annals of Tourism Research*, *43*(4), 942–961.

Olins, W. (2002). Branding the nation – The historical context. *Journal of Brand Management*, *9*(4/5), 241–248.

Olsen, M. (1991). *Strategic Management in the Hospitality Industry: A Literature Review*. London: Belhaven Press.

O'Neill, M. & Charters, S. (2000). Service quality at the cellar door: implications for Western Australia's wine tourism industry. *Managing Service Quality*, *10*(2), 112–122.

O'Neill, M., Palmer, A. & Charters, S. (2002). Wine production as a service experience – The effects of service quality on wine sales. *Journal of Services Marketing*, *16*(4), 342–362.

O'Neill, M. A. & McKenna, M. A. (1994). Northern Ireland tourism: A quality Perspective. *Managing Service Quality*, *4*(2), 31–35.

O'Neill, M., Palmer, A., Charters, S. & Fitz, F. (2001). Service quality and consumer behavioural intention: An exploratory study from the Australian wine tourism sector. *Conference Proceedings. Australian and New Zealand Marketing Academy Conference*, 1st–5th December 2001, Massey University.

Oppermann, M. (1996a). Visitation of tourism attractions and tourist expenditure patterns – Repeat versus first-time visitors. *Asia Pacific Journal of Tourism Research*, *1*(1), 61–68.

Oppermann, M. (1996b). Convention destination images: Analysis of association meeting planners' perceptions. *Tourism Management*, *17*(3), 75–182.

Oppermann, M. (1999b). Where psychology and geography interface in tourism research and theory. In A. G. Woodside, G. I. Crouch, J. A. Mazanec, M. Oppermann. & M. Y. Sakai, M. Y. (eds), *Consumer Psychology of Tourism, Hospitality and Leisure*. Wallingford: CABI.

Osti, L. & Pechlaner, H. (2001). Communication issues in NTO distribution strategies. In D. Buhalis & E. Laws (eds), *Tourism Distribution Channels* (pp. 231–242. London: Continuum.

OTSP. (2001). *New Zealand Tourism Strategy 2010: Summary of Recommendations*. Wellington: Office of Tourism and Sport.

PA Hotels and tourism. (1987). *Rotorua Promotions and Development Society: Development of a Marketing Strategy.* Auckland.

Page, S. (1995). *Urban Tourism.* London: Routledge.

Page, S., Clift. & Clark, N. (1994). Tourist health: The precautions, behaviour and health problems of British tourists in Malta. In A. V. Seaton, C. L. Jenkins, R. C. Wood, P. U. C. Dieke, M. M. Bennett, L. R. MacLellan & R. Smith (eds), *Tourism the State of the Art* (pp. 799–817). Chichester: John Wiley & Sons.

Page, S., Yeoman, I., Munro, C., Connell, J. & Walker, L. (2006). A case study of best practice – Visit Scotland's prepared response to an influenza pandemic. *Tourism Management, 27*, 361–393.

Page, S. & Wilks, J. (2004). *Managing Tourist Health and Safety.* Oxford: Elsevier.

Palmer, A. (1998). Evaluating the governance style of marketing groups. *Annals of Tourism Research, 25*(1), 185–201.

PATA. (2002). *Issues & Trends – Pacific Asia Travel. 7*(2), February.

Pattinson, G. (1990). Place promotion by tourist boards: the example of 'Beautiful Berkshire'. In G. Ashworth & B. Goodall (eds), *Marketing Tourism Places* (pp. 209–226). New York: Routledge.

Patton, M. Q. (1990). *Qualitative Evaluation and Research Methods* (2nd edn). Newbury Park, CA: Sage Publications.

Pearce, D. G. (1990). Tourism, the regions and restructuring in New Zealand. *Journal of Tourism Studies, 1*(2), 33–42.

Pearce, D. (1992). *Tourist Organizations.* Harlow, Essex: Longman.

Pearce, D. G. (1997). Competitive destination analysis in Southeast Asia. *Journal of Travel Research, 35*(4), 16–24.

Pearce, P. L. (1994). Fundamentals of tourist motivation. In D. Pearce & R. Butler, R. (eds), *Tourism Research: Critiques and Challenges.* New York: Routledge.

Pechlaner, H. (1999). The competitiveness of alpine destinations between market pressure and problems of adaptation. *Tourism, 47*(4), 332–343.

Pechlaner, H. & Abfalter, D. (2002). New challenges for NTOs – A multinational perspective with the example of cultural tourism in Italy. *Tourism, 50*(1), 5–20.

Pedro Bueno, A. (1999). Competitiveness in the tourist industry and the role of the Spanish public administrations: The case of Valencia Region. *Tourism, 47*(4), 316–331.

Perdue, R. R. (2000). Destination images and consumer confidence in destination attribute ratings. *Tourism Analysis, 5*, 77–81.

Pike, S. (1998). Destination positioning: Too many fingers in the pie? *NZ Tourism and Hospitality Research Conference Proceedings.* Christchurch: Lincoln University.

Pike, S. (2002a). Destination image analysis: A review of 142 papers from 1973–2000. *Tourism Management, 23*(5), 541–549.

Pike, S. (2002b). The use of importance-performance analysis to identify determinant short-break destination attributes in New Zealand. *Pacific Tourism Review,. 6*(1), 23–33.

Pike, S. (2002c). ToMA as a measure of competitive advantage for short-break holiday destinations. *Journal of Tourism Studies, 13*(1), 9–19.

Pike, S. (2003). The use of repertory grid analysis to elicit salient short-break holiday attributes. *Journal of Travel Research,* February.

Pike, S. (2004). Destination brand positioning slogans – Towards the development of a set of accountability criteria. *Acta Turistica, 16*(2), 102–124.

Pike, S. (2004). *Destination Marketing Organisations.* Oxford: Elsevier.

Pike, S. (2005). Tourism destination branding complexity. *Journal of Product & Brand Management, 14*(4), 258–259.

Pike, S. (2006). Destination decision sets: A longitudinal comparison of stated destination preferences and actual travel. *Journal of Vacation Marketing, 12*(4), 319-328.

Pike, S. (2007). A cautionary tale of a resort destination's self-inflicted crisis. *Journal of Travel & Tourism Marketing* (In press).

Pike, S. (2008). Destination image questionnaires: Avoiding uninformed responses. *Journal of Travel & Tourism Research* (In press).

Pine, J. & Gilmore, J. (1989). *The Experience Economy.* Cambridge, MA: Harvard University.

Press Pitts, B. G. & Ayers. K. (2000). Sports tourism and the gay games: The emerging use of destination marketing with the gay games. In M. Robinson, N. Evans, P. Long, R. Sharpley & J. Swarbrooke (eds), *Management, Marketing and the Political Economy of Travel and Tourism* (pp. 389–401). Sunderland: Business Education Publishers.

Pizam, A. (1990). Evaluating the effectiveness of travel trade shows and other tourism sales-promotion techniques. *Journal of Travel Research*, Summer, 3–8.

Pizam, A. (1999). A comprehensive approach to classifying acts of crime and violence at tourism destinations. *Journal of Travel Research, 38,* 5–12.

Plog, S. T. (1974). Why destination areas rise and fall in popularity. *Cornell HRA Quarterly, 14*(4), 55–58.

Plog, S. T. (2000). Thirty years that changed travel: Changes to expect over the next ten. Keynote address at the 31st Travel and Tourism Research Association Conference. Burbank, California, June.

Poetschke, B. (1995) Key success factors for public/private-sector partnerships in island tourism planning. In M. V. Conlin & T. Baum (eds), *Island Tourism.* Chichester: John Wiley & Sons.

Poon, A. (1993). *Tourism, Technology and Competitive Strategies.* Oxford: CAB International.

Popcorn, F. (1996). *Clicking.* London: HarperCollins.

Porter, M. E. (1979). How competitive forces shape strategy. *Harvard Business Review*, March–April, 137–145.

Porter, M. E. (1980). *Competitive Strategy.* New York: Free Press.

Porter, M. E. (1985). *Competitive Advantage.* New York: Free Press.

Porter, M. E. (1991). Towards a dynamic theory of strategy. *Strategic Management Journal, 12,* 95–117.

Porter, M. E. (1996). What is strategy? *Harvard Business Review*, Nov–Dec, 61–78.

Portorff, S. M. & Neal, D. M. (1994). Marketing implications for post-disaster tourism destinations. *Journal of Travel & Tourism Marketing, 3*(1), 115–122.

Pride, R. (2002). Brand Wales: 'Natural revival'. In N. Morgan, A. Prichard & R. Pride (eds), *Destination Branding* (pp. 109–123). Oxford: Butterworth-Heinemann.

Prideaux, B. (2000). The role of the transport system in destination development. *Tourism Management, 21*(1), 53–63.

Pritchard, G. (1982). Tourism promotion: Big business for the states. *HRA Quarterly, 23*(2), 48–57.

Pritchard, M. P. (1997). Evaluating the destination product with importance-performance analysis. *28th Annual TTRA Conference Proceedings.* Travel and Tourism Research Association. Norfolk, Virginia.

Pritchard, A. & Morgan, N. (1995). Evaluating vacation destination brochure images. *Journal of Vacation Marketing, 2*(1), 23–38.

Pritchard, A. & Morgan, N. (1998). Mood marketing – The new destination branding strategy: A case of Wales the brand. *Journal of Vacation Marketing, 4*(3), 215–229.

Prosser, G., Hunt, S., Braithwaite, D. & Rosemann, I. (2000). *The Significance of Regional Tourism: A Preliminary Report.* Lismore: Centre for Regional Tourism Research.

Quinn, J. B., Anderson, P. & Finkelstein, S. (1996). Managing professional intellect: Making the most of the best. *Harvard Business Review*, March–April, 71–80.

Rahman, F. (2003). New visa rule to boost Oman's tourism sector. www.eTurboNews.com, 29 July.

Reid, L .J. & Reid, S. D. (1993). Communicating tourism supplier services: Building repeat visitor relationships. *Journal of Travel and Tourism Marketing*, 2(2/3), 3–19.

Reynolds, W. H. (1965). The role of the consumer in image building. *California Management Review*, Spring, 69–76.

Richardson, J. I. (1999). *A History of Australian Travel and Tourism*. Elsternwick, Vic: Hospitality Press.

Richardson, J. & Cohen, J. (1993). State slogans: the case of the missing USP. *Journal of Travel & Tourism Marketing*, 2(2/3), 91–109.

Ries, A. (1992). The discipline of the narrow focus. *Journal of Business Strategy*, Nov–Dec, 3–9.

Ries, A. & Ries, L. (1998). *The 22 Immutable Laws of Branding*. New York: HarperCollins.

Ries, A. & Trout, J. (1982). The enormous competitive power of a selling product name. *Marketing Times*, 29(5), 28–38.

Ries, A. & Trout, J. (1986). *Positioning: The Battle for your Mind*. New York: McGraw-Hill.

Riley, R., Baker, D. & Van Doren, C. S. (1998). Movie induced tourism. *Annals of Tourism Research*, 25(4), 919–933.

Riley, R. & Van Doren, C. (1998). Movies as tourism promotion: a push factor in a pull location. *Tourism Management*, 13, 267–274.

Riley, S. & Palmer, J. (1975). Of attitudes and latitudes: A repertory grid study of perceptions of seaside resorts. *Journal of the Market Research Society*, 17(2), 74–89.

Ritchie, B. W., Burns, P. & Palmer, C. (2005). *Tourism Research Methods: Integrating Theory with Practise*. Wallingford: CABI.

Ritchie, J. R. B. (1996). Beacons of light in an expanding universe: An assessment of the state-of-the-art in tourism marketing/marketing research. *Journal of Travel & Tourism Marketing*, 5(4), 49–84.

Ritchie, J. R. B. & Crouch, G. I. (2000a). Are destination stars born or made: Must a competitive destination have star genes? *Lights, Camera, Action – 31st Annual Conference Proceedings*. San Fernando Valley, CA: Travel and Tourism Research Association.

Ritchie, J. R. B. & Crouch, G. I. (2000b). The competitive destination: A sustainability perspective. *Tourism Management*, 21, 1–7.

Ritchie, J. R. B. & Crouch, G. (2003). *The Competitive Destination – A Sustainable Tourism Perspective*. Oxford: CABI Publishing.

Ritchie, J. R. B., Crouch, G. I. & Hudson, S. (2000). Assessing the role of consumers in the measurement of destination competitiveness and sustainability. *Tourism Analysis*, 5, 69–76.

Ritchie, J. R. B. & Ritchie, R. J. B. (1998).The branding of tourism destinations – Past achievements and future challenges. In P. Keller (ed.), *Destination Marketing – Reports of the 48th AIEST Congress*, Marrakech. 89–116.

Rivard, P., (1974). *Samuel Slater, Father of American Manufacturers*. Providence, RI: Jo-Art Copy Service Inc.

Roehl, W. S. (1990). Travel agent attitudes toward China after Tiananmen square. *Journal of Travel Research*, Fall, 16–22.

Rogers, T. (2005). Destination management in the UK. In R. Harrill (ed.), *Fundamentals of Destination Management and Marketing*. (pp. 245–258). Washington: IACVB.

Roper, P. (2001). The case against tourism: Doubters and sceptics. In D. Jeffries (ed.), *Governments and Tourism*. (pp. 27–50). Oxford: Butterworth-Heinemann.

Rosemann, I., Prosser, G., Hunt, S. & Benecke, K. (2000). *Promoting Awareness of the Value of Tourism – A Resource Kit*. Lismore: Centre for Regional Tourism Research.

Rotorua District Council. (1992). *So, you want to be a Spa City!!* Rotorua: Economic Development Section, December.

Rubel, C. (1996). No mistake about it, Cleveland on a rebound. *Marketing News, 1*, January, 1, 8.

Rubies, E. B. (2001). Improving public-private sectors cooperation in tourism: A new paradigm for destinations. *Tourism Review, 56*(3/4), 38–41.

Ruddy, J. & Flanagan, S. (1999). *Tourism Destination Marketing: Gaining the Competitive Edge*. Conference Proceedings. European Conference of the Travel and Tourism Research Association.

Rusk, M. (1974). Innovations in travel research for Canada – The US vacation trip market segmentation study and its applications to the 1974 programs of the Canadian Government Office of Tourism. *Proceedings* (pp. 80–83). Salt Lake City: Travel Research Association.

Russel, J. A. (1980). A circumplex model of affect. *Journal of Personality and Social Psychology, 39*(6), 1161–1178.

Russel, J. A., Ward, L. M. & Pratt, G. (1981). Affective quality attributed to environments: A factor analytic study. *Environment and Behavior, 13*(3), 259–288.

Schoenbachler, C., di Benetto, A., Gordon, G. L. & Kaminski, P. F. (1995). Destination advertising: Assessing effectiveness with the split-run technique. *Journal of Travel & Tourism Marketing, 4*(2), 1–21.

Schultz, D. (2005). MR deserves blame for marketing's decline. *Marketing News*, February 15, 7.

Schultz, D. & Schultz, H. (2004). *Brand Babble: Sense and Nonsense about Branding*. Mason, Ohio: South-Western.

Schultz, D., Tannenbaum, S. & Lauterborn, R. (1993). *Integrated Marketing Communications*. Lincolnwood, IL: NTC Publishing.

Schur, Maxine (2007). Following my heart to Heidiland: Inside the landscape of a famous movie. Retrieved on 3/6/07 from: http://www.escapeartist.com/efam/43/In_Search_of_Heidiland.html.

Schwartz, P. (1992). *The Art of the Long View*. London: Century Business.

Sears, J. (1989). *Sacred Places: American Tourist Attractions in the Nineteenth Century*. New York: Oxford University Press.

Seaton, A. V. (1994). Public relations. In S. F. Witt & L. Moutinho (eds), *Tourism Marketing and Management Handbook*. Hertfordshire: Prentice Hall International.

Seaton, A. V. (1996). Guided by the dark: From thanatopsis to thanatourism. *International Journal of Heritage Studies, 2*(4), 234–244.

Selby, M. & Morgan, N. J. (1996). Reconstruing place image: A case study of its role in destination market research. *Tourism Management, 17*(4), 287–294.

Shaffer, M. S. (2001). *See America First: Tourism and National Identity, 1880–1940*. Washington, DC: Smithsonian Institution Press.

Sharpley, R. (2002). Tourism: A vehicle for development? In R. Sharpley & D. Telfer (eds), *Tourism and Development – Concepts and Issues*. Clevedon: Channel View Publications.

Shoemaker, S. (2000). Segmenting the mature market: 10 years later. *Journal of Travel Research, 39* (August), 11–26.

Sigaux, G. (1966). *History of Tourism*. London: Leisure Arts.

Sims, S. L. (1990). Educational needs and opportunities for personnel in convention and visitor bureaus. *Visions in Leisure and Business, 9*(3), 27–32.

Sirakaya, E., McLellan, R. W. & Uysal, M. (1996). Modeling vacation destination decisions: A behavioral approach. *Journal of Travel & Tourism Marketing*, 5(1/2), 57–75.

Slater, J. (2002). Brand Louisiana: 'Come as you are. Leave different.' In N. Morgan, A. Pritchard & R Pride (2002). *Destination Branding* (pp. 148–162). Oxford: Butterworth-Heinemann.

Smeral, E. (1996). Globalisation and changes in the competitiveness of tourism destinations. *AIEST Conference*. Rotorua: Waiariki Polytechnic.

Smeral, E. (2004). Evaluating leisure time travel source markets: An innovative guide for national tourist organizations for future competitiveness. *Leisure-Futures Conference*. Bolzano.

Smeral, E. & Witt, S. F. (2002). Destination country portfolio analysis: The evaluation of national tourism destination marketing programs revisited. *Journal of Travel Research*, 40, 287–294.

Smith, S. L. J. (1988) Defining tourism: A supply-side view. *Annals of Tourism Research*, 15, 179–190.

Smith, S. L .J. (2003). A vision for the Canadian tourism industry. *Tourism Management*, 24, 123–133.

Smith, V. L. (2001). Tourism issues of the 21st century. In V. L. Smith & M. Brent (eds), *Hosts and Guests Revisited: Tourism Issues of the 21st Century* (pp. 333–353). New York: Cognizant.

Sonmez, S. F., Apostolopoulous, Y. & Tarlow, P. (1999). Tourism in crisis: Managing the effects of terrorism. *Journal of Travel Research*, 38, 13–18.

Spotts, D. M. (1997). Regional analysis of tourism resources for marketing purposes. *Journal of Travel Research*, Winter, 3–15.

Spyri, Johanna (1996). *Heidi*. New York: Viking

Stafford, D. (1986). *The Founding Years in Rotorua: A History of Events to 1900*. Auckland: Ray Richards.

Stafford, D. (1988). *The New Century in Rotorua*. Auckland: Ray Richards.

Staniford, T. & Cheyne, J. (1994). The search for the perfect organisation: A New Zealand case study. *Tourism Down-Under: A Tourism Research Conference Proceedings*. Palmerston North: Massey University.

Stein, J. (2006). Borat make funny joke on idiot Americans! High-Five! *Time*, 13 November, 60.

Stern, E. & Krakover, S. (1993). The formation of a composite urban image. *Geographical Analysis*, 25(2), 130–146.

Supphellen, M. & Nygaardsvic, I. (2002). Testing country brand slogans: Conceptual development and empirical illustration of a simple normative model. *Journal of Brand Management*, 9(4/5), 385–395.

Swiss National Tourist Office (2007) Heidiland home page. Retrieved on 3/6/07 from: http://www.heidiland.ch/en/accessing_resorts.cfm

Tan, T. S. W., Barnes, D. J. & Smith, R. W. N. (1995). An overview of quality management practice in the New Zealand tourism industry. Unpublished report. Massey University.

Taylor, G. D., Rogers, J. & Stanton, B. (1994). Bridging the gap between industry and researchers. *Journal of Travel Research*, Spring, 9–12.

The Sunday Mail. (2007). Mad about daft and dangerous festivals. Escape (28/1/07), 9–10.

Thompson, J. R. & Cooper, P. D. (1979). Additional evidence on the limited size of evoked and inept sets of travel destination. *Journal of Travel Research*, 17(3), 23–25.

TNZ. (2001). *100 Years Pure Progress*. Wellington: Tourism New Zealand.

Tooke, N. & Baker, M. (1996). Seeing is believing: The effect of film on visitor numbers to screened locations. *Tourism Management, 17*(2), 87–94.

Tourelle, G. (2003). United tourism market mooted. *The New Zealand Herald.* 29 July.

Toffler, A. (1991). *Future Shock.* New York: Random House.

Tourism Auckland. (2002). *Presentation to the Auckland City Council.* October.

Tourism Rotorua. (1996). *Emergence of a New Spirit: An Introduction to Rotorua's Brand Identity Process.* Rotorua District Council.

Tourism Strategy Group. (2001). *New Zealand Tourism Strategy: 2010.* Tourism New Zealand. www.tourisminfo.co.nz. May.

Treacy, M. & Wiersema, F. (1995). *The Discipline of Market Leaders.* London: Harper-Collins.

Tribe, J. (1997). *Corporate Strategy for Tourism.* London: ITP.

Trout, J. & Ries, A. (1979). Positioning: Ten years later: *Industrial Marketing, 64*(7), 32–42.

Urde, M. (1999). Brand orientation: A mindset for building brands into strategic resources. *Journal of Marketing Management, 15,* 117–133.

Uysal, M., Chen, J. S. & Williams, D. R. (2000). Increasing state market share through a regional positioning. *Tourism Management, 21*(1), 89–96.

Vallee, P. (2005). Destination management in Canada. In R. Harrill (ed.), *Fundamentals of Destination Management and Marketing* (pp. 229–244). Washington, DC: IACVB.

Vanhove, N. (2002). Tourism policy – between competitiveness and sustainability: The case of Bruges. *Tourism Review, 57*(3), 34–40.

Vanhove, N. (2005). *The Economics of Tourism Destinations.* Oxford: Elsevier.

Vanhove, N. (2006). A comparative analysis of competition models for tourism destinations. In M. Kozak & L. Andreu (eds), *Progress in Tourism Marketing* (pp. 101–114). Oxford: Elsevier.

Van Middelkoop, M., Borgers, A. W. J. & Timmermans, H. J. P. (1999). Complimentarity, substitution and independence among tourist trips. *Tourism Analysis, 4,* 63–74.

Veal, A. J. (2006). *Research Methods for Leisure and Tourism.* (3rd edn). Harlow, Essex: Pearson Education.

Velas, F. & Bechell, L. (1995). *International Tourism – An Economic Perspective.* Basingstoke: Macmillan Business.

Voase, R. (2002). *Tourism in Western Europe: A Collection of Case Histories.* Wallingford: CABI.

Wade, P. (2006). Chairman's message. *TQ News, 8,* Spring, 2.

Wade, P. (2006). Five tips for driving sales through search engine optimised public relations writing. *Htrends.* http://www.htrends.com viewed 5/3/06.

Wahab, S., Crampon., L. J. & Rothfield, L. M. (1976). *Tourism Marketing.* London: Tourism International Press.

Walkley, I. (2005). Coming soon: Segmentation by DNA. *Marketing Update,* October Australian Marketing Institute.

Walters, J. (2005). Member care. In R. Harrill (ed.), *Fundamentals of Destination Management and Marketing* (pp. 161–172). Washington, DC: IACVB.

Walton, J. K. (1983). *The English Seaside Resort – A Social History 1750–1914.* Leicester: Leicester University press.

Walton, J. K. (2000). *The British Seaside: Holidays and Resorts in the Twentieth Century.* Manchester: Manchester University Press.

Wanhill, S. (2000). Issues in public sector involvement. In B. Faulkner, G. Moscard & E. Laws (eds), *Tourism in the 21st Century – Lessons from Experience* (pp. 222–242). London: Continuum.

Ward, D., Carter, H. & Topping, A. (2007). Shock on the Golden Mile over panel's 'bizarre' decision. *The Guardian*, 31 January.

Ward, S.V. & Gold, J.R. (1994). *The Use of Publicity and Marketing to Sell Towns and Regions*. Chichester: John Wiley & Sons.

Wargenau, A. & Che, D. (2006). Wine tourism development and marketing strategies in Southwest Michigan. *International Journal of Wine Marketing*, 18(1), 45–60.

Wason, G. (1998). Taxation and tourism. *Travel & Tourism Analyst*, 2, 77–95.

Watson, P. (2006). Net success comes in a blink. *The Courier-Mail*, 21–22 January.

Wax, C. (2006). How to…make the most out of search engine marketing. B & T, March 3, 9.

Weaver, D. & Lawton, L. (2006). *Tourism Management* (3rd edn). Milton, Qld: Wiley.

Wicks, B. E. & Schutt, M. A. (1991). Examining the role of tourism promotion through the use of brochures. *Tourism Management*, December, 301–312.

Wind, Y. & Robinson, P. J. (1972). Product positioning: An application of multidimensional scaling. *Attitude Research in Transition* (pp. 155–175). American Marketing Association.

Wine Institute of New Zealand. (2006). *Annual Report*. Retrieved 12/9/06. http://www.nzwine.com/intro/.

Wintermans, J. (1994). The problem of articulate incompetence. *Canadian Business Review*, Spring, 42–43.

Witt,, S. F., Brooke, M. Z. & Buckley, P. J. (1995). *The Management of International Tourism* (2nd edn). London: Routledge.

Witt, S. F. & Gammon, S. (1994). Incentive travel. In S. F. Witt & L. Moutinho (eds), *Tourism Marketing and Management Handbook* (2nd edn). Hertfordshire: Prentice Hall.

Witt., S. F. & Moutinho, L. (1994). *Tourism Marketing and Management Handbook*. (2nd edn). London: Prentice Hall.

Wockner, C. & Weston, P. (2006). Anger over 'sick' Bali prison tours. *The Sunday Mail*, 12 March, 9.

Woodside, A. G. & Carr, J. A. (1988). Consumer decision-making and competitive marketing strategies: Applications for tourism planning. *Journal of Travel Research*, Winter, 2–7.

Woodside, A. G. & Lysonski, S. (1989). A general model of traveler destination choice. *Journal of Travel Research*, Spring, 8–14.

Woodside, A. G., Ronkainen, I. & Reid, D. M. (1977). Measurement and utilization of the evoked set as a travel marketing variable. *The Travel Research Association Eighth Annual Conference Proceedings* (pp. 123–130). Salt Lake City: Travel and Tourism Research Association.

Woodside, A. G. & Sherrell, D. (1977). Traveler evoked, inept, and inert sets of vacation destinations. *Journal of Travel Research*, 16, 14–18.

Woodside, A. G. & Wilson, E. J. (1985). Effects of consumer awareness of brand advertising on preference. *Journal of Advertising Research*, 25(4), 41–48.

Woolford, L. (2005). Technology. In R. Harrill (ed.), *Fundamentals of Destination Management and Marketing* (pp. 125–146). Washington, DC: IACVB.

Wright, J. (2006). PNG tourism completely off track. *The Courier-Mail*, Business, 25 September, 79.

WTO. (1979). *Tourist Images*. Madrid: World Tourism Organization.

WTO. (1983a). *The Framework of the State's Responsibility for theManagement of Tourism*. Madrid: World Tourism Organization.

WTO. (1993). *Recommendations on Tourism Statistics*. Madrid: World Tourism Organization.

WTO. (1994). *National and Regional Tourism Planning*. Madrid: World Tourism Organization.

WTO. (1995). *Tourism to the Year 2000 and Beyond: Volume 1 the World*. Madrid: World Tourism Organisation.

WTO. (2002). *Thinktank*. Madrid: World Tourism Organisation. Accessed online: http://www.world-tourism.org/education/menu.html.

WTTC. (2003). *Blueprint for New Tourism*. London: World Travel & Tourism Council.

WTTC. (2005). *Progress and Priorities 2005/06*. London: World Travel & Tourism Council.

Zikmund, W. G. & Babin, B. J. (2007). *Essentials of Marketing Research* (3rd edn). Mason, OH: Thompson.

Index